POLAND SPRING

Revisiting New England: The New Regionalism

SERIES EDITORS

Siobhan Senier, University of New Hampshire
Darren Ranco, Dartmouth College
Adam Sweeting, Boston University
David H. Watters, University of New Hampshire

This series presents fresh discussions of the distinctiveness of New England culture. The editors seek manuscripts examining the history of New England regionalism; the way its culture came to represent American national culture as a whole; the interaction between that "official" New England culture and the people who lived in the region; and local, subregional, or even biographical subjects as microcosms that explicitly open up and consider larger issues. The series welcomes new theoretical and historical perspectives and is designed to cross disciplinary boundaries and appeal to a wide audience.

Becoming Modern: New Nineteenth-Century Studies

SERIES EDITORS

Sarah Sherman, Department of English, University of New Hampshire
Janet Aikins, Department of English, University of New Hampshire
Rohan McWilliam, Anglia Polytechnic University, Cambridge, England
Janet Polasky, Department of History, University of New Hampshire

This book series maps the complexity of historical change and assesses the formation of ideas, movements, and institutions crucial to our own time by publishing books that examine the emergence of modernity in North America and Europe. Set primarily but not exclusively in the nineteenth century, the series shifts attention from modernity's twentieth-century forms to its earlier moments of uncertain and often disputed construction. Seeking books of interest to scholars on both sides of the Atlantic, it thereby encourages the expansion of nineteenth-century studies and the exploration of more global patterns of development.

For a complete list of titles in these series, please see pages 304 and 305.

University of New Hampshire Press

Durham, New Hampshire

PUBLISHED BY

UNIVERSITY PRESS OF NEW ENGLAND

HANOVER AND LONDON

POLAND SPRING

A Tale of the Gilded Age,
1860–1900

David L. Richards

University of New Hampshire Press
Published by University Press of New England,
One Court Street, Lebanon, NH 03766
www.upne.com
© 2005 by David L. Richards
Printed in the United States of America

5   4   3   2   1

Nestlé Waters and the Poland Spring brand have provided generous support for the publishing of
Poland Spring: A Tale of the Gilded Age, 1860–1900. This support is intended to help preserve the interest in history of this glorious time in Maine. Nestlé Waters has neither influenced nor endorsed
content of this publication.

Library of Congress Cataloging-in-Publication Data

Richards, David, 1962–
    Poland Spring : a tale of the Gilded Age, 1860–1900 / David L. Richards.
        p. cm. — (Revisiting New England)
    Includes bibliographical references and index.
    ISBN-13: 978-1-58465-481-0 (cloth : alk. paper)
    ISBN-10: 1-58465-481-3 (cloth : alk. paper)
    1. Poland Spring (Me.)—History. 2. Poland Spring (Me.)—Social life and customs.
3. Springs—Maine—Poland Spring—History. 4. Resorts—Maine—Poland Spring—
History. 5. Poland Spring (Me.)—Economic conditions. 6. Hiram Ricker & Sons.
7. Businessmen—Maine—Poland Spring—Biography. 8. Ricker family. 9. Poland Spring
(Me.)—Biography. I. Title. II. Series.
    F29.P7R49 2005
    974.1'82—dc22   2005009924

To my family, and all of my other teachers.

Contents

POLAND SPRING

Introduction

From Country Farm to Summer City

Early on a Saturday morning in mid-July of 1860, a reporter for the *Lewiston Falls Journal* and a companion embarked on a daylong journey through central Maine. It took the pair on a circuit from the industrial city of Lewiston to the rural villages of Minot Corner, Hackett's Mill, Poland Corner, White Oak Hill, West Poland, and the New Gloucester Shaker community, before winding up back at the starting point in the early evening. One mile beyond the Shaker settlement and four miles short of the Grand Trunk Railroad depot at Empire Station, the duo made an additional stop. It was at Hiram Ricker's tired country farm, which looked as though it had seen better days. Four decades later, a promotional pamphlet published by Hiram Ricker and Sons referred to the same site as a "summer city."[1] In between, the Poland Spring resort gained national renown, as it became part family business, exclusive club, colonial homestead, social mecca, therapeutic spa, pastoral farm, natural Eden, recreational playground, and cultured city. This journey back in time explores how the transformation from country farm to summer city occurred and why it made the resort a "metaphor for progress." The consequences were profound—the spread to the countryside of the modern values that have continued to shape the nation's cultural landscape long after the passing of the Gilded Age.[2]

Even covering so brief a span as forty years, the story of the Poland Spring resort has much to tell. At one level, it is the history of a family, the Rickers, and their age-old American quest for success. At another level, it is the history of a business—one that tracks the ascent and eclipse of local entrepreneurial capitalism by a national corporate form during the nineteenth century in the United States. It is also part local history, with Poland Spring serving as an example of the dramatic economic and social forces that affected northern New England after the Civil War. Because these changes altered the rural landscape, the story is partly an environmental history as well. Moreover, the mix of class, gender, ethnic, and racial relationships also makes this a social history. Then, too, it is a case study of a major Victorian resort. Ultimately, however, this is a tale that illuminates the cultural history of the Gilded Age.

Given its name in 1873 by Mark Twain and Charles Dudley Warner, co-authors of the novel *The Gilded Age*, the period between the Civil War and the dawn of the twentieth century is one of the least remembered and admired eras in United States history. Yet, it was one of the most pivotal. During these years, remarkable technological innovations sparked revolutions in transportation, communication, and production that bound a nation of island communities into a truly national economy and created vast new accumulations of wealth. Railroads crisscrossed the continent. Streetcar lines wended through cities and extended into new suburbs. Steamboats plied rivers, lakes, and coastal waters. Telegraphs and telephones vanquished the barriers of distance. Machines turned out more cloth, more shoes, and more steel, sometimes too much; consequently, industry boomed and busted in periodic cycles. It also grew in scale and scope, integrating far-flung facilities into national enterprises. In pursuit of jobs, people flocked from the countryside to cities. Similarly and simultaneously, immigrants from overseas flooded into the nation's urban centers in search of opportunity. In sum, the forces of modernization—industrialization, urbanization, and migration—reshaped the economy and society of the United States during the last third of the nineteenth century.[3]

Such changes did not always progress smoothly. Severe business depressions gripped the country in the early 1870s and 1890s. Both times, violent labor unrest ensued. While cities strained to house, police, care for, and clean up after the multiplying masses, plaintive cries of abandonment, neglect, and exploitation arose from beset farmers in the countryside. Throughout the nation, the taint of greed, graft, corruption, and venality, often masquerading behind the sanctification of Social Darwinism, befouled the air as darkly and pungently as the sooty and smelly smoke billowing from factories. Responses to the crises of the Gilded Age varied. Grangers organized. Knights of Labor united. Rail workers struck. Anarchists rioted. Mugwumps reformed. Bellamy looked backward. Populists crusaded. Coxey's Army marched. Bryan campaigned. Meanwhile, the comfortable, although no less discontented and disconcerted, urban upper classes searched for solutions to society's ills as participants in the colonial revival, arts and crafts, social purity, country life, back-to-nature, strenuous life, and city beautiful movements.

Contemporary social critics and future historians have assessed the Gilded Age in a multitude of ways. Echoing Twain and Warner, Edwin Lawrence Godkin, editor of the *Nation* magazine, decried a "chromo-civilization" in which material prosperity gilded moral superficiality.[4] At the end of the century, economist Thorstein Veblen mocked the barbarous acquisitiveness of the age of excess.[5] Beginning the new century, historian Henry Adams characterized the previous one as an age of energy.[6] Commentators in the early twentieth century noted the colorfulness, or colorlessness of the Gay Nineties.[7] Writing amid the Great Depression, which made the economic downturns of earlier times seem mild by comparison, historians during the 1930s found the seeds of industrial capitalism's destruction in the class conflict and resource exploitation cooked up by the "robber barons" during the "Great Barbecue" of the late nineteenth century.[8] Just a generation later, however, the era had become the seedtime for the age of reform.[9] One historian has synthesized the extremes by arguing that the period was both an age of corruption and reform.[10] The consistent and dominant theme throughout the historiography of the Gilded Age has been modernization—the changes wrought by urbanization, industrialization, and immigration.[11] Since the late 1960s, historians have emphasized a variation on this theme, focusing on the organizational transformation of American society during the era.[12]

While each of these interpretations contributes to a fuller understanding of the Gilded Age, my read on the period is that faith in progress was the fundamental belief that underlay the sweeping transformations of the last third of the nineteenth century.[13] It even explains the development of the Poland Spring resort. With the central tenet of their culture called into question by the sporadic economic crises and myriad social problems of the late 1800s, many prosperous Americans retreated to the seashore, mountains, or countryside each summer. Some would argue they escaped. I, however, regard resorts as more constructive than evasive cultural creations. When patrons arrived on the hilltop each summer, they came bearing urban conceptions of status, consumption, health, nature, leisure, and culture. To accommodate these views and restore faith in progress, the proprietors and promoters of the Poland Spring resort attempted to create a perfect world—a mecca, an Eden, a paradise on earth. The middle landscape they constructed sought to bridge the disjunctions between cultural ideal and social reality by blending the best virtues of a nostalgic rural agrarian past and the modern urban industrial present. In short, the goal was to reform a corrupted urban vision by re-forming the rural landscape. Essentially, the project was more than escapist, for the ultimate destination of both the creators and participants was after all, the summer city, not the country farm.

As recent scholarship is making abundantly clear, the rise of resort culture was widespread during the nineteenth century. Many sites competed for the mantle of "Queen of Resorts" or moniker of "the Switzerland of America." The story of Poland Spring merits consideration not only because the resort featured a famous spring, but also because of the confluence of three factors that made the site unique: its location, its seclusion, and its proprietors. Most Gilded-Age resorts in the Northeast were located either along the Atlantic coast or in the mountains of the Appalachian chain. Poland Spring was in between, situated smack-dab in the countryside, and therefore already well on its way to being a quintessential middle landscape. The common location of many summer retreats gave rise to a larger resort community. Leading tourist destinations such as Bar Harbor, Maine, the White Mountains of New Hampshire, and Saratoga, New York, featured large clusters of hotels. In addition, a string of these resort communities located within convenient travel distance of one another ran from Downeast Maine to the Jersey Shore. In contrast, Poland Spring stood alone, lending to it an added element of isolation and exclusivity. Finally, while all resorts had owners and managers, some even as notable as the Rickers, few could claim a family dynasty that spanned several generations over the course of a century. The Ricker family was an essential element of the local color that made the Poland Spring such a unique resort experience, such a successful business enterprise, and ultimately, such a fascinating historical study.[14]

PART I

The People of Progress

In 1890 Henry A. and George W. Poole took time from their busy careers as newspaper publishers, book printers, and electrotype foundry operators in the Mechanic Falls section of Poland to reflect upon the sweeping changes that had taken place since the Civil War. The brothers observed that "old customs, habits, and ways of working, thinking, and speaking" had given way to new ones. The "progress of civilization" had transformed "gloomy forests" into "beautiful villages and populous cities." Moreover, it had annihilated distance through the introduction of steam power and the magnetic telegraph. The spinning wheel, fulling and carding mill, traveling tailor, and itinerant shoemaker had passed permanently into the annals of history. "Articles once wrought by hand, hammer, and hard and tiresome physical exertion," they noted, were "now turned out by machinery in a far more workmanlike manner, and at far cheaper rates." Rather than lamenting these changes, the Pooles celebrated the benefits brought about by "the inevitable law of progress." As the observations of the brothers suggest, faith in progress was the motive force of the Gilded Age. Seemingly everywhere Americans looked, they saw more signs of material advancement—signs that scribes and orators unquestioningly accepted and enthusiastically chronicled as progress. Significantly, their paeans to progress infrequently encompassed considerations of moral improvement. Progress meant cumulatively more production, more consumption, more money, and more leisure, with little consideration of the fairness with which the new riches were apportioned or the beneficence with which they were expended.[1]

For Georgia Drew Merrill, the multiplying production of shoe factories, textile mills, and paper companies in Mechanic Falls and the other towns and cities of Androscoggin County, Maine, demonstrated that it was one of the "most progressive of counties" in the state. For W. A. Ferguson, "rapid and beautiful growth" and "stirring manufacturing activity" provided ample proof that the county's legal center, Auburn, was "a city of energy and progress." For Richard Herndon, the legal careers of local at-

*torneys William H. Newell and George C. Wing qualified them as "men of progress."
Adopting a slightly less parochial but still provincial point of view, a Mechanic Falls industrialist turned local historian, John W. Penney, proclaimed that "men and women
from Maine" were "in the front of every progressive and honorable employment in the
wide world," as well as "a chief factor in humanity's upward progress."[2]*

*For another of Maine's men of progress, Congressman Nelson F. Dingley, Jr., the in-
exorable expansion of rail mileage was proof of national progress. Speaking at the town
of Poland's centennial celebration in 1895, Dingley marveled that a mere twenty-three
miles of track in 1830 had grown six decades later into a rail system of 180,000 miles that
grid-ironed the nation. Indeed, railroads led the vanguard of progress during the nineteenth century. The expanding transportation infrastructure not only fostered the development of the tourist industry, it also made possible a rise in industrial production.
Railroads hauled raw materials to and finished products from the nation's shoe, textile,
and steel factories. While the population of the United States almost doubled between
1870 and 1900, output in these three leading industries grew respectively by nearly three,
eight, and nine-fold.[3]*

*Progress touched Maine as well. As track mileage in the state increased from 472 in
1861 to 1,356 in 1889, so, too, did business activity and industrial output. In Poland, the
arrival of the railroad during the winter of 1849 proved to be "a great stimulator of
growth." By the close of the next year, eight new stores, three shops, and five mills had
opened at Mechanic Falls. The combination of rail service and waterpower brought one
of the age's "men of progress," Adna C. Denison, to the village the following year to
launch a new industry—papermaking. In 1851 Denison and a partner purchased a
parcel of land along the Little Androscoggin River where they built a mill. During the
1850s, the Eagle Mill produced about a ton of paper per day for books, newspapers in
Lewiston and Portland, and magazines such as the* Atlantic Monthly. *By 1890 the
five mills of the Poland Paper Company produced fifteen tons of paper daily, demonstrating what was termed the "continuous and rapid expansion of business interests" at
Mechanic Falls.[4]*

*Not far from where the Little Androscoggin flowed into its larger namesake, busi-
ness also boomed. In Auburn, located only a dozen miles from Poland, laborers in
twelve shoe factories turned out more than thirteen million pairs of shoes and boots in
1890. This represented more than a twenty-fold increase over the production total at the
end of the Civil War. Across the Androscoggin River in the thriving manufacturing city
of Lewiston, nine companies operated fifteen mills that employed thousands of workers
and annually produced millions of yards of textiles.[5]*

*Such growth in manufacturing required an expanding labor force. The prospect of
employment swelled cities with migrants from the countryside and immigrants from*

abroad. As a consequence, the population of Boston, New York, and Philadelphia doubled and tripled between 1860 and 1900, while in Chicago it multiplied over fifteen-fold. Much of this growth resulted from foreign immigration. Between the elections of presidents Lincoln and McKinley, more than fourteen million people came to the United States. According to the twelfth federal census, about one-third of the nation's population in 1900 was either foreign born or the offspring of immigrant parents.[6]

Urban growth in Maine was equally dramatic. The population of Auburn, Lewiston, and Portland soared. In 1860 Auburn contained 4,022 residents, Lewiston 7,424, and Portland 26,341; by 1900 the respective figures were 12,951, 23,761, and 50,145. As elsewhere in the industrial Northeast, foreign immigrants accounted for much of the increase. Commenting on the situation in his native Androscoggin County, Crosby S. Noyes, a regular patron of the Poland Spring resort, observed: "the foreign element began to come in with the advent of the great manufacturing establishments at Lewiston." A massive migration from the Canadian province of Quebec added to the city, whose population was nearly 40 percent foreign-born in 1900, a distinctively Franco-American cultural influence.[7]

The teeming urban areas of the Northeast supplied the majority of the resort's patrons, many of whom sought refuge from the "foreign elements" filling their home cities. Largely drawn from the families of businessmen and professionals, these people of progress were the disciples who carried out the transformations of the Gilded Age in their roles as builders, leaders, managers, teachers, preachers, and healers. So strong was the force of progress, it even seeped into the countryside and transformed isolated towns by exposing inhabitants to new "commodities, manners and modes of thought." As the Poole brothers observed, "the tide of progress" swept along Poland's "progressive" sons and daughters and led to the creation of the town's "gigantic institution," the Poland Spring resort. The creators of the town's "greatest industry" and Poland's most famous progeny were the Rickers.[8]

The Proprietors

"Jabez Ricker, God says 'you must give the Shakers your farm,'" commanded Father John Barnes, leader of the Alfred Shaker community, in the fall of 1793. "Well, if God says so, it must be so. But you shall pay me for it," replied Ricker.[1] Affirming the prevailing late-nineteenth-century view that progress was providential, Sister Aurelia G. Mace recorded this bit of oral history a century after its utterance. Despite the divine overtones, the exchange also revealed the ascendant secular ideology of the day. It was not religious idealism. It was not republican virtue. It was economic liberalism, the call for individual entrepreneurs to produce, profit, and progress. On behalf of the Shakers, Thomas Cushman did indeed wind up paying Jabez Ricker for his ninety-four acres. As a consequence of this transaction, a farm family moved deeper into the hinterlands of the District of Maine and began a century-long quest to make a hilltop in the town of Poland pay.[2]

Driven first by a sense of family obligation and propelled later by the allure of material wealth, successive generations of Rickers set to work. They became missionaries of liberal capitalism, helping to spread the principles of private property, resource commodification, individual opportunity, risk taking, and profit making into the countryside. In the process, they transformed their piece of the eastern frontier into a secure home, valuable legacy, inviting attraction, and lucrative commodity. In short, the Rickers became people of progress.[3]

In the years following the American Revolution, the Maine frontier, which was still governed by the state of Massachusetts, was neither secure nor inviting. Instead it was a region beset by economic uncertainty, social strife, political turmoil, and religious excitement. This made it fertile ground for converts to the many new doctrines of salvation preached by itinerant evangelists. Thus when Shaker missionaries showed up near Poland in 1783, they attracted many attentive listeners. The meetings so moved one of the local settlers, Eliphaz Ring, that he and his family converted to the teachings of Ann Lee and covenanted their property atop Range Hill to the communal United Society of Believers.[4]

A decade later, another group of Believers at the Shaker enclave in Alfred fixed their attention on the mill privilege owned by their neighbor, Jabez Ricker. After repeated attempts to convince him to join the religion failed, the community tried a new tactic. The Shakers proposed an exchange of property: the Ricker farm in Alfred in trade for the one formerly owned by Ring in Poland. The divine revelation of Father Barnes, along with the "Consideration of four Hundred and fifty Pounds lawful Money" sealed the deal. As Sister Aurelia remarked with the benefit of hindsight, "little did [Jabez] think that his posterity would become what they are, the greatest Hotel Proprietors in the world, and leading men in the state and nation."[5]

The Ricker Family

Sometime in 1794, probably soon after the winter snows had thawed and spring mud solidified, Jabez Ricker, his wife Mary, and eight of their ten children loaded an oxcart with family possessions and set out for their new home. The nearly fifty-mile journey through territory lacking well-traveled roads and often overgrown with thicket took three days. Upon reaching Poland, the weary group found a small house far removed from the nearest road and neighbor. The isolation of the spot unsettled the homesick daughters. According to family lore, the five girls "sat in by the Old Chimney Fire-Place and, placing their buxom cheeks in the palms of their hands 'boo-hooed and bawled' . . . until darkness shut down and they went away to their first night's rest in the new home."[6]

The next morning, or so the Rickers wanted people to believe, the family awoke to find two men at the door seeking breakfast. The hungry travelers, bound for Paris, Maine, had been turned away by the New Gloucester Shakers, whose village was located a short distance from Range, soon to be known as Ricker Hill. Unprepared to serve the strangers, the Rickers nevertheless invited in and fed the pair. This act of hospitality marked the genesis of the family's role as innkeepers. As Hiram Ricker related many years later, "that is how my father went to keeping public house. There was no other place for people to stop."[7]

Realizing the potential of the location as a resting place for farmers heading south to market in Portland and travelers bound as far north as Montreal, Canada, the Rickers began building a new larger house soon after their arrival. Putting "all their time and endeavor" into the project, they cleared additional land and then hand sawed all the lumber, built a kiln and fired each of the estimated twelve thousand clay mortar bricks, and forged every wrought iron nail used in the construction of the structure. At the same time, the family also built a stable large enough to accommodate eighteen oxen. Because of the scope of the tasks and primitiveness of the conditions, the pace of progress was slow. The eight-room, two-and-a-half-story, clapboarded structure, known first as the Wentworth Ricker Inn and later as the Mansion House, finally opened its doors in 1797.[8]

Wentworth Ricker, the son of Jabez and Mary and father of Hiram, ran the inn with great energy, drive, and foresight. He saw to it that the county road was extended through the family's property, thus ensuring a steady stream of passersby who plied "the great thoroughfare" between Portland, western Maine, northern New Hampshire and Vermont, and lower Quebec. Over the years, Wentworth improved the site in other ways as well. First came a woodshed and cider house behind the house. Then, using money earned as a teamster during the War of 1812, he built a barn. Finally, in 1825 he added a second larger stable. All the while, Wentworth Ricker managed the facility as "a tavern of the good old-fashioned sort where landlord was host. Hospitality was met at the threshold; Comfort and Good Cheer awaited the guest within."[9]

With his health failing, Wentworth Ricker turned management of the family homestead over to his eldest surviving son, Hiram, in 1834. Born in the house in 1809, Hiram had spent his youth helping his father operate the farm and inn. His business experience also included brief employment with a Boston clothier, where Hiram was working when called home by his ailing father. Wentworth died in 1837, bequeathing the family's 350-acre property to his two sons, Hiram and Albert, and spinster daughter, Mary. Albert Ricker conveyed his portion of the estate to his siblings, effectively leaving Hiram in charge.[10]

By most accounts, Hiram's greatest strength was his gregariousness. Described as "a good-natured, jovial man," Ricker was known as a "capital conversationalist" and "good story-teller." Although a bit of a character, he was nevertheless a man of uprightness and honesty. These traits suited him well for his new career as an innkeeper. There was, though, an unrelenting restlessness to Hiram. Imbued with the entrepreneurial spirit of the Age of Jackson, he never lacked for schemes to make his fortune, no matter how desperate his straits became. Many years after his death, one family friend characterized him as:

a dreamer and a visionary; a man of remarkable optimism; far-sighted; courageous; careless; a good buyer; a poor seller; always seeing bigger things than the profits at hand; always hanging on until the others sold out and left him to hold the bag—empty as they are sure to be after the others had had their hands in and taken what they could grab.

Another account offered a similar assessment, observing: "Mr. Ricker was a man who could plan great schemes but was unfortunate in putting them into execution."[11]

For the first decade under Hiram's stewardship, the Mansion House remained a busy place. An 1839 report described "the Temperance house" as "a pleasant spot to stop and look abroad." Many years later, Freeland Marble recalled that the inn did "quite a bit of business" during the mid-1840s. Farmers continued to travel the county road, driving livestock and hauling crops to market in Portland. Others remembered the "long lines of teams" that passed through Poland "at all hours of the day." Many of the "rollicking, jolly fellows" journeying to and from Maine's leading commercial center stopped on the hilltop and stayed the night with the Rickers. The family also took in guests for longer recreational stays. Following an initial visit in 1844, Freeman Wight of Roxbury, Massachusetts, returned to the Mansion House with his wife two years later. For Mr. Wight, picking blueberries and drinking spring water were the highlights of a pleasant summer vacation spent at Poland Spring. Over a half century after the stay, he reminisced: "I never had a better time in my life."[12]

Not content merely to care for the family homestead and carry on the family business, the ambitious Hiram became an agent of progress and began his long quest for financial success. Caught up in the market revolution of the mid-nineteenth century, Ricker started trading in sheep and wool. The reduction in protectionist tariff rates originally legislated by Congress in 1846 soon put an end to those speculative ventures. Increased foreign imports caused the value of wool to plummet from fifty to twenty cents per pound. In order to salvage his investment, Ricker rushed his burgeoning stockpile into production. Operating at full capacity for six weeks, the Mayall Mill in nearby Gray, Maine, wove the wool into more than eight thousand yards of cloth.[13]

Nostalgic images of Hiram and Janette Ricker, the noble patriarch and matriarch of the resort, greeted readers of *Poland Spring Centennial*, a souvenir history published by Hiram Ricker and Sons in 1895 to commemorate the Ricker family's first century on the hilltop. Poland Spring Centennial: A Souvenir (*South Poland, Maine: Hiram Ricker and Sons, 1895*), 6 (*author's collection*).

The hardship wreaked by this financial reversal could hardly have come at a worse time, for Hiram Ricker now had a family to support. On May 28, 1846, he had married Janette Bolster in Thompsonville, Connecticut. It was without a doubt the wisest partnership decision Hiram ever made. A native of Rumford, Maine, Janette came from one of the town's leading families. Her mother, the former Cynthia Wheeler, was described as "an exemplary woman, an excellent wife and mother, performing faithfully her duties to her family, to the Christian church, and to the community." Her father, Alvan Bolster, achieved distinction in the areas of business, politics, and the military. He prospered as a farmer and merchant, served as a state legislator for several terms and postmaster for over three decades, rose to the rank of general in the local militia, and held the highest state office in the Sons of Temperance. By the time of his death in 1862, Bolster was one of Rumford's most prominent citizens.[14]

Everyone seemed to admire Janette Wheeler Ricker. A booklet commemorating the family's centennial at Poland Spring remembered her as someone who "was very popular with guests of the Ricker inns, and idolized by her children." It also described Janette as "possessed of all those qualities which go to make the true woman." She was liberally educated, having studied at schools in Kents Hill and Bethel, Maine. She was good with children, lead-ing her to teach for a brief time. She was creative, prompting her to head off to Boston for art training. She also possessed a long list of admirable personal qualities: "uncompromising integrity," "uncommon business as well as ex-ecutive ability," "untiring perseverance," "great strength of character," and "a sunny and hospitable disposition." All of these attributes made her queen of the Mansion House, where she ably performed the roles of "the loved neighbor, the honored hostess, the devoted mother, and helpful wife." Assay-ing her many virtues, one biographer went so far as to credit Janette Ricker with having "had a large share in developing the famous Poland Springs."[15]

The newlyweds' first child, Edward Payson Ricker, was born in the family home in Poland two days shy of the couple's first anniversary. Sometime be-tween that event in 1847 and October of 1850, the family moved to Janette's hometown of Rumford. A local historian recorded that Hiram and Janette Ricker "remained in Rumford a short time after their marriage and were here with one child when the census of 1850 was taken." The couple's second offspring, Alvan Bolster Ricker, was born on October 25, a little over two months after the visit by the census enumerator. The remaining four Ricker children, born between 1852 and 1865, carried on the tradition of coming into the world in the Mansion House.[16]

With one exception, each child went on to play a role in the operation of the family business. Edward succeeded his father and oversaw the develop-ment of the property into a world-renowned resort. Alvan assumed respon-sibility for the farm and culinary departments. Hiram managed the spring water business. Sarah, the most retiring of the siblings, concerned herself with the welfare of the children staying on and living around the hilltop. Janette, who was called Nettie to avoid confusion with her mother, helped edit the resort newspaper and supervise its art gallery. Only the oldest daugh-ter, Cynthia, left Poland Spring. In 1873 she married Oliver Marsh and moved to Springfield, Massachusetts.[17]

The Revolution of 1849

As Hiram Ricker tried to provide for his growing family while recovering from the tariff policies enacted in far off Washington, D.C., he faced a sec-ond, more direct challenge to his livelihood closer to home. In February of 1845 the Maine State Legislature granted a charter to a group of Portland businessmen establishing the Atlantic and St. Lawrence Railroad. With much

During the summer of 1926, the six children of Hiram and Janette Ricker posed for group photographs. Seated are daughters Janette, Cynthia, and Sarah, who preferred to be known as Nettie, Ella, and Sadie. Standing are sons Edward, Alvan, and Hiram, or E. P., A. B., and Hi. *Courtesy Androscoggin Historical Society.*

fanfare and great ceremony, officials broke ground for the project on July 4. Soon thereafter, workmen began laying track at both ends of the route between Portland, Maine, and Montreal, Canada, which had brought prosperity to the Mansion House for over five decades. By 1849, rails on the American side reached Poland. On February 22, a train made the first thirty-mile run from Portland through a landscape that over a half century after the arrival of the Rickers still gave "evidence of having been won recently from a state of nature." The Grand Trunk Railroad leased the newly completed nearly three-hundred-mile rail link and commenced carrying passenger and freight traffic between the commercial center of Quebec and the leading port on the coast of Maine in 1853.[18]

The arrival of the Atlantic and St. Lawrence exemplified the transportation revolution railroads brought to island communities such as Poland. Because the company swung its line several miles to the east of the county road, "the direction of travel and transportation" changed, the economic development of the town shifted, and "Poland Corner was almost deserted." The beneficiary of this "marvelous progress" was Mechanic Falls, where the railroad located a new depot. That section of town blossomed and prospered. For the Rickers, the effect was quite the opposite. The procession of teams that once had made its way over the county road past their inn "at all hours of the day" suddenly ceased. Farmers in the hinterlands served by the railroad no longer had to make the arduous trip to Portland. Even local farmers could bypass Ricker Hill and head directly to Mechanic Falls. In addition, the introduction of the railroad curtailed travel by stagecoach and horseback. Isolated establishments like the one run by the Rickers thrived by providing convenient rest stops for weary drivers, riders, and steeds. The iron horse, however, was untiring. Looking back a half-century later at this difficult period of transition, the Rickers recalled: "the hotel business largely dropped off, as travel by the country road greatly diminished, and the house was distant from the railroad." Guests became so few and far between that Hiram abandoned Poland Spring and relocated his family to Rumford.[19]

Having held on for too long as a wool trader and innkeeper, Ricker next turned his attention to the lumber business. A few months before the arrival of the railroad in Poland, Hiram had purchased 265 acres in Rumford for two thousand dollars, half of which he had borrowed from his wife's father, Alvan Bolster. When Hiram failed to meet the terms of the mortgage by the first-anniversary deadline at the end of 1849, his father-in-law began placing foreclosure announcements in the local newspaper. Under pressure to repay the loan, Hiram borrowed one thousand dollars from David F. Brown of Peru, Maine, in February of the following year. He also busied himself "landing in wood." Apparently, the lumber business was not as rewarding as Ricker had anticipated, because by the end of the year he sought "to hire A Little Mony [sic]" to tide him over until he could "get it [money] out of my wood." Writing in December of 1850 to Dr. Augustus H. Burbank, the son of his sister, Sophronia, Hiram proposed a one-year loan, offering to give "a good Security" and handsome reward in return. Indicative of the wariness with which family members regarded his financial dealings, Hiram concluded the letter by instructing his nephew not to "say any thing to your Father About it." In the end, Hiram's other sister, Mary, bailed him out. On June 14, 1852, he conveyed his remaining half interest in the Rumford property to Mary for three thousand dollars, making a tidy 50 percent profit for himself in the deal.[20]

While in Rumford, Ricker also oversaw the surveying, cutting, and hauling of timber from the wood lots of Portland entrepreneur Francis O. J.

Smith. Smith's interest in the hinterland lying between Portland and Rumford grew out of a loan he had made in 1849 to the cash-strapped stockholders of the recently chartered Buckfield Branch Railroad. Two years later, Smith foreclosed on the mortgage and assumed full control of the struggling company. A grand plan to open up the region between the Androscoggin and Little Androscoggin Rivers for economic development began to unfold once Smith had maneuvered himself in charge. Undaunted by the unprofitability of the thirteen-mile stretch connecting Mechanic Falls and Buckfield, he proposed adding twelve more miles of track to extend the line all the way to the town of Canton. The complementary leg of the travel route would consist of a steamship line plying the Androscoggin River between Canton and Rumford. Smith envisioned that this transportation network would eventually make connections through communities in northwestern Maine all the way to the Province of Quebec.[21]

Freed from his mortgage entanglements in Rumford and optimistic that the transportation revolution, whose adverse economic impact he had already experienced firsthand, also presented ample opportunities for financial gain, Ricker prepared to invest in Smith's venture. In a letter written to Francis Smith on August 18, 1852, he apologized for not having given "any thing towards the Extension of the BB [Buckfield Branch] Railroad as yet." Ricker assured Smith he would contribute the next time the two met, adding that "I will due [sic] what I can towards the Extension for it must go through." Ricker did invest in the second part of the project, the Androscoggin Navigation Company. In 1853 the Maine State Legislature granted five men, including Ricker and his father-in-law, Alvan Bolster, but interestingly not Smith, the exclusive right to navigate steamboats between Canton Point and Rumford Falls. The twenty-year charter included one major stipulation. The corporation had to have at least one thirty-ton steamboat in operation within two years or else risk revocation of its monopoly.[22]

The partners wasted little time getting a boat on the river, the aptly named *Surprise*. On its maiden voyage, the steamer succumbed to the navigational hazards of the Androscoggin River, first running aground at Lunt's Upper Island and then having its tiller and wheel smashed by the swift current at Moore's Rips. The captain managed to maneuver the damaged side-wheeler back to Canton, where it remained, never to leave shore again. The accident forced the investors to abandon the enterprise. Once again, Hiram Ricker had met with failure.[23]

Unfazed by the steamboat ordeal, Ricker next got himself involved in a

plan to establish an axe factory in Rumford. In 1855 Mary Ricker sold the
dam and water privileges at Steep Falls, which were covered by the property
deed her brother had dealt to her three years earlier. Like all the previous ventures with which Hiram had been associated, this one also proved unsuccessful and short-lived. One chronicler described the demise of the factory as
"the crowning climax of Hiram Ricker's financial troubles."[24]

Meanwhile, back in Poland, Hiram had slowly been losing control of the
family homestead. In October 1851, about the time he was felling the forests
surrounding Rumford Falls, Hiram and Mary Ricker mortgaged the farm
for $2,500. Five years later, following failed investments and missed opportu-
nities in wool, real estate, lumber, the railroad, steamboat, and axe factory, the
threat of foreclosure loomed over the hilltop. The intercession of Eleazer
Burbank, the brother-in-law from whom Ricker had tried to conceal his loan
request back in 1850, postponed the day of reckoning by a few months. The
end, however, finally came in October 1856. The foreclosure culminated a
decade of financial decline for Hiram and opened two decades of legal limbo
for Jabez Ricker's legacy.[25]

The Birth of a Resort

The same market and transportation revolutions that had caused the closure
of the Mansion House also held the potential to resupply it with guests. An
expanding network of rail service in northern New England made scenic
outposts such as the White Mountains of New Hampshire and the Atlantic
Coast of Maine increasingly accessible. As a way of adding passenger traffic,
railroads actively encouraged the development of the vacation industry by is-
suing guidebooks promoting regional attractions. Entrepreneurs expanded
existing inns and built new hotels to accommodate the influx of visitors.
During the last half of the nineteenth century, more than 140 resort hotels
sprang up in the White Mountains alone. The development of the tourist
trade in Maine was similarly dramatic. During the 1850s and 1860s, railroads
conveyed visitors into the state who were bound for such newly popular summer coastal attractions as Old Orchard Beach, the islands of Casco Bay, and
Mount Desert Island. As lines branched inland, travelers also headed for
such scenic and recreational outposts as Rangeley and Greenville.[26]

The solitude of pine groves and purity of spring water attracted visitors to
places like Empire Grove in Poland as well. Beginning in 1858, Methodists
held annual summertime camp meetings there. Described as "among the finest

and most convenient" grounds in New England, this religious retreat provided a place for the faithful to restore both body and soul. Perhaps inspired by the success of this local attraction, Hiram Ricker came up with an idea to draw people back to the hilltop. His namesake youngest son recalled in 1894 that the family had operated a dance pavilion in the oak grove behind the Mansion House during the middle to late 1850s. The vagueness of young Hiram's recollection suggests that this undertaking met with about as much success as all the rest of his father's previous business ventures. The unabated string of misfortunes was about to end, however.[27]

A short distance to the north and slightly down the hill from the dance pavilion, water bubbled up from an underground spring. The Indians had known about the spot for ages. White settlers had stumbled upon it during a walk through the woods in 1785. Almost a decade later, Wentworth Ricker had channeled the flow into a trough to water his cattle. The first member of the family to experience the healing powers of the spring had been Hiram's uncle, Joseph Ricker. After unsuccessful treatments with blood blister and calomel in 1800, several eminent physicians had pronounced his fever a hopeless case and left him to die. The lone "humane" doctor who stayed on the case had heeded the patient's pleas for water and instructed an attendant to bring a jug from the spring. According to family lore, Joseph drank the pure water, made a rapid recovery, and lived for another fifty-two years. At the time, though, no one had attached any special significance to the circumstances surrounding Joseph's "miraculous" return to good health.[28]

The next cure credited in retrospect to the water was Wentworth Ricker's case of kidney stones. While helping hired men clear a field near the spring in 1827, Wentworth had sipped the water for refreshment. In time he had noticed that his pain had subsided and then that his ailment had vanished altogether. Yet as Hiram recalled, his father "never knew what cured him." Hiram Ricker claimed the title of discoverer of the "marvellous curative properties" for himself. In 1844 he had suffered an attack of dyspepsia so severe that "the most skillful and celebrated physicians" in Maine pronounced it incurable. While haying with his farm hands in July, he had tried the water without the usual added flavorings of molasses and ginger. Afterward, "much to his surprise and gratification, he was speedily cured." At first, he was unsure what had brought about the recovery. He guessed it had something to do with the water—a hunch he confirmed through investigation and experimentation. Subsequently, Hiram encouraged "all his friends, who were similarly afflicted, to drink freely of it."[29]

The advice was put to the test in the pivotal year of 1859. The first incident occurred in June when a friend brought his gravely ill daughter to Poland Spring for treatment. She was afflicted with a case of constipation that had confounded the best medical minds in Portland. Upon the girl's arrival, Hiram Ricker sent twelve-year-old Edward to the spring to fill a pail for her. After drinking the water for a few days, the patient was well enough to return home. At the same time, neighbor William Schellinger had two experiences that strengthened the Rickers' faith in the medicinal quality of the water. The first arose from Schellinger's habit of drinking from the spring whenever his work brought him nearby. He soon realized that the water quieted the kidney pains that had plagued him for two years. The second confirmation began in June when he received permission from the Rickers to turn a sickly ox into a pasture near the spring. Much to his surprise, the girth of the "emaciated" animal expanded six inches during the summer. The recovery was so complete that Schellinger was able to sell the ox to a butcher by September.[30]

Wishing to lend credibility to his folk remedy, Hiram Ricker went to Portland that same month to have a "reliable and scientific physician" test the water. He called upon Eliphalet Clark, one of the doctors who had attended the girl with the bound up bowels. Supported by anecdotal evidence of the water's medicinal properties, Ricker convinced Dr. Clark to prescribe the remedy on a trial basis. The first patient to receive the treatment was Nathan J. Miller. This "very pale, much emaciated" victim of kidney hemorrhages drank four glasses the first day and felt immediate improvement. In a short time, Miller had fully recovered. Impressed by the results, Dr. Clark placed a standing order for five gallons of the water to be sent to his office twice a week. Thankful that his life had been saved, Miller entered into a partnership with Hiram Ricker to develop the spring commercially.[31]

Ricker had larger ambitions than just selling water. In 1859 his wife's cousin, Dexter D. W. Abbott, had opened a hotel at the site of the Mt. Zircon mineral spring near Rumford. This might have been the example that gave Hiram the idea to promote the combination of the scenic setting and healing waters found at the family homestead. Or it might have been the advertisements placed in a Portland newspaper by the proprietor of the Eagle Hotel in Mechanic Falls, inviting "anyone who desired to partake of the famous mineral springs at Poland" to stay at the establishment. Whatever the source of inspiration, after fourteen years of one failed venture after another, Hiram Ricker, ever the dreamer and aspiring entrepreneur, had finally come up with a way to make the family legacy pay. The allure of the location brought the traveling public back to Ricker Hill. The resort era at Poland Spring was born.[32]

The Mansion House reopened its doors to the public in 1860. By the following year, its guest-rooms were filled to overflowing. In a letter to her youngest sibling, Alvan Augustine Bolster, Janette Ricker told "Guss" about the constant crowd of visitors from mid-June to mid-September, followed by a steady trickle of three to four boarders throughout the remainder of the year. The inn attracted the likes of James Harper, owner of a New York publishing firm, who made sketches of the Mansion House and Spring House during his stay. Joining the Harpers at Poland Spring during the summer of 1863 were the Merriams of Boston, as well as two lawyers from parts unknown and two professors from New York and Chicago. Recalling the appearance of the site six years later, a writer remembered a rough road leading up a steep hill, a spring overgrown with underbrush and "the 'Old Homestead' then, a big roomy country tavern, to which already some seekers for health were beginning to come."[33]

Ironically, the railroad, the engine of progress that had once threatened the very survival of the Mansion House, was now saving it. Trains put Poland Spring within convenient reach of vacationers from throughout the Northeast and Midwest. Travelers arriving in Boston had only to board the "Lewiston" car on northbound Boston and Maine trains. In Portland the car transferred to the Grand Trunk line that rambled three times daily "through one of the most attractive and picturesque sections of New England" on the way to Empire Station in Poland. With stops along the way, the thirty-two mile trip took about an hour and a half. After 1862, travelers also had the option of taking the Maine Central Railroad to Danville Junction located about five miles from Poland Spring. A third station within reach of the Mansion House opened at Lewiston Junction in 1876. In the early years of the resort, Hiram Ricker himself picked up guests at the depots. He brought them the final few miles to the hilltop in a tiny one-horse wagon that only had room for two passengers.[34]

Over time the Rickers increased the radius of their recruitment efforts. An 1883 catalog provided information on the best rail connections from New York and Philadelphia. It also targeted guests of other hotels in the region, explaining how they could reach the resort from the White Mountains. By 1889 promotional literature included travel tips for points of origin as far south as Baltimore, Maryland, and Washington, D.C. Vacationers could board Pullman cars in either city in the afternoon, be in Boston the next morning, and arrive at Poland Spring by the end of the second day.[35]

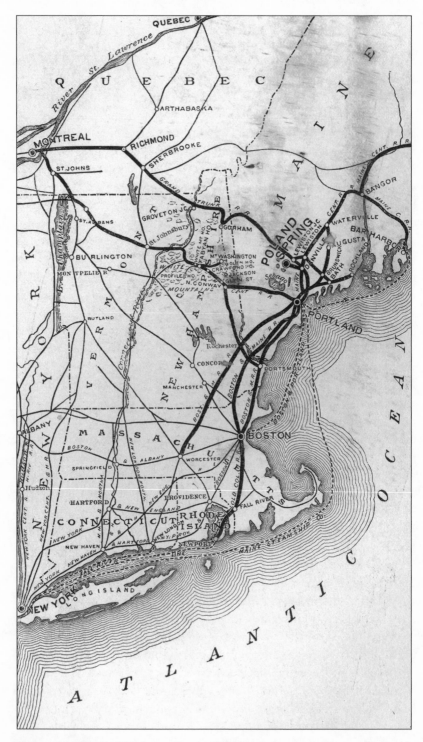

The map showing major Northeast rail routes to Poland Spring appeared in an 1890 pamphlet promoting Poland Spring Water. Poland Spring Water: Nature's Great Remedy and Its Marvelous Curative Properties *(South Poland, Maine: Hiram Ricker and Sons, 1890), [35]. Courtesy Androscoggin Historical Society.*

Another mode of conveyance in the unfolding transportation revolution—the steamship—also made Poland Spring more accessible. As early as 1883, catalogs advised vacationers departing from New York Harbor that they could reach Boston aboard Long Island Sound steamers. At the completion of this leg of the journey, they could either catch trains to Maine or transfer to a Boston and Portland steamer that left each day from India Wharf. Provided passengers made the proper train connections in Portland, they could be at Lewiston Junction by 9:00 A.M. the morning after leaving Boston Harbor. By 1889 travelers departing New York were able to bypass Boston altogether. The Maine Steamship Line offered direct service between New York and Portland, with vessels leaving three times a week from Pier 38 on the East River. Fourteen different steamship lines served Portland by 1896, giving prospective travelers to Poland Spring many options from which to choose.[36]

By train, steamer, stage, carriage, horse, bike, and even by foot, several thousand visitors a summer flocked to the family homestead a century after the Rickers had arrived in Poland. Over the course of the nineteenth century, the progress of liberal capitalism and transformations of the market and transportation revolutions had recast the hilltop, the proprietors who owned it, and the people who summered at it. As the values of liberal capitalism—private property, resource commodification, individual opportunity, and risk-taking and profit-seeking entrepreneurship—had penetrated into the Maine countryside along the banks of mighty rivers and tracks of powerful railroads, the outlook of the family's patriarchs had changed perceptibly. Valuing economic security above all else, Jabez and Wentworth Ricker had been content to pass on the family homestead to their heirs. Hiram Ricker had not been. He had been willing time and again to risk the family legacy—to mortgage property for access to capital—all in pursuit of greater financial rewards. He had been willing to let the imperatives of the marketplace supersede the needs of the lineal family—a family, ironically, that repeatedly interceded to bail the prodigal Hiram out of one misadventure after another. He had been willing to take advantage of the opportunities for personal profit made possible by the protectionist tariff policy of the federal government and a monopolistic charter grant from the state government. In summary, Hiram Ricker had been an entrepreneurial agent of progress. Most of the patrons who visited Ricker's resort shared the same attributes, values, and outlook on life, if not the same checkered path to success.

The Patrons

The Rickers catered to the beneficiaries of Gilded-Age progress—the families of prosperous businessmen, manufacturers, merchants, managers, and professionals. For this status-conscious and anxious group subject to the social flux, fragmentation, and competition attendant to the era's great redistributions of population and wealth, the opportunity to vacation with like-minded and mannered members of the upper middle class was one of the most inviting attractions of Poland Spring. To ensure the predictable social setting expected by patrons, the proprietors tried to maintain a rigid exclusivity at the resort. The Rickers' efforts at shaping the human environment met with mixed results, for controlling the contemporary class, ethnic, and racial conflicts of American society was difficult, even in the relatively homogeneous Maine countryside.[1]

"The Representative People of Our Country"

Although no comprehensive profile exists, statistical and anecdotal evidence suggests the resort's clientele was predominantly urban in origin, upper middle class in status, and white Anglo-Saxon Protestant in heritage. This evidence comes largely from the resort newspaper, the *Hill-Top*. Through its "Arrivals" and "Tid-Bits" sections, the periodical provided weekly lists of guests and occasional details about individual backgrounds. The paper did not, however, conduct a census survey of incoming visitors. While it regularly recorded names, family ties, and hometowns, and randomly reported the occupational status of patrons, it never remarked about their ethnic heritage or racial background. Circumstantial evidence—primarily the practice of religion and patterns of discrimination at the resort—does offer some insight into these two social characteristics of those who vacationed at Poland Spring.[2]

The source of information for the list of arrivals was the guest registers. In addition to containing basic personal information on visitors, the documents supplied the all-important attendance figures by which the Rickers charted the popularity and progress of the resort. In 1893, for instance, attendance totaled 25,682, which according to Edward Ricker actually represented between three thousand and four thousand guests. Although stays averaged between six and eight days, the duration varied in reality from the one day spent at Poland Spring by the loyal core of local patrons to the entire summer spent by guests from away. Most people traveled as part of a group. A total of 1,451 parties registered at the resort in 1894. They ranged from lone individuals joining family members who had already arrived to full families with servants including maids, valets, and coachmen in tow. A typical vacation pattern was for a wife and children to arrive for an extended stay, to be joined later by a husband whose "extensive business interests" permitted him only a week or two away from work, a trip referred to as a "flying visit."[3]

In 1894 guests hailed from twenty-seven states and three foreign countries. Over two-thirds of the arrivals came from three places: one-third from Massachusetts, one-quarter from New York, and a little over one-tenth from Maine. Seven years later, the resort drew 2,435 parties from a wider area, thirty-five states and four foreign countries. Nearly the identical total percentage still called the same three leading states home. Now, though, more local people frequented the resort, as indicated by an almost doubling of the percentage of visitors from Maine.[4]

In addition to its largely Northeastern cast, the clientele had predominantly urban origins. In 1894 well over a quarter of the visitors lived in cities with population in excess of one million. Over 60 percent lived in communities with 100,000 or more residents. In 1901, 10 percent more vacationers came from cities of 500,000 or more, although 10 percent less were from metropolitan areas of 100,000 and above. Residents of Boston, New York City, Brooklyn, and Philadelphia continued to be the resort's most frequent customers. Anecdotal reports confirm the statistical evidence. One observer who made a thorough survey of the Poland Spring clientele in 1892 noted the prevalence of Bostonians and Philadelphians. The journalist also commented on the skewed age distribution of the guests, exclaiming, "what a proportion after all of middle aged and gray-haired elderly people." The final characteristic that caught the reporter's attention was the loyalty of the group. Some of the Boston visitors had been among the earliest patrons of the resort and many members of the Philadelphia crowd had been regularly coming to Poland Spring for the past decade.[5]

In both 1894 and 1901, these two cities ranked among the top four points of origin for resort patrons. A comparison of the 130 Boston families that appeared on either the 1894 or 1901 guest lists with a roster of prominent Bostonians during the era offers insight into the caliber of clientele the Rickers attracted. The seven matches include a lawyer, Linus M. Child; the president of a music publishing firm, John C. Haynes; the co-owner of a rubber company, Rhodes Lockwood; the founder of a shoe manufacturing business, Augustus P. Martin; a dentist and Harvard faculty member, Dr. Eugene H. Smith; the editor of the *Boston Globe*, Charles H. Taylor; and the master of the Suffolk County House of Correction, John C. Whiton. Similarly, among the 145 families that visited from the City of Brotherly Love were the Peppers and Curtises. The family of William P. Pepper, the hard-driving, physically spent provost of the University of Pennsylvania, vacationed at Poland Spring in 1894. This was a departure for Dr. Pepper and his wife, who normally summered at Northeast Harbor, following most other proper Philadelphians to Mount Desert Island. Cyrus H. K. Curtis, in contrast, was the prototypical Poland Spring patron. Born in Portland, Maine, in 1850, he had set out to make his fortune in Boston in 1869, before relocating to Philadelphia in 1876. There, as head of Curtis Publishing, he oversaw publication of two of the most popular American periodicals during the late nineteenth century, the *Ladies Home Journal* and *Saturday Evening Post*.[6]

The resort was filled with many guests who shared biographies similar to Curtis's: a childhood spent in New England, often on a farm, followed by a move to the city, business success, and the struggle as an adult to gain social acceptance among the genteel urban old guard. In sum, they were real-life counterparts to the literary character Silas Lapham. Fashioned by author William Dean Howells as the archetype of the rising Gilded-Age self-made man, Lapham was a Vermont farm boy turned Boston paint magnate. While the Poland Spring resort did not attract someone with the stature and talents of Howells, it did appeal to many families like the fictional Laphams.[7]

The sons of Hiram Ricker actively recruited fellow newcomers to the entrepreneurial, managerial, and professional middle class. An 1877 promotional pamphlet specifically identified the spring's target clientele as clergymen, doctors, insurance executives, bankers, editors, lawyers, and merchants. Observing the following year that "all kinds of characters [are] here good, bad

Guests enjoy the sociability and exclusivity of the veranda at the Poland Spring House. *Maine Historic Preservation Commission.*

and indifferent," a guest was less certain of the respectable character of his fellow patrons. In contrast, advertisements and guidebooks variously characterized visitors to Poland Spring as "cultured," "distinguished," and "in the highest degree refined, aristocratic, and powerful." Hiram W. Ricker described them simply as "perfectly respectable people."[8]

Respectable but not rich, despite the report that Poland Spring swarmed with millionaires during the summer of 1893, the resort did not for the most part attract families representing either old money or the wealthiest new captains of industry. Nor did it attract the Gilded Age's celebrated politicians, literati, or intellectuals. The wealthiest Americans favored the grand hotels of Saratoga, New York, and Cape May and Long Branch, New Jersey; the private cottages on Maine's Mount Desert Island; and the mansions of Newport, Rhode Island. Poland Spring and many of the larger hotels in the White Mountains rated a notch below these more prestigious summer communities. As one journalist commenting on the social differences between the two leading Maine resort areas noted: "Bar Harbor's wealth is at the summer villas and club-houses. Poland Spring's is in the hotel parlor and rotunda." Such notable surnames as Morgan, Rockefeller, DuPont, and Pulitzer did not appear in the "Arrival" column until the opening decades of the next century. Likewise, visits by such prominent politicians as Presidents William Howard Taft and Warren G. Harding and Vice President Calvin Coolidge, as well as by such noted celebrities as actor John Barrymore and boxer Gene Tunney, date the emergence of Poland Spring as a hideaway for the nation's most famous and fashionable citizens to the early years of the twentieth century.[9]

The resort's clientele may not have yet ascended to the most elite national status, but that is the ideal to which many of the patrons aspired. Another of the loyal Bostonians, the Reverend T. A. Dwyer, expressed his lofty social ambitions in an 1896 *Hill-Top* article. He perceived Poland Spring and its guests in aristocratic, almost regal terms. The clergyman anointed the Rickers as descendants of an ancient line of noble Saxon knights. He likened their main hotel to "a majestic palace . . . crowning one of the hills like the princely home of some great potentate." This was to be the summer haunt of the class of vacationers whom the minister immodestly referred to as "the representative people of our country." That was as it should be, Dwyer implied, for only "men of influence and high social standing," certainly not mere farmer lads, could comprehend and appreciate the pleasure-giving and health-restoring powers of the resort.[10]

Dwyer was just one of many clergymen counted among the resort's patrons. The Rickers' policy of lowering room rates for ministers in exchange for their leading worship bolstered the clerical ranks. In 1894 the *Hill-Top* reported that "the priesthood is well represented at Poland by five of the leading members." This large roster of clerics, most of whom were Episcopalians, Congregationalists, or Universalists, afforded guests a wide range of religious services to attend every Sunday. On a typical Sabbath in August 1897, a minister from Washington, D.C. celebrated mass in the early morning and a clergyman from Philadelphia followed later with a sermon entitled, "A Day of Judgment." Julius Gassauer, assisted by a pastor from Chicago, rounded out the day by preaching from John 14:27 on the topic of peace. Gassauer, the resort's headwaiter, had introduced the custom of worship at Poland Spring. His regular Sunday evening meetings drew an "excellent attendance" of coworkers and patrons, who were eager to hear his "carefully-prepared sermons" that bore "testimony to the excellence of his discourses." The Rickers also made provisions for Catholics. Priests from Lewiston came to the Poland Spring House before dawn on Sundays to celebrate morning mass with employees and any interested guests.[11]

One of the most astute observers of the religious scene at the resort, as

well as of social life in general, was Jane L. Patterson, the wife of a Universalist minister. She and her husband, the Reverend Adoniram J. Patterson,
began coming to Poland Spring from their home in Roxbury, Massachusetts,
during the early 1870s. Later she chronicled her impressions of the resort
in a novel entitled, *The Romance of the New Bethesda*. The inspiration for the
book was no secret. An 1896 issue of the *Hill-Top* announced that "'The
New Bethesda' by Mrs. Patterson, will be recognized as located at Poland
Springs." The author's fictitious names for the Mansion House and Poland
Spring House—the Old Stage Tavern and New Bethesda House, respectively—clearly symbolized the stark contrasts she saw between olden days
and modern times. Surveying the spiritual life at the fictional version of her
favorite summer haunt, Patterson observed approvingly that the "opportunity of religious worship" was "ample and varied to meet the needs of all."[12]

Whether this ecumenical spirit extended to the followers of Judaism is
unclear and disputed. The Rickers had no publicly stated policy prohibiting
the admission of Jews, although discrimination could be as effectively practiced covertly. Yet, the family certainly was not shy about making its distaste
for other groups well known. It seems improbable the family barred Jews
outright given some of the surnames listed among arrivals between 1894 and
1901: Adler, Baumgardner, Friedberger, Goldsmidt, Guggenheim, Gutmann,
Kauffmann, Levy, Munchheimer, Naumberg, Nussbaum, Oppenheimer,
Rosenbaum, Schwartz, Stein, Sternberg, Strauss, and Westheimer. In all
likelihood, wealth opened the gates to the largely Gentile bastion for genteel
Jews, just as it occasionally did at even more exclusive resorts.[13]

Nevertheless, the heyday of the Poland Spring resort did coincide with a
period of rising resentment against Jews. Nativist reaction against foreign
immigrants generally and Jewish newcomers from Central and Eastern Europe specifically made the last quarter of the nineteenth century an era of increasing anti-Semitism in the United States. Resorts were one of many
places where Jews found gates formerly ajar now firmly slammed shut. For
some affluent well-assimilated German Jews this often brought an end to
long-established relationships with hotels that had once welcomed them. A
celebrated case in 1877 at Saratoga involving Wall Street financier Joseph
Seligman and hotel proprietor Henry Hilton brought out into the open the
shifting tide from toleration to discrimination. In time, restrictive "gentlemen's agreements" became commonplace in the resort trade and accommodations became rigidly segregated on the basis of religious beliefs.[14]

By at least the mid–1910s, this pattern of prejudice and institutionalized segregation had spread to distant Poland, Maine, too. Across the Range Ponds from the Poland Spring Hotel on Ricker Hill, the Summit Spring Hotel established on White Oak Hill in 1900 gained the reputation as the Jewish resort in town. Later generations of the Ricker family have steadfastly denied that their relatives forced Jews to journey across Poland to find a place to stay. Charles W. Ricker, a grandson of Hiram and Janette Ricker, recalled that Nathan Baum, the manager and then proprietor of Summit Spring, sometimes stayed at Poland Spring. Furthermore, he remembered Baum kidding that "he only took a certain class of Jews at Summit Springs and sent the rest over to us." George Ricker and Catherine Lennihan, the fourth generation to grow up around the resort, have been definite in their recollections that Jewish guests were welcomed at Poland Spring. The strongest evidence supporting the Rickers' claims of nondiscrimination is a pair of letters written by Simon Wolf. Wolf was an attorney, author, advisor to presidents from Abraham Lincoln to Woodrow Wilson, and an advocate for the "civic and religious rights of his persecuted coreligionists, the Jews of eastern Europe." In a note dated August 13, 1917, Wolf thanked Nettie Ricker for her "generous and liberal sentiments." He wrote: "To find in New England a woman all aglow for the history and people of the stock of Abraham and Moses is a revelation and gratification." Another letter written a month later makes clear that Wolf was not the only Jewish patron at Poland Spring that summer. In addition to Simon and Amy L. Wolf, five other guests, including New York merchant Jacob Gimbel and Belle K. Sondheim, who added her name "with pleasure," signed the note of gratitude.[15]

The Dickinsons: A Tale of Two Cities

Representative of the class of people who vacationed at Poland Spring was the family of Colonel John T. Dickinson. Dickinson knew of the resort in his capacity as secretary of the World's Columbian Commission, the body that oversaw the celebration held in Chicago in 1893 to commemorate the four-hundredth anniversary of the European discovery of the Americas. It was Dickinson whom the chairman of the Committee on Awards notified that Poland Spring water "was the only spring water east of New York that received an award at the World's Columbian Exposition." If Dickinson visited the second-floor gallery of the Agricultural Building, he would have seen in addition to the Rickers' towering Poland Water display, many "fine paintings and scenic views of their famous springs and grounds" that "added very materially to the decorative appearance" of the Hiram Ricker and Sons' booth. Dickinson's boss, Thomas W. Palmer, president of the Commission, had been impressed enough by the Rickers' lavish promotion of the resort to visit Poland Spring in July. In the end, recommendations by one of the leading physicians in the nation's capital clinched Dickinson's decision to travel to the site during the summer of 1893. The resort's healthful location, charming elevation, picturesque scenery, sumptuous accommodations, airy rooms, manifold attractions, and superior management so impressed Dickinson that he prepared to bring his family back to the hilltop again in 1894.[16]

This summer Dickinson's desire to leave Chicago was more urgent, and not only because of the uncomfortably sweltering midsummer weather. The nation was still mired in an economic depression brought about by the failure of several major railroads in early 1893. One of the places where the shock waves of the collapse were being felt most severely was the Pullman Palace Car Company. There on the southwest outskirts of the sprawling metropolis of Chicago, labor unrest was fomenting. Even in far-off Maine, the news from the Windy City was "the story of the week." The hard times that had befallen the overexpanded railroad industry had caused George Pullman to reduce wages 30 to 70 percent. Angered that the paternalistic industrialist had not commensurately reduced rents levied on company housing and prices charged at company stores, workers had gone on strike in early May 1894. When met several months later with two thousand federal troops sent to Chicago by President Grover Cleveland to end the widening protest, the strikers resorted to violence. Rioters tipped over rail cars, tore up tracks, destroyed freight, torched buildings at the World's Fair grounds, and generally laid siege to the guiding principles of the White City and Gilded-Age liberal capitalism. Only "the strong arm of the federal government" restored "peace and order," but not before blood was shed and lives lost. Coincidentally, the defeated strikers surrendered about the same time Col. Dickinson and his family retreated. Little did the Dickinsons realize that the social order of their vacation paradise would also need defending during this eventful summer.[17]

Propelled by the turmoil swirling around them, Dickinson, his wife, and his stepdaughter, Louise Mattocks, left their apartment in the Hotel Metropole located at the corner of Michigan Avenue and 23d Street and on a steamy Sunday afternoon in mid-July headed for Union Station. There they boarded a train bound for the safe environs and refreshing climes of Maine. Because of "all the *striking* effects" surrounding the Pullman dispute, the Dickinsons purposely avoided American rail lines as much as possible. Instead, they opted to take the Grand Trunk, a line that kept them in Canada for much of the journey. Ironically, the family likely boarded a Pullman car that the very strikers they were trying to avoid had produced. If so, they would have found themselves surrounded by an elegant decor of mahogany and vermilion woodwork, plush upholstery, Wilton carpets, and silk draperies in a color scheme of fawn, empire green, and steel blue that bespoke refinement and exclusivity. Moreover, the family would have had access to other equally luxurious specialty dining, drawing, sleeping, parlor, library, and observation cars on what amounted to a resort on rails.[18]

Departing Chicago at 3:00 P.M. on Sunday, the Grand Trunk's "Seaside and White Mountains Special" chugged out of the Windy City and was soon whirling through the farm country of Illinois, Indiana, and Michigan. Once in Canada and safely distanced from labor strife, the family took a quick side trip to explore the Thousand Islands region of the St. Lawrence River. Later on Monday, the Dickinsons found time to drive through Montreal and dine at the Windsor Hotel. That evening, they boarded the Grand Trunk's Portland Sleeper and departed the city at 8:40 P.M. After a ten-hour ride, the family arrived in Danville Junction. The last leg of their nearly forty-hour sojourn, "an exhilarating drive over the beautiful hills of Maine," delivered the Dickinsons to the entrance of the Poland Spring House early Tuesday morning, July 17.[19]

During the seven weeks the Dickinsons vacationed at Poland Spring they made quite a favorable impression. A native of the Lone Star state, John Dickinson came to Maine with a Texas-sized reputation befitting his ample girth. One biographer admiringly observed: "He is a man of commanding presence. Five feet ten and a half inches in height, of considerable magnetism, courteous and dignified in manner, kind-hearted, and generous, and always attracts those who come within the circle of his influence." Given this build-up, it is no wonder the *Hill-Top* identified Mr. and Mrs. Dickinson as regular participants in the wide variety of recreational activities available at the resort. They played lawn tennis and croquet. They went down to Middle Range Pond to row, sail, and ride the steam launch. On the few days it rained, they bowled and played pool. Walks through "bewitching wooded paths" and on the boardwalks leading to the Mansion House down one side of the hilltop and the Spring House down the other provided the couple with additional opportunities for "healthful exercise."[20]

Mr. Dickinson drank in the combination of pleasure and health thirstily. Part resort, part sanitarium, Poland Spring was, in his opinion: "the happiest

Before vacationing with his family at Poland Spring during the tumultuous summer of 1894, John T. Dickinson served as Secretary of the World's Columbian Commission, the body that organized the international exposition held in Chicago the prior year. *Julian Ralph*, Chicago and the World's Fair *(New York: Harper & Brothers, 1893). Courtesy Paul V. Galvin Library, Digital History Collection, Illinois Institute of Technology.*

dual resort for the seeker after health and the seeker after pleasure that can possibly be found in the United States." Dickinson especially appreciated the healing powers of the water, crediting it with curing suffering humanity "of all the ills to which flesh is heir." Commenting on his experiences, the Colonel cleverly paraphrased Julius Caesar: "I came, I saw, and I concurred." "Nature and the Ricker Brothers," he observed, had joined forces to create an ideal setting for a summer outing.[21]

Mr. and Mrs. Dickinson did not involve themselves very much in the social life of the resort. Mrs. Dickinson did chaperone a hop at which her daughter took the lead in dancing the Virginia reel. She also played cards on Friday evenings in the amusement room of the Poland Spring House. On August 3d, the same day, coincidentally, that the Pullman strike officially ended, she was even fortunate enough to win a lady's workbag as second prize during a round of the favorite card game of the people of progress, progressive euchre. Described as being "particularly well suited to social gatherings," the rules of euchre assigned players to tables of four, where teams of two competed against one another. Since partners changed at the end of each game, participants had the chance to intermingle extensively. The objective was to win as many games as possible and by so doing, to progress toward the head table. At the end of a prescribed length of time, usually two hours, the competition ceased and the hosts presented prizes to the contestants who had accumulated the most points.[22]

The social butterfly of the family was Louise Mattocks. This "most charming of Chicago's fairest daughters" spent much of her time with six young people: Rita and Blanche Todd of New York and Helen Stinson of Philadelphia, escorted by Allen M. Rogers of New York and John H. and Arthur A. Maginnis of New Orleans. Much like Miss Mattocks, the Maginnis cousins had escaped labor strife at home; only in this case the strike was against the family's cotton mill, the largest such enterprise in the entire South. Happily oblivious to the hardships faced by urban workers amid a depressed national economy, the "lucky seven" took drives to many of the featured escapes surrounding the Poland Spring resort, including Pope's kennels on White Oak Hill, the Wilson House in Raymond, and the State Fair in Lewiston. On Monday July 30th, Louise invited several of her new acquaintances on a carriage ride to the "secluded hamlet" of New Gloucester. According to the prescriptive promotional literature, the excursion was supposed to evoke sublime responses to the scenery of the countryside. In truth, the unsupervised trip was marked more by youthful horseplay than reflective romanticism. The group spent a "most enjoyable afternoon" blowing the coach horn, singing college songs, bellowing the Poland yell, and otherwise showing off for and making a nuisance of themselves to the locals.[23]

The exploits of Miss Mattocks and her friends made them centers of attention at the resort as well. On the 8th of August, they had "a jolly party" aboard the steam launch down at the Range Ponds. Several weeks later, the young people attended the Mother Goose costume party. Louise went as Jill. Her "most attentive" Jack was Allen Rogers. The impression "the beautiful young lady" made that evening "well sustained her reputation as the prettiest woman in the house."[24]

As the calendar turned to September and the first cool and bracing autumn days descended upon the hilltop, the family's time at Poland Spring wound down. During their stay at the resort, the Dickinsons had "won many friends." The *Hill-Top* was certain the family would be "much missed by a large circle of acquaintances." On September 6th, Col. Dickinson, his charming wife, and pretty daughter boarded a stage, beginning the long trip back to Chicago. Despite the natural beauties of Maine, the many friends they had made during their two visits, and all the social and recreational activities the resort offered, the family never returned to Poland Spring.[25]

Perhaps the assaults against social exclusivity experienced at Poland Spring during the summer of 1894 irreparably shattered for the Dickinsons the illusion of safe escape from the realities of the modern world. The list of incidents was disturbing. A group of "objectionable" men from Mechanic Falls had molested some guests one night. A white waitress had been caught walking in the woods with a black man. The Rickers had banished several members of the resort baseball team for rowdy behavior. These sporadic breaches of order paled, however, in comparison to the alarming possibility that the Portland and Rumford Falls Railroad might routinely transport carloads of "picnickers and excursionists" to the area.[26]

Guarded Gates

To the Rickers, the troubling events of 1894 pointed to the need for the family to exercise firmer control over access to its property. They feared that if they did not regulate the makeup of the human environment, their resort would lose the exclusivity demanded by the people of progress. Succumbing to "the excluding mania of the Gilded Age," which segregated by race, class, and ethnicity the nation's neighborhoods, schools, and clubs, as well as recreation spots, the family erected barriers, both visible and invisible, to better shape the social landscape of Poland Spring. Whom the Rickers kept under close tabs or kept out completely reveals a great deal about the prejudices of those they let in, the social upheaval of the Gilded Age, and the limits of moral progress during the last quarter of the nineteenth century.[27]

The Rickers made no attempt to conceal the fact they discriminated against many groups in order to maintain the exclusivity of the resort. Because of their proximity, local residents, with a few exceptions, headed the list of groups kept at a safe distance. While they were welcome to pass over the grounds, most knew better than to stop for a visit. Those who did not, such as a party from Casco, Maine, were halted at the guarded gates and told that excursionists were forbidden from entering the grounds. A local lawyer, Jesse M. Libby, was so sure "ordinary country people" knew their place that he offered to wager that fewer than a dozen residents of Poland had ever dined at the Poland Spring House.[28]

To preserve the social exclusivity of the resort, the Rickers had guarded gates installed at the entrances to the hilltop in 1894. Poland Spring Centennial: A Souvenir (*South Poland, Maine: Hiram Ricker and Sons, 1895*), 27 (*author's collection*).

The keepers of the gates worried far more about ordinary city people than county folk. The Rickers feared that "picnickers and excursionists," a euphemism for the predominantly Franco-American working class that populated the mill town of Lewiston, would take advantage of the cheap fares offered by the Portland and Rumford Falls Railroad to visit Poland Spring on day trips. Voicing the family's concern to a local reporter, Edward Ricker claimed that the influx of "large excursion parties and curiosity seekers . . . would ruin the reputation of my house and drive away the clientage that we have worked so long to secure." A friend and neighbor of the Rickers, Boston coffee merchant James S. Sanborn, concurred. Sanborn predicted that five- and ten-cent fares would attract a "certain grade of people." He did not mean to imply that this class of travelers lacked good character, only that they were not "people of wealth who spend their money." Sanborn based his opinion on reports of how rising tides of excursionists had adversely altered the character of Old Orchard Beach in Maine and Revere and Nantasket Beaches in Massachusetts.[29]

While the Rickers openly banned excursionists, if they practiced other forms of discrimination they did so discreetly. Class barriers, most notably in the form of the cost of admittance to the hilltop, were sufficient to screen out most undesirable elements. Thus, the Rickers did not bother to erect the formal racial barriers that Jim Crow laws established so effectively elsewhere in the nation. That did not mean everyone at Poland Spring was white. Native and African Americans were permitted beyond the gates of the resort, but only to fill specific and restricted roles.

Native Americans, the iconic Gilded-Age children of nature and exemplars of the arts and crafts ideal, were at the resort essentially for show. During a pilgrimage to most of the major Northeastern resorts in 1886, Charles Dudley Warner noted the prevalence of Indian traders. He complained: "the occupation of being a red man, a merchant of baskets and bead-work, is taken up by so many traders with a brogue and a twang at our watering-places that it is difficult for the traveller to keep alive any sentiment about this race." Untroubled by Warner's reservations about native authenticity, the Rickers allowed Penobscots from Old Town, Maine, to pitch tents across the road from the spring. From the spot, the Indians sold souvenirs to curious guests. Drawn by the opportunity to make some money, so many Native Americans initially showed up that within a few years they had "overrun" the place and become a "nuisance." At that point, Edward Ricker limited the encampment to just one family, refusing all other applicants. Ricker explained that he permitted the token appearance of the Indians because "they come there to sell their work and to a certain extent as long as they are quiet, they are an attraction."[30]

The *Hill-Top* actively promoted the commodification of Native American culture by encouraging guests to "hie to the tent of Hiawatha." At the campsite, they could watch Newell Neptune make bows and arrows, talk with him about moose and caribou hunts "in the great wilderness," inhale the fragrance of sweet grass boxes, examine "the neat construction" of his handiwork, and most important of all, purchase "pretty things" as souvenirs. This final act truly distinguished "the descendants of that great race" from the disciples of the leisure class. The antimodern "noble red man and his squaw" produced; the modern white man and his wife consumed. The middle ground where they could "bury the hatchet and smoke the pipe of peace" was the Indian encampment turned Gilded-Age bazaar.[31]

The encounter between the two races ultimately served as "an object lesson in the possibilities of human progress and development." The "end of the nineteenth-century red man" encountered at the campsite had shed the "yellow ochre, feathers and bear's teeth" worn by his "savage" progenitor. A conversation with Neptune revealed someone who was "well spoken, courteous, polite, graceful, tall, manly, vigorous and interesting." In short, he was a "civilized" person. Yet as a premodern symbol, he could not be considered fully modern and therefore, he could not be allowed any farther beyond the guarded gates than the grove surrounding the spring. That is where the proprietors stuck the Indians in their historical pageant of the progress of civilizations. In the grand social tableaux of the resort, Native Americans had not earned the privilege to ascend to the hotel on the hilltop. That exalted spot remained the exclusive domain of the people of progress.[32]

Showmanship in the form of musical talent did get some minorities beyond the gates and all the way to the top of the hill. During the 1890s, groups of African American students from Atlanta University, Hampton Institute, and Tuskegee Institute regularly came to Poland Spring to entertain during their annual tours of New England summer resorts. On July 28, 1896, for instance, a quartet from Atlanta University sang "darkey melodies" to the accompaniment of the mandolin, guitar, and banjo. For their efforts, the students collected $47.23 in donations. Two weeks later, a similar group from Hampton Institute in Virginia entertained. In addition to the musical program, several speakers from the school addressed the audience. The principal presented an overview of the organization; while a graduate offered the black student perspective and a Native American told about the good work Hampton was doing for "his people." Finally, Mr. Daggs spoke on other African American educational institutions in the South.[33]

Booker T. Washington also traveled the New England resort circuit seeking support for the advancement of Southern blacks. He justified the trips to the North on the grounds that they exposed his message to new audiences. The program typically included a musical performance by a quartet of students, followed by his stock lecture, "The Negro in America: His Conditions and Prospects." The receptivity of audiences to his harangues on the "Southern Question" surprised him. Washington made his first trip to Poland Spring in July 1895 and was an immediate sensation. His eloquent pleas, convincing statements, and clever anecdotes in support of "the training of colored youths" caused his wealthy white listeners to dig deep into their wallets. During his stay, he raised over $250 for Tuskegee Institute. The appeal and success of his mission ensured return visits for many years to come. In 1897 students from the school joined him. The following year,

Mrs. Washington, speaking on behalf of Southern black women, accompanied her husband. By 1900 the *Hill-Top* considered Washington "one of the most famous of colored men of this or any age."[34]

Being a famous African American was also Frederick Douglass's ticket to Poland Spring. Jane Patterson placed Douglass at the fictional New Bethesda during the summer of 1878, well before guests had decided whether a great black man should be welcome on the hilltop. In her novel, a Southern woman felt the resort had "no right to entertain negroes without asking the guests if it is agreeable." Much to the woman's dismay, her husband spoke in favor of the celebrated abolitionist's admittance: "That man is no ordinary bootblack. That is Fred Douglas [sic]. He is a great man, Frances. We don't mind the color of great men." Persuaded to address the resort's white patrons despite his reluctance to antagonize Southerners "with all their prejudices," Douglass mesmerized an attentive, standing-room-only audience with his eloquent oratory. According to Patterson, the "profound impression" this passionate defender of liberty made on guests caused many of them to regard him like a prophet of old.[35]

In spite of the esteem felt for Douglass, Washington's message of black self-improvement better salved patrons' consciences and fit their conception of post-Reconstruction racial progress. The *Hill-Top* praised an unnamed "very black man" in the South for preaching the liberal capitalist, *laissez-faire* doctrine of "work out your own problem" even more sternly than Washington did. Reminding his congregation that whites had contributed a great deal of money to educate freedmen, the speaker beseeched his audience to "get up and hustle for yourselves." He assured them that "there is room for you if you educate yourselves and don't fuss about being black." The resort newspaper rejoiced that a black man spoke the "good, plain, hard facts," or more bluntly, that he dared "to lash the 'nigger,'" for no white man could have done so "without creating a riot." Having seized upon an anonymous Uncle Tom to make their point of black self-help and white absolution, the editor was quick to disavow responsibility for use of a racial epithet whose use was inflammatory even more than a century ago. Besides setting it off in quotations, the paper added a parenthetical note stating that the black orator had peppered his talk with this slur instead of the more genteel appellations "colored man" or "negro." Naively believing that no "line of human activity" was closed to hardworking, well-behaved blacks, the editorial looked forward to the peaceful emergence of "the new negro" from an admittedly dark racial past.[36]

One of the lines of human activity open to African Americans at the resort was as workers. Patterson recalled that in 1881 "colored Dick" served as an elevator operator "with the courtesy of his race." A Poland Spring House breakfast menu from the same period featured an engraving of a black waiter on the cover, although it may have been a stock printing image. Besides the blacks employed by the Rickers, some guests brought along their African American domestic servants and carriage drivers. One of those workers brazenly disrupted the carefully guarded social harmony of the resort during the 1895 season. The culprit was the same "colored man" who had violated social taboo the previous year by going for a walk in the woods with a white table girl. This summer he had been spreading the rumor that one of the waitresses "had the clap [and] that he could have had connection with her, if he so desired." To make matters worse, the man had "freely expressed" that he owned a gun and would use it if any of the Rickers bothered him.[37]

Ironically, the unidentified man's greatest defiance of the social order came on August 28th, the date of the resort staff's masquerade party. This annual event marked the one time during the season when the social hierarchy differentiating proprietors and patrons from employees was overturned and workers "owned the house." Thanks to the generosity and goodwill of the Rickers and the support of the guests' amusement committee, bellboys and housekeepers escaped their own cares and worries for a few hours by dressing up and living out fantasies. The guest list of masqueraders typically included "a sprinkling of clowns, Chinamen, Indians, Monkeys, Harlequins, and Sailors."[38]

The 1895 event attracted more than eighty participants. At nine o'clock in the evening, the partygoers assembled before spectators and marched into the music hall of the Poland Spring House to begin an evening of dancing and dining. While the costumes of Bertha Jordan, who wore a dress emblazoned with Hill-Top banners, and Annie McCarthy, who covered her dress with Poland Water tags, surely pleased their employers, they did not receive top honors. Instead, prizes for best costumes were awarded to guests who came dressed as the King of Hungary, a snowflake, a pinecone, an Indian, and in shows of working-class solidarity, a washerwoman and a member of Jacob Coxey's Army. If this masquerade was anything like the one held the previous year, the employees enjoyed a program of dance music performed by the "ever superior" orchestra. Amid the order of dances, the revelers would have removed their masks and revealed their identities at the sound of the cornet. In both years, the "jolly" party concluded in the dining room with a late-night feast organized by the Rickers.[39]

While many of the employees of the resort prepared for the ball, the defiant black man and several of his companions were getting drunk in the stable. They became so boisterous that Hiram W. Ricker eventually came to investigate, although he dared say nothing to them. Later, in the midst of the party, the man made his way to the Poland Spring House, where he proceeded to smoke a cigar in the main dining room. When asked to leave, he at first refused and then "took his time about going out." His final act of defiance occurred during an encounter with a night watchman. The drunken troublemaker told the watchman he did not care what happened to him because he would be departing Poland Spring in the morning. The incident affirmed both the perceived utility and actual futility of the guarded gates. The disorderly conduct of the black man was precisely the type of behavior the urban elite hoped to leave behind when they passed through the entrance to the resort. Yet, because of their attachment to the luxury and status of servants, many guests inadvertently introduced festering racial and class tensions to the social landscape of Poland Spring.[40]

"The War of the Stages"

Maintaining exclusivity meant not only controlling the human environment of the resort, but also the means of access to it. When business rivals threatened to break the family's local monopoly on stage and train service, and lodging too, the Rickers reacted with consternation. The tumultuous year of 1894, with its many forays against the invisible barriers restricting entry to Ricker Hill, culminated in a bitter feud and the construction of very visible gates and guardhouses to protect Poland Spring as a preserve for the people of progress.

The Rickers' main adversary was the upstart Portland and Rumford Falls Railroad. Established in 1890 out of the remains of several earlier attempts to connect Mechanic Falls and Rumford, including the short-lived Buckfield Branch Railroad in which Hiram Ricker had once invested, the rail line was one fiefdom in the business empire presided over by Hugh J. Chisholm. A former newsboy on the Grand Trunk run between Toronto and Detroit, Chisholm had parlayed the job into a thriving publishing company based in Portland that specialized in production of pictorial travel guides promoting the Victorian tourist trade. To ensure the supply of paper for his enterprises, this quintessential Gilded-Age man of progress planned to transform the "forest-covered wilderness" around Rumford, where Hiram Ricker had once lumbered, into an industrial city. The transformation entailed four phases: erecting a dam across the Androscoggin River, excavating canals for water power, constructing three factories, and extending the former Buckfield Railroad to Rumford at its northern terminus and Auburn at its southern terminus. By the end of 1893, Chisholm's Rumford Falls Paper Company was producing over one hundred tons of pulp and paper per day. The railroad branch ensured a connection to the Maine Central, a trunk line that could ship the paper to markets outside the state.[41]

Initial plans called for the southern branch of the Portland and Rumford Falls Railroad to follow a direct route from Mechanic Falls through Minot Corner and on to Auburn. While the survey was under way, Chisholm and Edward Ricker met to discuss the possibility of bypassing Minot and instead swinging the line through Poland Spring. Ricker reportedly "entered heartily into the matter." In fact, according to George D. Bisbee, an official of the railroad, Ricker's support was decisive in convincing the directors to scrap the Minot route in favor of one that would run through Poland Spring. At first, Ricker took an active interest in planning the branch. In September 1892, he brought Bisbee to the top of the Poland Spring House's main tower and pointed out to the head of the railroad's committee on location and land damage several possible routes to pass through the town. Furthermore, Ricker used his influence to persuade local property owners to cooperate with the railroad. He also personally selected the location of the Poland Spring station at Poland Plains. Ricker preferred this site because it commanded the best view of the resort.[42]

A critical issue the two parties could not agree on was where the line should connect with the Maine Central. Edward Ricker insisted that it be at Danville Junction. This "advertised center" was where ticketing arrangements between the Rickers and passenger agents for various railroads called for most guests to arrive. Consequently, this was where the Rickers had located their stage service. Another depot a few miles to the north would only confuse passengers and might take business away from the store and two stables the family owned in Danville Junction. The Rickers protested that they could not afford to lose any business since their stage line already operated at a "dead loss."[43]

The directors of the railroad preferred a connection at Hackett's Crossing because it was closer to the large Lewiston-Auburn market. They rejected alternative routes to Danville proposed by Edward Ricker on the grounds that sharp grades would make construction too expensive. Although Ricker was clearly disappointed by the railroad's decision, he still supported the project, or so Bisbee believed. He was mistaken. Once it became clear in 1893 that track was not being laid to Danville, rumors began to circulate that the Rickers were contemplating building their own branch. Several attempts by Bisbee to discuss the matter with Edward Ricker were rebuffed with the response that he was away in New York.[44]

The Rickers were indeed planning to build their own rail line. Once the Portland and Rumford Falls Railroad made its connection with the Maine Central, the family allied itself with the rival Grand Trunk. On March 5, 1894, the Rickers filed articles of association with the State Board of Railroad Commissioners proposing to lay three and a half miles of track between their bottling plant and the Grand Trunk station at Lewiston Junction. Capitalized at $25,000, the Poland Spring Railroad was controlled by the three Ricker brothers who owned 243 of the 250 shares in the company. Their interest in the project cooled when they learned that state law would not permit them to run the branch as a private line. If the Rickers could not use the railroad to control access to the resort, it would be of little value to them.[45]

While this maneuvering was going on, the Portland and Rumford Falls Railroad inaugurated on February 12th its service over the eleven-and-one-half-mile branch connecting Mechanic Falls and Auburn. Now instead of getting off at Danville Junction, Maine Central passengers could continue on a few miles to Hackett's Crossing, which the railroad had renamed Poland Spring Junction. From there, a Portland and Rumford Falls train would take them to a station in Poland Spring. Guests of the resort could journey the final two miles by stage. To the directors of the railroad, the advantage of this new route was obvious. Reducing the length of the trip by one-half to two-thirds would reduce the amount of time the traveling public would have to spend in a hot, dusty, bumpy coach. The Rickers did not see the situation the same way.

With the summer travel season only a few months away, Bisbee and fellow director Waldo Pettengill sent the Rickers a letter in mid-March, explaining the preparations the company had made to receive passenger traffic. The railroad had negotiated ticketing arrangements with several carriers and had secured a contract with the American Express Company. The directors expected the Poland Spring station to be ready for business by June 1st. In the meantime, they wanted to discuss again the possibility of hauling freight for Hiram Ricker and Sons and asked for "hearty co-operation" in establishing stage service to the resort.[46]

The presumptuous tone of the correspondence irked Edward Ricker. The response he fired off a few days later registered his irritation. He declined the offer to operate the railroad's stage line, explaining later that running a second line would "double the expense and divide the business." Furthermore, Ricker informed the directors that he would deny the company's carriages access to the family's private property. He also warned that in all likelihood passengers who traveled on the Portland and Rumford Falls Railroad would be unable to find accommodations at the resort. Finally, Ricker stated his intention to place advertisements in papers warning people away from the line, unless the company changed the name of Poland Spring Junction.[47]

The letter caught officials of the railroad by surprise. According to Bisbee, this was the first time Edward Ricker had mentioned that he would deny passengers of the railroad access to the resort. The threat was especially disconcerting because the company had already begun to sell tickets for the fast-approaching summer season. Confident that negotiations could resolve the dispute, Bisbee visited Edward Ricker a few weeks after the exchange of letters. His peace mission failed. Ricker not only refused to budge from the positions he had already stated, he threw up another roadblock. Gates would limit access to the road leading to the resort. Subsequent appeals by Bisbee for cooperation, as well as further direct discussions with Hugh Chisholm, went nowhere.[48]

As far as the Rickers were concerned, the matter had moved beyond honest misunderstanding to deliberate attempts to undermine their business. The fact that the railroad had named two of its stations Poland Spring especially peeved the proprietors of the resort. Edward Ricker was certain it was part of a deliberate scheme to steal passengers away from his family's stage service. He was also concerned that the railroad intended to establish picnic grounds for day-trippers on the fifty-plus acres it had acquired between Poland Spring Station and Lower Range Pond. The half-mile shore frontage there would provide ideal water access for swimmers and boaters. In addition, three businessmen from a drug company in Philadelphia had formed the Wampole Hotel and Spring Company in 1891 and purchased the Colomy farmstead located directly across the county road from the Mansion House. The trio intended to invest $35,000 in the property and turn it into a rival resort. The plan called for the construction of a springhouse, bottling plant, observatory, and hotel with a capacity of 75 to 125 occupants. The best way to get guests to the proposed new hotel would be to bring them by stage from Poland Spring Station over Ricker Hill, right past the Poland Spring and Mansion Houses.[49]

The Rickers responded to the competition by doing everything in their power to frustrate the railroad's plans. As threatened, they placed advertisements stating that the Danville Junction stage was the only authorized means to reach the resort. Furthermore, they used their considerable influence to persuade—some said intimidate—railroad agents to ticket passengers exclusively by way of Danville Junction. When the Portland and Rumford Railroad tried to start its own stage line, the Rickers refused to allow the company to stable its horses at Poland Spring. After the directors made arrangements to board teams with Charles Nevens, the Rickers bought him out. Then when a petition began to circulate asking the county commissioners to take the road over Ricker Hill by eminent domain, the Rickers responded by drawing up a counterpetition. Hiram W. Ricker himself canvassed for signatures at the town's Fourth of July celebration. Finally, the family pushed for a special town meeting to enlist aid in defending its property "from the encroachments of objectionable excursion parties." Convened on August 16th, the session drew almost two-thirds of Poland's citizens. By a nearly unanimous vote, they instructed the selectmen "to use all fair and honorable means to defeat the petition" backed by the railroad. The show of support affirmed for the *Hill-Top* the "esteem in which the Messrs. Ricker are held by their townsmen."[50]

With the arrival of the season's first vacationers in June, what a local paper described as "a very picturesque little war" heated up. The Portland and Rumford Falls Railroad went ahead with its plans to carry passengers from Poland Spring Junction to Poland Spring Station and then, via stage, to the Poland Spring resort. The Rickers responded by declaring the main road through their property a private way and supplying instructions on who was not allowed passage. The gates would swing open with alacrity for "the elect"—"for the son of rural Poland, for the prim folk from Shaker town, for the curious visitor from the city, for all the folks from the country 'round who come passengerless." For stages of the railroad, however, the watchword would be "go 'round."[51]

A "titillating" air of expectation hovered over the hilltop on the first day of new stage service. "A large and critical audience" gathered on the piazza of the Mansion House to watch the drama unfold. As the Tally-Ho coach left the Wampole stable, "intense interest" focused on the driver and his passenger George Bisbee. A few moments into the journey and a few rods past the Mansion House, the two men found the road blocked by a new fence and gate. Under the watchful surveillance of Edward Ricker, his attorney William

Newell, and a small party of spectators, Bisbee bounded down from the coach and approached the gate as if he intended to open it. Racing from his vantage point beneath a nearby elm tree to the center of the road, Ricker barked out: "Don't open those gates, Mister." After a vain attempt to convince Ricker to let the coach pass, the railroad director "resigned himself to the inevitable." The retreat disappointed some of the onlookers, for crashing the gates "with whizzing lash and hoarse halloo," as one reporter observed, "would have made this story thrilling." Instead, the thrill seekers had to content themselves with "an absorbingly interesting topic of conversation."[52]

For the remainder of the summer, the railroad's stages could do nothing more than drop passengers off on the public highway running in front of the Mansion House. The Rickers did provide transportation from that point to the Poland Spring House. The controversy so infuriated some travelers that they refused the ride up the hill and instead walked the final quarter of a mile lugging their own gripsacks. As the directors of the railroad feared, the inconvenience did not appeal to the leisure class. As a result, business at Poland Spring Station was light. The Portland and Rumford Falls Railroad transported fewer than 190 guests to the resort during the contentious summer of 1894.[53]

"Railroad v. Ricker"

The war of the stages entered a new phase six days after the Dickinson family departed Poland Spring. In mid-September, the spat between the Rickers and the railroad moved from the guarded gates of the resort to the hearing room of the Androscoggin County Commissioners. Directly at issue was whether the county should make the private road running through the Rickers' property a public highway. The larger cultural issue was whether the government should defer to the invisible hand of liberal capitalism or use its regulatory power to determine the public economic good. Hanging in the balance, as the proprietors saw it, were the control of their property and the exclusivity of the resort.

The commissioners, attorneys, and petitioners began the day by touring Poland Spring Station. They then traveled both the direct route from the station to the resort and the alternate way the blockade had forced the railroad's stages to take. After peacefully dining together at the Poland Spring House, the parties inspected the spring and the area of the new road proposed by the Rickers. All concerned eventually made their way to the Poland

Town House where a large audience had assembled to observe the cause célèbre. It pitted the petitioners, who had to prove that access to the road over the hilltop was both a common convenience and public necessity, against the Rickers, who had cleverly planned to undermine the claims by counter-petitioning to have a highway built to the north of their property.[54]

Jesse Libby, representing both the original petitioners and the Wampole Company, addressed the commissioners first. In his opening statement, the attorney outlined the major points of his case. First, thirty years of public use established the convenience and necessity of the existing road. Second, borrowing a legal argument used in enjoining the sympathetic job action by the American Railway Union in the Pullman strike, he maintained that the passage of mail over the route made it a public post road. Third, because the Rickers operated a public hostelry, the road leading to it must be a public highway. Fourth, the Rickers' promises of Poland Spring passenger and freight traffic as inducements to alter the course of the line constituted a binding commitment to the railroad. The family's breach of "good faith," Libby contended, violated "the interests of right and justice."[55]

Anticipating the rebuttals of counsel for the Rickers, Libby assured the commissioners that there was no danger the railroad would bring excursionists and picnickers to Poland Spring. To point out the disingenuousness of this concern, he asked why the proprietors of the resort viewed the presence of a railroad station located two miles away with alarm, when they proposed to build one within a few thousand feet of the Poland Spring House. Libby also attempted to establish that in spite of recent claims by the proprietors, the hotel was a public, not a private accommodation. As evidence, he cited the "great flaming advertisements" that had appeared in the *New York Tribune*, *Boston Globe*, and *Lewiston Journal*, as well as in promotional literature for the Maine Central Railroad. In Libby's opinion, all of these points led to the conclusion that there was a "great crying public need, necessity, common convenience and everything else" for the road.[56]

In his opening statement, William Newell, one of the attorneys representing the Rickers, attacked the case Libby had built on several grounds. First, he charged that the real petitioners were "one class of people," the directors of the Portland and Rumford Falls Railroad. Newell delighted in contrasting the original petition signed by forty-eight people with the widely supported remonstrances and counterpetitions signed by 337 residents of Poland, 150 businessmen in Lewiston and Auburn, and five hundred guests of the resort. Second, he maintained that the petition was ultimately about competition, not public access to the road. Third, he rejected the contention that the proprietors operated a public hotel, noting that they did not serve a "transient patronage." Fourth, he dismissed as "mere bosh" the accusation that the family had misled the directors of the railroad. Finally and most important, Newell argued that infringement of the Rickers' right to control their property would impair the "quiet and seclusion" and "mar the beauty . . . and the exclusiveness" of the resort.[57]

Newell reiterated the private property rights and social control arguments throughout his examination of witnesses. They readily agreed that changing the status of the road would lead to more excursionists and less exclusivity. The consequence, they unanimously testified, would be fewer guests at the Poland Spring House. H. L. Pratt, agent for the Bates Manufacturing Company in Lewiston, for instance, stated his belief that the proposed road would be "almost fatal to the business of the house." He predicted that the railroad would "bring promiscuous parties there interfering with the quiet and seclusion of the place and be obnoxious to the guests who go there for rest and quiet." Seth D. Wakefield, a resident of Lewiston and long time visitor to Poland Spring, agreed that the road "would have the tendency of carrying excursion parties," which would "spoil the Poland Spring property."[58]

Newell's main witnesses were brothers Hiram and Edward Ricker. His questioning of the two covered their dealings with the railroad directors, the economic consequences of the road issue, and the need for the family to control its property. On the first point, both brothers testified that Edward had made known to representatives of the railroad his insistence that the branch run to Danville Junction as a condition of his continued support. Hiram went on to state the family's position that the Danville connection had to be maintained "at all hazards." Edward concurred with this point. Furthermore, he explained that his initial involvement in the project, despite the lack of a firm commitment on the location of the southern terminus, was intended to demonstrate his friendliness toward the railroad, not to induce the directors to alter their plans for his benefit.[59]

As for control over their property, the brothers insisted that any infringement of ownership rights would interfere with future plans to develop the grounds. Edward fretted that granting greater access would permit people to come and "do as they saw fit, and make it very unpleasant to guests." He valued control so highly because it was the means by which the family maintained the all-important exclusiveness of Poland Spring. He claimed that 99 percent of resorts in the United States failed when they lacked the element of exclusivity. He cited the Profile House in Franconia, New Hampshire, and the Old Orchard House in Old Orchard Beach, Maine, as examples of hotels that had lost business once railroads made them too accessible. Proud of the patronage his family had "catered and studied to get," he testified that the resort "is known today as having the finest class of trade that there is in any resort in this country or Europe." Edward did not want to see this carefully cultivated clientele driven away by the introduction of what attorney Newell referred to as a promiscuous "transient trade." Well aware that confirmation of the Rickers' absolute control over the road might alarm townspeople who had used it for years, Hiram offered assurances that the family did not "have any objection to any person in Poland going through there privately."[60]

In his closing statement for the remonstrants, Albert R. Savage, the second attorney representing Hiram Ricker and Sons, weighed into the dispute. Re-emphasizing that the road had nothing to do with common convenience or public interest, Savage countered that it had everything to do with competition between rival businesses. He dismissed the railroad-backed petition as an attempt "to invoke the strong arm of the state . . . to gratify the business interests . . . of a single corporation." Savage went on to equate the private interests of the Rickers with the public interests of the town, county, and even state. By building and maintaining the road in question, the family had saved the town and county money. Through their annual business expenditures, which Hiram W. Ricker estimated at well over $100,000, the family provided the area with a "source of great prosperity." By promoting the Poland Spring House and Poland Water, they carried the reputation of the town into the world. Moreover, by serving the summer tourist trade, they added to the state's chief source of income. Citing the harm increased public access had done to hotels in Old Orchard Beach and Bar Harbor, Savage warned that opening a public way through the Poland Spring resort might kill the goose that had been laying the golden eggs.[61]

George Wing, another attorney representing the Portland and Rumford Falls Railroad, rebutted the liberal defense of private property rights with a populist appeal to patriotic values. Wing's America was a place where roads were built to satisfy the public's curiosity; where a poor man had the right at least to look at the Poland Spring House, even if he could not afford to stay there; and where any barefoot boy could grow up to be a bigger man than "Ed" Ricker. Most of all, his America was a place where the "ground tier of sentiment" held that it was "the common people who must be served." Wing declared that no individual had the right either to obstruct "public convenience and necessity" or impede "the march of progress." He went on to attack the vaunted exclusivity of the resort as a "sham." After all, he noted, the Rickers allowed Indians and brawling Irish ballplayers on the grounds. Furthermore, they proposed to build a rail line that would come much closer to the Poland Spring House than the Portland and Rumford Falls Railroad did. Observing that water and oil cannot mix, Wing dismissed as idle talk suggestions that opening the road to the public would bring excursionists to the site.[62]

In his closing remarks, Jesse Libby pursued his colleague's assault on the "false issue" of excursionists, contending that financial circumstances and judicial protection would safeguard the Rickers "more effectually than the angel with the flaming sword protected the Garden of Eden in the beginning of our race." He also followed the lead of his co-counsel by employing an egalitarian patriotic rhetoric to assail the class discrimination attributed to the proprietors of the resort. He complained that control of the public interest by one man was "contrary to the spirit of American institutions." Appealing to the "public conscience," Libby likewise decried the policy of denying access to one specific group as "an anomaly in American institutions." He compared the social sorting that took place on Ricker Hill to the division of the public into sheep and goats and questioned whether such a policy was in keeping with "the spirit of Americanism." Libby even went so far as to equate with slavery the family's obsessive insistence on controlling the movement of travelers, reminding the commissioners that "since the emancipattion [sic] proclamation there has been no such property rights in persons."[63]

Responding to criticism that the petitioners were seeking public favor for a private interest, Libby argued that promoting economic development was good public policy. He had in mind the plan of the Wampole Company to develop the Colomy farm into a spring water business and resort hotel. Libby claimed the site possessed an outlook "just as good" and water "just as pure" as Poland Spring. Access to the road, he promised, would bring the town additional investment in the Wampole property and thus more taxable real estate. Libby concluded his remarks by making Edward Ricker the issue. He advised the people of Poland not to confuse a right with the "sufferance" of an individual. If they did, he warned: "the very next man who crosses the whim of any proprietor of this estate is liable to be shut out." Libby submitted to the county commissioners that the public's right of passage could only be guaranteed by finding that the road did meet the test of common convenience and necessity.[64]

After four days of hearings and several more days of deliberations, the Androscoggin County Commissioners rendered their decision on Tuesday September 18th. As the *Hill-Top* had predicted two days earlier, the commissioners rejected the petition, ruling that public convenience alone did not warrant changing the status of the road. The Rickers remained "the monarchs of Ricker Hill." Although the verdict settled the issue from a legal standpoint, the directors of the Portland and Rumford Falls Railroad and owners of Hiram Ricker and Sons continued to joust for many years afterward. Sixteen months later, the railroad was agitating to have the local mail route moved from New Gloucester to its own Poland Spring Station. An observer commented that the officers of the railroad had proposed the change "to work against the Rickers." In 1897 Hiram W. Ricker and Jesse Libby squared off once again—this time over Poland's seat in the State Legislature—before settling on a compromise candidate, Bert M. Fernald. Another of the railroad's allies, Henry K. Wampole, also joined the fray in 1898 by changing the name of his spring to Polsko, an obvious ploy to play on the name recognition of Poland Spring.[65]

As the ongoing squabbles with the Portland and Rumford Railroad and other incidents during the summer of 1894 illustrated, the exclusivity of the Poland Spring clientele did not exempt the resort from class, ethnic, racial, and even business conflicts. Despite their attempts to maintain a strict social order, the Rickers could not enforce rigid exclusivity. Guarded gates did not prevent a few excursionists from straying onto the grounds, local tough guys from roughing up some guests, Irish baseball players from becoming too rowdy, Indians from creating a nuisance, a black man from disturbing the peace and causing trouble for two white waitresses, or Booker T. Washington from raising the "Southern Question." The same diversity that made exclusivity more desirable for some made it less obtainable for all. If the people of progress could not entirely control the human environment, they could try to shape the built environment in such a way as to provide escape from the problems and perils of Gilded-Age society.

PART II

The Masquerade of Antimodernity

Toward the end of August in 1895, Dr. and Mrs. George Trowbridge of New York City threw "the most important social event of the season," a bal masque. The costumes the couple wore paid tribute to European aristocracy and colonial nobility respectively. The host of the event came as a Continental gentleman, while the hostess made her appearance as Martha Washington. Following the lead of the doctor, the ten young men in attendance likewise dressed in the Continental style. The costumes of the young ladies displayed much more diversity and creativity. One of the hosts' daughters, Theodora, wore the attire of "a modest little red-cross nurse," while the other, Julia, dressed "as a bewitching little Italienne." Miss Vose wore the most revealing costume of all that of "a typical summer girl with her engagement finger full of rings."[1]

The masquerade balls thrown at Poland Spring perfectly epitomized the cultural significance of the Victorian resort. Patrons did don the figurative masks of antimodernity. They did retreat from "the bustle and hustle of to-day" to the nostalgia, the domesticity and gentility, and the customs and traditions of "those halcyon days when the time-honored Mansion House first threw open its hospitable doors." Nevertheless, at the end of the evening, and the summer too, they removed all the "powder, rouge, and court-plaster" and doffed the dress and "decorations of monarchs." They changed back into typical summer visitors, into proud members of the leisure class, into conspicuous consumers, into the people of progress. In short, they reverted to being complexly and proudly modern.[2]

Paradoxically, becoming modern entailed being antimodern occasionally. Thus, the people of progress scurried each summer to leave behind the very world they had helped transform. Like the Dickinsons of Chicago and Trowbridges of New York, they fled the residential hotel, urban brownstone, or suburban estate; the office routine, medical rounds, and daily bustle; the specter of industrial unrest; and the sootiness, stench, and stickiness of summer in the city. Their destinations were seashore, lakeside, mountain-

top, and hilltop oases of antimodernity scattered throughout the country, but clustered most abundantly in the northeastern United States. To some extent, their vacations were a requirement of their status, affirming their identity as members of the exclusive leisure class. To a greater extent, however, the people of progress really were trying to escape, although not completely and not permanently, from the unintended byproducts of the seemingly uncontrollable urban-industrial dynamo they had a hand in creating and sustaining. At the Poland Spring resort, they could escape temporarily and therapeutically to the past, to a place of play and pretend, and to the ideal of purity.

The shorthand way of expressing these patterns of response is as antimodernism. The term should not be taken too literally. The people of progress were not against modernity by any stretch of the imagination. What they opposed, through summer travel rather than by political action, were the ill effects of modernization. The constructive ability to overcome contradictions, obscure contrasts, bridge dualities, and ignore ironies is how they could be nostalgic for a simpler past and yet not old-fashioned. It is how they could masquerade as aristocratic nobility by night and resume the role of plutocratic socialites by day. It is how they could mix romantic views of nature and history with empirical notions of medicine and science and come up with pure water. It is how, as Jackson Lears has explained, the "antimodern modernist" came to be.[3]

The fundamental conflict between faith in progress and anxiety about change, which often manifested itself as antimodernism, also gave shape to the prevailing Victorian values of the Gilded Age. As the restraining force of social institutions such as religion receded before the inroads of the market revolution and the allure of material prosperity, the expectation of self-control as opposed to social control increased. To restore and maintain order, there arose a set of attributes that defined the ideal Victorian individual, chief among them domesticity, gentility, propriety, sobriety, respectability, and purity. Aspirations to these qualities not only molded the people of progress, they also influenced the evolution of a new social institution, the Victorian resort.[4]

Because nineteenth-century Americans traveled for a variety of reasons, historians have assigned many motivations to Victorian tourism: imitation of European travel habits, pursuit of pleasure, romantic interest in nature, restoration of health, pilgrimages of spiritual revitalization, and the search for authentic experience.[5] Two interpretations have predominated—tourism as a search for identity and as a means of escape. Proponents of the former view assert that leisure travel contributed to the development of national, regional, and class identities. In sum, tourism helped make travelers more American, more middle-class, and more modern.[6] Despite the significance of the pursuit of identity, the theme that has most consistently run through historical studies of the subject is escape. Historians have defined the escape of tourism in three ways. Most common has been the generic evasive escape rooted in reaction to the problems of mod-

ern society. Variations on the theme are the transcendent escape of travel as pilgrimage and the ironic mode in which the desire to escape modern capitalist development has led right back into the clutches of consumer culture. I propose a fourth kind—the temporary and limited therapeutic escape of the masquerade in which antimodern sentiments masked modern intentions.[7]

The closest thing to a manifesto explaining the need to vacation at Poland Spring and outlining the values encompassed by the resort was an 1895 Hill-Top editorial. With its focus on the proliferating perils unleashed by economic modernization, the piece appealed specifically to readers' urge to escape. According to the newspaper, "toiling and seething masses" coursed through cities. An amorphous "great army," presumably filled with immigrants, invaded and permeated "all Boston." "The crafty plans of the leading spirits of political movements" ensnared unwary voters in tiny webs. "Great movements of warlike strife," such as the one seen the previous year during the Pullman strike, advanced and receded. These concerns, coupled with the daily "comings and goings of the busy world," pushed many urban dwellers out of the city.[8]

Offering relief from this modern morass, the Victorian resort also pulled the people of progress out of their homes. In many ways, the editorial portrayed Poland Spring as the antithesis of the pathological urban environment. "Remote from rails and highways" and cut off from newspapers, letters, and telegrams, guests could drink pure water, breathe clean air, eat fine food, converse with congenial companions, walk along shaded avenues, exercise with the golf club, read the Hill-Top, and be as happy as it was possible to be. Venturing into the "wilds of Maine," the paper avowed, would make a visitor feel as if a tremendous weight had been removed.[9]

Although it promoted an image of the resort as a refuge from modernity, the editorial recognized that travelers to Poland Spring were permanent residents of, as well as temporary refugees from, the modern world. Acknowledging patrons' engagement with contemporary society, the paper noted that "all eagerly seek the daily news" from the far away cities. It gave assurance that from their hilltop sentinel guests would still be able to keep track of distant affairs as if they were happening "in the valley below." "The hum of voices [and] the tread of hurrying feet" would remain within earshot. The activities of immigrants, unions, and political machines would remain within sight. The city scene would remain under the vigilant surveillance of the urban elite.[10]

The editorial's concern with the activities of the world beyond the hilltop suggests that Poland Spring was more than a bastion of escapism and that vacationers had more on their minds than the hedonistic pursuit of pleasure. Travelers could leave cities, but they could neither forget their obligations back home nor ignore the profound changes taking place all around them. Modernization, after all, had generated the very abundance of wealth, goods, status, and leisure that provided the rising middle class with a

new group identity and the wherewithal to travel, in addition to the new worries iden-
tified by the Hill-Top. Significantly, patrons of the resort did not check their faith in
progress at the front gate during their annual summer sojourn to Poland Spring. They
did not forego modern conveniences and technological innovations. They did not stop
consuming conspicuously and leisurely. They did not forget a new empirical and in-
strumental way of looking at and dealing with the world.

    In search of limited and temporary escape from the demands and disturbances of
modern urban-industrial life, the people of progress accepted the invitation of the Hill-
Top in all its dimensions. Dismayed by the changing complexion of Gilded-Age Amer-
ican society, they romanticized about the nostalgic nobility of a more culturally homo-
geneous past within the safe confines of the venerable Mansion House. Disquieted by
the burdens of business and busyness, they retreated into the sheltered domesticity and
gentility of the spacious Poland Spring House. Discomfited by the stress and strains of
the constant struggles for status and success, they imbibed therapeutic purity from the
healing waters protected by the Spring House. If guarded gates could not restore a har-
monious human environment, perhaps a built environment shaped by the colonial re-
vival movement, market and leisure revolutions, and social purity crusade could.

The Mansion House

"A Noble Inheritance"

By the time the *Lewiston Falls Journal* reporter showed up at the Ricker farmstead in 1860, the property had already lost its "celebrity in one direction." Thus, he nostalgically described the site as: "Once a well known stopping-place in the palmy days of stages and teams." Now it reminded passersby of "the 'good old times' when . . . the road was the scene of bustle and business." The writer summed up the transformation by observing: "Alas! times have changed, and with them the centers of trade and travel." The perceptive journalist had hit precisely upon the downside of progress. Unsettling change would always bedevil the faith of the people of progress. One popular antimodern antidote to the shifting centers of social and economic life in Gilded-Age America became fondness for good old times, especially for the colonial past. Because the masquerade of colonial revivalism was able to dampen the tension between progress and change, it ultimately enhanced rather than inhibited the development of the nostalgia travel that caused the "large house" of 1860 to grow into the "noble inheritance" of the Mansion House by 1900.[1]

The sometimes cult-like appeal of nostalgia during the late nineteenth century was not so much escapist as it was defensive and comparative. For people steeped in the "tradition of progress," the past was used as a yardstick to measure cultural advancement, badge to signify hereditary distinction, and cudgel to beat back the nation's newcomers and keep down its minorities. The version of the past the people of progress widely subscribed to affirmed the values of filiopiety, nobility, domesticity, and purity. It also exalted old-stock Americans as agents of progress by linking their celebrated Anglo-Saxon ethnic identity with misguided notions of evolutionary heredity. As a result, self-anointed native nobility became another route of escape for patrons of the Poland Spring resort.[2]

The preoccupation with the past initiated by the sectional crisis of mid-century, crystallized by the centennial of the United States in 1876, and propelled by the approaching conclusion of the nineteenth century coalesced into the colonial revival movement. Colonial revivalists broadly conceived the era as the period between the first permanent English settlements in the New World and the rise of industrialization during the early decades of the 1800s. The cherished values they associated with the years prior to the Age of Jackson were rustic simplicity, domestic order, economic self-sufficiency, social hierarchy, and cultural homogeneity. Stalwart Anglo-Saxon pioneers, who had planted American civilization in the form of homes, churches, schools, and even a few friendly inns, populated this imagined past. It was an age untainted by the perils plaguing modern society—political corruption, industrial depressions, labor strife, foreign immigration, and urban stress. Yet, the people of progress only wanted to look, not live backwards. As historian Karal Ann Marling has noted, the nostalgia of colonial revivalists was ultimately "part of the great American push forward: an edenic past bolstered the drive toward a utopian future."[3]

The ability of the Rickers to make old times on the hilltop seem good played into the retrospective mood unleashed by the colonial revival movement and, in turn, partly accounted for the improving fortunes of the resort. Between 1860 and 1900, the family promoted its genealogy and heraldry, as well as celebrated the centennials of the town of Poland and the resort at Poland Spring. The proprietors also transformed the Mansion House into a symbol of the colonial revival. For them, the past was both a foundation to build upon and legacy to pass on, not merely a refuge to retreat to—points they emphasized with repeated reminders that preservation did not preclude modernization. In effect, the Rickers turned the family's past, a sometimes ignoble one at that, into a usable "noble inheritance" that reaffirmed their patrons' beliefs in both the privileged status of colonial ancestry and the remarkable progress of Western civilization.[4]

"Sapientia Donum Dei"

During the Gilded Age, genealogy became one popular diversion from present problems. George W. Ricker of Boston produced the first surviving record of the family's past in 1851. His genealogical research traced the ancestry through four generations, from Wentworth Ricker back to George and Maturin Ricker. The latter two brothers had immigrated from the Isle of

Jersey to Dover, New Hampshire, in 1675. Not content to begin the story in Jersey, the latter-day George Ricker speculated on the family's European origins. First noting that the English-ruled inhabitants of Jersey preserved French "manners, customs, and language" and then surmising that the family surname was a corruption of the French Richer, Ricker deduced that his ancestors had hailed from France.[5]

George Ricker revealed the filiopietistic purpose of his genealogy when he claimed: "the New England progenitors of this family, if we may believe tradition, were large athletic men, endowed with great powers of physical endurance, which they had many opportunities of testing." The most important test came on October 7, 1675, when Indians ambushed George and Maturin in Somersworth, New Hampshire. Ricker's account recorded that the Indians carried away the firearms and garments of both brothers although only Maturin was killed. Significantly, George Ricker invoked the memory of past powerfulness in the face of peril to a generation increasingly confronting the kind of contemporary powerlessness Hiram Ricker had experienced in so many ways by 1851. Throughout the remainder of the nineteenth century, this empowering claim to old-stock status recurred in historical accounts about the family. The only part of the genealogy future publicists found necessary to revise was the Rickers' French origins.[6]

Nearly two decades later, Samuel Ricker wrote a letter congratulating his Cousin Hiram on the newfound prosperity brought about by the discovery of the healing powers of spring water. Another of the topics Sam raised was the history of the family. Scolding Hiram for having ignored a question from a previous correspondence, Sam asked once again for verification of their grandfather Jabez's land holdings in New Hampshire. He also inquired whether his cousin had ever heard a rumor "to the effect that there existed in Europe a large Ricker fortune," suggesting that the dream of striking it rich was not limited to Hiram. Sam was anxious to receive this information, because he was about to embark on a journey that over the next several months would take him from his home in Ohio to Louisiana, Georgia, Washington, D.C., and New England. He explained that the purpose of the swing through the Northeast would be "to perfect my 'Ricker History' and to put it in proper form for publication." Samuel died in 1874 without completing the task, but his records were passed on to his son.[7]

The family's history interested more than just the Rickers. In 1877 Maine's pre-eminent and prolific genealogist, Dr. William B. Lapham, took up their story. Described as "an enthusiastic and diligent delver among the records of the past, always inclining toward those relating to ancient or noted families," Lapham began his genealogy of the Rickers by recounting the emigration of George and Maturin from England to New Hampshire in 1670. Demonstrating his well known "painstaking, critical and conscientious" approach to history, Lapham then set the record straight on the outcome of the brothers' fatal encounter with Natives in 1706, not 1675. Basing his version of the incident on the entry in a journal from the period, he reported that they "were slain by the Indians; George was killed while running up the lane near the garrison; Maturin was killed in his field, and his little son [Noah] carried away." According to the version of the incident handed down from Jabez Ricker to his grandson Hiram, Noah "was taken into Canada, where he was educated to the priesthood." The family history prepared for the New England Historical Publishing Company in 1903 added that Noah never returned to the American colonies.[8]

Carrying on the family lineage, Lapham moved on to another of Maturin's sons, Joseph Ricker. By including the text of Joseph's will, the genealogy supplied the answer to the burning question Samuel Ricker had so urgently posed to Hiram seven years earlier. Jabez Ricker had indeed owned land in Dover, where his father, Joseph, had bequeathed him a legacy of a little over one hundred acres. Following the family into the nineteenth century, Lapham reported that "Wentworth Ricker, son of Jabez, kept a public house on Ricker Hill in Poland, for many years, and his hostelrie was a popular stopping place for farmers going to Portland, before the days of railways." In addition, he paid tribute to Wentworth's son, Hiram, who was now "the senior proprietor of the Mineral Springs and hotels at Poland."[9]

The interest in and value of family and local history that genealogists and amateur historians like Lapham promoted was not lost upon the Rickers. In the same year as the centennial of the nation, the proprietors of the resort began tapping into an ever-deepening reservoir of nostalgia for the early American past to boost sales of Poland Water and promote visitation to the newly opened Poland Spring House. Frequent inquiries from people who "wanted to know how this Spring was discovered" had alerted the Rickers to the possibility that relating the site's history would make drinking the water and traveling to the resort more appealing. From cursory mention of significant dates in the 1876 water catalogue, publicists revised the historical content of the promotional literature into a more detailed narrative that developed into the official family biography by the publication of the 1883 edition.[10]

The new pamphlet traced the history of Ricker Hill all the way back to the arrival in 1779 of the first white settler in the area, an individual who was characterized as a "worthy and sturdy New England yeoman." The 1883 water catalogue went on to give an account of the first Ricker settlers in the area by reviewing the creation of the Mansion House. An illustration depicting the site as it originally had appeared showed a two-and-a-half-story wooden building with an attached rear ell leading to a barn. Along a drive on the north side of the house stood two other farm buildings. Lest prospective patrons receive the mistaken impression that the Rickers intended to put them up in the same rustic facility pictured in the catalogue, the text assured them that "the old house has been remodeled and refitted with all the conveniences of a modern hotel." In addition to the contrasts of past and present, another advertised attraction of a stay at the Mansion House was the continuity of its ownership. The catalogue proudly pointed out that the inn had been "kept by the original proprietor until his death in 1837, then by his son Hiram Ricker until 1872, and since that time by the sons of the latter." To the promoters of the resort, this was "a remarkable instance, perhaps the only one in the State of Maine, of a public house, which has been maintained by the same family for fully three-quarters of a century."[11]

In 1890 William H. H. Murray combined the fact that three generations of Rickers had operated Poland Spring with his misunderstanding of genetics to promote the resort. Murray, a one-time minister who had become one of the nation's most vocal evangelists for the virtues of the Victorian vacation, instructed readers about "a biological force which transmits the characteristic qualities of ancestors to their descendants." He explained that it was "by the benign operation of this law of transmitted forces" that "the strong and vital" passed on to their children their physical appearance, mental and spiritual qualities, characteristic virtues, and distinguishing talents. In the case of the Rickers, he asserted, this theory meant that the "ancient family" had passed on "the gifts and knowledge of [the] hotel business." Murray concluded: "it is the 'hotel blood' in this Ricker family that enables them to manage their great Hotel as they do."[12]

Exhibiting a similarly misguided notion of evolutionary biology that flourished in the aftermath of the publication of Charles Darwin's *Origin of Species* in 1859, another promotional piece published by Hiram Ricker and Sons in 1890 railed against a perceived threat to the process of heredity—"mongrelization." The anonymous author admired ancient civilizations because "in architecture, in art, in government, in social life, their development was from one germinal force and true to it." The writer longed for a bygone

Patrons imbibing refreshing glasses of pure water in the modern 1906 Spring House were also reminded of the Rickers' "noble inheritance." The motto accompanying the family coat of arms, "*Sapientia Donum Dei*," translates as: Knowledge is the gift of God. *Maine Historic Preservation Commission.*

time when "the word Thoroughbred, was once applied to humans as well as animals" and when "each blood was true to itself and was kept pure." This social critic deplored the "base admixtures" and "neutralizing currents" that modern people had "allowed to enter those old systems of racial development." As a model of racial purity, the writer ironically revered the "red race"—a group on the brink of final subjugation at the hands of the dominant white race after centuries of resistance.[13]

Despite the admired pure bloodlines of Native Americans, Indians held as ambiguous a place in the colonial revival as they did at the resort. While they were sometimes praised for having lived in harmony with nature, they were also often vilified for their savagery. Resurrecting the well-worn story of George and Maturin Riccar, an 1892 article entitled "Birth of an Ancient Inn" enlivened the tale by highlighting the danger faced by the colonists in light of the treachery practiced by the Indians. In the retelling, Dover circa 1706 became a "beleaguered" town at war with the native population. Standing just outside the stockades of their fortified blockhouses, the brothers "within five minutes of each other heard with death-struck ears the shots from Indian muskets that summoned them both to their last long home." The heroic retelling of the story also included the version of the incident Hiram Ricker had heard from his grandfather, Jabez. Hiram described the conflict as a massacre and the attack on the second brother as an ambush. Expounding on the significance of this nearly two-century-old colonial tale, the article offered the "trite, but true" observation "that it is from sturdy stock alone, that sturdy sons and daughters are born." As evidence of the Rickers' sturdiness and thus entitlement to privileged status, the account supplied a list of their ancestors' accomplishments: "founding homes, building towns, establishing families of worthy name from Maine to New Orleans, and last but not least, upbuilding on a sunlit hill in the paradise of Maine, a summer home . . . known to all the world."[14]

Symptomatic of the Nordic ethnocentrism endemic to the era, use of the variant Riccar spelling of the surname in the article intentionally emphasized the family's Anglo-Saxon stock. Downplaying the claim by "some genealogists" that the family was "a branch of the French Ricards," the same article maintained, "this fact is not so interesting as the well-attested location of the ancient feudal and knightly family of Rikers in Saxony in the 14th century." With possibly a stopover in Holland, the "unquestionably" Saxon family had by the seventeenth century, the article noted, "drifted thence across the face of Europe into France, and finally settled down in that 'blest isle of Jersey.'" The account went on to describe a vignette of the family's Saxon coat of arms and to decipher its symbolism.[15]

The author of the article most likely gleaned the information about the family heraldry from the research of M. F. Jasper. In 1892 Jasper had received the twin assignments to verify the vitally necessary but tenuously substantiated Saxon ancestry of the Rickers and then to represent it in a coat of arms. Acknowledging the imprecision of genealogy due to the variety of spellings of surnames, uncertainty of identities, and absence of data, Jasper nevertheless sought to assure the family of the appropriateness of his selection. In a letter, he promised: "if the birthplace of the first American ancestor is known, it will not be difficult to trace the family throughout Europe." Working from the knowledge that Maturin Ricker came from the Isle of Jersey, and noting the similarity of the Jersey Ricard and Saxon Riker arms, Jasper concluded: "I am confident that both are of the same family only that this [the Jersey] arms got a modification, as well as the name [Ricard] by the strong admixture of french [sic] for which the isle of Jersey is noted." As an added inspiring and ingratiating touch, Jasper appended to the family's Saxon emblem of ethnic unity, class exclusivity, and cultural authority the motto found on its Jersey offspring, "*Sapientia Donum Dei*," which he translated as "Knowledge is the gift of God."[16]

Poland Spring Centennial: A Souvenir

Attuned to the interest in the past possessed by the people of progress, the Rickers shrewdly decided to commemorate the family's century-long residence on the hilltop by publishing a historical booklet. Emblazoned in the lower right-hand corner of the cream-colored cover of *Poland Spring Centennial* were the azure and argent Ricker coat of arms and gold-lettered Latin motto Jasper had chosen three years earlier. The souvenir publication included eight sections covering the genealogy of the family, history of the Mansion House, careers of Wentworth and Hiram Ricker, discovery and utility of the spring water, establishment of the Poland Spring House, main attractions of the resort, and life at Poland Spring. Using the historical information about the family that researchers and writers had circulated since 1851, the guide wove the various strands of the past together into one comprehensive colonial revival narrative aimed at making Poland Spring a more inviting tourist destination. The *Hill-Top* heralded it as a work of "remarkable elegance, comprising eighty-nine pages gotten up in the most exquisite manner known to the printer's art." The illustrations, the paper proclaimed, comprised "a history of progress in themselves." In addition, the written record of the Rickers was "one to look back to and admire." Highlighting the main contrasting themes of the publication—nostalgic nobility and modern progress, the periodical summed up the work as the history of "energy and pluck, combined with the sweet and gentle influence of a noble New England woman" that had created "a palace where but a short time ago was only a wilderness."[17]

Poland Spring Centennial opened with a revealing juxtaposition that accentuated the colonial revival's dual missions—respect for tradition and promotion of progress. On one page appeared an illustrated tribute to the noble woman, Janette Ricker, and her husband, Hiram, under the heading "The Past." Neither the matriarch nor the patriarch of the family had lived long enough to observe the centennial of the homestead. Janette had succumbed to heart disease on September 23, 1883, at the age of sixty-two. As the tribute reported, although somewhat incorrectly, "Hiram died January 4, 1893, full of years, having attained the ripe age of eighty-four." On the opposite page under the title "The Future" appeared the heirs to the family legacy, the "eldest sons of Hiram Ricker's sons."[18]

The booklet was replete with the principal topics of the colonial revival— Anglo-Saxon identity, colonial ancestry, and native nobility. After reviewing the spread of the feudal and knightly Ricker family from Saxony through Continental Europe and onto the Isle of Jersey, the souvenir history honored the "noble ancestral hill" and the colonial heritage of the hearty souls who had built it up. The oft-repeated story of George and Maturin Riccar's immigration to New Hampshire and later death at the hands of the "savage" Indians was rehashed once again. Jabez Ricker and his sons were lauded for laying the foundation that eventually enabled the transformation of "a hill-farm in the forest" into "the great New England Spa." An illustration of a sign bearing Wentworth Ricker's name and the date 1797 commemorated the important role one of those sons had played in opening the Mansion House to the public. Section one went on to provide genealogical information down to the seventh generation—the grandchildren of Hiram and Janette Ricker and the group specifically designated as the future of the family.[19]

Section seven of *Poland Spring Centennial* amounted to a virtual colonial revival tour of the resort. Revealingly, the section opened with an illustration of a fireplace, a symbol of domesticity, simplicity, and tranquility made popular by the colonial revival movement. The tour began at the Danville Junction railroad depot. Leaving the train, the reader stepped back into the era of stage travel by boarding a coach that covered the remaining distance to the resort. Arrival at the castle-like Poland Spring House was a scene reminiscent of the days when Wentworth Ricker had greeted visitors to the Mansion House. The reader was "by manner, if not in words, made welcome with something of the flavor, if not the exuberance, of the old time reception by landlord of guest."[20]

After an extensive examination of the Poland Spring House and a quick visit to the recently opened, thoroughly modern Maine State Building, the tour moved on to "the veteran Mansion House." Describing the facility as "an ideal country inn," the booklet offered assurances that alterations made to the building over the years had neither "destroyed its quaintness" nor caused it to lose "its mellow charm." The structure still featured "the spreading low studded office, the pleasant sitting-rooms, the cozy dining-room, with its cheerful outlook, the homelike rooms above stairs, the piazzas shaded by stately elms of Hiram Ricker's planting," yet it also offered "the conveniences which modern hotel methods afford." The contrasts between the "rare old tavern" and "modern hotel" combined "to make it a veritable house of contentment."[21]

From the Mansion House, the stroll proceeded northward along the old county road past other examples of early American architecture. The literary tour came upon a barn dating to 1813, the Albert Ricker homestead, and the Lane cottage, all three of which were pictured, before coming to the Jackson Inn. The souvenir guide explained that Daniel Jackson had built the inn in 1800, making it the second home in town, after the Rickers' Mansion House, to have offered public accommodations. As the current owners of the "venerable house," the Rickers were in the process of freshening and remodeling the "good example of early nineteenth century New England" architecture in order to retain "it as an unique feature of [their] many-featured resort."[22]

Leaving the county road for one that wound westerly around Middle Range Pond, the tour led to another part of the expanding Ricker estate, an old graveyard that attested to the family's deep roots in the area. Poland's first meetinghouse had once stood beside the cemetery grounds. When the building had been raised sometime in the mid–1790s, Molly Ricker, Wentworth's wife, had entertained and fed the workers, "doing all the cooking herself, using up seven bags of flour, with other things in like proportion." The second historical tie between the family and the cemetery was the unfortunate death of one of the people buried there. According to town lore, Dr. Nathaniel Morrill, a guest at the Jackson Inn, had gone out for a walk on the morning of May 8, 1807. Along the way he had encountered a man driving an ox. As the two parties had passed, the animal had unexpectedly pinned Morrill with his horns and violently thrown the doctor to the ground, breaking the man's back. A picture of Dr. Morrill's headstone in *Poland Spring Centennial* recorded "his sudden and melancholy death, Occasioned by an unruly ox." The driver of the ornery beast of burden had been none other than Alvan Bolster, the father of Janette and future father-in-law of Hiram Ricker.[23]

Besides reminding readers of the heroic struggles faced by colonial forbearers, another reason for coming to the burial ground was to offer a different visual perspective of the resort on the hilltop. With park-like rural cemeteries all the rage in Victorian cities, this authentic country antecedent provided the perfect setting to nourish romantic landscape notions. Creating a stark contrast between past and present, the colonial revival tour concluded in the "ancient graveyard," looking back across Middle Range Pond toward the modern Poland Spring House. As the souvenir guide pointed out and an illustration made clear, from this spot "through the vista of the trees the great house on the hill appears in the distance, presenting . . . a most charming picture." Standing in the cemetery, even if only imaginatively, it was as if the entire enterprise of transforming the hilltop had sprung forth from the heroic deeds of the ancestors buried beneath the headstones. What could be more romantic? How could the past be made any more usable for the people of progress?[24]

With the colonial revival tour ended and readers safely returned to the resort, the eighth and final section of *Poland Spring Centennial* revealed the purposes of the entire exercise. First, by virtue of their Saxon ancestry and American colonial heritage the Rickers were proprietors worthy of respect. As the souvenir booklet summed up the situation in its stirring conclusion, "when, in the fullness of time, the control falls into the hands of the sons of Hiram Ricker's sons, it will have become indeed a noble inheritance, a monument of sturdy enterprise and sagacity." Lest readers receive the mistaken impression that the resort wallowed in nostalgia, the booklet also made sure to emphasize the second function of the colonial revival—promoting progress. It did so by reviewing the great variety of thoroughly up-to-date entertainments available at Poland Spring. The final image readers were left with was a current picture of the Mansion House—an attraction made noble by virtue of its age, its state of preservation, its historic mission, its century-long ownership by the same family, and last but not least, its modern amenities.[25]

In addition to prospective resort patrons, *Poland Spring Centennial* had another enthusiastic audience. Members of the extended Ricker family, no matter how distantly related, were delighted to see their ancestors' exploits honored. A flurry of correspondence from long-lost relatives followed publication of the souvenir booklet in 1895. A recently widowed distant cousin from Ohio, Rosella Ricker Freeman, wrote a series of letters asking to be taken in by her prosperous Poland Spring relations. The family apparently heeded the advice of another cousin who warned that Freeman was a possible "opium eater," who "is very peculiar, in fact strange and you would not wish her ever come to Poland."[26]

In contrast to crazy Cousin Ellen, most of the correspondents wrote to revel in the noble lineage and ethnic identity of the Rickers. An 1897 letter from another family historian, Ernest H. Ricker of Illinois, linked the knightly Saxon Riccar ancestry to "a numerous, far-reaching" American clan that had produced more than its share of "professional men such as Judges, Ministers, Professors of colleges, Physicians, Bankers and Lawyers." C. E. Ricker of Oregon attributed the success of the family to the wisdom derived from its

German heritage and the beauty passed down "from the 'Jersey Lilly [*sic*].'" H. P. Ricker of New York added, "Till later years I had supposed I was English. But guess am full as proud over the Saxon. I *do* think the R[icker]s a *noble* set of people. I am proud of them." This pride also brought a call for the publication of Samuel Ricker's languishing family genealogy, a promise by Ernest Ricker to publish a twelve-hundred-page family history, and the preparation of a 175-page genealogical manuscript by Percival L. Ricker.[27]

None of these Ricker genealogies circulating within the family made it into print until the end of the twentieth century. In 1900, however, the Reverend John W. Hayley published a genealogy that included George Ricker's lineage. The minister did not completely neglect Maturin's line. He paid homage to a few prominent descendants of the younger Ricker brother, including "those enterprising gentlemen, Messrs. Hiram Ricker and Sons." Far from clearing up the mystery of the family's origins, Hayley further confused the ethnicity of the Rickers by associating the surname with similar Scottish ones.[28]

Poland Centennial: A Celebration

Two months after celebrating the centennial of Poland Spring, the three Ricker brothers played leading roles in the celebration of Poland's centennial. Alvan Ricker was one of the five members of the committee charged by the annual town meeting with planning the festivities to be held on September 11, 1895. Given his experience feeding several hundred guests of the resort each day, it is not surprising that Alvan assumed responsibility for organizing the centennial dinner. Over two-thirds of the estimated three thousand people attending the celebration crowded under the big top for the meal. The banquet featured contributions "prepared by the generous and public-spirited women of Poland," as well as Chase and Sanborn coffee supplied by summer resident James Sanborn. In the far from objective estimation of the commemorative book co-authored by Alvan B. Ricker, Bert M. Fernald, and Hiram W. Ricker, "the dinner was one of the finest ever served under a tent."[29]

In addition to his role in preparing the centennial publication, Hiram W. Ricker served as marshal of the centennial parade. In the midst of a brisk morning shower, he and his aides greeted guests arriving for the festivities at the Portland and Rumford Falls depot. Apparently, the auspiciousness of the occasion convinced the Rickers to set aside for the day their festering feud with the managers of the railroad. From the train station, the resplendent marshal, aboard his stately steed, led a procession of parade participants and onlookers from Poland Corner to the town cemetery. There, on what had turned into a morning of beautiful sunshine, the celebrants honored the "loyal dead." The final stop on the parade route was the large tent where the residents and friends of Poland assembled to listen to orations by a succession of speakers before and after the centennial dinner.[30]

First to address the crowd was President of the Day, Bert Fernald. In his welcoming remarks, he discussed what would be the two recurring colonial revival themes of the centennial celebration, the heroism of the town's settlers and the progress of civilization. Contrasting the past century with the era when the "savages" roamed the "primitive" surroundings, this native-born son of Poland commented that since the establishment of the town, "history is replete with the evidences of its progress." Fernald attributed this to the "sturdy" forefathers of Poland who had been "full of courage, ambition, enterprise, and perseverance, true to themselves, their country, and their God."[31]

Following his welcoming remarks, the delivery of an opening prayer, and the singing of the centennial hymn, Fernald introduced the Orator of the Day. W. W. McCann opened his talk on the history of Poland with a discussion of progress. To him, the word meant the "advancing forces of civilization," such as those that had enabled the conquering white man to triumph over the savage life of the Indian. According to McCann, progress, symbolized by the westward moving "star of Empire," manifested itself in Poland as "thought, ideas, the school, and the church—the best forces of New England civilization." He also touched upon the other main theme of the day, filiopietism, paying tribute to the "hardy, industrious New England stock." McCann contrasted the aims of this group, which had cleared farmland and built homes, with those of "the old Spanish explorers," who had pursued gold and glory instead. McCann left no doubt which group of colonists had left the richer legacy.[32]

McCann extended accolades to one Poland family of ancient lineage in particular. Referring to the recent centennial celebration at Poland Spring, the Orator of the Day acknowledged "the magnificent success of the Rickers." McCann related to the audience the story of how a century earlier the family had unwittingly entered the hotel business by taking in a "weary and hungry traveler" who had been turned away from the nearby Shaker community. While prosperity and fame had followed from that initial act of hospitality by the Rickers, McCann invited people to "recall on this our natal day, with greater pride and satisfaction, their honest, intelligent, generous, and patriotic citizenship." The agreeable audience responded with hearty applause to the request to honor these loftier old-fashioned and non-material-istic values.[33]

Explaining that men had neglected "the less noisy and unostentatious tri-umphs of women," McCann then singled out one member of the family for special tribute—Janette Ricker. Paying homage to the Victorian cult of do-mesticity, he expressed admiration for the maternal and domestic values the matriarch of the family had embodied by reciting the many duties Janette had assumed during her lifetime: landlady, hostess, cook, housewife, mother, and neighbor. McCann observed, "her wise counsel, executive ability, and un-compromising integrity did much in giving tone and direction to the affairs on Ricker Hill." The claps and cheers that arose from the gathering affirmed the accuracy of the speaker's assessment. He summed up his brief biography of and tribute to Janette with the comment that "her life and work remain, not only a precious memory, but an inspiration to wives and mothers who shall succeed her in those splendid homes."[34]

Despite his warm praise for this remarkable woman, McCann ended the lengthy oration on the history of Poland by celebrating the separate spheres that rigidly defined gender roles during the pioneer past. He recalled with pride "the early struggles and sturdy manliness of those of an earlier day." He also romanticized about "the manly, determined bridegroom," who toiled in the summer heat, braved the storms of winter, enlarged his fields, improved and beautified his home, and unmurmuringly endured hardships. As for the "fair and no less determined bride," he loved to think of her "singing merrily as the birds," plying the shuttle, preparing the frugal meal, teaching the first-born to talk, and "instructing him in his letters." The distinction was clear. Colonial men were builders; their brides were nurturers. McCann's epitaph for "the pioneers of these Northern woodlands" was: "They did the best they could with their surroundings—angels could do no more."[35]

After a break for dinner, Maine Congressman Nelson Dingley addressed the sons and daughters of Poland on the power and purpose of studying the past. He began his speech by defining history as "philosophy teaching by ex-ample." Therefore, he reasoned: "the story of the past is valuable only as it il-luminates the path of the future." There was no idle escapism in his histori-cal examinations. Instead, Dingley dwelled on the dual themes of filiopietistic respect and progressive advancement. When the congressman speculated about what lay ahead for a nation on the brink of imperial adventures, he foresaw only continued progress, measured by the growth of population, the increase in wealth, the advance of national power, and the spread of Anglo-

Saxon civilization. He encouraged his listeners to carry on this legacy by assuring them that "the noble blood which coursed in the veins of our forefathers has not lost its vigor or character." Dingley concluded his address by
urging people to "be true to the great principles which animated the fathers."[36]

Next to the podium stepped Edward Ricker, a disciple of both colonial revival principles on speakers' lips and listeners' minds that day. Introduced as
a "distinguished and progressive son of Poland" and "her greatest benefactor,"
the ailing resort proprietor expressed to the crowd his "love of our forefathers
and the good old town." The remainder of his abbreviated presentation consisted of two prophecies about the year 1995. The first was that during the
next one hundred years, Maine would see tenfold progress and development,
eventually making it "the great playground of this country." Ricker's second
prophecy was more universal. He predicted that by the end of the second
millennium, "the form of our Republican Government will be established
throughout the world." Appropriately enough, Edward Ricker concluded his
"few rambling remarks" by drinking a toast of Poland Water to the health of
all in attendance.[37]

The Reverend J. Albert Libby followed Ricker and honored Poland with
a poem he had composed for the occasion. This lyrical review of the town's
notable citizens and historic places included forty lines devoted to the Ricker
family. Although Libby generally celebrated the century of progress that had
brought prosperity to the Ricker boys and pride to the townspeople, he also
expressed a certain longing for olden days. On Ricker Hill the poet found the
stability of the past preserved in two places, the Mansion House and the
spring. About the former, Libby mused:

> The Ricker Hill, what early used to be,
> Must now be known with all antiquity,
> Though hidden in the mansion pile, we know,
> Is the old house of ten decades ago.

Similarly, the minister's tribute to the unchanging constancy of the water observed that "The living spring, however, yet remains, / The one unfailing
source of all the gains."[38]

Presenting the final toast of the day, John Penney spoke on the topic of
Poland's early settlers. This member of the Maine Historical Society opened
his talk by commenting on the importance of reviving the colonial past. Penney quoted English historian Thomas B. Macaulay's dictum that "a people

which takes no pride in the noble achievements of remote ancestors, will never achieve anything worthy to be remembered by remote descendants." Linking history with heredity he added, "the people who do keep green the memory and deeds of their ancestors, are a people in whose veins runs the noblest and richest blood of the earth." Penney used the development of the "trait" of historical awareness as a gauge by which to measure the "plane of civilization and refinement" attained by groups of people. Highly developed civilizations produced histories, he reasoned; lesser-developed ones perpetuated myths and legends.[39]

Overlooking the many myths and legends told about Poland, particularly the ones flowing from the hilltop, Penney made clear on which plane he placed the history of New England. The Mechanic Falls machinist turned local historian reverently proclaimed:

> To the New Englander of to-day, there is a halo of exquisite romance that entwines the memory of the early settler, so full of stirring incident, heroic achievement and sublime faith, that it charms and thrills and stirs the emotions of the soul, promoting patriotism and love of country, and inciting to nobler living.

When it came time to praise the town's principal mythologizers, Penney noted that the Rickers' "ancestral tree sprang from Saxon soil." Assessing a century of hotel keeping at Poland Spring, he congratulated the family for having "developed the rugged old hill into a sanitarium, world-renowned, a paradise of health, a thing of beauty and a joy forever." Penney concluded by honoring Poland's unknown heroes, the early settlers who, like the Rickers, were "descendants of the Puritan stock . . . God-fearing, brave, patriotic, honest, lowly toilers."[40]

Following the reprinted texts of the thirteen addresses, orations, prayers, poems, and toasts, the compilers of *Poland Centennial* added a brief tribute of their own to the resort. It lauded the "celebrated Poland Mineral Spring," commended the energy of the three Ricker brothers, complimented "the noble dimensions of the Poland Spring House," and praised the wealthy and intelligent patrons of the establishment. The tribute also invoked for the final time the two main colonial revival themes of the centennial celebration, filiopietism and progress. Wentworth Ricker was acknowledged as having opened "the quaint and hospitable Mansion House" in 1797, while his grandson, Hiram W. Ricker, was cited for his interest "in advancing the educational interests and all that pertains to the welfare of his native town."[41]

Old Home Week

In addition to genealogy, heraldry, and commemorative celebrations, another interest of colonial revivalists was the preservation of old homes. This made the oldest building at Poland Spring—the Mansion House—the focus of much attention. The venerable structure's place in the built environment was more complicated than as a repository for nostalgic antimodernism. Instead, like so much else at the resort, the building was a study in contrasts. Its antiquity gave it an undeniably proud past. Yet, the proprietors wanted to make perfectly clear that the facility also featured the latest modern amenities. Thus, the Mansion House functioned simultaneously both as a preserve of old-fashioned values of domesticity and piety in its roles as home and Sunday School, as well as a promoter of modern leisure, consumption, and commerce in its roles as resort hotel, business office, and post office.

The transformation from home and inn to hotel and home began after the 1869 season. During the ensuing fall and winter, workmen raised the roof and added a full third story to the Mansion House, increasing its room count to fifteen and boarding capacity to about twenty-five. Two years later, removal of the old wood and cider houses and extension of the ell at the back of the structure added seven more rooms. Even after the construction of a new hotel on the hilltop in 1876, the Rickers continued to expand the Mansion House to meet "the business requirements" of running such a popular resort. The building was enlarged again in 1883, bringing the number of rooms to sixty-six. A visitor to the facility nearly a decade later was immediately struck by its contrasts. The journalist described the facility as "ideal in its adoption of modern notions, and in the quaint, beloved associations with the days of sweet Lang Syne." The reporter observed that this combination made the inn "especially dear to some of the older folks, who do not care for the bustle and life of a modern, fashionable hotel such as that set on the hill."[42]

In large part, a homelike atmosphere gave the Mansion House its distinctive charm. Even after all the expansions to accommodate the growing legion of guests, the building still served as the residence of Hiram and Janette Ricker and all their children. Whether for use by family or visitors, the architectural features of the facility added to the ambience of domesticity. Enormous fireplaces, comfortable rooms, a beautiful little dining room, and towering elms created a cozy, quiet, and serene setting that made the inn a home away from home, beloved by all who stayed there.[43]

The craze for cycling dates this photograph of the Mansion House to the mid- to late 1890s. A century after the construction of the family's colonial homestead on the hilltop, the original structure, which corresponds to the front left section of the building, had grown into a sprawling hotel complex. *Maine Historic Preservation Commission.*

The same attributes of domesticity that made the Mansion House such an inviting place to escape the hustle and bustle of the mundane world also made it an ideal spot for the piety Sarah Ricker brought to the hilltop through the introduction of formal religious instruction for children. In 1896 Sarah, who went by the nickname Sadie, organized the Hill-Side Sunday School with the help of the aptly named Grace Hall and the personal secretary of Hiram W. Ricker, Pamela Leonard. The trio held sessions in one of the parlors for as many as twenty-seven students from January through June. The school closed for the tourist season, reopening when the summer traffic died down at the end of September. Concluding that the Mansion House was not big enough to accommodate both the children and the guests, Sadie soon moved the Christian endeavor to a nearby schoolhouse. She continued to serve as superintendent until 1928. During her long tenure, the motherly Aunt Sadie, who never married and thus had no children of her own, became dearly beloved for the deep interest and sincere affection she lavished on her pupils. They remembered with special fondness the picnics and Christmas parties she organized for them.[44]

Outward appearances of domesticity and piety disguised the more commercial, behind-the-scenes activities that took place in the Mansion House. The facility also served as the headquarters from which the younger Hiram Ricker managed the operations of both the inn and the spring. From a suite of four rooms behind the front desk, he and his staff recorded the "immense sales" of Poland Water. As local postmaster, a position either he or his father held from 1870 to 1900, Hiram also presided over the South Poland post office based in the building.[45]

Given the contrasts embodied in the Mansion House, how to promote the facility often confounded publicists. One season the *Hill-Top* described it as "a roadside inn, erected by sturdy pioneers," "an object lesson in enterprise," and a monument to the old-time virtues of thrift, perseverance, and good judgment. A few years later, the "time-honored Mansion House" and "ancient hostelry of by-gone days" was *passe*. In its place, stood "the Mansion House of to-day." Guests during the 1898 season found that electric illumination had replaced gas; new baths had replaced old; and Falstaffian room proportions had replaced straight-laced precursors. In addition, among the twenty-seven rooms added to the sprawling complex were a sun parlor and kitchen designed to fulfill the therapeutic needs of the "inner man." The paper imagined that if Wentworth Ricker could return and see the transformation of his inn, the presence of all the modern innovations and improvements would astound him.[46]

Such a reincarnation was no more the point of the colonial revival as practiced at Poland Spring than was trying to recreate for patrons some version of the good old days. The ultimate aim of the movement was to make modernity less bewildering to moderns. In the case of the built environment, one manifestation of the contrasting amalgamation between nostalgia and progress was the quaint yet modern Mansion House. By the end of the century, promotional literature repeatedly harped upon this duality. An 1899 announcement described the inn as "improved and modernized," while still preserving "that air and architecture so quaint and attractive in these old houses." Similarly, an 1899 article referred to "The Old Homestead" as "this modernized yet quaint old hostelry."[47]

In the retrospective mood befitting the approach of a new century, the *Hill-Top* attempted to explain the seemingly paradoxical juxtaposition. The crux of the matter was the American "desire for change," and more specifically, for it to be progressive. Likening change to "parting with old friends," the paper used the example of a reconstructed fireplace and chimney to offer assurances that "a careful hand preserved each specimen of the handicraft of early times." The all-purpose concept of purity, which was never specifically defined but often mentioned in conjunction with the spring, ensured that change became progress. An unaltered and fixed absolute, much like the "pure" water of the spring, the purity of craftsmanship produced a new fireplace without sacrificing any of its old character. The same principle also kept producing a new, more modern Mansion House that maintained the most elemental and essential qualities of the old—quaintness, hospitality, and domesticity—despite continual alterations. Preserving purity and protecting fundamental values, while combining the contrasts of past and present, distinguished mere change from true progress.[48]

Colonial revivalists often linked the ideal of purity with the past through the medium of architecture. During Maine's annual Old Home Week in 1900, the *Hill-Top* elaborated on the concept of purity as it related to colonial revival architecture. Observing that "the architecture of old New England is a sermon that is too often neglected," the paper commended the Massachusetts commissioners to the Columbian Exposition for having decided to reproduce the colonial Hancock mansion as the state's exhibit hall. The periodical maintained that "it typified not only the austere and pure mind of John Hancock, but of a whole nation whose being is due to the era of our puritanical forefathers." The writer conjured up the specter of Hancock in the article and imagined him pointing to the mansion and saying: "There you see symbolized the true democracy—quiet, elegant and refined, and capable in itself of arousing a love for the pure and an abhorrence of the fickle in life." Despite the sermonic tone, the allusion to Puritans and obsession with purity had less to do with the theology of a puritanical past and more to do with colonial revivalists search for cultural order and stability.[49]

The tribute to the Massachusetts exhibition hall at the world's fair served as a prelude to the intended focus of the *Hill-Top* article—the remodeled Mansion House. Although filled with more modern conveniences, the "old wayside inn" still retained "its colonial aspect." Entering the office from the front entrance, guests saw to the right the oft-mentioned new fireplace made of old bricks. The walls throughout the room were still held together by the original hand-forged nails and hand-hewn timbers. At the foot of the staircase leading to the second floor was the entrance to the old parlor, "where even the ancient finish" was preserved. Ascending to the next level, visitors found two "charming old rooms," the guest and family chambers. The former still featured the same old rail, wainscoting, and framing. The latter continued to evoke nostalgic memories as the birthplace of so many Ricker children. Drawing the tour to a close, the author informed readers: "it is the effort of the owners to enhance, to perfect, and to idealize the home of their ancestry—to make a modern inn, still preserving the atmosphere of the old." The Rickers stated that they did this not only to satisfy their guests, but also "to make real the traditions of those who went before us, and whose sturdy and magnificent character and courage was the foundation on which was laid all the great enterprises which have startled the older world."[50]

The themes addressed in the article explain the appeal of the colonial revival at Poland Spring. The movement was about love for the pure, for timeless values, and abhorrence of the fickle, of change for the sake of change. The permanence of purity was associated with the past; the ephemerality of fickleness was associated with the present. Furthermore, it was about preserving the best features of the old ways while simultaneously promoting the progress of the modern age. Finally, it was about honoring and carrying on the traditions and traits—in short, the noble inheritance—passed down from heroic ancestors.

Use of the term "noble inheritance" suggests the meaning the present generation attached to the past. The value placed on the colonial era derived from its perceived nobility. In the midst of the unprecedented influx of foreign immigrants during the late nineteenth century, many old-stock Americans were reminded that their colonial forbearers had paid a high price for the opportunity to pursue happiness. Those ancestors had struggled mightily against hardships to civilize the wilderness. Sometimes they even had sacrificed their lives to vanquish Natives they regarded as savages. As a consequence, colonial revivalists firmly believed that the Anglo-Saxon and early American ancestry of families such as the Rickers ought to convey exalted status upon them, for both hereditary and historical reasons. In effect, people such as the Rickers used the notion of an ethnically pure past not only to define the social exclusivity of the resort, but also to defend their cultural authority in American society.

The children of Hiram and Janette Ricker laid claim to this portion of their legacy by researching their genealogy, telling and retelling their family history, displaying their coat of arms, celebrating local centennials, and preserving old buildings. By reviving the past, they also added to the contrasts that gave character to the Poland Spring resort. More than escapist antimodern nostalgia drove the colonial revival movement. It was also informed by the desire for progress. Out of the noble inheritance embodied by the Mansion House, therefore, came the equally noble dream to crown the hilltop with a more modern hotel.

The Poland Spring House

"Mecca of the Fashion, the Wealth and Culture of the Country"

In contrast to the Mansion House, which primarily evoked a noble past, the Rickers intended the Poland Spring House to be a monument to progress. Heralding its "magnificent proportions," beautiful design, and perfect appointments, the proprietors promoted the hotel as one of the leading "modern summer houses." Nevertheless, behind the fashionable facade of modernity went on more of the masquerade of antimodernity. In its idealized roles as a private domestic space and exclusive aristocratic enclave, the building served as a sanctuary from the rapacious outside world. At the same time, the so-called "Mecca of the fashion, the wealth and culture of the country" also celebrated sociability, commodified leisure, kindled consumption, spotlighted technology, fostered commerce, and in short, embraced Gilded-Age life. As the market revolution played out within the walls of the Poland Spring House through a quarter century of renovations and additions, the contrasts between antimodern genteel home and noble castle on one side and modern social mecca, pleasure palace, technological showplace, and commercial counting house on the other helped transform the resort into a "veritable paradise" for the people of progress.[1]

A Dream Hotel (1860)

As early as 1860, a local reporter writing about the newly popular water source at Poland Spring observed: "a hotel on the spot is what is wanted." Several years later, Jane Patterson attributed a premonition expressing a similar sentiment to a fictional character based upon Hiram Ricker. Speaking to his son Ellison, Dr. Rossville predicted: "People will swarm here like bees, and you must make preparations to receive them. You want to build a new hotel right on the highest point here." According to a family friend, Edward Ricker did indeed dream of building "a boarding-house of a little larger scope on the Hill."[2]

Lack of funds made fulfillment of the dream infeasible for many years. Under his stewardship, Hiram Ricker had "encumbered" the property with crushing debts. By the time he entrusted the claim to the legacy to his firstborn in 1869, Edward received little more than "a vague title to an embarrassed farm," which he had to defend "against those who wanted to secure the property away from the family." With the homestead mortgaged to the hilt and its ownership in dispute, securing credit and finding investors was difficult. Local banks refused to loan money to Edward. Mechanics Savings Bank in Auburn approved a $5,500 mortgage on the farm in 1875 only when his uncle, John R. Pulsifer, a man of "inflexible integrity," agreed to cosign. A year later, Edward and Alvan Ricker persuaded Albert S. Young, the well-known co-proprietor of the successful Elm House in Auburn, to finance their plan for a new hotel at Poland Spring. The brothers entered into a partnership with Young that called for him to pay half the construction and operating costs in exchange for half ownership in the venture. The Rickers reserved, however, the option to buy him out within six years.[3]

With the finances of the project seemingly squared away, attention turned to construction. On January 26, 1876, the Rickers contracted with Hiram Dinsmore and Jeremiah Philbrook to build the proposed hotel. Following plans rendered by architects John Calvin Stevens and George M. Coombs, craftsmen worked with "speed and thoroughness" to complete the structure in time for the fast approaching summer tourist season. Masons laid the foundation and built seven chimneys. Carpenters framed and sided the structure using 337,000 feet of lumber and 125 casks of nails. Plasterers covered 15,000 yards of lathe. Plumbers hooked up miles of gas piping, steam fixtures, and water works. Painters brushed uncounted gallons of white and green paint over clapboards and shutters. In all, eighty craftsmen and laborers contributed nineteen hundred workdays to the project, completing the building in less than four months.[4]

Getting the work done at such breakneck speed did not come cheap. The structure cost $23,000 to build. Finishing and furnishing it brought the total to between $35,000 and $40,000. In order to pay for the project, the Rickers had to mortgage the farm to the Union Mutual Life Insurance Company in Portland for $12,000 repayable over five years at 8 percent semiannual interest. Even this loan, some of which was used to repay Uncle John Pulsifer and settle the year-old mortgage from Mechanics Savings Bank, could not cover all the remaining expenses. With funds again running low and the summer season drawing near, Edward Ricker relied on credit from a Lewiston furniture store to outfit the hotel. To save shipping costs, he even hauled some of the one hundred carpets and chamber sets back to Poland Spring aboard the family's hay wagon.[5]

The Poland Spring House opened on June 21, 1876, with little fanfare. Only one line announced the event in the Lewiston newspaper. The following day, Edward Ricker and Albert Young "politely escorted" seventeen guests from the Sabbathday Lake Shaker community "through the whole establishment." They toured through a building composed of two perpendicular wings that met to form an L. One wing measured 114 feet and faced north; the other measured 148 feet and faced west. Within these confines, the facility provided accommodations for an additional two hundred guests on the hilltop. Outside, piazzas totaling 450 feet, 360 feet at ground level plus another 90 feet on the upper floors, adorned the front of the hotel. The wings joined at the visual centerpiece of the structure, the prominent six-story tower capped by a French Mansard roof.[6]

With its commanding architectural elements, fine domestic furnishings, and latest technological innovations, the new hotel enhanced Poland Spring's growing reputation. One of the first visitors to view the building declared it a "first-class" hotel "worthy of Long Branch and Newport," two of the leading resort communities in the Northeast. In contrast, long after the novelty of the original edifice had faded, the *Hill-Top* unflatteringly remembered it in 1903 as having been a "crude, square, unornamented structure of four as plain stories as any beach resort, with a square, simple tower." To retain its coveted first-class designation, the Rickers had to renovate, reinvent, and modernize the Poland Spring House repeatedly in the quarter century after it opened.[7]

Genteel Home: The Poland Spring House (1876)

In its original manifestation the Poland Spring House was a genteel home, a place where domesticity reigned supreme. For Victorian adults like Jane Patterson, the ideal home was "the shrine of the family affections" glorified by God. As this perennial Poland Spring patron expressed the sentiment, "to elevate and purify the life of the home ought to be an ambition worthy of the highest endowments." Social convention typically assigned primary responsibility for this goal to women, who were deemed the "true guardians" of the home, willing to place familial duty above personal pleasure. For Victorian children, the cult of domesticity presided over by pious, wise, and tender mothers created a "walled garden" that shielded them from corrupting worldly influences. With each remove into the interior of the house, the family retreated further into a realm of privacy and purity. This conception of domesticity gave to the Victorian home an air of antimodern escape.[8]

The proprietors of the Poland Spring House relied on more than the name of the building to create an appealing Victorian homelike setting for their patrons. Although laid out on a much grander scale, the hotel contained most of the rooms found in a typical house owned by an urban, upper-middle-class family during the Gilded Age. The piazza, or veranda, marked the passage from the public world of the street to the private world of the home. Both residents and guests entered into a ceremonial room—a hall in a house, the lobby in the hotel—where acquaintances and strangers alike exhibited their best genteel behavior. In each type of building, the first floor contained specialized rooms for socializing, dining, and entertaining. Upper floors provided space for more private functions such as sleeping and bathing. The remotest regions of the Victorian house, whether it was a single-family dwelling or a multifamily hotel, were the unseen work places and living quarters of the servants responsible for most of the domestic chores. Ideally, the spatial specialization built into the late-nineteenth-century genteel home, regardless of scale, mediated occupants from the experience of the competitive secular world.[9]

For many houses, the Poland Spring House included, the veranda served as a transitional space. It separated the natural outdoors from the artificial indoors, the informal resort grounds from the formal hotel interior, and the world from the refuge. There, patrons gazed, gossiped, chatted, eavesdropped, daydreamed, smoked, dozed, and in short, relaxed. Seizing on the centrality of the location, the Ricker brothers often strategically stationed themselves on the "hospitable piazza" to greet new guests as they arrived by stage at 10:30 in the morning, 1:00 and 3:30 in the afternoon, and 7:30 in the evening. Edward Ricker made guests feel welcome with his "hale, hearty and whole-souled" greetings and assurances "that the whole house" was theirs. After exchanging pleasantries with the proprietors, patrons could take in the sights, human as well as natural. With its rows of comfortable rocking chairs, the veranda provided an inviting setting for people watching. A reporter surveying the piazza in 1892 noted that the site was "alive with young folk's talk," as well as a favorite after-dinner haunt of the older set. As visitor Lida A. Churchill described the scene two years later, the entire world conversed like brothers on the veranda. In an account reminiscent of a passage from *Little Women*, she claimed to have found at Poland Spring "the military Russian, the urbane Frenchman, the practical German, [and] the count of Italy" engaged in fraternal discussions. Churchill also encountered other stock characters as she traversed the nearly quarter-mile-long piazza: "languorous, handsome daughters and chivalrous sons" of the South, New Yorkers putting aside their commercial cares, and "cultivated, Ibsenistic" Bostonians laying down abstruse volumes to drink in the "mysterious elixir of life."[10]

In 1876 guests could enter the Poland Spring House in two places. The west entrance led into the lobby where Leander Stevens, an experienced hotel manager and the father of one of the building's architects, attended to affairs. In Victorian fashion, the room of "first impressions" sought to grab the attention of patrons with a "fine counter" and equally elegant walnut and ash columns that terminated "at the ceiling in a broad cornice of the same woods." Beyond the front desk, a wide stairwell ascended to the upper floors. In the opinion of one reporter, it was "probably the finest hotel office in Maine." Not fine enough to suit the Rickers, however. In order to create "a homelike air" amid the vastness of the "great office hall," they had the lobby entirely renovated and reconfigured for the 1887 season. Workmen pushed the entrance out four feet to create space for bay windows, moved the location of the front desk to the back of the room, and constructed a rear entrance for easier access to the baggage elevator. They also laid a floor with alternating bands of light and dark hardwoods; added "highly polished, massive, modern oak counters," desks, and stairways; and finished the room "with oak in antique design." Between the new counter and central stairway appeared a six-foot-wide "huge domed fireplace" finished in terra cotta. Resident painter William Thresher added a "much admired" United States shield above the mantel.[11]

The north entrance to the hotel placed guests in a spacious corridor that separated the ladies' parlors. Described as the "quintessential Victorian room," parlor design, decor, and deportment was shaped by the values of domesticity and rules of gentility. The rooms also exuded a modern mix of cosmopolitanism and consumerism that led to a riot of fabrics and furnishings. The resulting "bricabracomania" unleashed by this materialistic bent came to define the visually busy palace parlor. In such "cozy corners," Gilded-Age "parlor people" conversed, read, wrote, and rested. In the parlor of the Poland Spring House, large plate glass windows provided "unequalled scenic pictures" of the landscape. As the setting sun reflected off the western sky, its

OFFICE FROM DINING ROOM ENTRANCE. PARLOR.

OFFICE AND NEWS STAND PARLOR LOOKING INTO OFFICE

INTERIOR VIEWS OF POLAND SPRING HOUSE.

MUSIC ROOM.

OFFICE.

DINING ROOM.

INTERIOR VIEWS OF POLAND SPRING HOUSE.

The montage of interior views of the Poland Spring House appeared in a souvenir booklet published in the mid-1880s, about a decade after the social "mecca" of the resort opened. *Poland Spring: Souvenir. Poland Spring, Maine: Hiram Ricker and Sons, [1885]. Courtesy Androscoggin Historical Society.*

light seemed to turn the windows into masses of "almost liquid diamonds, rubies, emeralds, and turquoise." Stained glass windows added to the kaleidoscope of color. Opposite the scenes of natural beauty hung artistic representations. Paintings of poppies by Abbott Graves, New England autumn and springtime scenes by John J. Enneking, and apple blossoms by Adelaide Palmer adorned parlor walls. Decorations painted by William Thresher contributed to the elegance of the rooms. The ceiling of the ladies' writing room featured the motif of a Maine pinecone intertwined with an oak leaf. Guests admired the creations of both nature and artists from "grand and sumptuous" chairs, sofas, and divans that invited repose and suggested "the sweet and entrancing music of the 'unspeakable Turk.'"[12]

The Turks may have been unspeakable, but the people of progress admired their textiles. The rage for Mediterranean, Middle Eastern and Far Eastern items in Victorian decor reflected the "domestication of exotica." Another example of such exotic taste, in the form of an Oriental portiere hanging from a Moorish archway, screened the parlor from the front office to the Poland Spring House. In contrast to the patriotic republican mantelpiece over the lobby fireplace, the one in the parlor paid tribute to ancient Roman decadence. "Tastily finished in tile," the oak mantel featured a richly carved scene entitled "The Feast of Bacchus." Fittingly, guests passed this symbolic tribute to hedonistic indulgence on their way to the dining room.[13]

The rules of gentility also governed the dining experience at the Poland Spring House. From the decor of the forty-by-eighty-foot dining room to the watercolor paintings on the menu covers to the gowns "stately dames and dowagers" wore to breakfast to the white dresses of the table girls to the presentation of the food, everything about mealtimes reflected refinement. As one reporter put it, "dinner here is no vulgar wish." The Ricker family watched over the room from the first table to the right of the entrance. An adjoining private dining area seated up to forty honored guests. It connected to a third chamber reserved for the children and servants of guests. Up to three hundred diners assembled for breakfast from seven to nine in the morning, although the leisurely pace of resort life often extended the hours. Liberation from the tyranny of the clock, coupled with New England custom, accounted for the lateness of the midday meal from one to two-thirty in the afternoon. The final meal of the day was served from six to eight in the evening.[14]

Despite all the attention devoted to refinement, the main fare of the dining room was still food. A veritable cornucopia awaited guests at every sitting. A menu from 1887 offered diners the choice of four soups; two fish varieties; five boiled and five roasted meat selections; five entrees; four kinds of cold cuts; a dozen vegetable dishes; nine relishes; five pastries; and sixteen desserts. To supply such prodigious quantities, the kitchen in just one day during the height of the 1894 season served up quite literally a ton of food: 440 pounds of beef, 300 pounds of lamb, 205 pounds of fish, 200 pounds of duck, 150 pounds of chicken, 100 pounds of fowl, 90 pounds of ribs, 75 pounds of turkey, 40 pounds of ham, and 35 pounds of lobster, 18 pounds of coffee, and 200 pounds of sugar, plus 120 dozen eggs, 16 gallons of cream, 80 gallons of milk, 3 bushels of berries, and 3 barrels of flour. Despite the staggering tally, the *Hill-Top* assured readers that the larder was inexhaustible.[15]

The resort newspaper attributed the Gilded-Age gluttony on display daily in the dining room to two gastronomic philosophies: "eat, drink, and be merry" and "the way to a man's heart is through his stomach." Ravenous diners could guiltlessly gorge their appetites, for even if their consumption doubled, the paper informed them, "the welcome is the same." Not surprisingly, excesses at the table caused many patrons to "gain flesh." Ironically, it also undoubtedly exacerbated cases of a widespread disorder of the day—dyspepsia—the very malady that drew many patrons to the spring in the first place. Obfuscating the matter, the *Hill-Top* sent a curiously self-evident and thus meaningless message to diners, assuring them that if they survived the overeating, they would "live to grow old and gray."[16]

Diners did need to practice moderation in what they drank. Of course all the water they wanted was always available, but aside from that offering, tea and coffee supplied exclusively by Chase and Sanborn were the only other choices. Beverage selections were not as extensive as food because sobriety ruled at Poland Spring. The hilltop went dry sometime after the mid-1820s. A receipt recording the purchase of fifteen gallons of rum, four gallons of gin, and one gallon of Madeira wine from a Portland merchant attests that Wentworth Ricker kept the tap room of the Mansion House well stocked at least until 1825. Thereafter, Hiram Ricker's discovery of the healing power of spring water, Alvan Bolster's leadership of the Sons of Temperance, and Albert Young's support of "the cold water principle" at his Auburn hotel joined forces to shut off the flow of liquor on the hilltop. When asked whether whiskey would be served at the new Poland Spring House, Young assured a "guileless" reporter in 1876 that this hotel, too, would be water powered. As late as 1904, the business was still described as "a thoroughly temperance hotel." It was a policy the genteel patrons of the resort heartily supported, at least publicly.[17]

The family delegated responsibility for procuring provisions to Alvan

Ricker. To ensure freshness, he oversaw the production and cultivation of some of the foodstuffs on site. Area farmers and local food wholesalers also sold provisions to the resort. In addition, A. B. made frequent trips to Boston, where he gained a reputation for being "one of the shrewdest buyers" in the city. Merchants knew that showing him less than the best produce was a waste of time. For his part, Ricker kept a detailed account of purchases made for the culinary department. From 1896 to 1903, he meticulously recorded data on the quantities and costs of more than one hundred foodstuffs served at the resort, everything ranging from anchovies to vermicelli. Indicating the budgetary limits that constrained even a luxury hotel, his cost consciousness resulted in the procurement of cheaper fare for employees and experiments to determine which brand of flour produced the most bread. Ricker's calculations determined that 196 pounds of Washburn flour yielded 145 loaves weighing on average 32 to 33 ounces, while the same amount of the King Arthur brand yielded 145 loaves weighing only 31 ounces each.[18]

While Alvan Ricker reigned over the larder and kitchen, the dining room was the domain of the headwaiter. For many years, Julius Gassauer, an Austrian native training for the ministry, masterfully handled the duty of serving a clientele accustomed to receiving first-class treatment. A demeanor epitomizing European culture and refinement that caused patrons to regard the headwaiter as a peer abetted his work. At meal times, Gassauer and his assistants seated each party at one of sixty tables that accommodated anywhere from six to fourteen people. For status-conscious patrons, seating was no simple matter of first come, first served. Regular visitors expected to dine at a favorite table, while fashionable guests wanted places at the end of the hall so they could parade past their fellow patrons. The ability to satisfy every preference was the true test of the headwaiter's skillfulness. Gassauer orchestrated the flow of events in the dining room so smoothly that the *Hill-Top* observed in 1896, "Mr. Julius's friends are limited only by the capacity of the house."[19]

The headwaiter also supervised the table girls who served diners. Overseeing this crew was no small task either, for the wait staff numbered sixty women in 1889 and grew to ninety by 1900. The headwaiter had the responsibility of making certain everyone knew the rules governing "time of service, general behavior, and manner of waiting on table." Waitresses were expected to adhere to a rigid dress code. The uniform for breakfasts and teas was a dark dress with an "ample" skirt and a large white apron. For dinners, the uniform was a white dress, "neatly arranged," and an apron. Regulations also directed waitresses "at all times to have their hair neatly arranged." Failure to "conform strictly to the rules of the Dining Hall" provided grounds for "immediate discharge." Although the waitresses agreed to abide by the terms of an agreement that dictated the maintenance of "good order" down to the minutest detail, they were far from docile uninformed workers. While a little less than a third were Irish, Canadian, or English immigrants, most of the women were from Maine and many were teachers or students. In the opinion of Jane Patterson, the educated backgrounds of some table girls made them "as scholarly as the ladies they serve."[20]

Patterson attributed the constantly improving "class of servants" to the "excellent care" the Rickers provided their employees. In 1892 waitresses worked for $2.50 per week, less the cost of their uniforms and travel expenses. In addition, they received free room and board in the "comfortable accommodations" of the help's quarters located behind the hotel. In return, the proprietors expected workers to keep their rooms in good order, do their own washing and ironing, obey a 10:00 P.M. curfew, and comport themselves "quietly and civilly." The obligations of gentility, if not the privileges, governed the back of the house, too. To ensure the full and faithful performance, the standard employee contract stipulated that dismissal or early departure risked forfeiture of half the season's wages. The clause had force behind it, because the Rickers withheld final payment until an employee's service had concluded. No worker skipped out early without paying the price.[21]

Unlike the very public first floor of the Poland Spring House, the upper floors encompassed many private realms. From the original 120 bedrooms in 1876, the hotel expanded to a capacity of over four hundred beds two decades later. Descriptions of the apartments characterized the scale as spacious, the decor as tasteful, the furnishings as comfortable, and the ambience as inviting. Suites offered the most amenities: large closets, broad windows, cozy verandas, open fireplaces, and most desirable of all, private bathrooms. As an 1898 newspaper account proudly put it, the hotel's "private suites and apartments are furnished with all the elegance that money can command." Adding to the allure, the geographic orientation of the building exposed most rooms to generous amounts of summer sunshine and cooling breezes. Thus, the apartments abounded in both radiant light and fresh air. The proprietors promised that there were no poor rooms in the hotel and "none without something of a view."[22]

For the geriatric element among the clientele, the bedroom—a place of relative peace and quiet—provided the ideal setting for convalescence. Although the Rickers promoted the promise of good health to attract patrons, they simultaneously sought to dispel the image of the hotel as a hospital. An 1887 pamphlet demonstrates the mixed message that resulted from the contrasting images of the Poland Spring House as a peaceful genteel home and active social mecca. It opened by declaring that the resort was "one of the most charming spots . . . for invalids in search of health." A few pages later, the tract abruptly changed tack, advising readers not to get the idea that Poland Spring "is a resort for invalids only." To accentuate the point, a lengthy list of social and recreational activities followed. An 1892 article conveyed the conflicting messages the opposite way. It first forcefully stated: "Poland Spring is not a hospital. It is no invalids' home." In case anyone missed the point, the writer added, "the idea that Poland Spring is the abode chiefly of the lame and the invalid is wrong." Yet, the piece closed with a detailed account of how a "weak and tottering" New York businessman had come to the resort in 1888 to restore his health.[23]

The Rickers did employ a local physician, Dr. Milton C. Wedgwood, to attend to the medical needs of guests. Wedgwood's informal and sporadic visits to Poland Spring beginning in the 1870s gradually evolved into a more formal and permanent relationship by 1886. The doctor traveled from his practice in Lewiston to the resort three to four times a week during July and August to attend to his summer patients. Given his long experience, no one knew the aches and pains of guests better than he did. Commenting on the general health of the clientele in 1894, Dr. Wedgwood observed that "the majority of the people that come to Poland Spring are middle aged and there is hardly a floor in the house that doesn't have two or more sick people in it, and they have come there because it is retired and because they want quiet." The prospect of peace and rest, coupled with the sociability of the piazza, cosmopolitanism of the parlors, refinement of the dining room, and privacy of the bedrooms, became the hallmarks of the genteel Poland Spring House for sick and sound alike.[24]

The Refinement of the Music Hall (1884)

In their never-ending quest to create a paradise that could please everyone all the time, the Rickers began making costly improvements to the Poland Spring House only a few years after it opened. In 1881, for example, the family spent $20,000 on alterations. A $15,000 mortgage, the third taken out on the homestead in five years and the second received from Philander S. Briggs of Boston, partially financed the renovations. In a move to gain full control of the management of the resort, the Ricker brothers used some of the money to buy out Albert Young's interest in the hotel valued at nearly $24,000. The agreement between the partners also specifically obligated the Rickers to cover an outstanding balance of $280 still owed for the hotel's original furnishings. Keeping the dream alive, while remaining solvent, carried with it very real and heavy expenses.[25]

To add to the refinement of the genteel Poland Spring House, the proprietors made more improvements to the building in 1884. The first part of the project, alterations to the exterior, made the structure more stylish by adding two towers, several ornamental chimneys, and a less monotonous facade. Phase two, the construction of a 40-by-125-foot extension to the west wing of the hotel, not only increased the number of bedrooms in the facility by sixty-four, it also included a "dainty" new music hall. The latter facility, measuring thirty-six feet wide by seventy-two feet long, became a place where patrons could experience the high culture of orchestral music, the mental stimulation of educational lectures, and the moral uplift of religious worship. In sum, it was a space where the people of progress could exhibit the refinement of gentility.[26]

Musical entertainment on the hilltop predated the music hall. Even before the establishment of the resort, there had been the ill-fated dance pavilion of the 1850s. Many years later, a trio, consisting of a fiddler, pianist, and cornet player, comprised the first group to perform at the Poland Spring House. During the hotel's inaugural season, the musicians greeted new arrivals in the lobby with a repertoire of dance tunes. At night they played for guests who merrily reeled, jigged, and waltzed to the music. A succession of local musicians entertained at the hotel over the next decade. A four-piece group led by another "old-time" fiddle player replaced the original trio in 1877. After several seasons, the quartet gave way to brass bands. With the arrival of the more mobile musicians, the venue for serenading inbound travelers shifted from the hotel veranda to the Spring House. After the last stage had arrived for the day, the music playing moved to the hotel lobby, where guests listened while gathering for the evening meal. Jane Patterson recalled that the musical prelude especially appealed to the young people who danced informally while waiting to head into the dining room. When the weather permitted, the band also performed outdoors in the hotel courtyard.[27]

The addition of the music hall quickly changed the tradition of local musicians, informal dances, and outdoor concerts. In 1886 the Rickers hired eight professional musicians from the Boston Symphony Orchestra (BSO) at a cost of several thousand dollars. Led by pianist J. Howard Richardson, the orchestra performed concerts, complete with printed programs, at 11:30 A.M. and 8:00 P.M. on weekdays and at 3:30 P.M. on Sundays. At these sessions, a repertoire of music "culled from the finest literature" supplanted once-popular dance tunes such as "Sweet Marie" and "Ta-ra-ra." Patterson termed it "music to satisfy the artist"; while a spectator described the scene at a forenoon concert in 1892 as an audience of elderly ladies sitting "with folded hands and some with needle work." Leadership of the orchestra passed to Daniel Kuntz in 1894. A violinist with the BSO, Kuntz was no stranger to the resort. He had played under Richardson for several seasons, during which time he had become one of the most popular performers. The *Hill-Top* touted the Kuntz Orchestral Club as a group that "music lovers from any of the large cities will feel well acquainted." Indeed, one Bostonian staying at the hotel believed the group was equaled by few and excelled by none.[28]

The orchestra performed what cultural arbiters considered the best works of all the great composers, including Beethoven, Wagner, Mozart, Rossini, Bach, and Strauss. Concerts typically offered between five and eight arrangements, one or two of which might be performed solo. Visiting artists, usually singers, also contributed their talents to the presentations. In July 1897, for instance, the "large dramatic voice" of contralto Katharine Ricker, a relative of the proprietors, filled the music hall with songs of "thorough musical and artistic feeling." A performer with the Central Congregational Church in Boston, Ricker "was heartily encored in all selections." Guests even volunteered a song from time to time. In 1895 D. J. Griffith surprised concertgoers with an exquisite rendition of "*Die Uhr.*" A "most hearty and deserved" response from the audience elicited from Griffith a double encore of songs by eminent European composers.[29]

The new formality of the music reflected the ongoing differentiation of the arts into high and lowbrow cultures during the nineteenth century. Where once guests had happily danced to "popular" tunes, the *Hill-Top* now derided it as too commonplace. Music hall audiences wanted something more than mere frivolity and physical stimulation from performances. They wanted cultural refinement and moral uplift. Consequently, patrons now politely listened rather than spiritedly danced to music. More important, they expected their appreciation of the orchestra, with its emphasis on the European classics, to help fulfill their genteel aspirations.[30]

The highbrow tone of concerts carried over into many of the lectures presented in the music hall. While the presentations had no intentional unifying theme, they essentially amounted to training in gentility. Mrs. Bailey's programs, "Harmony of the Body," "Voice in Speaking," and "Dress," which interested parties could supplement with private lessons at five dollars per individual session or fifteen dollars for ten group sessions, instructed women how to be more well mannered, well spoken, and well dressed. Talks on the Battle of Gettysburg, theory of the flat earth, and Mark Twain's *Innocents Abroad* enabled guests to sound better educated. Illustrated lectures on the gold rush in the Klondike and war in Cuba made them better informed. Poetry recitations and dramatic performances made audience members better cultured. Presentations on the Grand Canyon, Alaska, India, and the Matterhorn made the vacationers seem even better traveled. A sermon on a Christian school established in Syria, which concluded with the passing of the collection plate, made the stewards of wealth feel better intentioned. A reading by Shaker Sister Aurelia Mace from her manuscript "The Aletheia" allowed the "noble class of people" she addressed to feel more pious.[31]

Noble Castle: The Renovations of 1889

In 1889 the Rickers reimagined their dream hotel. Amid the colonial revival movement, the Poland Spring House became another setting for the masquerade of aristocratic nobility. With a major $70,000 expansion and renovation financed by a third mortgage on the hotel lot, the genteel home of domesticity and refinement began an imaginative metamorphosis into a noble castle. Competition within the resort industry made the move a virtual necessity. By the last decade of the nineteenth century, palatial hotels had become the standard by which wealthy travelers judged the merit of vacation spots. On its face, the alterations to the building were only rudimentary. The plan submitted by architects John Calvin Stevens and Albert Winslow Cobb simply extended the north wing 116 feet to the east and increased both the size of the dining room and number of apartments. It also sought to upgrade "the architectural style of the great house" by incorporating Queen Anne and colonial revival motifs into the design. More important, the project aimed to transform the image of the Poland Spring House from home to castle, thereby elevating the status of its clientele from families of self-made people of progress to heirs of a self-perpetuating native aristocracy.[32]

Edward Ricker took an active interest in the redesign of the hotel. Recognizing the opportunity presented by the tree-shrouded approach to the hilltop, he devoted a great deal of consideration to the first impression made by the profile of the building as it suddenly burst into the sight of arriving coach passengers. Study of other resort accommodations had convinced Ricker of the desirability of artistry in architecture. A replica of the huge barn-like structures that passed for hotels in Bar Harbor would not do at his resort. Ricker's determination to add more character to the Poland Spring House led to close consultation with the architects. Dissatisfied with their plan to renovate the main tower, E. P. telegraphed his revisions to Stevens and Cobb at their Portland office. Writing from Boston, Stevens assured his "anxious" client that "satisfactory arrangements" for the contemplated changes could be fixed up. They were. The architects added bays on the upper stories and a cap to the roof of the remodeled tower. Four new towers, symbolizing the ascension of the hotel's image from house to castle, also crowned the addition.[33]

As concerned as Ricker was with the exterior details, the main focus of the project was the expansion of the dining room to "grand and palatial dimensions." The addition increased the length of the room to 183 feet and its capacity to four hundred diners. On the surface, architectural elements such as new sideboards, bays, Corinthian columns, and fireplaces, some with "old-fashioned, colonial mantels," improved upon the refinements of genteel domesticity. A vine motif appeared along the top of the nearly sixteen-foot-high walls in the form of an embossed pattern stenciled by one of the foremost mural painters in the country, Albert Haberstroh of Boston. In the light from the gas chandeliers, the reflected glow of the pure cream white walls created an ambience of rest and comfort and the polished oak floor shone like satin. Upon closer inspection, the addition of an orchestra platform, stained-glass decorations, and an immense eight-by-fourteen-foot plate-glass window signified the incursion of not just luxury, but also new values into the space. The new decor and furnishings represented the intrusion of the modern marketplace into the illusion of a domestic space. Diners now sat in leather-seated oak chairs specially designed by Edward Ricker and at tables "richly clothed" in the finest linen. They ate off Haviland china decorated with "exquisitely painted vines in woodsy suggestion," using luxurious Reed and Barton silverware that was "so well known and in designs especially adapted for Hotel, Steamboat, and Dining Car Service."[34]

Above the dining room, the addition made way for fifty-five new apartments. A tour of the third floor conducted by "Landlord" Ricker led through suites comprised of bed, sitting, and bath rooms. For the princely sum of seventy dollars per week, the likes of Richard H. Stearns, "the great dry goods dealer of the Hub" and the epitome of a modern merchant spreading the new gospel of conspicuous consumption into the Victorian home, rented such palatial quarters. The rooms featured "exquisite" carpets, "sumptuous" brass and oak furniture, hot and cold running water, steam heat, open fireplaces, "superb" views, and "closets enough to make every lady smile." The Rickers proudly advertised that the remodeled Poland Spring House was now "first-class in all its appointments, and second to no Summer Hotel in the United States, a perfect home for its patrons."[35]

Lest guests fail to appreciate fully the intermediary stage easing the transformation from genteel home to social mecca, publicists added their finishing touches to the creations of the architects, carpenters, decorators, and other craftsmen who had worked on the renovation. In an 1890 essay, William Murray lauded the "noble hotel nobly located" on a "noble" hill, noting that "it becomes, as a crown becometh a king's head." The interior of the hotel impressed him as well. Murray appreciated the "noble" appearance of the lobby, spaciousness of the corridors, and abundance of atmosphere. He reserved his most glowing comments for the dining hall. The room's size, "noble" height, gleaming floors, and magnificent views reminded him of the halls where old Norse kings "met for feast and wassail." Moreover, the sweet music, fragrant flowers, and beautiful furniture created a cultivated setting that Murray considered as vital to an enjoyable dining experience as "victuals deftly prepared." He complimented the hosts for honoring their guests "as people of refinement and civilized tastes" rather than as brutish swine. The Rickers, Murray concluded, exalted "the noble art of entertainment."[36]

Other publicists joined the chorus in praise of the nobility and majesty of the renovated hotel. An account published in 1891 depicted the Poland Spring House as a palace of beauty, wealth, and fashion. Three years later, Lida Churchill characterized it as "a veritable castle of liberty and expansion." In the same year, George H. Haynes dubbed Poland Spring the "Queen of Resorts" and portrayed its main hotel as "a veritable castle on the hill." Also in 1894, the editor of a New Hampshire newspaper paid tribute to "the mammoth palace on the hill." The *Boston Daily Globe* told its readers in 1897 about "the castle-like Poland Spring House" that crowned the "noble hill." For its part, the *Hill-Top* compared the edifice to a palace "with all imperial magnificence." The Rickers had apparently realized their noble dream.[37]

Social Mecca: "The Invasion of Fashion"

A funny thing happened on the way to the masquerade of aristocratic escape. Constantly updating the architecture and adding to the accommodations also altered the atmosphere of the hotel. Although the ideal of the Victorian resort as genteel home or noble castle envisioned flight from worldly considerations, creating a completely private refuge in an inherently public setting ultimately proved impossible. Filled with hundreds of guests from many different places and staffed by hundreds of working-class employees, the Poland Spring House could neither preserve the private realm of domestic tranquility nor protect the ideal of social exclusivity. Nor could it keep out new values of modernity such as fashionability, sociability, and theatricality. Governed by the conventions of fashion, customs of social interaction, and codes of public display, the new resort culture looked outward more than inward. The resulting social mecca provided the people of progress with a grand new stage where they could preen, promenade, party, play, and perform.[38]

One guest who understood early on the transition to modernity taking place at Poland Spring was Jane Patterson. Before the construction of the new hotel, an informal, homelike atmosphere had reigned on the hilltop. Women had come for rest, not for dress parades. In her novel, the opening of the New Bethesda House changed everything. Commenting on the state of affairs by 1878, Patterson lamented:

With the new house, a new order had unconsciously crept in. Ladies appeared at the supper-table in full dress, and radiant with laces and diamonds. Calico and gingham still prevailed in the morning, but every lady must look her prettiest at evening. Even the gentlemen laid aside their business suits and conformed to the new order. The at-home atmosphere so charming at the Old Stage Tavern seemed a little chilled by the invasion of fashion.

A letter writer staying at the resort during the summer of 1878 concurred with Patterson's harsh assessment. The correspondent succinctly differentiated the clienteles of the Mansion and Poland Spring Houses as respectively "the solid ones" and "the fashionables." Fashionability had trumped domesticity and gentility.[39]

Indeed, fashion increasingly preoccupied the thoughts of guests, especially the women. While dining one evening in 1894, a patron observed "the many elegant costumes and the costly jewels worn." During a conversation on the veranda later that evening, the same person remarked: "the ladies know that they must bring their finest plumage to the backwoods of Maine." The statement recalled for another "old sojourner" the story of a prominent Philadelphia socialite who during a visit to Poland Spring in 1886, had hidden in her room virtually the entire time because she had not brought her best silks and satins. Believing that Maine was one vast forest and the resort little more than a farmhouse in a clearing, the woman had mistakenly assumed that she could leave behind the worldly cares of fashion during her escape to the countryside.[40]

With even greater disappointment, Patterson contended that other elements of the invasion of modernity had also caused the resort to outgrow "the family ideal." The domestic atmosphere that had once bound guests together in "a union of sentiment" had disappeared. In its place arose a less congenial setting that emphasized the status and pleasure of individual families. Diamonds now sparkled "like rain-drops on an April day." "Portly and well-kept men, and care-free women . . . clothed like queens" clogged the halls and piazzas. Unknown figures flitted about in perpetual motion. Strange faces appeared at every turn. In Patterson's view, the New Bethesda House had ceased to be a home away from home where genteel middle-class families shared a sense of community. Instead, it had become a hotel where acquisitive leisure-class tourists paid a high price to buy a measure of social exclusivity. The *Hill-Top* termed the transformation the "social whirl."[41]

One of the grandest and most stylish social events ever held at the Poland Spring House was a reception in honor of General Benjamin Franklin Butler. A Massachusetts lawyer and politician of great flamboyance, controversy, and popularity, Butler had gained notoriety during the Civil War for his authoritarian command of Union-occupied Louisiana. After the war, he had served in the United States House of Representatives, where he had aligned himself with the Radical Republicans and joined the campaign to impeach President Andrew Johnson. Although he had become an immensely wealthy man by parlaying his extensive government contacts into contracts for his business interests, Butler had always played the part of populist politician. After many failed attempts, he finally had won election as Governor of Massachusetts in 1882. Two years later, he had run as the presidential nominee of both the Greenback-Labor and Anti-Monopoly Parties.[42]

To many of his contemporaries, Butler symbolized the worst attributes of the Gilded Age. His strong-armed rule and suspected looting of New Orleans had earned him such uncouth alliterative epithets as "Beast," "Brute," and "the bag-eyed bullion bagger." The general's distinctive appearance contributed to the impression of a man prone to excess. Butler was short, stocky, bald, cross-eyed, and had a droopy eyelid. One critical historian unflatteringly described him as being a man who was "oily and puffy and wheezy . . . [and] who yearly added more flesh." Butler's cultivated lack of gentility added to his persona. His habits of tucking his napkin under his chin at meals and chewing or smoking the wrong end of cigars attracted notice. Yet, his status, not to mention stature, mitigated the unconventional behavior. As an admiring commentator put it after one of Butler's visits to Poland Spring, the general had earned the "right" to do what he did.[43]

Butler's health had taken an unexpected turn for the worse following a fall at a Philadelphia railroad station in February of 1887. The mishap had left the general with a dislocated right shoulder. The injury had required surgery, during which, the patient complained, the surgeons had pulled him all to pieces. Still suffering from lameness several months later, Butler had decided the relief he needed could be found at Poland Spring. Sailing from Boston aboard his yacht *America*, the general arrived in Portland on a Sunday evening in mid-July. The next morning, he and his traveling party boarded a special Pullman car and headed for the resort. Met at the Lewiston Junction railroad depot, the entourage was conveyed to the resort by the Messrs. Ricker themselves.[44]

Hiram Ricker and his sons could not let the arrival of such a distinguished guest go unnoticed. Judging by the program featuring General Butler's ample profile and the amount of press coverage received by the visit, plans for the reception and promenade concert must have been in the works for a while. From the moment Butler and his party arrived at nine o'clock in the morning on July 18th, the resort was astir. Well-wishers from Lewiston and Auburn descended upon the hilltop throughout the day. Corridors, reception rooms, and parlors of the Poland Spring House were filled with "unusual chatter and bustle." The general did not disappoint his admirers. Encamping on the piazza with an after-dinner Havana cigar in hand, Butler entertained his company with amusing "anecdotes and interesting reminiscences." The eagerly anticipated reception commenced at 8:15 P.M. in the music hall. During the evening, Butler personally greeted between four and five hundred guests. The event brought out ladies dressed in their most elegant toilets and displaying the most beautiful floral arrangements. After a brief concert, the orchestra played eight selections that sent "everybody who knew how to dance" onto the floor. The evening concluded with "an elegant collation" served by the Rickers in the dining room.[45]

The ball in Ben Butler's honor was more than just about being fashionable and being seen, or being sociable and mixing with peers. The point was also to be theatrical and put on a display—a show of status, wealth, power, privilege, and self-importance. In addition to the formal balls, energetic hops, youthful cotillions, mirthful masquerades, and dramatic tableauxs provided forums for "public theatricality"—for the wearing of costumes, the assumption of roles, the following of scripts. The events customarily commenced with grand processions from the lobby to the music hall that permitted elegantly attired couples to display their fashionability to other admiring guests. The dance card further invested the affair with an air of "stately dignity." The intricate precision of carefully conceived orders of marches, quadrilles, waltzes, Schottisches, Lanciers, gallops, and fancies made it "hard to recognize the usual jolly dancers of Saturday night."[46]

Among the jolliest dancers were the young people at the resort. Their Saturday evening hops filled the music hall with young ladies attired in "tasty" costumes and young gentlemen in "regulation black," watched over by matrons in "more sober shades." The ostentatious show of wealth included glittering diamonds, beautiful pearls, and other choice jewels that accentuated colorful gowns made out of the finest satin, crepon, muslin, chiffon, silk, organdy, velvet, taffeta, and lace, and decorated with colorful brocade and ribbons. The "entrancing strains" struck up by the orchestra summoned the young people onto the dance floor for "dreamy" waltzes. All this pageantry offered escape from "the trials and the sober realities of life" to the youthful partygoers, whose credo reportedly was: "Let us be gay." It was just the sort of hedonistic sociability Jane Patterson abhorred.[47]

Patterson understood that young people were the prime movers of the shift in social relations. Their affairs drove much of the action in *The Romance of the New Bethesda*. As with the Raynor family in her novel, many children accompanied their parents to the social mecca on the hilltop. In fact, one report in 1892 claimed that there was proportionately "more of the youth of swelldom at Poland Spring than at any other resort in America." The presence of so many adolescents with doting mothers and fathers in tow helped shape the social agenda of the hotel. It also expanded the bounds of propriety and added an air of romance, making the vacation community "a children's paradise."[48]

All of these changes—the invasion of fashion, the social whirl, and the theatrical spectacle—portended for Patterson a waning of the moral piety and religious sentiment that had once underpinned Victorian domesticity and gentility. In her novel, Maud Raynor, a woman who has entered the ministry, notes how young people are the first to succumb to the new rules of modern sociability. Raynor voices alarm that children have become "so volatile, so given to the pursuit of pleasure, with small evidence of that serious undertone which swayed and fashioned her own youth." Furthermore, it amazes her "that the Sunday-school takes on the air of a holiday party, with scarcely a sign of the reverence suggested by the place and the work it is set to do." Given the rising secular spirit, the New Bethesda House becomes the playground of pleasure seekers, not the promised land of the pious people of progress.[49]

Pleasure Palace: Constructing the Casino (1887)

As Jane Patterson had astutely observed, over the course of a decade from its opening, the Poland Spring House had evolved from a secluded domestic refuge into a public pleasure palace. The leisure revolution had lightened the social atmosphere. Victorian social life became less like work. There was some relief from the demanding requirements of fashionability, sociability, and theatricality. Many occasions now called for more fun than fashion, more release than refinement, more play than display. Besides the serious business of concerts, lectures, and worship services, and intense socializing at hops, cotillions, masquerades, and balls, the music hall was also a place where patrons could partake of "entertainments of a light and pleasing nature." An annex constructed in 1887 to serve as a casino provided numerous opportunities for more relaxed recreation. In addition, an amusement room added a few years later became the center of what became one of the most popular light and pleasing entertainments at the resort—card playing.

Responsibility for providing leisure activities did not rest solely with the proprietors of the Poland Spring House. An amusement committee composed of and funded by guests supplemented the social life at the resort. Each season patrons pledged to the cause by signing a subscription list posted near the news counter in the hotel lobby. The $1,200 collected in 1893 paid for a full schedule of musical and literary programs, as well as the resort baseball team. The size of the fund enabled the committee to attract the finest acts working the summer-resort circuit. With money already in hand, committee members could guarantee performers set fees rather than the uncertain contributions from a post-performance collection plate. Poland Spring was one of the few resorts to adopt the practice, which enabled the resort to attract a class of entertainers "a hundred percent better than those usually heard at a summer hotel."[50]

The cast of characters that took to the stage was diverse. One of the high-class acts was the impersonator and humorist Charles Williams, who paid his Harvard College tuition with the money he earned during the summer.

Lacking the status conferred by an Ivy League education, many veterans of the resort circuit sought to legitimate their talents by assuming professional titles and the authority they conferred. The *Hill-Top* described the work of Professor Zanoni as the science of thought transference. The paper likened the sensitive nervous system of "the greatest mind reader of the nineteenth century" to "the sensitized plate of the photographer."[51]

To make a living, these entertainers traveled from hotel to hotel during the summertime. The visit to Poland Spring by monologue artist William R. Page in early September 1899 marked his forty-second resort appearance of the season. His successful solo performance of the comedy "Aunt Matilda's Suitor" drew "one of the largest audiences of the season" to the music hall. Every once in a while, the amusement committee booked a highbrow act. Reflecting its genteel bias, the *Hill-Top* described the drama performed by Ella Chamberlin and Emma Tuttle-James in 1898 as "one of the most satisfactory given by the various entertainers who visit Poland Spring." Thorough refinement distinguished the duo's work and in contrast to the "clever" magicians, mind readers, and monologuers, earned them accolades as consummate artists.[52]

With the addition of the Casino, space for leisure activities at the Poland Spring House expanded considerably. Unlike earlier additions, the thirty-by-sixty-foot, three-story annex was a freestanding structure connected by a long and wide, covered walkway that swept in a ninety-degree arc so that the building stood aside the west wing of the hotel. The ground floor contained game rooms and a barbershop. A clubroom on the second floor offered gentlemen a cozy hideaway where they could relax on comfortable furniture and peruse "the leading newspapers of the day." Even though guests had left their urban homes, many of them wanted to keep abreast of current events. Papers such as the *New York Tribune* promised to provide vacationers "away from the city . . . the exact truth of what is going on at home, without distortion, inaccuracy, or hysterics." Twenty-four apartments filled the remainder of the upper two floors and increased the capacity of a facility "taxed to the utmost."[53]

Guests who felt overly taxed, perhaps by the news of the day, could indulge themselves with a therapeutic massage. In 1894 Horace Ettridge, a trained nurse and masseur from New York City, brought his dozen years of experience to Poland Spring. The next season, the highly respected Elizabeth Robinson, a graduate of the "celebrated" Posse Gymnasium in Boston, replaced Ettridge. Skilled in the art of Swedish massage, Lizzie Robinson had the ability to revivify "the system when fatigued" and restore "full muscular activity and strength." Her "refined and gentle manner" especially pleased the sick and "those of nervous temperament," making the "massage artiste . . . a pleasant and agreeable companion for the invalid." In 1899 masseuse Hilma Haglund took up residence in Room 320 of the Casino. A graduate of the institute operated in Stockholm, Sweden, by Professor Unman, the so-called Edison of massage, Miss Haglund relieved muscle tension, headaches, fatigue, and nervousness through the application of her "deft" fingers. Promotional announcements for her massage and medical gymnastic sessions advised clients: "to continue these treatments regularly is to throw medicine to the dogs, for you will have no use for it." Many patrons put the claim to the test, as Haglund's services were "in constant demand."[54]

After exercising and massaging their muscles, guests could have their bodies beautified in the Casino. As the *Hill-Top* reminded readers in 1898, "manicuring is a necessity these days when every attention is given to personal appearance and comfort." Women entrusted their hands, as well as their feet, faces, and hair, to "that most estimable and artistic little lady, Miss Jacobs." Her skillful fingers clipped and filed nails, massaged feet, cleansed facial pores, and shampooed, cut, curled, and arranged "hair in the most charming manner." More to the point, the "artistic taste and extensive experience" of the "indispensable" Jacobs transformed her customers into "particularly attractive" ladies upon whom "gentlemen like to look." Gentlemen had a much easier time of it. Since physical appearance composed less of their identity, the *Hill-Top* did not attempt to coax them into a battery of weekly beauty treatments. A visit to the barber, M. J. Frazier, for a haircut, possibly a shave, and maybe a manicure made a man sufficiently presentable to participate in the leisurely social life of the Poland Spring House.[55]

Renovations undertaken in 1893 reaffirmed the Rickers' commitment to provide their patrons with opportunities for the modern pleasures of social interaction, leisure, and consumption. In order to offer even more entertainment facilities, the proprietors extended the west wing of the hotel another one hundred feet. Designed by Lewiston architect George Coombs, the addition off the music room created space for an amusement hall and store on the lower level. On the upper floors, twenty "handsome" bath suites were added to the expanding room count of the Poland Spring House. Other improvements included the placement of awnings over the piazza and many of the windows, plus construction of a *porte cochere* at the front entrance.[56]

Compared to the adjacent music hall, the amusement room was "smaller and cozier." This made it an ideal place for small group gatherings such as card parties. Among the favorite leisurely pastimes was the "noble" game of whist. The lessons offered by Misses Noble and Trist helped promote the "subtle" art of whist playing; so, too, did the lectures illustrated with stereopticon views presented by the "whist queen," Miss Kate Wheelock. Once guests mastered the intricacies of the game, they found it possessed the virtues required of a Victorian parlor competition—the chance to wile away a leisurely evening, to share the company of friends, and to win prizes. Contestants vied for a wide assortment of examples of Gilded-Age material culture, everything from bon-bon spoons to moustache combs.[57]

On occasion card playing took on a calling higher than pleasure and guests showed their engagement with, rather than escape from, the affairs of the world. Following the sinking of the USS Maine and outbreak of war against Spain in 1898, the cause was patriotism and the game was progressive euchre. Organized by Mrs. Arthur Maginnis, the event was "one of the largest and most successful euchre parties ever held at Poland Spring." As the price of participation, ninety-two players subscribed $152 to the local branch of the Women's Patriotic Aid Society. Patriotic fervor infused every detail of the event. The resort florist and his assistants decorated the stage with a six-by-nine-foot flag made out of red geraniums, white asters, and blue verbenas. They also hung American flags from every chandelier. The scorecards bore an illustration of the flag and were bound together with red, white, and blue ribbons. The playing cards featured the Stars and Stripes on the back. Finally, the prize table featured a two-pound drum of candy covered with red, white, and blue satin, a tricolor sash belt with military buckle, a silk American flag, and a book entitled Poems of American Patriotism. The master of ceremonies made a special point of assuring the audience that all of the souvenirs had been purchased with donated money, not with the funds subscribed to "the noble cause" of war relief. The evening ended with a hearty rendition of the first and last verses of the "Star-Spangled Banner," all through which one participant spiritedly and proudly waved the flag he had been awarded for his second place finish.[58]

Technological Showplace: Opening the Photo Studio (1894)

The rise of fashion and leisure, as well the creeping in of the news and events of the day, were not the only ways that the outside world intruded into the Poland Spring House. Beneath its aristocratic facade and homey decor, the sprawling building was a marvel of modern machinery. From its opening day, the Rickers promoted the hotel's state-of-the-art lighting, plumbing, and sewage systems. A Springfield gas machine located underground a hundred feet to the north of the building produced the fuel that lit the building. Running water flowed from a sixteen-barrel tank on the uppermost floor. A steam pump located in the barreling house moved the water from the spring up the hill to the hotel through hundreds of yards of enameled iron pipe. Wastewater drained into a common cesspool and then passed through another network of pipes to a sewer located well away from the building. Each of these modern mechanical marvels provided the conveniences that appealed to the people of progress and made the hotel a technological showplace.[59]

As business people whose success depended upon the healthfulness of the resort, the Rickers paid special attention to sanitation. Long before the incidence of urban travelers returning from their summer excursions with cases of "vacation typhoid" plagued Maine's tourist industry, the brothers moved to protect the integrity of their chief asset—the water supply. In 1885 they contracted with Portland civil engineer Edward C. Jordan to devise a new plumbing and sewage system. An authority on hydraulics and sanitary science, Jordan was one of the Gilded Age's new sanitarians whose scientific knowledge and professional credentials became hallmarks of the modern era. In 1886 he submitted a plan that called for the storage of water for washbowls and water closets in separate holding tanks on the fourth and fifth floors of the hotel. Exhaust pipes connected to the plumbing vented fumes to stacks on the roof. Drains and cement sewer pipes carried waste from both the Poland Spring and Mansion Houses over a half-mile underground to irrigation fields on the west side of the county road, far removed from the site of the spring.[60]

Put in place over two years and at an expense of several thousand dollars, the system met with favorable reaction. At a time when sanitary laws throughout the country were "tumbled up," "piecemeal," and "antiquated," Dr. A. G. Young of the State Board of Health praised the wisdom of resort proprietors like the Rickers, who, without any official prodding, realized the value of protecting guests' health. His report on summer hotels specifically cited the new drainage system at Poland Spring as a model sanitary plan. The resort physician, Dr. Wedgwood, concurred. His testimonial, along with those of medical men from Portland and Washington, D.C., complimenting the Rickers on the "perfectness" of the site's sewerage and ventilation, appeared in the hotel's 1887 promotional catalog. A report in the *Sanitary Inspector* affirmed the assessment. The professional journal admired the model sewage system, describing it as just one of "the sanitary arrangements of the establishment" that made Poland Spring such an "ideal resort."[61]

In the opinion of publicists, the inclusion of this and many other such "modern devices for comfort and luxury" made the hotel "A Perfect Home for Its Patrons." Innovative features of the facility included a steam-powered passenger elevator, a fire-escape system, and electric annunciators for signaling the front desk. In ensuing years, the Rickers also had workmen add electric lights, automatic fire alarms, and fire-extinguishing equipment fed by rooftop water tanks. Thus by 1898, the annual announcement for the summer season could proudly proclaim that the hotel featured "every convenience of the most modern metropolitan house."[62]

The *Hill-Top* reinforced for readers the benefits of modern technology by hearkening back to aboriginal times. The paper contrasted the Indian wrapped in skins warming himself beside smoldering embers at the spring and the ancient stagecoach traveler slumbering in the old Mansion House with the present-day guest residing in a royal apartment outfitted with "furnishings of the most modern and expensive production." The constant across the ages was comfort. The difference was the impact of accumulated innovation. According to the editors, "constant vigilance and unceasing effort in the line of progress" had over time resulted in ever "greater conveniences for comfort."[63]

Fascination with technology, combined with an abundance of leisure, led to the construction of another annex in 1894. The primary purpose of this addition was to house a photographic studio. Designed in the Queen Anne style, the "exceedingly handsome" structure was connected to the Casino by a covered veranda. The new facility made obsolete an observatory darkroom on the roof of the Poland Spring House that had existed since at least 1889. The addition of three darkrooms for use by guests greatly stimulated photographic activity at the resort. The *Hill-Top* reported in 1894 that "now it is no uncommon sight to see parties of a half dozen or more starting out through the country, all with cameras in their hands." Patrons embraced the medium of photography, as it permitted them to memorialize and objectify their vacation experiences.[64]

For the less adventurous and technologically savvy, the building also included a professional studio, where guests could purchase stock views of the resort and its surroundings. They could also have their leisure-class status and identity affirmed by having their portraits taken. The Notman Photographic Company, a renowned Boston firm in the "van-guard" of the new

technology that wed art and science, managed the business. Mr. Ness oversaw the operation during the first summer and relieved the resident photographer, Denys B. O. Bourdon, for brief periods in subsequent years. Bourdon,
a longtime employee of the company, had earned a reputation as an accomplished portrait photographer able to combine accuracy with artistry. Evidence of his "exquisite" work graced the walls of the hotel. It also frequently
illustrated the pages of the *Hill-Top* and the promotional literature published
by Hiram Ricker and Sons. Pointing out that "there is a little vanity in us all,"
the newspaper encouraged visitors to take advantage of Bourdon's superior
skill at fixing happy expressions on glass plates. The pitch for the modern
technology of photography also included the antimodern observation that it
was easier to look one's best away from "the hurry and bustle of city life."[65]

Commercial Counting House: Shopping at the Art Store (1897)

Beneath the photographic and promotional images of the hotel as genteel
house, refined home, noble castle, social mecca, pleasure palace, and technological showplace lay the economic reality. For the proprietors of the Poland
Spring House, commerce was king and consumption its handmaiden. Even
the grandiloquent promoter William Murray acknowledged that the noble
art of entertaining guests was also a "noble business." Members of the
Gilded-Age leisure class obliged their hosts by conspicuously consuming in
myriad ways during their stays. Despite their patrons' largesse, financing the
enterprise and maintaining the solvency of the resort remained a constant
struggle for the Rickers.[66]

An observant reporter cut through the illusion of escape to see telltale
signs of business activity all about the hotel in 1896. At the front counter, the
desk clerk assured new arrivals that he had saved them the "most desirable
room in the house" and the express clerk promised prompt delivery of baggage. Meanwhile at the news counter, the popular attendant informed guests
about the selection of cigars, schedule for the resort baseball team, and availability of the *Hill-Top*; while the smiling postmistress sold souvenirs and con-
fections in between sorting and distributing the mail. Those visitors requiring more immediate contact with the outside world than either a newspaper
or letter could provide visited the bright-eyed and rosy-cheeked Miss Anderson at the adjacent telegraph office. Far from abetting escape from modern life, Western Union service afforded "business men every opportunity of
having immediate connections with their places of business and all stock ex-

changes." On the other side of the main stairway, a student from nearby He-
bron Academy in Buckfield dispensed hundreds of free samples at the water
counter. The payoff would come later when guests would order cases of water
to tide them over at home until their return to Poland Spring the next season. A fire and burglarproof safe for the keeping of the guests' valuables and
the Rickers' receipts anchored the lobby.[67]

Sometimes the hotel lobby had additional commercial bustle to it. A year
earlier, the one Ricker sibling who did not earn a living from the family business, Cynthia, had placed a tablecloth and vase of sweet peas on the radiator
at the center of the room and used the space to hawk two cooking utensils of
her own invention. Designed to improve drainage of fat from food, her fryers turned out less greasy doughnuts, fish balls, crullers, croquettes, and frit-
ters. Following a successful stint at Jordan and Marsh's department store in
Boston a few months earlier, Cynthia demonstrated the benefits of improved
culinary technology at Poland Spring one Friday afternoon in mid-August
1895. As a result of her pitch, she sold several of the devices. The *Hill-Top* gave
a boost to the marketing campaign by carrying illustrated advertisements for
the fryers throughout the remainder of the season.[68]

The eldest Ricker daughter was not the only person to put ingenuity and
salesmanship on display at the Poland Spring House. The Shakers regularly
sold their wares at the hotel. The coming together of the religious and resort
communities highlighted the contrasts between antimodernity and modernity. Akin to the tradition of female fundraising fairs, the Shakers' fancy goods
trade promoted sentimental commerce and virtuous consumption that eased
the transition to the modern market economy. Unlike the Shakers, who set
themselves apart from the world, venerated the work ethic, and rejected materialism, the patrons of the resort embraced Victorian sociability, legitimated the leisure ethic, and consumed conspicuously. To sate the last com-
pulsion, traders from Sabbathday Lake began making the three-mile trek to
the resort several evenings a week during the summer of 1888. Besides bringing along a refreshing air of old-fashioned tranquility and simplicity, Sisters
such as the kindly and popular Aurelia Mace arrived bearing valises filled
with poplar ware boxes, plush rugs, fir balsam pillows, horsehair brushes, and
many other fancy goods produced by "their industrious and deft fingers." For
patrons who wanted access to genuine and authentic items made manually
rather than mechanically, the arrangement was ideal. They could be part of
the arts and crafts movement without any of the stitching. Moreover, trade
with Believers allowed the people of progress to salve their consciences through

a commercial transaction of Christian charity, as proceeds from the sales went straight "into the general coffers of the Shaker community."[69]

Guests did not always cloak their consumption as charity. In a far corner of the hotel beyond the music and amusement rooms, shoppers could satisfy their souvenir-hunting, gift-giving, and craft-making needs in a makeshift store. For a time, a salesman from Portland came every Friday to take orders for "high-class needlework, decorative novelties of original design, prizes, cotilion [sic] favors, etc." Remodeling work done in preparation for the 1897 season turned the space into a more formal art store. Rather than dealing with an outside merchant, the Rickers employed the friendly and exotically named Mrs. Nasseem Mallouf to run the shop. This well-stocked, "perfect" facsimile Oriental bazaar displayed abundance, showcased beauty, promoted domesticity, celebrated consumption, and transformed luxury into necessity. On the "overflowing" racks and shelves, shoppers found "myriads of articles essential to a lady's happiness." The store stocked jackets, kimonos, wraps, belts, lace, ribbon, and dress trimming "calculated for the decoration of the person," as well as Baghdad curtains, Persian rugs, and Turkish and Syrian hand embroideries calculated for the decoration of the home.[70]

Overseeing all the social and commercial activity of the Poland Spring House was Edward Ricker. From a private office located across the hall from the water counter, he presided over not only the counting house, but also a family empire that encompassed over a thousand acres, scores of buildings, and hundreds of employees and guests. Although he was the eldest son of Hiram and Janette Ricker, Edward had earned his position by deeds as much as by birth. Possessing both a vision of greatness and a willingness to work hard, the "chief architect" of Poland Spring had rescued the family farm from creditors and fashioned it into one of the nation's leading resorts. The *Lewiston Journal* attributed his success to tireless energy, supreme genius, prophetic faith, good judgment, thorough wisdom, and executive ability. Columnist Arthur G. Staples described his friend as a consummate "hotel-man"—gentle, attentive, and kind. These qualities brought the "brown-bearded genius" of the hilltop a wide circle of friends and a loyal clientele.[71]

Although he possessed the requisite "perfect business talents" to create Hiram Ricker and Sons, Edward, like his father, could not keep his pursuit of personal wealth in check. Not content to have constructed a successful tourist mecca, his brain brimmed with plans to develop the hilltop further. It also percolated with schemes to gain him a fortune rivaling those of his well-heeled guests. During the monetary debates and gold rushes of the

1890s, Ricker invested heavily and disastrously in mining stocks. On the eve of the tumultuous 1896 presidential election, he speculated in grain futures. His ambitions, however, never quite kept pace with his resources. Despite the popularity of the water and the resort, huge expenses kept the corporation's accounts in a perpetually mortgaged state and put his personal finances in an increasingly precarious condition. By 1913 financial advisor Charles Sumner Cook of the Fidelity Trust Company in Portland was pleading with Edward to reduce personal and business debts that amounted to a staggering $600,000.[72]

Building and running a first-class summer city was a capital-intensive endeavor. In 1892 a reporter estimated that the Ricker family had already invested $300,000 in the resort. The following year, the family spent somewhere between $115,000 and $120,000 operating the two hotels. According to Hiram W. Ricker, the annual costs came to $84,000, which partially included a payroll of $37,000, miscellaneous expenses of $19,000, and food purchases of $16,000. Capital expenditures amounted to $31,000, almost evenly split between labor and material costs. Property taxes increased the total outlay by several thousand dollars. During the fiscal year ending in February 1902, for example, the real estate owned by Hiram Ricker and Sons amounted to 29 percent of Poland's total valuation. Consequently, the Rickers' $4,000 tax bill accounted for 26 percent of the town's revenue. Continuing hikes in assessments had prompted a ninety-minute-long harangue on "awful taxes" by Edward Ricker at the Poland town meeting only a few years earlier.[73]

A slim profit margin fired Ricker's frustration with property taxes. Revenues from bookings could have only modestly exceeded expenditures in some years. Attendance at the Poland Spring House in 1893, despite the onset of a nationwide business depression, came to 25,682, an average of 208 guests for each day of the eighteen-week season from early June to mid-October. If everyone had paid the highest daily "transient" rate at the height of the season, five dollars, the Rickers would have grossed a little over $128,000 and might have netted only a few thousand dollars after making the interest payments on their considerable mortgage debts. In reality, guests paid weekly rates ranging as high as $150, depending upon the time of season, type of suite, and level of service. In 1892 one guest had even reportedly paid forty dollars a week to put up a pet dog in a room of its own. Nevertheless while the hotel was often full to its maximum capacity of between 450 and 500 guests, as it was during much of the 1896 and 1898 seasons, visions of "overflowing coffers" were only an illusion.[74]

This was the look of the front facade of the Poland Spring House by the end of the nineteenth century. Note the arrival of golfers on the scene, and at the spot where baseball had been played only a few years earlier. *Maine Historic Preservation Commission.*

Of course, the Rickers had many other revenue streams—the Mansion House, souvenirs, the photo studio, the art store, and most important of all, the water. Whatever profits the entire business earned, however, usually went right back into improvements to the resort. This aggressive reinvestment strategy built up a property valued between $700,000 by a newspaper in 1887 and $1.25 million by a prospective buyer in 1892. It also left the constantly cash-strapped Rickers dependent on creditors to finance the continual construction, renovations, and expansions required to keep the Poland Spring House up-to-date. Ironically, what the proprietors of Poland Spring most lacked was liquidity.[75]

By 1889 the Ricker brothers had taken out five mortgages, two on the family farm and three on the Poland Spring House and hotel lot, from three lenders amounting to $76,000. During the 1890s, one regular patron of the resort, Boston businessman Nelson Bartlett, emerged as the lone creditor. In 1892 Bartlett provided a $25,000 mortgage on the hotel lot. He then bought out the interest in three mortgages held by other lenders. Six years later,

Bartlett allowed the Rickers to refinance and consolidate their loans by extending them a $65,000 mortgage due in five years with 5 percent interest payable semiannually. Indicative of their ongoing cash-flow struggles, the Rickers missed the deadline. The Bartlett mortgage was not retired until 1911.[76]

Nelson Bartlett's money helped finance the last major renovations to the Poland Spring House during the nineteenth century. In time for the 1898 season, the Rickers had "that dry goods box of a tower . . . rounded out majestically" to give the resort's centerpiece hotel a more "prosperous and inviting atmosphere." The collaboration of architects George C. Coombs, Eugene J. Gibbs, and Harry C. Wilkinson also resulted in the removal of the "ungainly piazzas" surrounding the main tower and their replacement with artistic balconies from which "Juliets might be wooed." Reflecting the cultural tensions that constantly fed the need to transform the dream hotel, only a year later the antimodern allusions to Shakespearean romance gave way to pride in modernity. The remodeling work of 1899 added more graceful proportions to the central tower, more tasteful decoration to the office lobby, more luxurious elegance to the first-floor parlors, and more sumptuous suites to the upper floors. Assessing the latest makeover of the Poland Spring House, the *Hill-Top* attributed the charm of the new "royal" apartments to "furnishings of the most modern and expensive production."[77]

It is fitting that a building that grew to incorporate such contrasts and reflect such ambivalence stood at the center of the resort. Like the Mansion House, the Poland Spring House was shaped by the values of both antimodernity and modernity. For some guests, the hotel, in its guises as genteel house, refined home, and noble castle, provided an ideal stage for the masquerade of escape from the modern world of social diversity and competitive commerce. For other patrons, the facility was a modern manifestation of the market revolution, a mecca of fashion, wealth, and culture that affirmed status, celebrated sociability, legitimated leisure, encouraged consumption, and promoted progress. Finally, for the proprietors, the hotel was both a family legacy to be cherished and a financial commodity to be mortgaged. The same contrasting values that shaped the architecture of the built environment at the resort also transformed the landscape of the natural environment on the hilltop. It was at the spring that the powerful and opposing forces of antimodernity and modernity most significantly intersected to define quite literally the Poland Spring resort.

The Spring House

"The Ministry of Pure Water"

The writer from the Lewiston newspaper who stopped at the home of Hiram Ricker during a mid-July afternoon in 1860 came to see what had already become known as the "famous mineral spring in Poland." In a field located a short distance from the future site of the Poland Spring House, water bubbled up at the rate of eight gallons per minute from crevices in a ledge of hard black trap. The journalist reported: "we never tasted of purer, clearer water than this." The article attributed the water's freedom from "foreign substances" to the natural filtration process it went through and the careful handling it received from Mr. Ricker. Noting the significance of the find, the reporter remarked "the very pureness of the water" had affected "remarkable cures."[1]

In the four decades after this visit, the Rickers and their publicists followed the lead of the local journalist and made purity the primary asset of Poland Water. To do so, they first constructed a deeply layered historical landscape of purity made up of geological convulsions, natural surroundings, aboriginal associations, and colonial settlers. After laying the foundation, they then built their commercial empire on four corner posts of purity: miraculous healings, medicinal virtues, scientific analysis, and sound business practices. Ultimately, they promoted pure Poland Water as possessing the power to cleanse the body of "evil humors," clear the mind of "distorted fancies," and transform the soul. As a consequence, for many guests of the resort, the path to paradise passed directly through the Spring House.[2]

The Rickers' appeals to purity tapped into two deep currents of concern in Gilded-Age America. The first was the safety of the nation's food and water. The second was the state of the country's moral well-being. With respect to the former, periodic cholera, typhoid, and yellow fever epidemics aroused fears about the impact of urban congestion and pollution on the cleanliness and healthiness of public water sources. Meanwhile, reports about adulterated and mislabeled products, which culminated in the muckraking exposés of the meatpacking and patent medicine industries during the early twentieth century, raised doubts about the safety of the nation's food and drug supplies. In this atmosphere of anxiety, the Rickers found a receptive audience when they warned in the 1880s that "modern modes of living" and the consumption of impure water brought many thousands to "Death's door." Historian James Harvey Young has argued that reform movements of the era, such as the crusade for food and drug control, grew out of "a deep worry about 'purity.'" The widespread perception was that "business, government at all levels, social conduct, even the bloodlines of the nation's populace seemed threatened with pollution and required cleaning up." At a more fundamental level, anthropologist Mary Douglas has argued: "purity is the enemy of change, of ambiguity and compromise." The quest for purity, thus, becomes a means of restoring social order and unity, as well as of atoning, particularly during periods of rapid social change.[3]

Amid the profound changes of the Gilded Age, "deep worry" gave way to full-fledged obsession, with purity becoming as ubiquitous a cultural metaphor as progress at Poland Spring. Consequently, Chase and Sanborn supplied the resort with tea of "healthful and delicious purity." The head clerk at the Mansion House offered patrons "absolutely pure olive oil" for cooking and medicinal purposes from his brother's grove in California. The pages of the resort newspaper carried advertisements for an alternate source of pure olive oil sold by the S. S. Pierce Company in Boston, pure drugs carried by pharmacist O. W. Jones of Auburn, and pure chocolates made by Winthrop M. Baker of Boston. Of course, the epitome of purity was Poland Water. An 1895 Hill-Top article entitled "Crystal Purity" preached that "to the pure all things are pure, hence the most impure may imagine themselves pure when they gaze into the pure crystal of the Poland Spring Carafe, and witness the purity of its contents; and become purer for the vision and the thought." The message could hardly have been stated any more crystal clearly.[4]

The Prophets of Purity

The lead spokesman and chief salesman of Poland Water was Hiram Ricker. One journalist described Hiram as "the conscientious expounder of the virtues of this Spring." Another wrote that "he rather talk Poland Water than eat or sleep." According to family lore, one of Hiram's favorite techniques for

In this posed scene at the 1883 Spring House, Hiram Ricker with his trademark long-flowing, mutton-chop beard hands a glass of Poland Water to an appreciative patron. *Maine Historic Preservation Commission.*

drumming up business was to meet trains arriving at the Danville Junction depot and then walk through the cars handing out free samples. As Ricker "talked up" its "wonderful virtues," the spring reportedly "acquired a local reputation." Hiram, ever the man on the make, had finally found his calling.[5]

In the early years of the business, friends, acquaintances, and "seekers for health" came from all directions to partake of the spring water that "flowed from the rock and made its way down the hill-side, unchecked by the hand of man." At the site, they found "only a rough little shed" in the midst of a pine forest grown up with underbrush. Inside the crude shelter, the water collected in a crevice formed in an outcropping ledge. Over the years, the Rickers enlarged the opening in the rock until it had a capacity of about thirty gallons. Because "at that time all comers were free to take away as much of the water as they desired for their own use," parties arrived bearing big earthenware jugs that they filled from the pool by means of a dipper, which was later replaced by a pail. The charge for this privilege was three cents per gallon. To serve local consumers unable to travel to the spring, the Rickers established a delivery route. Hiram drove the green express wagon pulled by an old white horse. More distant customers could have barrels of water sent by rail.[6]

Following a brief flurry of interest in the spring, "local excitement" eventually subsided. During their second year in business, Hiram Ricker and Nathan Miller reached the high-water mark of their partnership, shipping one thousand barrels. Thereafter sales decreased and Miller lost interest in the project. Lacking the finances to distribute Poland Water widely on his own, Ricker had to scale back operations. By 1870 shipments from the spring stood at a meager three hundred barrels. Nevertheless, the reputation of the water had spread well beyond Maine during the preceding decade. Correspondence from Sam Ricker mentioned that Hiram had been invited to New York in 1870 "to explain the virtues of the Poland water." Assuming that his cousin would be dealing with physicians, Sam advised Hiram to "take counsel of medical men of undoubted reputation." Sam Ricker also offered to do his part to promote the product by distributing circulars in the region surrounding Cincinnati, Ohio.[7]

Although many observers credited Hiram Ricker with being the "most active and potent" force behind the discovery and development of the spring, Edward played a vital role, too. It began with his advice to end the unproductive partnership with Nathan Miller. By 1868 Edward had persuaded his father to buy out Miller's share in the business. As compensation, Miller received a bond issued by the newly created partnership, Hiram Ricker and Son, headed by Edward. Miller's death complicated the transaction. Dissatisfied with the proposed arrangement, his heirs filed a lawsuit seeking to take control of the spring. After a five-year court battle, two arbiters finally ruled in favor of the Ricker family. In the aftermath of the settlement with the Miller estate, Alvan Bolster Ricker joined the reorganized firm that became known as Hiram Ricker and Sons.[8]

Hiram Weston Ricker, the youngest of Hiram and Janette's three sons, was made a partner in 1880. His preparation for the responsibility began as a youth. During breaks from school, young Hiram worked at the spring and sold jugs of water in Auburn and Lewiston. As he reached adulthood, Hiram stood five-feet and ten-inches tall. His passport described him as possessing a round face and chin with a straight nose and mouth, a high forehead, a light complexion, and blue eyes. His most prominent facial feature, however, was a long flowing beard. Considered to be the "natural mechanic" of the family, Hiram was placed in charge of the water business where he could use his talents to make certain the bottling process and shipping routine ran smoothly.[9]

Some hard feelings soon arose among the brothers turned business partners. In a carefully worded letter written in 1880, brother-in-law Oliver Marsh mentioned Edward was having "trouble" settling upon the value of the property with his father and youngest brother. Marsh hinted that the dispute typified a pattern of favoritism the patriarch of the family had shown over the years toward his namesake at the expense of his two older sons. Siding with Edward, he sympathized: "They don't seem to consider that you have had [to] work so hard to save it [the property] for them and they ought to [be] very gratefull [sic] to think that they have got so good a home but they are like everybody else the more they get the more they want." Marsh extended to the beleaguered Edward the offer "to do anything in my power to help you settle the trouble."[10]

Apparently the brothers shielded their domestic squabbles well from the public, as biographers only lavished praise on family members. The Lewiston newspaper lauded the "lusty sons of the old stock" for their executive ability, enterprise, energy, and untiring labors. As for the youngest of the three brothers, Hiram W. Ricker was characterized by Arthur Staples as "an angel with whiskers—a man of tenderness and gentle manner." Another account described him as an individual possessing a congenial personality and quick wit, traits that won him many loyal friends. Hiram's wide interests, uncanny foresight, and daring aggressiveness served him well in his role as lead salesman following the death of his father. The younger Hiram was credited with being an unselfish and proud worker who devoted "his entire time . . . to the promotion of Poland water sales, which he guided until weekly shipments aggregated thousands of gallons." Having set aside any lingering family disputes, the diligent Hiram and his two brothers decided to dissolve their partnership and incorporate as Hiram Ricker and Sons in 1894.[11]

"Poland Mineral Spring Water, History of Its Discovery"

Even before the death of the gregarious elder Hiram Ricker, the primary way the prophets of purity promoted Poland Water was through pamphlets. The first objective of the booklets was to relate the history of purity to potential customers. One of the earliest examples, an 1876 publication, opened with the statement that "many have wanted to know how this Spring was discovered." The Rickers obliged inquirers by recounting their ancestors' "purely accidental" determination of the water's efficacy. Over the next several years, the scope of the history expanded to include coverage of the geological, natural, and aboriginal landscapes, leading up to the family's appearance on the colonial landscape and eventual development of the spring into an industrial landscape. Moreover, the focal point of the history became better defined. The Rickers remembered the past not only as the basis of progress and origin of nobility, but also as the exemplar of permanence and source of purity. In this historical narrative, purity preserved the past and paved the way for progress. It also paid dividends for the promotion of the water.[12]

By 1883 the Rickers settled on an official history of the spring. In the water pamphlet for that year, they took readers back to a time when the "pristine forces" had forged the geological landscape of the hilltop. During the "era of upheaval," molten granite had flowed into fissures created by the folding and tilting of gneiss slates. In the subsequent old red sandstone era, porphyritic rock had smashed its way through the bedrock forming veins ranging in thickness from a few inches up to fifteen feet. Percolation through one such vein accounted for the water's "renowned freedom from organic matter, and its medicinal properties." Following the flow back to its source "at the center of the world," an 1890 pamphlet contrasted the geological formations of "primeval creation" through which the spring rose with the contemporary "superficial earth." The latter could taint the water with impurities. The former gave to the water its "first and foremost characteristic"—purity.[13]

Although he substituted a more general romantic notion of Nature for the specific scientific forces of geology, William Murray likewise traced the spring's purity and healing powers back to the prehistoric past. In 1890 he wrote that Nature had created the hilltop at Poland Spring ages ago. "From a fissure near the crest of this magnificent mound of oldest rock," Murray continued, "she poured, from deepest depths beyond the guess of man, a stream of water so pure that he who sees remembers it ever after as a marvel." The marvelous spring's properties included the ability to bring dying people back to "health and vigor." Similarly, fellow resort promoter George Haynes first traced the origins of the water all the way back to the age of the dinosaurs and then noted, "the health-giving water flows to-day the same as it did then."[14]

The permanence highlighted by Haynes was another positive byproduct of the primeval antiquity of the geological landscape. During an age of rapid and revolutionary social change, the "eternal" nature of the spring's geology became the unshakable bedrock upon which to construct the empire of purity. Guests eagerly drank up the illusion of timelessness bottled at the spring. When Mr. and Mrs. T. D. Elsbree of Valley Falls, Rhode Island, returned to the Mansion House in 1897 after an absence of eighteen years, they were heartened to find that amid all the changes that had taken place on the hilltop, Poland Water had remained the same.[15]

According to the Rickers' history, the geological past was followed by an era when "wild beasts" and "aboriginal savages" benefited from the water. Local legend held that Chief Poland, who "possessed the leading characteristics of his race, treachery and bravery, united perhaps with more than ordinary sagacity," had been known to "appease his burning thirst" at the spring. Plows and spades had turned up physical evidence of the aboriginal landscape in the form of "the arrow of flint, the hatchet and chisel of stone, the spear-point of quartz, [and] the fish-hook of bone." The 1890 water pamphlet surmised that the ancients had come to the site to cure their infirmities centuries before the arrival of white settlers. Furthermore, it speculated that the spring was "fashionable a thousand years before the Norsemen discovered America" and so well known that it had drawn from "distant nations and tribes" visitors in search of health and life. In more recent times, a well-known itinerant Pigwacket medicine woman named Moll Locket had continued to frequent the spot even after the Rickers had taken up residence, reportedly because she had grown "as fond of . . . Poland Water" as she had of "ardent" spirits.[16]

Even though Moll Locket had fallen prey to one of the evils of the white man's world, Native Americans were typically praised for remaining faithful to their traditional customs. The 1890 pamphlet complimented the "red race" for recognizing that the natural remedies it used were "gifts of the Great Spirit." In addition, the author praised the Aborigines for keeping close to Nature, observing her closely, and living in harmony with her laws. In contrast to moderns, who were chided for despising "the healing qualities of pure air, pure water, [and] pure sunshine," "these closest students of Nature" were deemed "disciples of a true, natural hygiene." The sight of the Penobscot encampment at Poland Spring inspired similar praise of Indians by publicist George Haynes, who was transported back "in imagination to the primitive days when the spring was to their ancestors a sacred fount, and they partook of the sparkling water at this, nature's reservoir."[17]

Despite the conflicting messages about the legacy of Native Americans, the ancient race was generally regarded as a protector of the spring's purity. For this reason, the Rickers highlighted the Indian history of the hilltop. In a sense, the accolades to Native naturalism and illustration of the chief served to symbolize the passage of the spring's stewardship to the people of progress and the layering of the colonial landscape over its aboriginal precursor. The torch had been passed from the likes of Chief Poland and Moll Locket to the Rickers—first, as the spring water broke Joseph's fever in 1800; then, as it healed Wentworth's bout with kidney stones in 1827; and finally, as it healed Hiram's dyspepsia in 1844. Although the family knew about the healing powers of the spring for many years, the business of selling the water did not begin in earnest until 1859. In that pivotal year, the water produced several "notable" cures; the first doctor began prescribing its use; and Hiram Ricker made his first sale. From that point onward, the use of the "truly wonderful Spring Water," or so the Rickers claimed, "increased in a ratio unprecedented in the history of any other mineral water on the globe."[18]

An 1894 *Hill-Top* article entitled "Poland Spring in the Past" well summarized the Rickers' version of the site's history. It alluded to a geological past when the "pure, sparkling, and health-giving" waters flowed from solid rock "as they had flowed from the beginning of time." The geological landscape was part of a more expansive natural landscape attributed to a "benign Creator," who had created a "pleasing land" from which "the pure and healing flood" poured forth. Humans entered the picture during the aboriginal past, when Indians visited the spring "long before the advent of the white man." During the colonial past, the Rickers discovered the "medicinal properties of the spring." In more recent times, Hiram Ricker's faith in the water, whose virtue lay in its "absolute purity," brought it worldwide acclaim. The lesson readers were supposed to draw from this history was to "drink Poland water."[19]

"This Great Gift of God"

After laying the foundation of the spring's history, religious sentiment was the first cornerstone upon which the Rickers built their empire of water. Since purity was fundamentally a moral issue for Gilded-Age Americans, publicists often used religious language and symbols to promote Poland Water. The moral dimension of the search for purity held out the promise of fulfilling the spiritual needs of modern man in addition to healing the physical maladies associated with modern life. A verse from "A Drinking Song" making the rounds of the resort in 1895 expressed this belief lyrically:

> The inner man will be refreshed;
>   The eye will find relief;
> And as I quaff from the carafe,
> Shall down all cares and grief.

Of course, the elixir the poem praised was the "purest" water of Poland Spring.[20]

The carafe mentioned in the rhyme was a triangular glass decanter that Nettie Ricker had designed. The three sides depicted images of the Mansion, Poland Spring, and Spring Houses. The stopper was formed in the shape of a cow's head and was meant to represent the first unwitting beneficiaries of the water following the arrival of the family on the hilltop. The proprietors encouraged guests to take carafes home in order to "remind them of the place the water comes from, the rock-riven crystal fountain of health, pure and eternal." Patrons could also take away another symbolic reminder of Poland Spring's healing powers, a "Moses" spoon that the talented Nettie had also created. This souvenir was intended to recall for resort visitors their pleasant walks and drives, good dinners, and "unsurpassed Poland Water."[21]

Before the introduction of the carafe, the Rickers chose as one of their first bottle designs a twelve-inch-tall quart container shaped in the form of a bearded man wearing a robe. The "Moses" bottle honored the prophet, who "in Biblical history, 'smote the rock and the waters gushed forth.'" Jane Patterson explained the symbolism of the container in *The Romance of the New Bethesda*. In the novel, Dr. Rossville, the character based upon Hiram Ricker, responded to an inquiry about the meaning of the bottle with the statement, "No man can bring water out of a rock without help. It is the Lord's doings, and it is marvellous in our eyes. It was marvellous then, and a good deal more so now." Besides their common marvelous origins, the sacred pools of pure water found at Horeb and Poland Spring were also linked by miraculous powers. Patterson wrote that like the Bethesda of biblical times, "the New Bethesda heals the sick, and restores the lame, and makes the blind to see." Surprisingly, the *Hill-Top* was less fervent about the religious symbolism, instead joking that "the Rickers sell Moses bottles because there is a *prophet* on them," an obvious allusion to the double meaning of the statement.[22]

Hiram Ricker took the Moses revival at Poland Spring quite seriously, so much so that he adopted the archetype of biblical patriarch as his own distinctive role to fill. To look the part of prophet, Hiram grew shoulder-length, mutton-chop whiskers. Two of his three sons, Edward and Hiram, likewise sported long flowing beards, which led to speculation that one of them had posed for the design of the original Moses bottle. More than looking the part, however, the elder Hiram played it. He received the revelation of "the power of Poland Water." He ministered to the faithless. He restored the lame. He healed the sick. He even prophesied the future. The two noteworthy predictions Hiram Ricker reportedly made during his tenure as

patriarch of Poland Spring were that the water would become known throughout the world and that the spring would eventually be exhausted.[23]

From 1859 until his death in 1893, Hiram worked to make sure that at least
the first of his prophecies came true. According to an 1876 newspaper article,
Ricker's ability to discourse nobly on the virtues of the water attracted pale
and emaciated invalids and "lean, lank and cadaverous persons" to Poland
Spring. The account credited his ministrations with "redeeming from the
thraldom of disease" the rich and poor, as well as the high and low. The reporter was so swept up by Hiram's evangelism he speculated that the apostle
Paul would have advised substituting Poland Water for wine to relieve the
sick if only it had been available in biblical times.[24]

Another article attributed Ricker's success to a conviction that "lent faith
to others." The journalist explained that as a result, "the book of life is full of
testimonials from invalids whom Hiram Ricker, Sr., induced to drink of the
spring." One of those invalids was a gentleman whom Hiram remembered
meeting in 1862. Because of a sore on his ankle, the man had been reduced to
hobbling around. After drinking and bathing in Poland Water for three
weeks, the patient was instructed to throw away his cane. To the man's great
joy, he found that he could walk unassisted for the first time in three years.
Hiram recounted a similar story about a Mr. Smith from Charlestown,
Massachusetts, who was able to walk freely again after drinking the water for
only six days in 1876.[25]

The 1877 water pamphlet included several testimonies to the growing
faith in the healing powers of Poland Water. Drinking it had enabled Samuel
A. Parker to renovate his whole system, Henry C. Thiemann to cure his case
of kidney stones, and Job Prince to relieve his urinary troubles. In addition,
Moses E. Osgood was convinced that his life had been saved from the rav-
ages of an acute affliction of Bright's disease by the use of Poland Water
under God's direction. Another convert to the faith was Mrs. Webster Teel.
For five years, her daughter's health had been deteriorating. Hoping to rid the
eleven-year-old girl of the pain associated with bladder and kidney ailments,
Mrs. Teel finally decided to buy a barrel of the water in 1876, even though she
"did not have an atom of faith" in it. Within ten weeks the "pure, life-giving
water" had cured Lula Teel. Her grateful mother urged "every one suffering
from any of these terrible diseases . . . to try this great gift of God to man."[26]

When the Reverend A. J. Patterson had been introduced to the water in
August 1873, he, too, had shared Mrs. Teel's initial skepticism. At the time,
the minister suffered from inflammation of the kidneys. His condition had

degenerated to the point that one of the leading physicians in Boston had advised him to retire. A dejected Patterson traveled to Poland Spring expecting to find only rest, not relief. He dismissed Hiram Ricker's claims about the water as those of "an interested advocate." When Hiram told him to drink three pints in three hours, Patterson was certain the proprietor of the resort "must be a subject almost ready for an insane asylum." Nevertheless, he obeyed, deciding it would be better to die "from an over-drink of pure water" than from kidney disease. When the deadline set by Hiram arrived, the minister noticed, "the obstructions were at once entirely and permanently removed" for the first time in eight months. In a testimony recounted ten years later, Patterson referred to the work of Providence that had prolonged his life as "little short of a miracle."[27]

Like the testimonies written by satisfied customers, the advertising produced by Hiram Ricker and Sons also made extensive use of religious vocabulary to describe Poland Water. The 1890 pamphlet referred to the product as a "gift of God." The "miraculous" water was credited with reviving dead organs, restoring health and strength, delivering mankind from "the aches that torture, and the ills which destroy," and saving the public from "pain and death." Extending this line of thinking, the inaugural issue of the *Hill-Top* suggested that the water could improve people spiritually as well as physically. The author, Holman Day, instructed visitors to Ricker Hill to engage in the following meditative ritual:

Place your face to the west and love the Lord. Then drink Poland water. Then contemplate Heaven, descended on earth, and listen to the low sweet communings of Earth and Sky, the droning sounds of Peace and the laughter of happy human souls, and then I should solemnly advise you to drink more Poland water.

According to Day, transformation, if not outright transfiguration, were the rewards that awaited the faithful water drinker.[28]

"Wonderful Medicinal Virtues"

The second cornerstone of Poland Water was the linkage of its purity with its "wonderful medicinal virtues." The Rickers regularly placed periodical advertisements and published promotional pamphlets to proclaim the healthfulness of pure water. To them it was "evident that the health of the body depends in a large measure upon the purity of the water that is drank by each individual." Poland Water's "perfect purity," therefore, made it a valuable medical agent. It served as a counteracting medicine for invalids, a tonic and restorative for convalescents, and a preventative for the healthy.[29]

Highlighting the water's medicinal use, instructions in the pamphlets directed patients to drink it at prescribed times throughout the day: before breakfast, at 10:00 A.M., before dinner, then again at 3:00 P.M., before tea time, and finally, one last time before bedtime. Tea time was a curious designation since the beverage was one guide books sometimes warned people to avoid. Also discouraged or banned outright were coffee, cider, vinegar, wine, and liquors. In their place, the prescriptive literature advised the daily consumption of at least four to ten glasses of water, served no colder than forty-five to forty-eight degrees. The truly committed were challenged to break the record of Poland Spring's champion water drinker, George Innis of San Francisco. During the 1893 season, he had downed forty glasses of water in one twenty-four hour period.[30]

The Rickers were quite specific and confident about the maladies their prescribed water regimen could remedy. One of the first ads placed by Hiram Ricker, a circular in an 1860 issue of the *Brunswick (Maine) Record*, identified Poland Mineral Water as a cure for liver and kidney complaints, dyspepsia, and gravel. It also described the water as a blood purifier. Anyone requiring proof was invited to contact the local agent, Dr. J. R. Haley, or to "visit the Spring and use the water." A postscript notified prospective visitors that they could obtain board at the site for a fee ranging from $2.50 to $3.50 per week. Over the decades, the list of ailments for which the Rickers recommended Poland Water as a "sure cure" expanded to include dropsy, rheumatism, scrofula humor, appetite loss, general debility, indigestion, constipation, diabetes, urinary problems, and "many of the peculiar diseases of women."[31]

Given the emphasis on the medicinal uses of the water, it is no wonder that the first impression locals had of the resort was as a health spa. A county atlas published in 1873 described the site as providing "accommodation of invalids desiring to avail themselves of the medicinal virtues of its water." Furthermore, the author of the entry on Poland, Jesse Libby, observed that the resort's clientele was made up of hundreds who came during the summer months "to throw down their burden of disease and seek health and vigor from this panacea of Nature." They left, Libby claimed, attesting to the water's virtue and giving thanks to "the kind Providence which has provided this reservoir of life."[32]

Rather than relying solely on glowing tributes from promoters, the Rickers substantiated their therapeutic claims by providing scores of "testimonials" from former patients. Instead of calling it advertising, the family preferred to describe what it was doing as submitting "testimony" about the water's "healing virtues" for the public's consideration. Using correspondence from satisfied customers had several advantages. First, it made more personal the "curative virtues" of the "great and valuable remedy." Commendations came from "persons in all conditions of life, of the highest respectability," men such as Isaac Emery, vice president of John Hancock Life Insurance, who was esteemed as "one of the oldest and most influential merchants of Boston." Second, it fostered a sense of community among consumers by introducing the public to new "neighbors." They ranged from Elder Otis Sawyer of the Sabbathday Lake Shaker village, who hailed the product as "the Water of Life flowing from the fountain of the Lord," to prominent members of the national community such as President Ulysses Grant, who, it was claimed, would drink no other water. Finally, the testimonials were presented as being "true as truth," not as commercial endorsements prone to exaggeration and hence, subject to disbelief. Readers skeptical of the authenticity or veracity of the letters were invited to view the originals, which were kept in a book available for examination at the office counter in the Poland Spring House.[33]

One of the most highly prized personal testimonials came from one of the first patients cured by the spring water, Ezekiel C. Jackson. This cattle driver from Norway, Maine, had been troubled by kidney stones for many years when Hiram Ricker paid his friend a visit in 1859. Ricker wanted to conduct an experiment on one of the 503 pieces of gravel that a Boston surgeon had removed from Jackson in 1853. Ricker placed a specimen in a vial of the spring water and observed that it dissolved almost instantaneously. Additional tests with other fragments produced similar results. When Jackson's affliction returned in January of 1860, he showed up at Poland Spring vowing tearfully never to be operated on again. Hiram comforted his disconsolate patient and sent him home with a supply of water. According to an affidavit supplied by Jackson, he "experienced immediate relief, and within four weeks was entirely cured." Three decades later, the Rickers prominently featured the handwritten letter, along with a typescript copy, in a water pamphlet. They also had the pleasure of extending a "genuine, hearty welcome" to Jackson on August 14, 1897, when he made his first visit to Poland Spring in a quarter of a century. Jackson reported that in the thirty-seven years since he had first tried the water, his kidney troubles had never reappeared.[34]

Even as testimonials extolled the medicinal virtues of the water, they subtly indicted the medical profession. Doctors were criticized for being expensive, ineffective, misinformed, and just plain wrong. In 1884 Hiram Ricker recounted over twenty cases in which conventional medicine had failed patients. His business partner, Nathan Miller, had despaired that doc-, tors could do anything for him after five months of treatment. Ezekiel Jackson had not been cured by his operation. A minister from Lynn, Massachusetts, charged doctors had "humbugged" him. A Maine sea captain had spent $650 at a Boston hospital without receiving any relief. Hiram, in contrast, had cured Captain Brooks's case of dropsy in less than three weeks and for less than twenty dollars. The point made by such cases was clear. Patients should turn to Poland Water and abandon the "nauseating pills, powders and potions" prescribed by physicians.[35]

The Rickers had to be careful that criticism of the medical profession did not go too far, since many people preferred to place their trust in trained professionals, rather than put their faith in folk healers. Hiram Ricker's decision to seek the approval of Dr. Eliphalet Clark during the formative stages of the water business suggests that he recognized the respectable status the emerging medical profession was earning in Gilded-Age America. Moreover, it was no accident that the Rickers paid tribute to "the first physician to prescribe Poland Water" by including a photograph and biography of Dr. Clark in *Poland Spring Centennial*. Far from being confused or hypocritical, the Rickers distinguished between "true" and "scientific" physicians. The former group was acceptable because its members recognized the "vital and physical elements of man" and enlisted in behalf of patients "all the powers of external nature as well as the quickening influences of faith and hope." The latter group was unacceptable because its members treated "the human body as if it were so much brute matter, to be subjected to analytical and synthetical reagents for the purpose of evolving definite results."[36]

Early pamphlets made sparing use of endorsements from doctors of either classification. The 1876 and 1877 editions each included only two letters from members of the medical profession out of a total of fifty-one. By 1883 the list of physicians in Maine, Boston, and New York recommending the "beneficial effects" of Poland Water had grown to forty-two. Compared to the detailed, often emotional, recovery narratives written by patients, the correspondence from men of medicine tended to be terse statements identifying specific maladies alleviated by use of the water. A Boston doctor needed only six lines in an 1872 letter to recommend the water for those afflicted with dyspepsia or urinary diseases. It took a Philadelphia physician a little longer to prescribe use of the remedy in all cases of nervous derangement. His 1883 letter required nine lines because he felt compelled to explain that the water's "remarkable purity" outweighed his aversion to making product recommendations. By 1894 the Rickers had worn down the apprehensions of enough members of the medical fraternity and set aside their own reservations about the medical profession to be able to boast, "one of the best advertisements that Poland water can have is the endorsement of the same by physicians."[37]

The most avid medical promoter of Poland Water was the resort's consulting physician, Dr. Milton Wedgwood. After careful investigation of claims made for the water, he wrote a testimonial in 1879 asserting that its purity and curative properties had been established beyond doubt. Wedgwood declared the product useful for all forms of dyspepsia and kidney disease. Later he expanded the scope of his recommendation in "Diseases of the Urinary Organs," a four-page paper published in its entirety in the 1883 water pamphlet. Based upon his work with patients at the resort, Wedgwood was confident that drinking the water could give "a new lease of life" to sufferers of kidney and bladder diseases, benefit people afflicted with rheumatic or scarlet fever, and save mothers from the "evil" results of the "frightful" complications of pregnancy.[38]

"The Light of Science"

The Rickers' new reliance on medical endorsements reflected the changing times. So, too, did the advent of inspections of the resort by regulators and analyses of the water by scientists. Each of these innovations suggests that at the turn of the century, "raw empiricism was on the way out," as was "knowledge based on faith." In their place, a scientific epistemology was gaining ascendance. This "alternative way of knowing" was based upon standardized procedures, logical argument, and replicable evidence. To certify the safety and purity of Poland Water, the Rickers called upon the expertise of chemists. These men of science not only identified the quantities of minerals such as potash, soda, lime, magnesia, and chlorine in the water; more important, they established "the purity and excellence, as well as the medicinal qualities" of the product. In sharing these reports with the public, the proprietors of the spring specifically appealed to "an instinctive curiosity, common to everybody, to 'know what the water contains.'" Although somewhat reluctantly, they had come to realize that "the light of science" made good business sense. Thus, the Rickers made it the third cornerstone of their empire of pure water.[39]

Chemists had thoroughly analyzed the composition of Poland Water by the early 1860s. In 1861 the Laboratory of the Survey in Portland identified silicates of potash and soda as the principal salts found in the water. In the same year, the Maine Board of Agriculture reported similar results and concluded: "it can be safely recommended in all cases where a pure water is required." A year later, a Harvard scientist prepared a report comparing the chemical constituents of the waters from several Maine springs, including the one in Poland. For good measure, the Rickers had the assayers for the states of Maine and Massachusetts test Poland Water in the early 1870s. On the basis of "a careful qualitative examination," the Maine assay judged the product "a most *wholesome* and *delicious* drinking water." The report from Massachusetts identified alkalinity, aeration, and purity, above all else, as the main characteristics. The official in charge gave an enthusiastic endorsement, stating: "this water having been extensively used for medicinal purposes for ten or fifteen years, does not require any further comments from the analytical chemist, other than to classify it as a water of great purity."[40]

"Closely in accord" with these earlier findings was the analysis of Abram A. Breneman, a former chemistry professor at Cornell University. In December 1894, he commended "not only the great purity of Poland Water, but its constancy of composition during long periods." His familiarity with the product dated back at least a year earlier to 1893 when he had judged the three hundred mineral spring waters exhibited at the World's Columbian Exposition. Breneman had awarded the Rickers' entry a medal, citing it as a "water of great purity" and a "valuable medicinal agent." Claiming that their water was the only one out of the hundreds from throughout the world honored on both counts, the Rickers launched a new advertising campaign in 1895. Entitled "Poland Water Leads Them All," it pointed to the product's effectiveness as an eliminator of bladder and kidney ailments, superior sales compared to the waters of Saratoga Springs, and exposition award as evidence of past success and future promise.[41]

Despite the regular inclusion of chemical analyses in pamphlets, the Rickers were ambivalent about their utility. While they established the purity and supported the efficacy of the water, they also facilitated deception and failed to explain the water's "secret." In an 1883 pamphlet, the Rickers admitted they placed "no particular stress on our published analyses." Furthermore, they complained that "published analyses have indeed done injury; for they have induced parties to announce other springs, located in different sections of the country, as possessing 'all the qualities of the POLAND SPRING WATER.'" The problem had become so commonplace that hundreds of people had urged the company to do something about it. The Rickers responded that they could do little "except to make known, as far as we are able, our claims for the genuine POLAND WATER." The best the company could do in the impersonal modern marketplace was provide customers with accurate information and trust they would both believe it and put it to good use.[42]

To prevent readers from being seduced completely by the presumed authority of scientists, the 1883 pamphlet repeatedly reminded readers of the limitations of science. The Rickers made it clear that instead of "any preconceived theories or arbitrary assumptions of chemists," the empirical evidence attested to by "thousands of intelligent persons scattered all over this broad land" served as the basis for their therapeutic claims. While chemists could identify the mineral constituents of the water, they could not "account for its almost miraculous curative properties." This secret remained "with the Creator of all things." As far as the Rickers were concerned, testimonials stating that the water healed were sufficient. Knowing how or why it worked was irrelevant.[43]

The 1890 water pamphlet took a more stridently dim view of the "light of science." The text ridiculed modern science for being "intensely egotistical." Chemistry was dismissed as a discipline only able to "tell [how] much that there is; so much of this and so much of that, but, when it has made its formula of substances, it is no nearer the secret of the *healing* than before." When a chemist tried to explain the unique purity and absorbent quality of the water, he stood in "bewilderment." His analysis was "powerless to detect" these and other mysteries of nature. "Not a man living," the pamphlet maintained, could "tell why this Poland Water has done for them what it has done." A decade later, the Rickers acknowledged "strained" relations with the medical and chemical professions because of the family's insistence that knowledge of the water's power had come by divine revelation, not scientific analysis.[44]

One scientist who shared concerns about the limitations of his discipline was Maine State Chemist Frank Bartlett. Although he had conducted a "complete and exhaustive analysis" for the Rickers in 1877 and 1892, he had his reservations about their usefulness. Bartlett confided: "I have always believed that there is more in the combination of the Poland Water, or, I may say, in its physical properties, than people have been inclined to allow." He recognized that scientific examination could only identify elements. It could not tell how or why they combined, or what their effects would be. The professor ended an 1892 letter to Hiram Ricker and Sons with the admission that some things "surpasseth man's understanding."[45]

Government inspectors from the Maine State Board of Health also shone the light of science on Poland Spring. In the wake of growing public health concerns throughout the country, the State Legislature had created the board in 1885, granting it the authority to study and investigate, although not regulate. One of the first concerns the Board of Health identified and addressed was the safety of drinking water supplies. As early as its second annual report, the board warned, "spring water is not necessarily pure." In the next decade, the board plunged into the national debate over a proposed pure food and drug bill, deeming "it its duty, in the interest of the health of the people and of public economy, to use its influence for the support of the measure."[46]

With these concerns in mind, eight members of the Board of Health arrived at Poland Spring on June 27, 1897, for an inspection. During the three-day stay, the delegation fanned out to search the resort for dangerous microbes. A summary of the board's findings commended the Rickers for appreciating "the meaning of chemically clean" and understanding "recent bacteriological discoveries" related to the germ theory of disease. As Marcia Jordan, the wife of board member Edward Jordan, reported in the Hill-Top, "it is very certain that the officers of the board carried away delightful impressions of the health, exquisite cleanliness, and fine appointments of this peerless summer resort."[47]

Despite the vote of confidence, the board inspected the entire premises again in 1899. The sanitary improvements made during the intervening two years impressed Dr. Wallace K. Oakes in particular. The Rickers had installed a new scientific plumbing system in the Poland Spring House and improved the sterilization process at the bottling plant. Every bottle was now rinsed in an alkaline solution, washed with a rubber plunger, and sterilized with steam heated to 250 degrees. In Oakes's estimation, use of a sterile bottle and a perfect cork made it impossible for contaminating germs to pollute the pure water. Pronouncing board members "thoroughly satisfied" with the inspection, Oakes commented that the "delightful summer home" was as safe as it was beautiful.[48]

"A Fountain of Health and a Mountain of Wealth"

The final cornerstone of Hiram Ricker and Sons' water empire was the business of purity. The proprietors needed to convince consumers of what Dr.

Oakes had determined—that under the stewardship of the Rickers, the water sold in barrels and bottles was as pure as the water flowing from the spring. Informing the public that the company used state-of-the-art manufacturing procedures was one means of providing assurance. Another message influential with Gilded-Age consumers was the gospel of success. Achievement measured by statistical and anecdotal comparisons served as an indicator of merit. Combining sound salesmanship with "enterprise, good judgement, and mental capacity" the Rickers transformed the spring not only "into a fountain of health," but also "a mountain of wealth." [49]

Momentous changes came to the hilltop in 1876. In addition to opening the Poland Spring House, Hiram Ricker and Sons introduced the "Moses" bottle, registered a trademark for Poland Mineral Spring Water, and expanded production facilities. In the nation's centennial year, the company also issued its first pamphlet promoting the water. This and subsequent editions blended Hiram Ricker's personal style with the commercial techniques befitting the modern business his sons had established. The format typically consisted of a history of the family and the spring, details about the business, descriptions of the natural surroundings, information about the water's medicinal powers, and endorsements from dozens of patients and doctors. Through this medium, the Rickers conveyed two intertwined messages: Because Poland Water was natural, it was pure; and because it was pure, it possessed miraculous healing powers.

The reliance on promotional literature to communicate with consumers appealed to the instrumental consumer behavior that became the basis of modern commerce during the Gilded Age. As national and even international markets increasingly subsumed local commerce, the familiar relationship between producers and consumers stretched to the breaking point. In the new marketplace, customary behavior based upon the traditions of local community and personal contact was not possible. Replacing it was market-oriented, profit-maximizing, and rational business practice. Providing reams of historical, medical, chemical, and commercial information about Poland Water through scores of annual pamphlets allowed customers, at least theoretically, to make informed decisions about its merits even at distances far removed from the spring.[50]

Attempting to resist the changing nature of commerce, the Rickers made clear in the 1877 water pamphlet that they still wanted readers to think of themselves as part of a community. The 1879 edition went even further in attempting to translate the tradition of personal contact between merchants and customers to the mail order business by including a friendly engraved illustration of Hiram Ricker that greeted readers as they opened the catalog. Four years later, a handwritten letter accompanied the picture. The message from Hiram Ricker and Sons expressed the wish that the public might carefully read and conscientiously consider recommendations firmly establishing "the healing virtues of the Poland Water."[51]

In spite of these attempts to preserve customary marketplace relationships, the pamphlets really served as primers in the cultivation of instrumental consumer behavior. When "unscrupulous" and "ambitious" competitors started introducing imitations of Poland Water to the market in the late 1870s, the Rickers used the forum provided by the pamphlets "to make known, as far as we are able, our claims for the genuine POLAND WATER, in language that everybody cannot fail to understand." They also instructed consumers to look for the trademark introduced in 1876. Absence of a seal bearing the interlocking initials PMS was "*prima facie* evidence of fraud and imposture." As an additional safeguard, the Rickers urged the public to buy from "no person except our duly authorized agents, or directly from the Spring."[52]

Agents were important extensions of the Poland Spring community. From the outset of the business in 1860, Hiram Ricker relied upon representatives in Lewiston, Brunswick, and Saccarappa (Westbrook), Maine, to distribute the water. The apothecary firm of Harris and Chapman provided entry into the Boston market. These two enterprising salesmen cleverly primed demand by sending sample bottles to every physician in the city. They also invited doctors to examine depositions from patients whose ailments had been remedied by use of Poland Water. From five agents in 1860, the distribution network grew to twenty-four in 1879. Two-thirds were located in New England, the remaining one-third in cities within the area bounded by New York, Washington, New Orleans, and Chicago. By 1895 the network had expanded to forty-one agents, only five of whom were based in New England. Hiram Ricker and Sons was now a fully national enterprise with representatives spread from Bangor, Maine, in the East to Los Angeles, California, in the West and from Minneapolis, Minnesota, in the North to Jacksonville, Florida, in the South. It was also an international company with five agents in Canada and one in Bermuda. A year later Poland Water was for sale even in London.[53]

In time, the company dispensed with the middlemen in large cities, establishing instead its own offices in Boston, New York, Philadelphia, and Chicago. Begun in 1877, the Boston water depot was managed by Alonzo H. Briggs, who for a time held the mortgage on the Poland Spring Hotel. By

The Poland Water Depot in Boston was located at 175 Devonshire Street during the 1890s. Commercial outlets and retail agents extended the reach of Hiram Ricker and Sons across the country and around the world. *Courtesy Androscoggin Historical Society.*

1892 business was so good that nine workers staffed the enterprise. Pleased with this success, the Rickers opened a second regional distribution center in New York during May of 1883. Within a few years, annual sales reached three thousand dollars. By 1887, however, revenues had slumped to a third of the former level. To rekindle interest in the water, Edward Ricker traveled to the city intending to relocate the company's office. He chose space in the Tribune Building on Nassau Street, a prime location for which he was willing to commit to a rental rate nearly double the revenue generated by New York sales during the preceding year. Ricker's confidence was richly rewarded. In 1892 six people staffed the New York office and orders amounted to over $100,000. Sales continued to increase even amid the "hard times" that followed the Depression of 1893. By 1897 annual receipts totaled nearly $150,000. Customers could dial 6050 Cortlandt on their telephones and have Poland Water delivered anywhere in the city and as far away as Brooklyn and Jersey City.[54]

The increasing demand that resulted from the widening distribution network led to the enlargement of the Spring House and the addition of a thirty-by-sixty-foot plant for barreling and bottling in the fall of 1876. Featuring such attention to detail as glass tubing "so as to preserve the purity of the water," the new facility was acclaimed to be "as fine a structure for the purpose as there is in the country." By 1885 "business had so expanded" that an ell designed to serve as the packing department was built onto the north side of the building. Improved bottling machinery, aerating equipment, and a new storage tank were added to the operation. Made out of polished granite, the two-thousand-gallon tank measured four feet deep, four feet wide, and fourteen feet long. In 1892 Hiram Ricker and Sons turned out large quantities of Poland Water in what a local reporter called "the largest and best equipped barreling and bottling establishments in the United States." The operation duly impressed Professor Robinson of the State Board of Health. This "scientific man" found it refreshing and reassuring to observe all the "pains-taking" efforts the Rickers went through to bottle the water, especially at a time when "adulteration and hurry to get things on the market" were all the rage. To keep up with changing technology and increasing demand, the Rickers began circulating plans for a new "richly designed and costly stone house at the Spring" only three years later. Although the proposed spring house and bottling plant were slated for completion in 1897, the new facilities did not open until 1906.[55]

One measure of the success of Hiram Ricker and Sons came from the statistics the company disclosed. In 1886 the Rickers proudly noted that sales of Poland Water had multiplied from 20,000 gallons in 1870 to an annual total of 340,000 gallons. Income from water sales had increased commensurately, from $1,250 in 1870 to $25,000 in 1886. With consumption reaching the 400,000–gallon plateau in 1890, the Rickers trumpeted the fact that the output of their spring doubled that of all the springs at Saratoga, New York, combined. Sales continued to increase through the rest of the decade until the company was sending the water "throughout the

United States and Canada; to South America, Cuba, England, the continent of Europe, India, [and] Egypt."[56]

It was no accident the Rickers singled out Saratoga as the standard by which to measure the success of their spring water empire. The town was home to some of the oldest, most prominent, and most successful spas in the United States. Although this tourist center attracted many more visitors than the lone resort at Poland Spring, the Rickers could honestly lay claim to owning a spring water more popular than anything bubbling up from the ground in Saratoga. In part, their supremacy was rooted in the perceived superior medicinal advantages of the water from the Maine hilltop. As early as 1860, a minister declared in a Boston newspaper that "as a medicine the Poland Water was of greater value than the water of all the Springs in Saratoga." For its part, the *Hill-Top* boasted the Poland Spring resort was the "Saratoga of New England."[57]

For many mineral water aficionados, world-renowned European spas set the standard for excellence. Consequently, an 1890 advertisement pointed out that Hiram Ricker and Sons' sales surpassed not only those of "all the Springs at Saratoga combined," but also of "any other Medicinal Spring in the world." Another promotional piece published in the same year praised Poland Spring as both the Saratoga and "Baden-Baden of New England." It even went so far as to compare favorably the spring's "God-given water" with that of the "sacred Ganges" in far off India. In 1894 the *Hill-Top* observed that Poland Spring was "rapidly gaining a national reputation as the Carlsbad of America." Three years later the paper printed the testimonial of a guest who maintained that Poland Spring provided "much better facilities" than any of the renowned spas in Europe. By 1899 the Rickers claimed: "the majority of physicians all over the United States and many in the most famous European Spas recommend Poland Water as 'the purest and most valuable medicinal water known.'" While an article in the *Boston Daily Globe* concurred that the family operated the "foremost of American Spas," the writer was only willing to concede that Poland Spring rivaled, not surpassed the older mineral springs of Europe."[58]

In spite of their obvious economic self-interest in promoting the spring, the Rickers routinely denied suggestions that ownership brought them financial gain. Indeed for Hiram the elder, dispensing the healing water to the ill was such an important calling that he sometimes felt compelled to give it away. One beneficiary of his charity was Susan Noble, a twenty-four-year old woman whom he met in Lewiston. Having been treated by fifteen physicians to no avail, Noble's throat had become so swollen by scrofulous humor that she was unable to turn her head. Although she could not afford to pay for treatment, Ricker invited the woman to the spring anyway. In exchange for her labor, she was permitted to drink and bathe in the water for six weeks in July and August of 1866. When the condition flared up again the following year, Ricker invited her to return to the spring on the same terms. Noble was not the only person touched by Hiram Ricker's generosity. When money became tight in 1876 for Olive Martin, whom the ablest doctors in Boston had deemed doomed to succumb to Bright's disease, Hiram came to the rescue and supplied her with a complimentary barrel of water. This kind gesture won the ill woman over as a faithful visitor to the hilltop for many years afterwards.[59]

Even when it came to paying customers, the Rickers denied having a "speculative," "mercenary," or "commercial" interest in the spring water. The family dismissed irreverent remarks that "the spring [was] rippling away dreamily into—bank notes" with protestations that any money derived from sales of the water was an "inconsequential accident of possession." While the Rickers did not dispute they wished "to prosper, to thrive, to extend our business," they insisted they had been "lifted above the plane of selfishness." A "worthy and generous impulse" in their hearts, the proprietors maintained, motivated them "to spread the knowledge of what this water will do for suffering humanity, for the sake of humanity." Yet again, the family resorted to modern media techniques to promote the image of the benevolent good neighbor and the illusion of customary economic relations. More important, the Rickers had firmly laid the final footing for their empire of pure water.[60]

Fifty-seven years and one day after the *Lewiston Falls Journal* hailed the "great purity" of Poland Water, the Maine Medical Association honored the Rickers' "ministry of pure water." The organization presented the family with what was described as the "perfect tribute," a bronze plaque showing in bas-relief an Indian kneeling beside a wilderness spring. The *Hill-Top* explained that the image symbolized "the complete harmony of modern medical science and work done by this pure and potable spring water toward the physical betterment of the world." Walter Graham, the editor of the paper at the time, added that "for more than a century the water of a clear Maine spring has been performing its silent ministry of refreshment and healing thruout the world."[61]

While the quantity of the promotional literature distributed by Hiram Ricker and Sons between 1860 and 1900 calls into question the claim for the silence of the ministry, the numerous pamphlets and catalogs do resoundingly confirm that the company tirelessly preached the refreshing and healing virtues of the water's purity. As the Rickers developed the water business, they rooted the source of its purity in a timeless geological past governed by the laws of Nature. They then followed its history through layers of landscapes corresponding to ancient aboriginal, progressive colonial, and modern commercial times. Along the way, they offered abundant personal testimonials, medical endorsements, and scientific evidence verifying the therapeutic value and healing properties of the water. They also assured customers that their responsible stewardship and scrupulous business practices protected the purity of the water as it flowed from the spring into the marketplace. Finally and fundamentally, the Rickers' ministry asked the faithful to believe that drinking pure Poland Water could cleanse the Gilded-Age impurities of modern life from the inner self. Other changes on the way to the Poland Spring landscape championed similar antidotes to modernity.

PART III

The Search for a Middle Landscape

"A City of Vivid Contrasts"

The ambivalence produced by the tension between faith in progress and the desire for escape epitomized the fundamental dilemma many Gilded-Age vacationers faced. They urgently wanted to get away from the problems of urban-industrial society. As patron Marcia Bradbury Jordan poetically put it, her prosperous peers wanted to flee the city where the "newsboys' cries were rife"; and they wanted to leave behind "the crowded thoroughfare/And every sound of strife." Yet, they did not want to forsake the benefits of modern civilization. Thus by vacation's end, inevitably "fate led back to modern city ways/Where all the world's at work and nothing pays." When Jordan and other members of the urban elite packed for their summer migrations, their cultural baggage overflowed with firmly held thoroughly modern notions about the inevitability of progress, utility of technology, desirability of leisure, and necessity of consumption, none of which they were about to leave at home. The solution to their predicament was to find places where they could enjoy the advantages of progress by quarantining themselves from its unpleasant mutations; where they could re-create the city while recreating in the countryside; where they could ease not erase the transition to modernity. The search for such an accommodating middle landscape brought the people of progress to sites like Poland Spring, and the hilltop would never look the same ever after.[1]

In time, promoters came to understand that the varied landscape of reading, rowing, and rambling extolled by Jordan in her "summer letter" had transformed the resort into "a city of vivid contrasts." This city blended both rural and urban forms and features. Thus, a modern train trip ended with an old-fashioned stagecoach ride, a primitive Indian encampment greeted guests to the luxurious resort grounds, the quaint old Mansion House stood in counterpoise to the state-of-the-art new Poland Spring House, and the natural spring was sheltered by the technological wonders of the Spring House and Bottling Plant. By 1898 the Lewiston newspaper summed up the contrasts on the hilltop as being between the "condition of rural peace and simplicity" on the one hand and "urban elegance and the abode of wealth and fashion" on the other.[2]

What this perceptive account acknowledged, and what historians have also noted, is that the middle landscape was not some fixed entity shaped equally by rural and urban values. Over time, a more "complex environmental vision" influenced by the progress of modernization moved the molders of the landscape from a "complex pastoralism," which melded memories of a romantic past with modern reality, "toward an urban vision" that ushered in the urbanization process by tempering it with liberal doses of rural nostalgia and natural beauty. The eventual ascendance of a modern urban culture brought with it many "striking contrasts" that needed to be balanced. The hotel apartment furnished realms for the modern distinctions between public and private life. Newspapers addressed the desire for individual identity amid mass anomie. Gendered spaces differentiated between the male world of commerce and the female spheres of domesticity and consumption. Popular entertainments promoted community amid diversity. At Poland Spring, the sociability downstairs in the parlors accompanied by the privacy upstairs in the bedroom, the popularity of the Hill-Top with its fill of informative gossip and titillating tidbits, the separate creations of the Casino for men and the art store for women, and the offering of "darkey melodies" and employee masquerades in the music hall, which reinforced social exclusivity by containing cultural diversity, were just some of the resulting elements of the urban vision and urbane culture that produced the "city of vivid contrasts."[3]

Such assertive use of the city metaphor by promoters of the essentially rural resort was very revealing. Although established in response to the profound social and cultural changes that accompanied the processes of modernization, the resort functioned as more than simply a place to escape urban reality. In effect, it represented the effort to create an idealized setting of "urban pastoralism"—an alternative landscape that blended the past and the present, balanced tradition and progress, and offered the best of both country and city life. At the "city of vivid contrasts," a nostalgic air intermingled with a contemporary ambience, natural beauty complemented cultural refinement, and romanticism merged with modernism. Acting like a flywheel on the whirring dynamo of progress, the contrasts that abounded among the resort's middle landscapes made the many manifestations of antimodernity little more than masquerades and the march to modernity more manageable.[4]

At Poland Spring, the Rickers provided the people of progress with a highly complex layering of cultural landscapes. If the city slickers wanted a dose of country life, they could take up a scythe, tour the resort's dairy barn, or take a carriage ride and view the many local farms in the area. If the urban rusticators wanted to get back to nature, they could admire the natural surroundings from verandas, balconies, boats, or pathways. If *the urban sportsmen and women wanted a taste of the strenuous life, they could head to a fishing hole, the tennis courts, the baseball diamond, or the golf course. At the same time, these idealized landscapes masked certain modern realities, specifically the commercialization of agriculture, the commodification of nature, and the competitiveness of sports. What the resort really offered patrons, therefore, was a kaleidoscope of middle landscapes that layered an urban ideal over rural reality by blending together a wide mix of modern and antimodern values. When urban dwellers tired of their pretend pastoralism, but before they were ready to depart for home, they could find a reminder of the cities beautiful they had left behind by retiring to the Maine State Building. There they could partake of the presumed civilizing influences and cultural uplift brought about by studying museum exhibits, browsing through library books, reading the* Hill-Top, *and admiring the art gallery. This juxtaposition of pastoral farm, natural Eden, recreational playground, and cultured city highlights the breadth and depth of the search for a middle landscape that took place at Poland Spring during the Gilded Age. It is yet another indication of the powerful and persistent cultural forces that gradually transformed the country farm into the summer city.*

✻ 6 ✻

The Farm

"Lovely Pastoral Country"

According to literature promoting the Poland Spring resort, one of the most alluring features of the surrounding landscape was the pastoral panorama that encircled the hilltop. It included "the various colors of orchards, green pastures and golden grain, dotted here and there with the houses and barns of the prosperous farmers." Viewing these scenes from the veranda of the Poland Spring House or from a carriage on a break ride, reading about it in the *Hill-Top* or a popular novel, or seeing it in landscape paintings recalled for many patrons memories of an idyllic rural past. Swayed by the appeal of pastoralism, they linked the landscape lying before them with an agrarian golden age when Americans had presumably lived closer to the land and had been inherently more virtuous. While at first appearances replete with antimodern associations to nature and nostalgia, the late-nineteenth-century agricultural landscape in Maine was, in fact, more influenced by the imperatives of modern commerce. At Poland Spring the tug of antimodern myth and modern reality ultimately produced an agricultural middle landscape where visitors could vicariously experience country life in a setting of urbane leisure.[1]

Between 1860 and 1900 the state of agriculture in Poland, in Maine, and in New England transformed significantly. Many farms closed and much of the rural population moved away to industrial cities and the agricultural West. Remaining farms consolidated and specialized. New commercial enterprises such as dairy creameries and canning factories further altered the practice of farming and the look of the landscape. Many people viewed these changes with alarm. They feared that the continued abandonment of farms and decrease in rural population would lead to the wholesale bankrupting of the rural economy and complete desolation of the countryside. Moreover, those who rooted national character and strength in virtues derived from till-ing the soil worried that the perceived decline of New England agriculture might sap the vitality of the nation.

The problem of rural depopulation was one of the most vexing social issues of the day. Because of the diverse economic opportunities available in Poland, however, the town experienced only a slight loss of population. Between 1860 and 1890, the number of residents decreased from 2,746 to 2,472, a reduction of 10 percent. During the most recent decade of that period, six farms, representing nearly fifteen hundred acres, had been abandoned. Elsewhere in the state, the consequences of abandonment and depopulation were far more pronounced. During the 1880s, nearly 3,400 farms, over 5 percent of the total at the beginning of the decade, had ceased operations. Census figures, which decreased nearly 20 to 40 percent between 1860 and 1900 in most of the communities bordering Poland, tell the tale of the toll taken on small towns. What concerned observers like Henry and George Poole was not how many people were leaving the area, but rather, who was leaving. Disproportionately, it was intelligent and enterprising youths. Yet, even these departures were not "wholly irreparable," the brothers believed, for machines more than made up for the loss of labor.[2]

Spurred by demographic decline and informed by the mythology of the yeoman farmer, the legacy of Jeffersonian agrarianism, and the ideology of pastoralism, calls for agricultural reform eventually coalesced into the country life movement. The general tenor of the solutions offered to the perceived crisis was to operate farms in a more efficient manner—in short, to modernize them. Reformers advised farmers to think of agriculture not only as a way of life focused on feeding people and fostering virtue, but also as a business concerned with profit and loss. Preserving the past called for facing the future—a prescription, ironically, that only exacerbated some of the disconcerting trends already underway in New England agriculture. Paradoxically, the grafting of pastoralism and progressivism largely served to alienate country life even further from the very agrarian virtues many in the movement idealized and sought to preserve. Nowhere did this disjunction become more apparent than on the hilltop in Poland Spring. There the vivid contrasts of nostalgic pastoral fantasy and commercial agricultural reality came together to produce a vision of "lovely pastoral country."[3]

"A Very Fine Farming Region"

From a vantage atop White Oak Hill in the town of Poland, the reporter for the *Lewiston Falls Journal* provided a baseline by which to measure the agricultural changes to come in the decades after 1860. The observant journalist noted that "a very fine farming region" spread out before him. It was beginning to wilt, however, as the result of a yearlong drought. Perhaps, as agricultural experts warned, the lack of precipitation was related to the shrinking pine forests, which, the writer explained, had "succumbed to the rapacity of the speculator and the woodman's axe" during the first half of the nineteenth century. Whatever the cause, local farmers noted with concern that the hay crop was not half as large as the year before. Although they remained green and promising, corn stalks and potato plants also thirsted for a good soaking rain. Only the apple trees "loaded with fruit" appeared to be weathering the prolonged dry spell unscathed.[4]

The reporter was entering a town that was still growing and productive. The population had increased nearly 4 percent during the past decade. Still, livestock far outnumbered people in Poland, Maine. Pastures were populated and barns occupied by 1,157 sheep, 927 milk cows, 570 pigs, 537 oxen, 368 horses, and 607 assorted other cattle. In 1860 the sheep produced 4,006 pounds of wool, while the cows gave enough milk for the manufacture of 12,773 pounds of cheese and 63,476 pounds of butter, both of which took "the lead in all the markets." Despite the drought, the summer hay crop totaled 4,992 tons of hay. The fall harvest yielded 14,014 bushels of oats, 13,991 bushels of corn, 2,509 bushels of rye, 1,610 bushels of wheat, and 244 bushels of barley. In addition, gardens supplied 1,249 bushels of peas and beans and 62,722 bushels of potatoes that possessed "invariable reputation abroad." Blessed by a favorable climate and fertile soil, the apple trees bore fruit "as close of fibre and richly flavored, as juicy and longkeeping as any in America." For added bounty, the farms of Poland produced 2,420 pounds of honey, 689 pounds of maple sugar, 244 gallons of molasses, and 43 pounds of beeswax in 1860.[5]

On his way to Poland Spring, the journalist visited the "fine" farm of Daniel P. Atwood, an energetic republican who was busily bringing in what hay there was. He also toured for several hours the building and grounds of the Sabbathday Lake Shakers. When he finally reached the Ricker farmstead, the reporter found a "large house and still larger barns" that had once garnered in bountiful crops. Amid the drought, he now found a farmer awash with water and abuzz with big plans for the future. Hiram Ricker, ever the seeker of wealth, was already dreaming in 1860 of bringing back the heydays of yesteryear by cultivating a new crop on the thirty-acre field where his mineral spring flowed—tourists. Where cattle now grazed, he envisioned building a hotel.[6]

During the last quarter of the nineteenth century, Poland remained "principally an agricultural town," but one dramatically reshaped by an entirely new economic force. The rise of tourism, epitomized by the "commodious hotel" that arose on Ricker Hill in 1876, offered an alternative livelihood for the Rickers, who turned their farmstead into a resort. It also provided a quick source of cash for the many families that sold their property to summer people. Other families benefited by welcoming guests into their farmhouses or by building cottages on their property. For those people who continued to raise livestock and grow fruits and vegetables, tourism provided many opportunities to supplement their income. From the day the doors of the Poland Spring House opened, the Rickers made it known that the lamb and poultry served in the dining room "will be procured in Poland." At the resort, local farmers also found "a convenient market for their summer vegetables, spring chickens, eggs, [and] butter." Farm families in town profited not only from the direct sale of goods to Poland Spring, but also from the indirect transactions through local businesses such as dairy cooperatives and canning factories.[7]

In the forefront of the agricultural revolution marked by increasing cooperation and commerce was Bert Fernald. In 1878 at the age of twenty, Fernald took over the family farm that had fallen on hard times following his father's death a few years earlier. From these hardscrabble beginnings, he gradually developed one of the best Holstein dairy herds in the state. Admirers more familiar with the image than the reality of "Down East" agriculture praised the ambition and perseverance that enabled him to turn a "rocky farm" with sterile soil into a "very good farm" with "a more prosperous appearance." His success eventually earned him leadership in the local Patrons of Husbandry, where Fernald's fellow farmers selected him to serve on the committee charged with supervising the construction of the Lake Grange meeting hall.[8]

The Grange was supposed to be in the vanguard of promoting cooperative efforts among hard-pressed farmers. Two chapters of the group had organized in Poland in 1874. In March families around Harris Hill had come together to form the Excelsior Grange. Two months later, thirty-two people in West Poland had started the Lake Grange. Meetings served as forums for the exchange of ideas and promotion of fellowship. Less well received was the group's economic agenda, which "met with violent opposition." Arrangements made with suppliers to sell to Grangers at reduced prices did not work out. Neither did cooperative purchases. In 1895 the Lake Grange voted to abandon the practice and to refund the money remaining in the trading account. More popular was the life insurance provided by the Patron's Mutual

Aid Society. Begun in 1875, the organization served forty-five local Grange members fifteen years later. In spite of the limited economic achievements of the Patrons of Husbandry, Henry and George Poole judged the social, moral, and intellectual influence of the group to have been of "vital importance to the prosperity and well-being" of Poland's farm families.[9]

Undaunted by the mixed success of the Grange's economic programs, Fernald helped organize a new dairy cooperative in 1884. The eight-member Poland Dairy Association united the interests of farmers with those of mill owner John S. Briggs. Briggs, who served as president of the cooperative, had installed butter making equipment in the lower floor of his steam mill at Poland Corner. From the cream produced by local dairy herds, Superintendent J. W. Mitchell manufactured an average of three hundred pounds of butter daily. Sales of butter at an average price of twenty-eight cents per pound added up, as the factory paid out nearly twelve thousand dollars to local farmers in 1886. Production capacity more than tripled when the dairy moved to a new location at Poland Corner that had been purchased from Alvan Ricker in 1899. By this time, the facility was supplied by twelve hundred cows, which never thought of holidays, unions, walking delegates, or strikes, the *Hill-Top* playfully pointed out in a swipe at contemporary labor unrest. From an "ocean" of golden cream, the factory churned out up to a half ton of butter of "immaculate purity" each day.[10]

Fernald's next agricultural venture was investing in the nascent canning industry that was flourishing locally. He learned the business in his role as bookkeeper for Poland Packing Company, a "model canning establishment" that Portland's "pioneer packer," J. Winslow Jones, had established in 1873. Based upon reports from his wife's brothers, who had recently returned from a cross-country trip that revealed a large untapped market for canned goods, Fernald borrowed one thousand dollars from his aunt and decided to go out on his own in 1886. He built his first factory in West Poland near Tripp Pond. By 1897 Fernald, Keene and True was the third largest canning establishment in the state. It eventually grew to include seven factories with a combined capacity of 500,000 cans per day. Thanks to orders solicited by chief salesman Bert Fernald, the company shipped its products to grocers in Boston, New York, Philadelphia, and even as far away as San Francisco.[11]

In time, Fernald parlayed his success in farming and business into an impressive political career. It began in 1897 when he was chosen to run for a seat in the State Legislature "to straighten out a difference" between Hiram W. Ricker and Jesse Libby that dated back to their adversarial positions during the heated railroad dispute several years earlier. Following one term in the

Maine State House and two in the State Senate between 1897 and 1903, Fernald went on to serve as Governor of Maine from 1909 to 1911 and as United States Senator from 1916 until his death in 1926. Widely regarded as the power behind the politician was the Ricker family. William R. Pattangall, a contemporary political pundit, explained the relationship this way: "Bert M. Fernald was born in West Poland in 1858; he still lives in West Poland. West Poland is in the town of Poland. Poland Spring is in the town of Poland. The Rickers run Poland Spring. Thus you have the origin of Bert M. Fernald fairly accounted for." The alliance dated back at least to 1895 when Fernald helped the Ricker brothers plan the commemoration of the town's centennial.[12]

Because of the efforts of progressive farmers and modern businessmen like Fernald and the Rickers, agriculture prospered in Poland. By 1895 Poland Dairy Association supplied over one thousand pounds of butter to the Poland Spring resort each week. Even after the season ended, the dairy shipped standing orders to patrons of the hotels. Charles Fargo of Wells Fargo in Chicago, for one, left instructions that the cooperative should send him Poland butter wherever he might be. In addition, the association sold butter to customers in Maine, Massachusetts, and Rhode Island. Attributing the quality of the product to the chemistry of the local soil, the Poole brothers boasted that Poland butter took the lead in all the markets where it was introduced.[13]

For local farmers, the booming agricultural trade brought about by the increasing resort business had the benefit of "bringing metropolitan prices" to the area. They prospered by selling the Rickers some of the 2,500 quarts of milk, 81 bushels of potatoes, 10,080 eggs, 1,813 pounds of chicken, 34 lambs, 345 pounds of veal, and 29 bushels of berries consumed at Poland Spring each week. Hiram W. Ricker estimated that the family purchased nearly sixteen thousand dollars worth of Maine farm goods in 1893 alone. One local man matter-of-factly assessed the economic impact of the resort this way: "It creates a demand for what I can raise on the farm." From the standpoint of the Rickers, not enough farmers were willing to deal directly with them. As one member of the State Board of Agriculture pointed out in 1896, most of the resort's total annual food expenditure of forty thousand dollars was transacted with merchants in Boston. Accounting for this fact, one of the Rickers, probably Alvan, complained that there were only "two or three men in Poland and New Gloucester whom I can rely on . . . to furnish me with so many eggs." The same was true for poultry. The unnamed brother maintained that he would have greatly preferred to pay local farmers the profit rather than sending it off to wholesalers in the city.[14]

Even as modernization in the form of markets, merchants, manufacturing, machinery, and mergers transformed the nature of agriculture, observers still attributed the prosperity of successful farmers to time-honored traits of individual endeavor. Horace J. Brown, for instance, was credited through "diligence and proper cultivation" with increasing by four-fold the fertility of the farm he had purchased from Daniel Atwood. Where the property once had been hard pressed to support four cows, it accommodated a dairy herd of eighteen by 1890. Yet, neither degrees of hard work, intelligence, thrift, nor industry distinguished Atwood from Brown. What really made the decisive difference were the increased opportunities made possible by the presence in Poland of the resort, the dairy, the canning factories, and the railroad. The greater access to markets provided by rail service integrated farms into the world of modern commerce and forced farmers to become businessmen. The family-oriented, independent yeoman of Atwood's era was being replaced by the market-driven, interdependent, capitalist farmer of Brown's day. Nevertheless, the rhetoric of pastoralism clung to the ideal of agrarian republican virtue long after it ceased to accurately reflect reality.[15]

"This Process of Sorting and Sifting"

Henry and George Poole well understood that the "manner of conducting farm affairs . . . materially changed" during the latter half of the nineteenth century. Great improvements in agricultural implements, stock breeding, and transportation facilities had transformed agriculture, so much so that the brothers warned: "The farmer who persists in following the ruts of his grandfather will find himself far behind in the struggle for success." Perceptively observing that a new process had taken root, the Pooles proposed a surprising explanation for the recent progress in agriculture—monopolies. Asking readers familiar with the harangues of Populists to hear them out, the brothers explained that combining three or four unprofitable farms into one successful venture was desirable. It led to more work, higher wages, better skills, and less poverty. They noted,

This process of sorting and sifting, this policy of giving farms entirely over to crops for which they are best fitted, or finding out what they are made for, and respecting the answer, of treating nature as an ally rather than as an enemy, are going on, and will continue to go in spite of the efforts which may be made to arrest or defeat them.

In short, they were pointing out that progress, in the guise of modernization, touched agriculture, too.[16]

The brothers had no illusions about a bygone golden age of agriculture. To the contrary, they remembered mid-century as a time when the self-dependence and isolation of farmers had frequently led to hardship and uncertainty. It had been an era when most farmers were more likely to be visited by a deputy sheriff serving a foreclosure notice than by a newspaper reporter seeking a story. In 1850 getting local produce to market had meant traveling to Portland, the only sizable trading center in the region. The Pooles painted a bleak, albeit sympathetic, portrait of men who loaded their one-horse pungs with hogs, chickens, turkeys, butter, cheese, applesauce, and dried apples and then headed out into the cold on the two-day, thirty-five mile journey, four to five times a winter. The scarce profit they made was not enough to keep most farmers out of debt and most families away from poverty. A more unflattering side of country life during this period was the scene at the corner store. The Pooles portrayed it as the hangout of the town's loafers, idlers, and dissipated men, who "met to talk politics, drink rum, fight and swap horses."[17]

The golden age of agriculture, according to the Pooles, was the present. Because of improved access to expanding urban markets, the same pung-load of goods that brought twenty-five to fifty dollars in merchandise in 1850 was worth three times that amount in cash in 1890. Rather than being in debt, a farmer was now likely to have money invested in savings banks, government bonds, and railroad stocks. The times were so good that the Pooles could not imagine that any wise Poland farmer would trade places with one of his counterparts in the West. Although this assessment of the state of agriculture was decidedly bullish, it was neither naive nor romantic. The brothers readily acknowledged that even for the most successful farmer, the vocation was "somewhat irksome in some respects, making long days and causing close confinement." Nevertheless, they were certain that given the current economic conditions, farmers stood to earn "handsome profits" if they were thrifty, industrious, and good managers.[18]

In a sign of some of the new dimensions the sorting and sifting process took in reshaping Gilded-Age agriculture, Edward Ricker headed for Boston with a plan to speculate in grain futures on the eve of the pivotal 1896 presidential election. The contest pitted the Republican defender of the gold standard, deflation, creditors, and industrialists, William McKinley, against the Democratic champion of free silver, inflation, debtors, and farmers, William

Jennings Bryan. Edward was convinced that the interjection of "politics" into the market was about to lead to a "big drop" in commodity prices as election day on the first Tuesday in November drew near. He planned to take full advantage of the opportunity.[19]

Commenting on the state of affairs in Chicago, Ricker reported in his first letter back home on October 26 that "it looks *Bad*." A spike in spot interest rates from 10 to 50 percent on Wall Street two days later convinced him that the commodities market was about "to go to pieces." Seeking to benefit from the financial volatility, he had already shorted wheat futures. His scheme did not end there. He was certain that once wheat prices plummeted, they would quickly "jump again like a Rocket." Intent upon timing the market perfectly and profiting on both the way down and the way back up, Edward camped out for a week near his broker in Boston, ready at a moment's notice to give the orders to buy low and sell high.[20]

The stress of waiting began to wear on Ricker and affect his health. As he described the situation, not knowing which way the market was headed "keeps one on their nerves every minet [sic]." When New York banks rallied to pump more liquidity into the monetary system, thereby bringing down short-term interest rates and supporting stock prices, his disappointment was palpable. Only a few days earlier he had been certain financial markets were about to break downward. Now in a letter back to Brother Al, Edward wrote about trying to keep his nerves in the "best shape" he could. The following day he described how "hard" it was being away from home, having so much on his mind, and "going through what I have to go throu [sic]." Nevertheless, he closed this correspondence by assuring Alvan that his health was holding up and that he was "feeling as well or better" than he had for several days. That is where the correspondence concludes. There apparently was no culminating letter proclaiming the success of the speculative scheme.[21]

The sorting and shifting brought about by the commercialization of agriculture exempted no one, not the wheat farmers of the Great Plains, whose produce was the source of speculation, and not the communal Shakers, who lived within sight of the Poland Spring resort. They, too, eventually became the focus of Edward Ricker's penchant for financial wheeling and dealing and the family's quest for empire building. As owners of one of the largest farming establishments in the area, the Shakers at various times supplied the Rickers with many of the foodstuffs they served their guests, including cream, eggs, chickens, celery, peas, cabbage, potatoes, tomatoes, apples, pears, blackberries, and currants. A decrease in membership that was similar to but even more precipitous than the depopulation of nearby towns made it increasingly difficult for the group to maintain the scale of its farm operations. Between 1860 and 1900, the number of Believers at Sabbathday Lake dropped by 60 percent, from one hundred three people to forty-one.[22]

To alleviate the strain on the dwindling resources of the community, Shaker leaders closed the Poland Hill family and had its members move in with the Church family a short distance away in New Gloucester. The abandoned property was immediately put up for sale. An aggressive marketing campaign boasted that the site was "one of the most desirable estates in New England and one which for sightliness, pure air and water, cannot be surpassed." The Shaker Hill Farm was indeed estate-like in scope. It consisted of 150 acres of timberland, an equal amount of "first-class" tillage, 260 acres of pasture and woods, and "a large orchard of grafted fruit." In addition, it included about a dozen buildings, the most prominent of which was a recently completed three-and-a-half-story stone dwelling house. Finally, it featured two springs that thorough analysis showed were "substantially the same as the famous Poland mineral water." In the estimation of the Shakers, these assets made the site an ideal location for a summer resort.[23]

Fearing that his new neighbors might soon be the proprietors of a rival resort or worse yet, inmates of a state reformatory, Edward Ricker offered fifteen thousand dollars for the property. Seeking a price of fifty thousand dollars, which was still a bargain in their estimation, the Shakers summarily rejected the bid. Leaders of the community believed Poland Hill could "easily be made to exceed the value of the Ricker property," which was estimated at between seven hundred thousand and one million dollars. Apparently no one else saw as much potential in the property, as no other parties met the asking price. Despite an exhaustive sixteen-page pamphlet filled with glowing newspaper accounts, positive personal testimonials, and a favorable scientific water analysis, the "Unusual Real Estate Opportunity" at Upper Shaker Village remained unrealized year after year.[24]

What the Shakers were seeking in this era of "sorting and sifting" was a financial savior like James Sanborn. He was representative of the new breed of farmer sprouting up on the landscape—a wealthy urban businessman for whom agriculture was a leisurely diversion rather than financial livelihood. A native of Greene, Maine, he had made his fortune as a partner in Chase and Sanborn, the Boston-based coffee and tea import company. As "the New England Coffee King" looked homeward for a summer place, the Pulsifer farmstead caught his eye. John Pulsifer, the husband of Janette Ricker's sister, had built up the three-hundred-acre site into one of the largest and most prosperous estates in Poland. Following his uncle's death, Edward Ricker sold the property to Sanborn for four thousand dollars. Within two years, the Coffee King had constructed at the summer home he named Elmwood Farm one of the largest and most attractive barns in New England. This showcase became the place Sanborn retreated to when he preferred: "His country quiet to the city stirs."[25]

Gentleman farmers such as Sanborn advanced the cause of reform by bringing a more scientific approach that transformed their rural estates into "experimental agricultural stations." Thanks to a herd of thoroughbred Holstein cows, most of which Sanborn had imported from Germany, Elmwood produced large quantities of milk. It also annually produced two hundred fifty barrels of apples, sixty tons of hay, and six acres of ensilage corn. The farm achieved its prominence, however, as one of the leading breeders of French coach horses in the United States. The prize of the stable was a bright bay Arabian stallion that Sanborn had purchased for the same price as the entire Elmwood property. The princely sum was worth it, for the thoroughbred possessed an impeccable ancestry, reportedly tracing back ninety-four generations to the most renowned horses of Arabia and North Africa. Over two hundred years of careful breeding had produced Gemare, standing sixteen hands tall, weighing 1,250 pounds, and possessing a symmetrical build, fiery eyes, and an intelligent face with a white star on his forehead.[26]

With his entry into equine breeding, Sanborn was responding to the "earnest" demand of the marketplace for well-bred coach horses. As the Pooles noted with amazement in 1890, there was "no source of supply" for these animals. Aware of what breeders at Elmwood were attempting to accomplish, the brothers anticipated the emergence of "the people's horse." The "horse of the future" would be a cross between native-stock mares and French stallions with blood "clean and straight from the desert" flowing through their veins. In light of the emphasis placed on maintaining pure human bloodlines during the era, it is interesting that "the mingling of the blood of the Arab, Barb, and Thoroughbred" to produce "half-bred French coach carriage horses" was regarded as desirable. The Pooles had high hopes for Elmwood's hybrid equines, predicting that "in a few years the finest carriage-horse in the world and a noble class of roadsters would be seen in our city and on our suburban roadways."[27]

Sanborn expected that some of the best customers for his 150 horses would be the prosperous urban and suburban patrons of the Poland Spring resort, located only three miles from his country estate. Advertisements and articles in the *Hill-Top* hailed the horses offered for sale as stylish, well be-haved, fearless, courageous, durable, and swift—in sum, as ideal candidates to pull a wide variety of carriages. The newspaper earnestly encouraged guests to go to Elmwood, assuring them that they "would find it decidedly interesting to visit the Sanborn stock farm at such times as the horses are on exhibition." Visitors were welcome to watch the animals go through their daily exercise sessions between 10:00 A.M. and 12:00 P.M. any day except Sun-day. To accommodate travel-weary patrons, Sanborn even occasionally ar-ranged to bring a cavalcade of coach horses led by Gemare to Poland Spring. After one such "very attractive exhibition of fancy horse flesh," the *Hill-Top* proclaimed that "the perfect horse is as pretty a piece of animal nature as it is possible to find, and Mr. Sanborn is a true horseman."[28]

"The Very Heart of Life"

Gentleman farmers such as James Sanborn were not alone in having the financial means to operate "model farms" in Poland. During the era of sort-ing and sifting in New England agriculture, the Rickers built up an operation that rivaled Elmwood in scale, if not in kind. Apart from the pastoral refer-ences read in promotional literature, visitors first became aware of the agri-cultural landscape of the resort as the stage brought them past fields of corn on their ascent of Ricker Hill. The importance placed on conveying guests swiftly and comfortably in horse-drawn vehicles, as well as on serving them pure and fresh food, led to the proprietors' conviction that farming was not only one of the "indispensable adjuncts of pleasure and health resorts," but also "the very heart of life."[29]

As the hobby of Sanborn, livery business of the Rickers, and transporta-tion needs of patrons made clear, care of horses was one of the most impor-tant functions of the farm. The main stable was located across the county road from the Mansion House and dated back to 1825 when Wentworth Ricker's inn had catered to stage traffic. In 1887 a "modern" addition measur-ing 125 feet by 40 feet was built on to the older structure. The expanded fa-cility housed all the work and some of the livery horses, much of the harness and tack equipment, as well as the drivers and stable workers. Constructed a few years later, another stable near the Poland Spring House served guests and the Rickers' livery operation. In 1895 the guest stable accommodated nine private carriages and thirty-four private horses. Responsibility for the entire equine department was assigned to Hiram W. Ricker.[30]

Hiram's mettle was tested at the end of August 1894. Wild cries of "Fire! Fire!" rang through the air during the mid-evening hours of Tuesday the twenty-first. The crisis began when a stable hand noticed a small blaze in the hayloft. Flying into action, he aroused the drivers, hostlers, and stable men, who had already retired for the night to rooms above the stable office. The workmen scurried to save what they could, but fueled by eighty tons of hay and gusty winds, the building was soon "a roaring furnace of fire," forcing everyone to flee. Within an hour the structure had largely been reduced to a heap of smoldering ashes. The final death knell was the collapse of the chimney that unleashed a shower of sparks. Fearful that the wind would blow live embers toward the Mansion House, Hiram W. Ricker's private residence, or the nearby woods, men with buckets of water guarded rooftops and patrolled the grounds. Forty people kept a vigil throughout the night and prevented the spread of the disaster.[31]

With the dawn of the new day, the Rickers tallied their losses. Gone were the entire stable, a large collection of valuable harnesses, a substantial supply of hay, two carriages, and twenty-seven horses. Edward Ricker estimated the total loss amounted to fifteen thousand dollars, only two-thirds of which was insured. On Wednesday, Hiram called in replacement horse teams from the surrounding area and headed off to Portland to buy new equipment. By Friday morning, the *Hill-Top* reported that the livery department was back "in complete running order," a remarkable achievement attributed to the fact that "the Rickers spell hustle with a big H." They also hustled with the rebuilding. By the end of the winter, a double stable nearly twice as large as the original had risen phoenix-like from the ashes. Built at a cost of between ten and twelve thousand dollars, the "handsome" new structure included a metal roof and firewalls in an attempt to forestall future conflagrations.[32]

Besides "Equine Poland," another prominent feature of the resort farm was the dairy herd. The cows were kept in a barn located to the southwest of the main stable. This placed the building too close to suit the proprietors of the Wampole Hotel and Spring Company. Demonstrating that the two competitors could cooperate at times, Henry Wampole offered to convey some of his property to the Rickers for one dollar in 1896 if they would agree to move the location of the cow barn well out of view. The memorandum of agreement called for the Rickers to relocate the structure to the nearby Brown property within one year, grass over the old barnyard, build a private way connecting the Ricker and Brown properties, and haul all dressing and swill over the new road. The fifth stipulation gave Wampole the right to approve all the proposed improvements.[33]

The Rickers probably agreed to remove the nuisance for their arch-rival not out of any newfound sense of neighborliness, but rather because they had grand plans for expansion that the old site simply could not accommodate. In 1898 the proprietors of the resort had a massive new Cow Barn built for a dairy herd that had grown to a size ranging from sixty-five to one hundred cows, about fifty of which would be in production at any one time. The herd supplied some of the milk, cream, and butter, whose purity and freshness the culinary department promoted so proudly. In addition, some of the calves were destined "to delight the epicure with sweet and delicate chops of veal." In 1899 milk production from an assortment of registered Aryshires, Jerseys, and Holsteins varied from eight to twenty quarts per animal each day. This amount supplied less than half the four hundred quarts of milk, one hundred quarts of cream, and one hundred fifty pounds of butter consumed daily at Poland Spring. Purchases from local dairy farmers, the Poland Dairy Association, and Boston made up for the shortfall.[34]

Constructed at a cost of seven thousand dollars, the Cow Barn was nearly as expansive as one of the resort's hotels. As was the case with the Bottling Plant, the Rickers were so proud of the barn's modern sanitary conditions that they invited guests to inspect the dairy operation, so long as they did so before five in the morning or after five in the evening. Two Shaker Brothers took up the offer and came to Poland Spring on January 16, 1899, to see the "regal" facility. While walking through the 128-foot-long, 44-foot-wide main portion of the barn, they viewed the milk room and haymows. At the end of this section, an adjoining perpendicular wing, measuring 112 feet long by 42 feet wide, stretched to the left and toward the south. There the two Shaker brothers could have inspected the silo, granary, calf pens, and cow stalls, which gave the facility the appearance of royal luxury. Returning outside, the visitors would have noticed that the area between the two wings was fenced off to form a large barnyard. Beyond the barn complex, a separate building housed the creamery. "Numerous keepers in their clean white coats" kept the area so tidy that a delightful odor reportedly filled the air. Inspectors from the State Board of Health were duly impressed. Giving the dairy herd clean bills of health in both 1896 and 1897, the board praised the "fine cow barn" as an example of "the best modern practice" that all "intelligent and progressive" dairymen should adopt.[35]

The new Cow Barn was constructed in 1898 on property made available by rival hotel proprietor Henry K. Wampole. The move placed the pastoral landscape on the fringes rather than at the center of the resort landscape. *Maine Historic Preservation Commission.*

A similar sense of order and efficiency could be found amid the gardens, orchards, and fields. With nearly two hundred fifty acres available for agricultural purposes, the Rickers set aside twelve acres for potato fields, an acre and a half for a squash patch, and eight acres for assorted other garden vegetables. An eight-acre orchard yielded a thousand barrels of apples. Another eighteen acres were planted in oats. Much of the remaining farmland was used for pasturage and hay. In 1898 the hayfields produced 225 tons.[36]

Overseeing the operation of the farm was Alvan Ricker. The middle son of Hiram and Janette Ricker differed from his older and younger brothers in both appearance and demeanor. Save for a modest moustache, clean-shaven Alvan was "The Ricker Without Whiskers." Edward and Hiram had very public roles at the resort and were remembered as being perfect gentlemen. The middle brother, in contrast, labored behind the scenes and earned a reputation for being "a rough talking man" given to "unrestrained use of cusswords." Nevertheless, a "directing mind" and "exceptional memory for details" well suited him for the vital and difficult task of making sure enough food

was supplied and prepared to serve several hundred patrons three sumptuous meals a day. Reportedly, the so-called "Commissary-General of Poland
Spring" conducted the farm operations "with the regularity of clock work."[37]

Alvan Ricker gained his martial moniker and reputation for profanity
from his dealings with the workers under his command. "A.B." supervised between eleven and twenty farmhands, who tended vegetable gardens and fruit
orchards, sowed and harvested corn, oat, and hay fields, shepherded sheep,
tended the stables, slopped the hogs, and cared for the dairy herd. His lieu-
tenant was his only son, George. The *Hill-Top* reported in 1899 that although
the boy was only nine years old, he was already familiar with all aspects of the
farm, down to where every seed was planted. George's cousins, Charles and
Hiram W. Ricker, Jr., also took an interest in the work. In the summer of
1901, they laid out a thirty-by-fifty-foot garden in which they planted a variety of vegetables. The young entrepreneurs sold the first few quarts of peas
to their parents. With their ambitions whetted, the boys moved on to sell
beet greens to the hotel kitchens and cucumbers to the Lewiston market. Impressed by the involvement of the next generation in the affairs of the resort,
the resort newspaper confidently predicted that "there is little likelihood of
the place passing from the Ricker name for many, many years."[38]

As the nineteenth century drew to a close, the sorting and sifting process
in agriculture continued. Still languishing on the market, the Shaker farm on
Poland Hill attracted the attention of several potential gentlemen farmers
from large cities. In 1895 two men from New York, General W. N. Coles and
Henry A. Spaulding, the latter of whom had recently retired from a career as
a renowned international jewelry merchant, came to Poland to look at the
site. A year later, J. W. Thompson of Philadelphia paid the Shakers five hundred dollars for a six-month option to buy the property. Elder William Du-
mont had offered first option to the Rickers, but they had declined on the
grounds that they had "their hands full." In 1899 Elder William tried to
push the sale of Poland Hill along by sending a sample of Shaker Crystal
Spring Water to the former owners of one of the local canning companies.
Even more enticing, the community dropped the price of the property all the
way down to twelve thousand dollars. Nevertheless, none of the interested
parties was willing yet to make the Shakers a final offer.[39]

The possible sale of Poland Hill did rekindle the concerns and interest of
the Rickers. In February of 1899, Edward and Hiram called at the Shaker village to discuss buying the property. After three weeks of negotiations, the
trustees of the community agreed to the proposed terms—$7,500 at 6 per-

cent interest to be paid over ten years, plus the Shakers had to throw in another pasture on Range Hill bringing the total transfer to 644 acres. Three months later on May 26, 1899, both parties signed the agreement that had been a dozen years in the making. In this one corner of Poland, the sorting and sifting was finally over. The Shaker farm had at last become incorporated into the Rickers' resort empire.[40]

About six weeks after the transaction, the *Hill-Top* proudly announced the transfer and offered some insight as to what might be in store for the property, particularly for the massive stone house. In the near future, the new owners planned to "astonish the annual visitor to Poland Spring by inviting him to step inside a magnificently equipped electric palace car, and a minute later emerge in front of this ancient edifice which they will have transformed into something luxuriant and beautiful." That never came to pass, but Poland Hill did hold great agricultural value for the Rickers. Under the family's management, the former Shaker farm supplied the resort with apples and potatoes. Eventually, it housed a piggery with a capacity of two hundred fifty hogs and a hen house quartering two hundred Rhode Island Reds. As for the Shaker dwelling house, it became home to the farm help instead of a palace for resort patrons.[41]

Lapping the Cream of Country Life Without the Milking

The transaction between the Rickers and the Shakers exemplified the new reality of agriculture in New England during the late nineteenth century. Marginal farms were either being abandoned or consolidated with more successful ones. Agriculture was becoming ever more competitive and commercial. Nevertheless, promoters of the Poland Spring resort perpetuated an idealized depiction of the countryside that masked the changes taking place. This disconnection between the pastoral ideal and commercial reality of agriculture epitomized what Hal S. Barron has described as "the divergence of urban and rural culture during the second half of the nineteenth century." Ironically, the Rickers heightened the disjunction between antimodern image and modern reality by promoting the pastoral landscape even as the tourist industry contributed to the further modernization of agriculture and transformation of rural America.[42]

The program of pastoral preservation took many forms at Poland Spring. Inviting guests to "walk down through the 'farm' in front of the Hotel" or to seek out the lambs in the pasture or to admire a three-and-a-half-pound potato on display were among the ways the Rickers highlighted the agricultural dimension of the resort landscape. Byron P. Moulton, a regular visitor from Philadelphia, took the invitation even further. Moulton was yet another patron with a Lapham-like pedigree that spanned from humble birth in Vermont to "his keen insight and ready recognition" in later life that "his progress and prosperity" lay in "the opportunities of large cities." Given this background, a summer vacation at Poland Spring represented for Moulton the ideal opportunity to get back to his agrarian roots. As the *Hill-Top* reported in 1894, the former farmer boy was "exceedingly proud of his skill with the scythe and can cut a fine swath." Despite the pride this purely nostalgic exercise inspired, the skill exhibited was of little value to modern farmers who now for the most part used mowing machines to cut their hay.[43]

For those guests more inclined to spend their time reading a newspaper on the veranda than swinging a scythe in a field, the *Hill-Top* periodically recalled pastoral scenes from the agrarian past. The author of an 1897 article fondly remembered the "happy days" of health and comfort he had spent on Uncle Nat's farm working in the hayfields, clambering about the great beams of the old barn, and sleeping in the "pleasant old farmhouse." The following year, the paper reminisced about the carefree days of youth when boys would race a pet lamb from a farmhouse down to a dusty roadside and back again. An editorial on the charm of country roads that appeared several years later invoked the image of a newly abandoned farm to recall "happier days" when the owners husked corn and sipped cider.[44]

To recapture the nostalgia of the vanishing rural past, the resort newspaper promoted "Old Home Week." Originated by the citizens of Portsmouth, New Hampshire, in 1853 as a way of getting people who had moved away to return for a visit, the success of the innovation prompted the state of Maine to institute its own version of community reunions in 1900. While there was no formal celebration at the resort, the concept underlying old home week—luring the country-born members of the urban middle and upper classes back to their virtuous rural roots—did attract many guests to Poland Spring. Crosby Noyes, for one, stayed at the resort in 1900 because it provided him with the chance to be "among his native hills, and the scenes he loved when a boy." Born and raised on a farm in nearby Minot, Maine, he went on to become the publisher of the *Evening Star*, the "most influential newspaper in Washington." Noyes returned to the resort again the next year to attend the reunion of the school he had attended as a child.[45]

In 1902 Noyes made what was becoming an annual sojourn to Poland Spring in order to participate in Minot's centennial celebration. In his address at the event, he described his birthplace as a farming community surrounded by the "beauties of nature" and populated by families "from the sterling old Puritan stock." The combination of the natural environment and Puritan heritage found there and in the other towns of "the little southwest corner of Maine" produced, according to Noyes, "a mighty host of able and worthy men." Among others, he had in mind Hiram Ricker. Noyes praised the patriarch of the family for having built "the best hotel in the world," featuring "the great essentials of good air, good water, good food, and good attendance." He attributed this impressive achievement not only to the assistance of Janette Ricker and the couple's three sons, but also to "the never-say-die grit of the southwest Maine Yankee."[46]

Another program designed to celebrate the true grit of country life and bridge the growing gulf between rural and urban America was the "Fresh Air" fund. This charity raised money to send poor children on vacations from the city to the country. It was a trip whose benefits the patrons of Poland Spring knew well; consequently, they supported the cause generously. In August 1899 the Superintendent of the Boston City Missionary Society came to the resort and preached on the "fresh air" ministry. After his sermon, guests donated over four hundred dollars to cover the cost of bringing "a large number of poor and sick people summer recreation." Two years later, the same solicitation raised over six hundred dollars. Patrons of the resort also supported the "Country Week" program sponsored by the Boston Young Men's Christian Union (YMCU). This organization provided the urban poor with the opportunity for rest and recreation at "some proper place in the country or by the seashore." The program had the added feature of bringing city dwellers and country folks into direct contact with one another by placing participants with host families.[47]

As a way for guests to experience direct contact with the agrarian landscape and recapture "all the blessed memories of early days," the Hill-Top recommended carriage rides through "quiet country places." Trips to Pope's dog kennels or Sanborn's horse farm were popular destinations. Further to the north in Oxford, Maine, lay an inviting pastoral scene filled with farmhouses, frolicsome calves, orchard trees, barn cats, and pasture walls. Meanwhile, journeys through Poland featured sights of fields, fences, and farmhouses that seemed as though they had been there "all the time"; sounds of tinkling bells emanating from cow pastures; and smells of new-mown hay, clover, and ripening fruit. The setting was said to have the potential to invigorate visitors, as well as to inspire poets and artists.[48]

One author who was inspired by the agricultural landscape surrounding the hilltop was Jane Patterson. Her novel contained many nostalgic pastoral references to rickety barns, haymakers whetting their scythes, enjoyable hayrick rides, fields of delicious sweet corn, and the old-time smell of fresh-cut hay. The sentiment that Patterson sought to convey was best expressed by one character in particular, Charles Raynor. Soon after his arrival at the Poland Spring–like resort, Raynor observes that "these rural places nurture the virtues." "They draw life from the virgin soil, as the trees do," he continues. Lamenting that "the vicinity of cities is soon glossed over by the hand of cultivation," attorney Raynor goes on to wish that his chosen profession would permit him to live in the country.[49]

Other commentators also used the venue of Poland Spring to link virtue with the geography of the countryside. The author of *Poland Spring Centennial* asserted that a byproduct of the Rickers' forest farm was the family's "sturdy, rugged New England stock, inbred in the soil, hard working, persistent, energetic, alert, enterprising." Journalist Arthur Staples concurred with this assessment. He described the Rickers as a "stout old family that got their fibre and fullness of life off a hill-top on a farm of granitic substratum." He especially complimented Edward Ricker who had grown up calculating when the ground would be dry enough "to sow our grain." Staples characterized his friend as an old-fashioned, hardworking farm boy, possessing the thoughtfulness, resourcefulness, purposefulness, and vision to see beyond "the tops of his potato-patches."[50]

The *Hill-Top* used similar pastoral rhetoric when it lauded Maine Grange official Solon Chase as "a product of the soil, a typical Yankee, honest, energetic, and earnest." By this time, the octogenarian from Turner was a relic of the "lean and hungry years" of Maine agriculture that had followed the Panic of 1873. Chase had advocated inflation of the money supply as the solution to plummeting farm prices and had run for governor in 1882 as the nominee of the Greenback Party. One of his staple stump speeches on the campaign trail had been "Them Steers." To illustrate the effect of deflation, Chase would bring a yoke of oxen to a rally and then explain that he would be hard pressed to receive fifty dollars for steers he had purchased for one hundred dollars. More than two decades later, Chase was still giving the speech, but now as a quaint pastoral relic for the entertainment of cosmopolitan resort patrons rather than as a populist politician for the edification of beset local farmers.[51]

Another sign of the changing times was "them steers" of Cyrus A. Leach. This enterprising showman from Casco brought his famous trained steers to the hilltop and put on exhibitions in front of the Poland Spring House. The animals had learned many maneuvers. They could stand with all four hooves on a tub, walk the plank, seesaw, and jump over one another. When the tricks were done, they posed for photographs to the delight of the resort's amazed and appreciative patrons. After a few decades of sorting and sifting in agriculture, the mighty steer had been reduced by progress from a puller of pine trees, ploughs, and carts to a performer at exhibits and fairs and most revealing of all, to a subject of photography "like all notables."[52]

Amid the mix of commerce and circus that was the new reality of modern agriculture at the Poland Spring resort, the pastoralist project to validate the virtues of old-time farm life continued. One of the most prolific promoters of rural nostalgia at the turn of the century was Charles Asbury Stephens. From his home in Norway, C. A. Stephens wrote about the country life he had experienced as a boy growing up in the western part of the state at mid-century. Set in "a typical Maine farming community" of the 1860s during a time "when life was simpler," his Old Squire stories followed the homely romance and wholesome adventures of a "wonderfully harmonious family circle."[53]

In a typical display of the pastoral nostalgia Stephens was so adept at evoking, one of those adventures brought three plucky youths to Poland Spring in 1867. Against the advice of the wise Old Squire, whose "weather eye" detected an approaching storm, Addison, Theodora, and Kit planned to embark on one of the mid-century trading trips to Portland the Poole brothers had described. The children's load included dried apples, eggs, oats, butter, preserved plums, knit socks and mittens, dried sage, and coriander seed. In tow behind the cart, eight Durham veal calves pulled up the rear. The goal of the journey was for the children to earn enough money to pay their tuition at the local academy. Times were hard, however. Farm prices were falling and "nobody seemed willing to part with money." Armed only with "faith in the future," the siblings set out on the sixty-mile trek. The traveling party made it as far as the Mansion House before the onset of a drenching northeast rainstorm. In a display of old-fashioned neighborliness, Hiram Ricker, a boyhood friend of the Old Squire, came to the rescue of the rain-soaked youngsters. He put them up for the night before the continuation of an adventure that included troubles with runaway calves, an encounter with thieving gypsies, and the kidnapping of Addison on the way to the big city.[54]

Although they lacked access to the adventurous narratives permitted to authors by literary license, artists were also important promoters of the pastoral ideal. One of the most accomplished and notable visual recorders of the rural landscapes of Northern New England was Stephens's contemporary, Delbert Dana Coombs. A native of New Gloucester, D. D. Coombs had a close relationship with the Rickers. In addition to designing water bottle labels for the family, he regularly displayed the cattle paintings, for which he had "received considerable distinction," at the resort's art exhibitions. The *Hill-Top* praised the artist as "an excellent painter of the pastoral," adding that "his cattle live and move in green pastures, so naturally does he treat his subjects." Guests thought highly of his creations, too. His appropriately titled "In Green Pastures" was the first painting ever sold at the Poland Spring art gallery. When the friends of Mr. and Mrs. James Sanborn went looking two years later for the perfect housewarming gift for the couple's new home at Elmwood, they also selected a Coombs painting. It was just one more of "his cows" that could be found "adorning the walls of many an elegant Maine residence." [55]

The Rickers so esteemed Coombs's work that they commissioned the artist to paint one of his pastoral landscapes for permanent display at the resort. Completed in 1896 at a cost of two hundred dollars, "Ricker Hill" measured four by six feet and presented an interesting perspective from a hillside located across Middle Range Pond. In the immediate foreground, the artist's trademark cows lay contentedly. In the distant background, stood the stately resort, represented most prominently by the Poland Spring House. It looked like some palace in a pasture, like some faraway city upon a hill. The image of pastoral tranquility may have been appealing to the proprietors and patrons of the hotel and the direction of the gaze may have been revealing, but by reversing the order of agriculture and tourism, the picture distorted the prevailing trend in the local economy.[56]

Coombs did eventually record more accurately the transformation he was witnessing. In 1907 he sold a second large Poland Spring landscape to the Rickers for three hundred dollars. Entitled "Calling the Cows," this time the vantage was from the grounds of the resort. Once again, the foreground focused on cattle in a pasture, but in this scene, buildings — the Cow Barn and the Poland Spring House — loomed large in the background. In addition, the artist included two tiny figures, the farm workers who were in charge of calling the cows. Their obscurity amid the dozens of cows, the massive buildings, and the expansive landscape encompassed by the painting made an im-

D. D. Coombs painted "Calling the Cows" in 1907. The Rickers purchased his depiction of the pastoral landscape, which featured in the background the Cow Barn on the left and the Poland Spring House on the right. (From a post card of the painting.) *Maine Historic Preservation Commission.*

portant statement about the insignificance of their labor. Generally, hard work was one of the values celebrated by pastoralists. Coombs, however, understood his urban audience. Notwithstanding Byron Moulton's brief foray into the hayfield, the closest most members of the leisure class wanted to get to farm work was a picture on a wall. The landscape of leisure had supplanted the landscape of labor. A 1921 *Hill-Top* editorial summed up the transformation of the agricultural countryside of the farmer into the pastoral middle landscape of the tourist in memorable metaphorical terms: "visitors may lap all the cream of country life and do none of the milking."[57]

Actually, the *Hill-Top* became attuned to the excessive romanticism of the pastoral outlook much earlier than the 1920s. In the midst of another Old Home Week celebration in 1903, the paper scoffed at the notion that olden days, when nine out of ten people lived on a farm, could have been so good, noting that seven out of ten of those farms were now abandoned. Furthermore, it wondered with bemusement why painters and photographers went "into raptures over the dilapidated, tumble-down structure" rather than

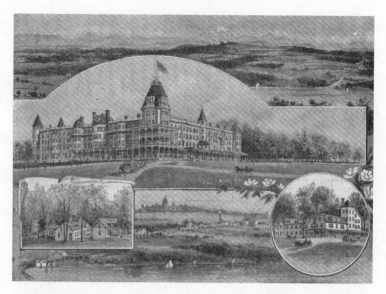

This montage of the built and natural environments that made up the middle landscape of the resort appeared in several travel guidebooks produced during the 1890s by "descriptive writer" George H. Haynes. *Sources: George H. Haynes,* The Charming Inland Retreats of Maine *(Portland, Maine: Self-published, 1890), 6;* Maine's Health, Pleasure and Sporting Resorts *(New York: A. H. Kellogg, 1894);* Specimens of Illustrations in Books Written by Geo. H. Haynes, Descriptive Writer *(Portland, Maine: Self-published, 1893), [5]; and* The State of Maine, in 1893 *(New York: Moss Engraving Company, 1893), 40. Courtesy Androscoggin Historical Society.*

seeking out "an architecturally fine, well-kept set of farm buildings." Finally, the periodical ridiculed the stock figure of Old Home Week stories. It dismissed the rich moralist who stood before the ruins of a farmhouse ready to trade his oil and railroad bonds for the happy days of his youth when as a barefooted boy, he had herded cows, hunted woodchucks, attended the red schoolhouse, and run off to see the circus. At least momentarily, reality triumphed over sentimentality in the pages of the *Hill-Top.* The clock had stuck midnight on another masquerade of antimodernity at Poland Spring.[58]

The pervasive, persistent, and deep-rooted appeal of pastoralism could not be reined in so easily. Even as the sorting and sifting process in agriculture and the rural migration to cities continued unabated during the opening decades of the twentieth century, nostalgia for a simpler past, romance for a pastoral landscape, and belief in the enduring virtues of agrarian republicanism retained their cultural power. While the allure of rural life faded away for many farm families, demonstrations by Byron Moulton and Cyrus Leach, speeches by Crosby Noyes and Solon Chase, books by Jane Patterson and C. A. Stephens, and paintings by D. D. Coombs kept the image very much alive for the urban patrons of Poland Spring. So, too, did the Ricker family's country farm on the hilltop. In this middle landscape, the leisure class enthusiastically lapped the cream of country life without actually having to live it. Patrons participated in a similar masquerade of antimodernity in the process of incorporating the natural surroundings of Poland Spring into the middle landscape of the resort.

7

The Grounds

"Out of a Country Farm an Eden"

In the view of the people of progress, the landscape of Poland Spring in 1860 consisted of a collection of natural resources awaiting development. Wood-cutters felled pine trees to clear land and produce lumber. Farmers plowed fields on which to raise corn and potatoes. Mill owners dammed the outlet of Middle Range Pond and the waters of the Little Androscoggin River to supply power for grinding grain and sawing clapboards. And, of course, Hiram Ricker bottled spring water to heal the sick. Given such a thoroughly utilitarian view of the environment, its potential as natural landscape whose aesthetic beauty might possess commercial value was scarcely imaginable. Over the next four decades, the Rickers and the urban clientele they served came to adopt a new view of nature. They regarded it not only as a collection of resources to process and consume, but also as scenes to view and contemplate, moments to experience and enjoy, and assets to promote and preserve. In the process, they did not simply discover nature. They constructed it into an Edenic middle landscape.[1]

At first glance, the new natural landscape of Poland Spring looked more antimodern than middling. Publicists for the resort promoted nature's timeless temporal permanence, aesthetic beauty, therapeutic healthfulness, and spiritual inspiration principally, and related issues such as regional identity, sensory stimulation, romantic innocence, and contemplative solitude collaterally. Cleverly, each characteristic of the new nature stood in contrast to the corresponding characteristics of the Gilded-Age city, with its incessant change, architectural artifice, contagious disease, rampant materialism, imposing anonymity, aesthetic blandness, cosmopolitan pretension, and constant commotion. It was not the message, therefore, that introduced the machine into the garden. It was the modern media and means the Rickers employed to promote and purvey nature that revealed the masquerade of antimodernism. As the ax gave way to the pen, the plow to the paintbrush, and the saw to the camera, a host of resort promoters used modern communication methods to turn utilitarian nature into romantic Nature. For their part, the Rickers furnished a variety of ways to experience this blend of two natures that contributed to the creation of the resort's middle landscape. Guests could admire pastures and fields from coaches and carriages, mountains and hills from the veranda, flora and fauna along wooded paths, grounds and gardens from boardwalks, ponds and lakes aboard the steam launch, and flowers and plants in the greenhouse.

The Edenic view of nature, which produced this socially constructed "tourist landscape," owed its origin to the influence of romanticism. Inspired by the European romantic movement, many American authors and artists produced works throughout the nineteenth century that brought the aesthetic qualities of nature to the foreground. The grandeur, sublimity, and picturesqueness they recorded in their creations were intended to remind readers and viewers of the divinity of God's creation. For many people, the return to nature represented the restoration of the link between the mundane manmade and the sacred natural worlds that the artificiality of modern urban industrial life had eroded. In such a mind-set, experiencing nature often took on moral implications. The back-to-nature movement spawned by the ideology led Americans, especially those who resided in cities, to watch birds, read nature books, camp in wilderness parks, and even vacation at scenic resorts. Subtly but effectively, travel promoters played upon the new Arcadian view to objectify and commodify nature.[2]

The Message: "This Land of Heavenly Favors"

Short of having inherited real estate along the coast, the Rickers could hardly have been blessed with a more ideal location for a successful summer resort. In addition to the health and wealth-giving spring, Ricker Hill also featured groves of oak and maple, as well as stands of pine that covered much of its eastern slope. At the base of the north side of the hill were Upper, Middle, and Lower Range Ponds. Rising eight hundred feet above sea level, the hilltop provided a commanding view of the surrounding landscape. In the immediate vicinity, an undulating countryside of broad fields and rocky pastures rolled toward distant hills and mountains. Plainly visible were nearby Black Cat and Rattlesnake Mountains, plus Shaker and White Oak Hills. Farther away rose the Oxford Hills to the north and Ossipee Hills to the southwest. By defining nature, describing its attributes, and detailing how it should be approached, promoters set about constructing from this raw material a "land of heavenly favors."[3]

Typically in publicity about the Poland Spring resort, nature meant visually attractive scenery. This came in five forms. The first was the landscape of the hilltop, whose main features included the lawns, gardens, trees, and spring, as well as the surrounding diversified and charming patchwork of fields and forests that receded in waves toward the hill country. The Rickers had a hand in shaping these settings and guests spent most of their time in this realm of nature. Expanding out in concentric circles from Ricker Hill were three different panoramas: the hillsides, ponds, and mountains. In general, the western foothills exhibited "dignity and rugged grandeur"; while the pine-covered Oxford Hills stood as a reminder of "the rugged mental timber" the natural environment had bestowed upon the region's inhabitants. Tucked within this territory were scores of lakes, including the three local ponds. On the distant western horizon, the peaks of the White Mountains appeared like the "jagged teeth of a giant saw." Overarching the topography of the region was the spherical dome of the sky, where the interplay of sun and clouds created an ever-changing light show of kaleidoscopic beauty.[4]

Nature was also defined by what it was not in the eyes of the resort's promoters. Given their preference for superficial mediated encounters with natural surroundings, wilderness settings were of little interest to most patrons of Poland Spring. Few visitors wanted to test their mettle against the elements or their wits against game. They were quite content to distance their contacts with wild animals. Thus, they watched sedately as deer grazed along the road to Danville and robins dashed across the lawn at the resort. In addition, they listened contentedly as bees buzzed about flowers and crickets chirped in the grass. Befriending the chipmunks Skip and Trip or the duo of Tom the turtle and Jerry the toad provided sufficient proximity to wildlife for these urban rusticators. Most guests preferred a tame and domesticated middle landscape, where primeval forests had been turned into shady groves, wild flowers were arranged into attractive bouquets, hunts were discussed with visiting Indians, game was mounted on walls, and even the lowly sumac was exalted as a thing of beauty.[5]

Guests such as William H. Wingate of Boston, who yearned for wilderness, represented the exception rather than the rule. After his stay at Poland Spring during the summer of 1894, Wingate made his annual camping trip to Northern Maine. There he successfully hunted moose, including the one whose head eventually came to hang above the fireplace in the rotunda of the Maine State Building. The *Hill-Top* directed parties interested in bagging big game to take the Bangor and Aroostook Railroad to the northernmost region of Maine. In Aroostook County, the paper reported, "the moose and caribou are so plentiful, you almost have to push them apart." Indicating the quarry the leisure class more routinely hunted during the Gilded Age, the periodical also advised adventurers to outfit themselves with fashionable furs and sealskins before heading out on their wilderness expeditions.[6]

Guests who wanted to experience wilder forms of nature less adventurously could travel to the Rangeley Lakes. Advertised as offering "Every Condition of Nature that is conducive to the creation of contentment," the region had developed a reputation for the excellence of its fishing and hunting. A large part of the appeal came from the ease and comfort with which sightseers and sportsmen could travel to this wilderness outpost. In August 1901, thirty Poland Spring patrons led by Mrs. Hugh Chisholm went to Poland Corner where they boarded a special Portland and Rumford Falls rail car that took the party on a memorable journey. After a four-hour ride through a pastoral landscape of prosperous farms and primal scenes of wild beauty, the group arrived at Bemis, Maine, on the southern end of Lake Mooselookmeguntic. Aboard the steamer *Florence E. Barker*, the contingent admired the lake, gazed at the surrounding mountains, watched for deer and bear, and checked out the camps at the Birches.[7]

Following the wilderness excursion to "Poland on the Rangeleys," the party headed home, but not before making a stop at Rumford Falls to see the epitome of the industrial harnessing of nature's bounty. As the visitors watched "the angry waters of the Androscoggin" send logs tumbling over the spectacular series of three falls, they saw what Hiram Ricker and Francis Smith had recognized long ago. Nature had "endowed this place with one of the best water powers in the State." During a tour of the local paper mill, the group observed the miraculous mechanical transformation of logs and pulp into bags and newsprint. The *Hill-Top* credited the "marvelous" progress on display to one person — Hugh Chisholm, the man who had founded an industrial city in the wilderness of Maine. After traveling from the outskirts of wild nature to the heart of its industrial counterpart, the excursionists returned to the Poland Spring resort and settled back into the middle landscape of Edenic nature. Thanks to the ultimate Gilded-Age machine in the garden — the train — they had made the whirlwind tour through the wide range of western Maine landscapes in less than half a day.[8]

Having determined the parameters of acceptable nature, promoters of the resort next set out to describe its leading attributes. During an age of rapid and revolutionary progress exemplified by Chisholm's transformation of Rumford Falls from forest wilderness to integral part of the International Paper trust, the fundamental appeal of romantic nature was its permanence. A pamphlet promoting the Poland Spring House paid homage to nature as an enduring and powerfully creative historical force. "She" had moved the primeval rock that formed the noble hilltop, sifted the rich soil that created the primitive forest, and opened the marvelous springs that supplied the lovely Range Ponds. Looking around at all feminine nature had borne, the *Hill-Top* wondered whether the "delicate texture" of a far away hillside had been there for all time. Similarly, the topic of country roads reminded the resort newspaper of highways lined with pine trees that had "stood guard, and watched the coming and the going of generations." Even in decay, the ghostly outline of an ancient pine stump conjured up "the majesty of its original grandeur." While these elements of the environment changed with the seasons and aged with time, "Dame Nature" was portrayed as a wise old lady who never grew older.[9]

The dame's ageless and seductive beauty was another quality that commended her to lovers of nature. The infatuation commenced with the addition of the Poland Spring House to the built environment. After touring the new facility, a local journalist pronounced that the views were of the "very finest order." The site commanded "most sweeping panoramas of ponds, streams, cities, villages and the fresh country side." From the veranda, visitors could see as far as the White Mountains to the northwest; while from the top of the hotel's six-story tower, they could gaze all the way to Casco Bay and the Atlantic Ocean to the southeast. In back of the building stood the visually pleasing stands of oak and pine that carried refreshing "out-of-door air" through the hotel corridors. Because of this natural diversity, the reporter recommended the resort as the ideal destination "for Lewiston and Auburn folks, hankering for a drive or a day's siesta." Furthermore, he predicted on the eve of the opening of the Poland Spring House that the beauty of the scenery," plus "the popularity of the Springs," would make the hotel a financial success.[10]

The changing seasons added to the diverse beauty of the natural landscape. During the summer, splendid sunshine, pure tonic air, fresh breezes, bowing daisies, dreamy blue mountains, and enchanting skies were "among the many joys of beautiful Poland" that might greet "the faithful pilgrim to the Mecca of the Pine Tree State." Autumn brought forth scenes likened to "a picture upon an artist's easel"—clear mountain ranges, multicolored leaves, bountiful corn stacks, plentiful pumpkin piles, and the luminous harvest moon. With winter came new "transcendent beauty" for viewing by the hardy guests who visited the Mansion House during the off-season. Boughs weighed down by snow and branches coated with ice produced a "symphony in white" and reflected "iridescent light."[11]

Another way promoters touted the magnificence of the site's natural beauty was by comparing it to other well-known tourist attractions. The earliest boasts about Poland Spring claimed its pre-eminence in the constellation of New England resorts. Over time the points of comparison ranged farther afield and the claims became bolder. By 1887 a pamphlet maintained that the hilltop commanded views of "one of the most beautiful and diversified landscapes" on the entire American continent. It also favorably compared the Range Ponds to Loch Katrine in Scotland. For the wife of art photographer Louis Alman, the view from the veranda of the Poland Spring House was reminiscent of an Italian landscape. The *Hill-Top* weighed in with its opinion that the scenery rivaled the lake country of Ireland and Switzerland. The latter country eventually became the highest standard of scenic comparison for inland American resorts. Thus, it was with great community pride that Louise M. Waterhouse's centennial poem, "Greetings to Poland," proclaimed to the world: "A Switzerland of America is here."[12]

Beauty, either in splendid aesthetic isolation or in self-promotional geographic comparison, was not a sufficiently redeeming quality of nature. Quite to the contrary, the *Hill-Top* warned in 1894 that man could not "find complete enjoyment . . . in feeding the aesthetic sense alone." The paper, therefore, also preached the therapeutic value of nature—its capacity to improve both the mental and physical health of true disciples. An article revealingly entitled "A Summer Shrine" advised readers that they needed to appease "the cravings of the inner man" and enjoy "every-day comforts" in order to appreciate most keenly the "manifold beauties of nature." Readers were called upon "to forget the care and turmoil of the outside world, and to study the harmonies of nature." Moreover, they were instructed to exchange "the impediments of daily toil" for "the garb of pleasure pilgrims." The article recommended several selections from the resort's varied menu of middle landscape offerings in the pursuit of "inspiriting restfulness." Guests could go on carriage rides. They could read in a shady nook on the veranda. Or, they might choose to muse beneath the shade trees at the spring. Finally, they could listen to the symphony of singing birds, or admire the lily pond, oak groves, and forest glens.[13]

Besides its ability to bring about mental relief, nature was believed to be physically beneficial, and not only because of the medicinal properties attributed to the mineral water. Few sources failed to link Poland Spring to the healing powers of nature. An 1887 pamphlet promoted the resort as a shrine where patients could receive the medicinal ministrations of nature. Several years later, Henry and George Poole pointed to Maine's "health-giving and restoring climate" as one of the prime attractions of the hilltop. Another history of Poland published in 1890 cited the combination of "the magic virtues of the water, the loveliness of the scenery, and the purity of the air" as additional natural blessings. Singling out the fresh country air, an 1897 *Hill-Top* editorial claimed that its "invigorating effect" made "the weak become strong, and the well, stronger." In its tribute to the therapeutic effects of nature, "A Summer Shrine" prescribed a regimen consisting of drafts of mineral water from bubbling fountains, breaths of the pure air of the hills, and gazes upon "the beauty and grandeur of the surrounding landscape" as the basis for good health.[14]

Attention to the healthful value of nature also gave rise to emphasis on the spiritual dimensions of the middle landscape. Descriptions of Poland Spring as a heaven, shrine, paradise, Eden, and "Mecca of many a summer pilgrimage" reflected the strong religious connection many patrons made between the resort and its natural surroundings. Many nineteenth-century vacationers regarded tourist attractions as sacred places that offered contact with transcendent reality, the hope of physical regeneration, and the promise of spiritual renewal, often "through the aid of a sacred or medicinal spring." These elements formed the essence of nature's appeal to many of the guests who came to Poland Spring to absolve "their citified souls." The scenic and medicinal gifts of nature provided access to the full range of therapeutic well-being—physical healing, mental relief, and spiritual rejuvenation.[15]

In addition to defining and describing the attributes of nature, promoters of the resort detailed for patrons how they should approach it. The *Hill-Top* did much of the work preparing the people of progress for their encounters with the outdoors. Of primary importance was readying the senses. According to the paper, the power of nature lay in the ability of scenery to activate the eyes, nose, ears, tongue, and skin. An editorial suggested that what made the day after a period of cloud and mist so perfect was the delight the beauties of nature brought to the senses. While sight was most often used, there were other ways to perceive surroundings. Nature lovers could smell the perfume of the pine and hemlock, hear the twitter of birds, taste the freshness of the air, and feel the texture of the ripening berry. The result of such sensory experiences, readers were instructed, was supposed to be the feeling of joy.[16]

Besides instinctive senses, the *Hill-Top* called for the application of deeper mental faculties to gain a true understanding of nature. Key to this was a sense of innocence. Singled out as models for imitation were children with their perceived innate appreciation of nature. Young enough to be largely free from the conventions of "civilized usage," children were admired for their ability to approach natural surroundings with simplicity. For the young, the outdoors was a vast playground where they could splash in puddles, jump from stone to stone, walk upon fence rails, picnic in open air, camp out beneath pines, play house on a rock ledge, and "enjoy their innocent games without fear of molestation or annoyance." As the paper wistfully and nostalgically remarked, "there is a charm about the woods the town can never wholly eradicate, and those who never made mud pies have lost a sweet and simple pleasure of their lives." Promoters of the resort implied that patrons could rediscover such natural simplicity at Poland Spring.[17]

Realizing that most guests had long ago lost the innocence of youth and outgrown appreciation of nature, the *Hill-Top* encouraged them at least to become reacquainted with its serenity. An 1898 article invited readers to check out a pine grove on the shores of Lower Range Pond "where solitude dwells." "Away from the click of golf clubs, or the clatter of non-desuetudinous tongues," the paper asserted, quiet reigned as it had since aboriginal times. Adding to the spot's loveliness was the fact that such "obnoxious" mediators of nature as pagodas, swings, and merry-go-rounds built by the "improving hand of man" had not despoiled the hideaway. Unlike so much of the middle landscape of the resort, the secluded spot remained an untouched, although not entirely unmediated, place of peacefulness, gentleness, and calmness.[18]

The Media: "Nature and Art, Art and Nature"

In addition to the omnipresent *Hill-Top*, the Rickers employed a variety of other media to advance the message of escape from the hectic artificial cityscapes of the urban Northeast to the restful natural landscape of rural Maine. Pamphlets, poems, paintings, photographs, and lectures each conveyed messages about nature's manifold virtues. Through these media, the promoters of the resort staked out "the aesthetic proprietorship of nature." To mask their essentially antimodern construction of nature, the Rickers relied ironi-

cally on modern means of mass communication. Out of this curious alchemy
of antimodernity and modernity, of preservation and promotion, of romanticism and commercialism, of nature and art came the tourist landscape, the
distinctive middle landscape that made the resort such an appealing Eden to
so many Gilded-Age tourists.[19]

Supplementing the ubiquitous weekly resort newspaper were the annual
water and hotel catalogs pressed into service to promote the joys of nature.
To fill out the 1890 edition of a pamphlet heralding the attractions of Poland
Spring, the Rickers called upon William Murray to contribute an essay. This
former Congregationalist minister brought great expertise to the project.
Drawing upon his vacation experiences in northern New York, he had written *Adventures in the Wilderness* in 1869 and then taken up a new career as a
travel writer. In his work for Hiram Ricker and Sons, "Adirondack" Murray
presented a more domesticated version of his usual message of "muscular
Christianity," which preached the gospel of mental and spiritual regeneration
through physical exertion. His major task for this client was to portray the natural surroundings of the resort in such a way that they would invite rather than
repel urban rusticators. He primarily did so by persuading readers that it was
possible to experience the beneficial effects of the outdoors within the comfortable confines of a grand hotel. Indicative of this tamer middle-landscape
version of nature, Murray equated a stay at the resort to "camping out under
a roof." Highlighting the proximity of the Poland Spring House both physically and aesthetically to nature, he emphasized the "friendly alliance" between the hotel and the nearby oak and maple trees that provided patrons
with shade and vitalized air. In addition, he noted that the hilltop location
of the structure permitted the free access of hygienic solar rays. Finally
with great literary flourish, Murray invited guests to view "the vast expanse
of country, the clustering farms, the emerald hills, the shining lakes, and
those majestic peaks of the White Mountains, behind which the sun sinks
from view as a ship disappears, sailing below the horizon in crimson seas."[20]

To appeal to patrons with highly refined tastes, who might have been
overwhelmed by the vastness of the panorama and closeness of nature, Murray made use of a reassuring metaphor. He compared the experience of nature to viewing art. While gazing out the large window at the end of the dining room in the Poland Spring House, guests took in a "plate-glass picture"
of moving life. Murray reported that "as you eat you look out upon shining
lakes and blue skies, green lawns acres in extent, and forest-covered hills, still
valleys far below you, and more silent peaks which penetrate the stillness of

remoter skies." What distinguished the canvas of God the Artist from those produced by mere mortals was the movement — the motion of swaying trees, fluttering leaves, soaring birds, and floating clouds. Lest readers miss his message, Murray related an anecdote about a celebrated Boston art connoisseur who had dismissed such a real-life nature scene as a "daub." Vain individuals and "rich noodles," he warned, needed to set aside their over-cultivated urban sensibilities in order to truly appreciate "Nature's own charming and realistic presence."[21]

Like Murray, George Haynes was a prolific "descriptive writer" who shaped perceptions of the natural landscape during the era for urban tourists with overcultivated social sensibilities and underdeveloped natural appreciation. From his publishing office in Portland, Haynes helped the Rickers promote their rural resort. His five-page spread on Poland Spring in *The Charming Inland Retreats of Maine* called attention to the site's "grand mountain, forest, and lake scenery." It typified a natural landscape that the author contended: "develops the love of the beautiful, refines the taste, and cultivates the imagination." An illustration of the hilltop from the vantage point of White Oak Hill provided readers with a panoramic glimpse of the natural beauties whose charms led Haynes to judge the resort one of the most prominent in the nation. Five years later in 1896, the site still looked to him like a "veritable paradise." In a talk presented to the Maine Genealogical Society, he cited the expansive grounds, sloping lawns, flowerbeds, forest groves, and lovely ponds as elements that made up the "picturesque hill farm." In addition, he praised the Rickers for improving their "princely domain" with rare skill and taste. The family's "pious" efforts to preserve and foster the natural beauty of the hilltop, Haynes maintained, had made Poland Spring "one of the most enchanting spots in all picturesque New England."[22]

More than merely enchanting, the natural surroundings, according to Haynes, invested the resort with a spiritual dimension as well. Attempting to stimulate interest in autumn vacations with the 1894 summer season drawing to a close, Haynes touched upon the full range of themes that made nature appealing to urban rusticators. The crystal spring, which carried people back in imagination to primitive times, symbolized the permanence of nature. A magnificent panorama, which was "frescoed with colors ever changing and never reproducible," demonstrated the "wild beauty" nature lavished on the resort. Drinking the "nectar of life" and breathing the pure mountain air offered nature's therapeutic promise of rest, comfort, and health. Moreover, it held the power to free weary saints and sinners from the cares and

troubles of life and to relax the bonds fettering them to the treadmill of business. "The endless variety of scenery," which awakened thoughts of the power
and grandeur of God's creation and "put new life into the jaded pilgrim," revealed the inspirational value of nature. For Haynes, the presence of "invigorating breezes, pure water and ozone laden with the perfume of fir and balsam" made Poland Spring the "Garden of Eden."[23]

Such a natural paradise inspired some observers to poetic constructions
of the resort's middle landscape. At Poland's centennial celebration, the Reverend J. Albert Libby invited visitors to surmount "the lofty domes" of the
Poland Spring House and take in views of the Range Ponds:

> Below, as well as from our many hills,
> Surpassing beauty all the vision fills,
> Their lovely water sheet the sight will please,
> A mirror for the clouds and towering trees.

Another Poland centennial celebrant, Louise Waterhouse, also paid tribute
in verse to the area's natural surroundings. In "Greeting to Poland," she especially praised the attractions that made the resort so famous: the smiling
ponds, stately hilltop, healing spring, and lordly grove. The poet concluded
her tribute with the declaration:

> Then hail to Poland, whose grand scenery fills
> Each son and daughter with a filial pride!
> Dear to each heart are all her rocks and rills,
> Long may her honor in each heart abide!

No mere antimodern romantic, Waterhouse prefaced the verse by calling
upon her hometown to "be strong and fearless—true as steel,/In the front
ranks of Progress always found."[24]

Complementing the words of journalists, publicists, and poets, the Rickers also employed a full range of artistic and photographic images to promote
the middle landscape of the resort. Although admittedly limited in its power
to "truly duplicate" the resplendence of nature, painting was nevertheless regarded as a powerful representational medium. Following the lead of William
Murray, the *Hill-Top* was replete with metaphorical references that spoke to
the inspirational artistry of the surrounding landscape. One article likened
the panorama encircling Ricker Hill to a "canvas for the sky to paint its picture on." In "A Summer Shrine," the writer described the abundant scenery

as a "perpetual feast of beauty" that might inspire a painter. Yet another article in the paper specifically listed the "groves of fragrant pine" and the "living
pearly stream" at Poland Spring as subjects worthy of artistic consideration.[25]

The *Hill-Top* freely associated art and nature based upon the belief in the
symbiotic relationship between the two. An 1896 editorial explained that Nature instilled a love of Art and that Art, whether photographic or impres-
sionistic, recorded "Nature, true Nature." The approximation to authenticity
was measured by the artist's ability to record the entire range of sensory experience. It was not enough to see nature in art; viewers also had to feel emo-
tions such as peacefulness. Reflecting the marriage of message and medium,
the editorial concluded with the incantation: "Nature and Art. Art and Nature. Life companions. Forever hand in hand."[26]

One of the artists who most successfully married the two companions was
John Enneking. Considered by many authorities to be one of the leading
American painters of the day, Enneking had served as a juror for the fine arts
exhibit at the World's Columbian Exposition. The eight pictures he sent for
the resort's inaugural art exhibition in 1895 surveyed the landscapes of New
England from a spring morning in Skowhegan, Maine, to a cloudy day in
North Bridgton, Maine, to summer twilight in Winthrop, Massachusetts.
The *Hill-Top* admired the genius of an artist who had perfected the authentic re-creation of nature. The paper praised his close study of subjects, mas-
terful skill with the brush, true fidelity to the principles of art, and acute ability to evoke the full range of sensory experiences. The result of Enneking's
immense talent was that viewers could "feel the grandeur," "breathe in the
cooling atmosphere," see the "rich, mellow glow," and bask in the "warmth
and cheerfulness" his scenes radiated.[27]

The development of photography and advances in printing during the
nineteenth century made it possible to employ a whole new medium of visual representation in the construction of the resort's middle landscape. In
their earliest promotional pamphlets, the Rickers had relied on engravings to
depict the landscape. The 1879 edition, for example, featured a scene of guests
resting in the grove at the Spring House, as well as strolling, horseback riding, and traveling by coach along the tree-lined drive to the Poland Spring
House. By 1887 the innovation of photoengraving made possible sharper illustrations of the oak grove behind the Poland Spring House and guests
rowing on Lower Range Pond. The lavishly illustrated 1890 water pamphlet
marked the full ascendance of published photography. The opening pages
featured a vignette that framed a view of the countryside lying between

White Oak and Ricker Hills. In the lower left-hand corner of the scene appeared a palette, brushes, and a partially painted canvas leaning against the successor to these tools of the artist — a camera. The illustration marked the transition from landscape drawing and painting to landscape photography, at least for promotional purposes.[28]

With the inception of the *Hill-Top* in 1894, high quality photographs of the natural surroundings began to appear in print regularly. The combination of pictures and text presented another way for the editors to mediate the experience of the tourist landscape for readers. A photograph of a country road in the vicinity of the Shaker village summoned up a verbal cornucopia of natural images: the dancing shadows of the playful sun, the whirring wings of a frightened partridge, the clear waters of a purling brook, the nodding caps of tiger lilies, the sere and yellow hues of the autumn woods, and the clear crisp breath of mountain air. Another photo, this one of the Range Ponds, served as a reminder of the range of natural scenes visible from Ricker Hill. The accompanying article concluded with the poetic couplet: "Ever charming, ever new/ When will the landscape tire the view?"[29]

Not soon, apparently, for the next week a picture of a sunset graced the front page of the *Hill-Top*. The paper used the illustration to explain the advantage photography had over the media of writing and painting. Quoting the renowned English art critic, John Ruskin, the article asserted that a sunset produced "colors for which there are no words in the language and no ideas in the mind, — things which can only be conceived while they are visible." That was the key to the camera's special power. Like the eye, it witnessed, rather than imagined, the visible. Unlike the eye, however, the new technology enabled photographers to record the moment permanently. This was a critical factor since nature did not hold its pictures steady for an instant "in fear some mortal would successfully reproduce it." Because nature was fleeting, no artist could do "perfect justice" to a Poland Spring sunset. According to the *Hill-Top*, even so great a landscape painter as Joseph M. Turner could only feebly reproduce the crimson, golden, and purple-tinged "kaleidoscopic combination of western clouds and low disappearing sun." Similarly, the paper observed that Turner's contemporary and fellow Englishman, William Hunt, lacked a palette that could equal "the pictures painted by the Master hand upon the western sky." The virtually instantaneous camera now allowed the promoters of the tourist landscape to control and reconstruct scenes of nature in ways previously unavailable to the masters of art.[30]

Visual images, enlivened by the spoken word, were the stock and trade of

several travel lecturers who spoke at Poland Spring. One of the era's most acclaimed oratorical interpreters of nature, Edward C. Swett, came to the resort in 1897 to deliver his highly regarded presentation on "Picturesque
Maine." Using 125 lime-light pictures, Swett took a large and attentive audience on an illustrated "flying" tour of the state's mountains, woods, shores,
homes, and hotels. His commanding presence, resonant voice, clear delivery,
distinct and graceful manner, and interesting views made a favorable impression on those who filled the music hall. The following season an equally esteemed landscape lecturer visited the resort, Henry G. Peabody of Boston. At
the beginning of August, he gave a "beautifully illustrated and well-delivered"
talk entitled "Tour of the White Mountains." Peabody returned a month
later to present "Along the New England Seashore," a program that featured
not only "the finest views of any lecturer before the public to-day," but also
"some fine views of Poland Spring."[31]

The Means: Nature and Ricker, A Firm All-Powerful

Befitting proprietors committed to keeping up with progress, the Rickers furnished the most modern means to experience nature, in addition to using the
most modern media to promote the tourist landscape. Guests rode through
the countryside on newly constructed roads and in finely crafted coaches, observed panoramas from the strategically situated veranda, walked the grounds
on well-engineered paths, sailed the ponds in the steam-powered launch,
and admired plants and flowers in the state-of-the-art greenhouse. The Hill-
Top was aware of the part promotional material played in constructing visitors' perceptions of nature. It also recognized the role the venues and con-
veyances provided by the Rickers played in mediating patrons' experience of
nature. Commenting in 1895 on the popularity of the Poland Spring resort,
an editorial observed: "Nature has done much, but nature cannot do everything, but when a combination of Nature and Ricker is formed it is a firm
all-powerful."[32]

As the proprietors well understood, the mediation of experience began
from the moment travelers set foot on the stages that shuttled from Lewiston and Danville Junctions to Poland Spring. In the early days of the resort,
"execrable" roads made this a "purgatorial journey." Jane Patterson remembered that undertaking the bone-rattling passage had required "a large infu-
sion of faith." Despite her best efforts to suffer stoically the "mundane shak-
ing," the trip had only served to remove her "farther and farther from the

spiritual realm." Aware that this was no way to introduce visitors to the resort, the Rickers petitioned local authorities to build an improved road to Poland Spring in 1886. The county of Androscoggin, city of Auburn, and towns of New Gloucester and Poland expended over five thousand dollars on the project, which not only improved the drive, but also reduced the traveling time by twenty minutes. To make the trip even more comfortable, the Rickers also improved the mode of transportation. "The high-seated spacious, easy-riding Poland wagon," either a Concord or Tally-Ho coach, replaced "the cumbrous hot and stuffy vehicle of former days." Smoothing out the jolting journey permitted stage passengers such as Patterson to enjoy the elixir of the country air free from "the shocks of the stony way."[33]

The Rickers paid such close attention to the stage service because they knew it offered visitors their initial impression of the area's natural landscape. Unlike the "arrow-like velocity" of the train trip that brought most travelers to Maine, the meandering coach ride gave "passengers time to fill their lungs with the pure air and ozone of the hill country." The more leisurely pace also welled up in riders "the desire to chat and laugh." Having set the mood, publicists highlighted "the swift unrolling picture" on view during the nearly hour-long journey. After leaving the "thrifty little village" of Danville, passengers watched pictures of leafy lanes, ponds "gemmed" by lily pads, and sweet, cool mists hovering over hollows sweep past the stage windows. Nearing the end of the narrow and winding main road, they caught the first glimpse of the towers of the Poland Spring House "rising like castle turrets above the trees." Once the gatekeeper admitted the stage onto the grounds, it began the mile-long ascent of Ricker Hill, wending its way through deep woods, over bridge and culvert, around corners, past birch-bark Indian camps, and right up to the Spring House. There the driver might stop to allow an attendant to supply the riders with a refreshing glass of sparkling water. A few moments later and a thousand feet farther, the long journey came to an end as the well-seasoned driver halted the team of four to six "sleek, plump, well-fed, well-groomed" horses in front of the hotel. If the driver and mediators of nature each had done their jobs effectively, the "exhilarating ride over a picturesquely undulating country" should have been a "pleasurable experience" that left passengers "beatifically translated."[34]

Once guests had settled in, carriage rides through the surrounding countryside could produce effects similar to those experienced on the stage ride. In 1894 the *Hill-Top* recounted what it described as "that exhilaration of feeling that always accompanies a ride on a brake." Setting out first for White Oak

Hill, the "merry" party enjoyed the scenery and landscape on the road to the Pope estate. At the next stop, the Lower Village of New Gloucester, "a broad expanse of meadow land" unfolded before the passengers. Passing over shady roads to Upper Gloucester, the group headed for the remains of an old saw mill, where "the grand sight" of "the sparkling water" cascading over "the beautiful falls" held everyone spellbound. "After tearing themselves away from this inspiring spot," the members of the party made their way to Bald Hill, where another awesome sight awaited. As the carriage crested the hill, "the setting sun hanging in the heavens like a huge ball of fire" began its slow descent behind Mount Washington, the tallest peak in New England. The ideal and enjoyable afternoon concluded with passage through "shady woods and picturesque valleys" on the way back to the Poland Spring House.[35]

At the hotel, the veranda provided an ideal vantage point from which to take in a variety of delightful vistas—an opportunity that was "a most essential factor in connection with the summer outing." Given the primacy of the space, an early promotional announcement invited guests to check out from the piazza: "the most beautiful landscape scenery in New Eangland [sic]". What Lida Churchill saw nearly two decades later as she gazed outward from the spot were peaceful Maine homes, the "shrubbery encircled" Range Ponds, "noble forest trees," and the piercing White Mountains. Imagining the view of a July sunset from the veranda, Holman Day wrote about winds wafting across clover blossoms, stirring the oak and maple groves, and scenting and vitalizing the heavy summer air. As this imaginary scene unfolded, shadows crept across the ponds and lawns, making the flowers appear spectral and the fountains seem like mist-wraiths. As the sky faded to crimson over the mountains, night came placidly to the New England countryside. At such moments of grand solemnity, Day observed, Poland Spring was a spot far lovelier than any other on earth.[36]

Miles of walkways awaited those guests who preferred ambulatory rather than sedentary encounters with nature. The *Hill-Top* recommended the path from the Bottling Plant to Lower Range Pond as the best route. It terminated at one of the loveliest spots at the resort—a shore-side pine grove made all the more accommodating by the presence of benches. Another popular walk was one "no well-regulated summer resort would think of existing without"—Lovers' Lane. Located near the spring, "the long shady path" featured seats at regular intervals. At these secluded rest stops, the "summer man" could whisper "soft nothings" to the "summer girl," making the woods a truly romantic paradise.[37]

Constructed in 1896, the Conservatory functioned as a greenhouse, supplying flowers for outdoor plantings and indoor displays. It was one of the means by which the Rickers attempted to transform the hilltop into a natural Eden. *Maine Historic Preservation Commission.*

The man responsible for the network of pathways on the hilltop was civil engineer and man of progress Edward Jordan. Following his successful design of the resort's "unequalled facilities for drainage," Jordan's next assignment in the construction of the middle landscape was to prepare "a plan for the development of Poland Spring property by means of paths and trees." Guided by the tastes and desires of guests for restful and healthful settings, he planned a park-like landscape, a map of which appeared in the 1887 promotional pamphlet for the Poland Spring Hotel. Jordan intended for the promenades running between buildings and the walks wending their way through the woods to heighten the attractiveness of the hilltop and bring guests into closer contact with the natural surroundings. In effect, he intended to engineer the experience of nature.[38]

The proprietors not only framed nature from the veranda and bounded it with paths; they also sheltered and displayed it in the Conservatory. Constructed as a greenhouse during the winter of 1896 and 1897, the building measured one hundred thirteen feet long by twenty feet wide. The interior of the heated structure contained five hot beds and a potting room with a capacity of ten thousand plants. Extensive flower gardens abutted the building. Overseen by anywhere from three to five gardeners, the center of "floral culture" at the resort supplied seedlings for the farm, plants for the ornamental gardens, and flowers for the hotels. Colorful roses and carnations found their way into urns, rockeries, and decorative beds that adorned the extensive lawns. Supplementing these staples with sweet peas and lilies grown by the Sabbathday Lake Shakers, floral arrangers also placed fresh cuttings in vases that brightened tables in the dining halls. The most spectacular floral creation was a bed of *Alternanthera* laid out in the shape of a large bottle with the words "Poland Water" spelled out in *Sempervivum*.[39]

With the flora of the grounds cultivated, conserved, and controlled, the next step in the taming of nature was to instruct guests how to appreciate some of the fauna found on the hilltop. During the summer of 1900, someone well versed in the teachings of naturalists Alexander Wilson and John Burroughs embarked on an extensive campaign to open patrons' eyes to "the rich and beautiful world" generally and the paradise that was Poland Spring specifically. The series of five full-length articles that appeared in the *Hill-Top* started by trying to awaken in readers "love for the birds." Recounting early morning explorations around the grounds, the anonymous amateur ornithologist named the species sighted and identified some of their distinguishing characteristics. The newspaper dutifully printed the list of forty-five birds ranging from Baltimore Orioles to Yellow Warblers that inhabited the woods, fields, orchards, and ponds within a ten-minute walk of the Poland Spring House.[40]

When the birds ended their courtship rituals and became scarce with the arrival of midsummer, the ornithologist metamorphosed into an entomologist in pursuit of butterflies. Although not as endearing as birds, the colorful flying insects still added "much of beauty and joy to the lover of 'meadow, grove and stream.'" With only slightly diminished enthusiasm, the nature lover provided detailed descriptions of fourteen kinds of butterflies, everything from Clouded Sulphers to Wood Nymphs, and pointed interested guests toward places "where the sun shines and flowers are plenty." The call came with the imparted wisdom to revel in the simple joy and pure delight of nature study, like boys at play. Apparently, the message resonated with at least one Mansion House guest, who, with the assistance of a boy named Charlie, assembled "a fine collection of beautiful butterflies."[41]

Although the Rickers and their fellow nature lovers fairly well domesticated the grounds, their power was perhaps exerted most forcefully with respect to the Range Ponds. The proprietors' active interest in the three interconnected bodies of water did not come until late into the development of the resort. The family did not really provide patrons with a reliable means to enjoy the ponds until 1894. In that year, the Rickers acquired a steam launch to ply the waters it controlled by virtue of exclusive navigation rights granted by the Maine State Legislature. The "staunch and substantially built" *Poland* weighed over six tons, measured thirty feet in length, and had a capacity of twenty people. The first time the limit was tested by the well-fed "heavy-weights" of the resort the vessel ran aground. As the "natty little" launch made the rounds of Middle and Upper Range Ponds twice daily, passengers took in ever-changing scenery "of the grandest and most picturesque nature." It was enough to impress upon passengers the "mightiness and graciousness of the All-Powerful in bestowing upon Poland" such vast and rich natural beauty.[42]

Despite the God-given appeal of the scenery, the ponds lacked something. "Dame Nature," the *Hill-Top* reported, had indeed supplied the Ranges with "a generous and unfailing supply" of water, a setting of "absolute solitude," and natural surroundings that gratified the eye. The Rickers had done their part, too. They had promoted the message that the ponds were lovely and charming through pamphlets, periodicals, photographs, and poems. They had also provided the means to appreciate the bodies of water in the form of sailboats, canoes, and the steam launch. Still, something was missing.[43]

The *Hill-Top* finally solved the mystery in 1903. The problem was that the Range Ponds were "orphans." The incorporation of the three foundlings into the all-powerful Ricker firmament of nature and their subsequent transformation into more fully developed natural attractions began with new names. Upper Range Pond became Lake Edward; Middle Range became Lake Alvan; and Lower Range became Lake Hiram. In addition, the paper assigned the lakes individual characteristics related to the recreational and natural landscapes emphasized at the resort. Lake Edward boasted sportive bass; Lake Alvan claimed the sail and oars; while Lake Hiram mirrored wooded shores. An illustrated article publicizing the adoption announced the makeover by reminding readers of "the value of water in a landscape." Unspoken yet understood by the people of progress was the belief that this value was not only aesthetic, therapeutic, and even spiritual, but utilitarian, commercial, and economic as well.[44]

The Reception: "These Passionate Lovers of Nature"

Given the array of media employed by publicists of Poland Spring and the vast amount of promotional material produced, guests could hardly have missed the message that nature was permanent, beautiful, healthful, and inspiring. They certainly used the means made available by the Rickers to experience nature at the resort. Written accounts and illustrations show that the coaches, carriages, and steam launch were well traveled, the veranda and groves well populated, and the paths and walks well worn. Although precisely what the vast majority of vacationers were thinking while they toured the countryside, viewed the mountain ranges, surveyed the grounds, ambled through the woods, and cruised the ponds is largely unknown, scattered evidence indicates that patrons did admire the permanence and beauty of the resort's natural surroundings. Moreover, many of them also left behind testimonials to the restful, healthful, and spiritual benefits of the Edenic middle landscape created on the hilltop.

Jane Patterson's novel provides the most extensive insight into how guests experienced nature at Poland Spring. As her story opens, the main characters wrestle with the distinction between wild and civilized nature. The year is 1873 and the Raynors have gone on vacation because Charles has overworked himself to the verge of death. Husband and wife are about to disembark from the train that has brought them from their home in Pennsylvania to their refuge in Maine. When Catharine Raynor takes her first look around, she is startled to discover that she has landed in a wilderness, not in "some lovely and cultivated portion" of the state as she had expected. Her husband attempts to set her mind at ease by assuring her that the resort is still another four to five miles from the railroad station. Once the couple reaches the hotel and settles in, the effects of nature are felt almost immediately. Kate takes in a magnificent sunset, which begins to relax her heart and mind. The next morning, Charles feasts his eyes on lovely mountain scenery, which helps to make him feel contented.[45]

In the days and weeks to come, the Raynors experience most of the dimensions of nature promoted at the resort. The couple revels in "the beauty of the sylvan solitude." Gathering plants and climbing from rock to rock during a walk along the path to the spring rekindles in the pair "the invigorating pulse of youth." The therapeutic value of nature comes to Charles as he naps on a hammock strung up in a pine stand, where the soothing air and complete quiet bring calm to his nerves. For Kate, it is the picturesqueness of the

scenery that relieves her cares and anxieties. With summer and their time at
the resort both drawing to an end, the spiritual value of nature is finally revealed to the pair. One day during their return from the spring, the couple
decides to stray from the tree-sheltered paths and venture instead through
the tangles of the unexplored forest. Along the way, the two reverentially
gather specimens of beautiful mosses and vines to bring home to their children. No sound disturbs them. Not so much as the chirp of a bird or buzz
of an insect is heard. The Raynors become "so attuned to the harmonies of
the universe by their harmony with each other and with God that all things
vocal and inanimate served their will and wish."[46]

After recounting three other visits by "these passionate lovers of Nature,"
Patterson concluded the novel by affirming the permanence, beauty, healthfulness, and spirituality of nature. As summer warmth gives way to fall
frosts, the Raynor's final vacation at New Bethesda draws to a close. The
change of seasons cannot "obliterate the handwriting of Providence" on the
hill country, however, for the divine presence in nature is enduring. Natural
beauty will continue to brood above the heights and healing water will continue to flow beneath the ground. Patterson, ever the Universalist minister's
wife, believed that those people who obeyed the call of the Eternal Voice to
come up to the higher place symbolized by New Bethesda would gain access
not only to "the elixir in rarefied air," but more important, to God's redemp-
tive power.[47]

The glowing accounts of Poland Spring by Jane and the Reverend A. J.
Patterson persuaded at least one of their acquaintances to check out the resort. Recalling his own initial impressions of the area, the Reverend T. A.
Dwyer imagined a stranger's initial reaction to the natural surroundings:
"Beautiful, beautiful!" The encircling mountains would make him feel as
though he were within a fortification that shut out both "the busy noises of
the world" and "the bustle and hum of business life." Then shifting from the
hypothetical realm to his actual experience, Dwyer described how nature
could also inspire spiritual transformation. One of the most glorious moments during his vacation had been an evening when the soft glows of the
setting sun had bathed the surrounding hills with a radiant splendor and had
flushed a nearby pond with reddened light. This self-described lover of nature recalled that "it was the sort of scene in which one could most readily
forget his own existence and feel melted into the general life of God's creation." Dwyer concluded his thoughts about all the "dreamy delights" he had
viewed from the hilltop with several lines from an Irish poem:

> In that Eden of the West
> Angels fold their wings to rest.
> Angels often wandering there
> Doubt if Eden were more fair.

Another urban rusticator had found paradise at Poland Spring.[48]

One did not have to be a minister to see the divine hand of nature touching the hilltop. In 1889 Benjamin Butler told a local reporter that he liked the resort because it presented "God's earth just as God made it." Besides admiring the permanence of natural creation, the general loved its beauty and championed its healthfulness. From his seat on the west veranda of the Poland Spring House, he could see the best of the mountains, "symbolic of purity and peace," as well as the countryside, "the spot favored of the Creator in summer." Citing the healing power of the water and the quietude of the setting, Butler paid tribute to Poland Spring as "the resort of men and women who need rest, comfort and renewed strength."[49]

One weary man of progress who ventured to the resort for revitalization was Terence P. McGowan, publisher of the *Board of Trade Journal* and agent for the Trans-Atlantic Steamship Company. During the summer of 1899, this resident of Portland, Maine, gladly quit the hot and crowded city and headed for the cool and refreshing hilltop to be with "the representative families and men of the nation." Based upon his experiences at Poland Spring, he concluded that nature had lavished this region of "the dear old 'Pine Tree State'" with many gifts, including the life-restoring elixir, lofty pines, a picturesque countryside, and beautiful panoramas. The means the Rickers provided to enjoy these natural assets—specifically, the palatial well-equipped hotels and splendid well-constructed carriages—made the site, in McGowan's estimation, an ideal resort.[50]

Not all the testimonials to nature came from enervated middle-aged men on the mental mend. For the younger generation, or maybe it was from the female perspective, the experience of nature was not primarily about relaxation and revitalization. After her brief visit to the resort during the summer of 1891, Helen C. Weld expressed feelings of joy and fun with regard to her outdoor adventures. She and her companions had availed themselves of several of the means provided to gain an appreciation of the natural surroundings. They had walked to the Spring House and taken in the beautiful views, followed "a pretty woody path to one of the line of lakes," and gone on a "lovely drive" to the Pope estate and the Shaker settlement. At the conclusion of her two-day stay, Weld recorded in her diary that she had enjoyed her time at Poland Spring immensely.[51]

An anonymous poem by "A Guest" well summarized the contributions that nature added to a vacation at the resort. It supplied the "spacious grounds" and "beauties round" that made the middle landscape aesthetically pleasing. It also supplied the fresh air, pure water, and carefree atmosphere that made the site therapeutically beneficial. The tribute closed with a toast:

> Nature's done so much for thee,
> Fair Poland Spring;
> And thou in turn dost much for me.
> We drink to thy prosperity.

What the Rickers added to the partnership was the insight to conceive of these natural attributes as marketable commodities and the skill to manage and promote these assets for the benefit of their nature-starved patrons. As Lida Churchill summed up the arrangement, Nature had "poured out its treasures as clouds pour out rain," but the Rickers had given the resort its soul.[52]

The Rickers' project to shape impressions of the natural surroundings began by defining the rural setting of Poland Spring as a middle landscape that would appeal to their urban clientele's desire to return to nature without forsaking the comforts of modernity. They then interpreted this experience into the subtly but inherently antimodern message that nature offered the benefits of temporal permanence, aesthetic beauty, therapeutic healthfulness, and spiritual inspiration. They promoted this message through the modern media of periodicals, pamphlets, paintings, photographs, poems, and lectures. They made available to patrons the most modern means to enjoy nature: wilderness excursions, luxurious stages and carriages, relaxing verandas, secluded walkways, a verdant greenhouse, and a state-of-the-art steamboat. Looking back admiringly in 1923 at the resort on the hilltop, Arthur Staples credited the proprietors with having created an Eden out of a country farm. For some patrons of the Poland Spring resort, however, "the feeling of passive content" produced by such mediated contact with nature did not suffice. To please those people of progress expecting a more strenuous brand of outdoor activity, the Rickers had to tame nature into a recreational playground, too.[53]

The Playing Fields

A Picturesque Recreational Landscape

In late August 1899, guests gathered in the music hall of the Poland Spring House to watch the presentation of prizes to the leading golfers at the resort. The ceremony began with remarks by Byron Moulton, who recounted that when he had first visited the hilltop in 1876, recreation had consisted of a ride on an ox-drawn hayrack. Among the many changes he had seen since that time was the laying out of the "most beautiful golf grounds in the country." The transformation of pastureland into playing fields led Moulton to put down the hay scythe he had wielded a few summers earlier and to pick up in its place the golf club. The exchange of implements symbolized the ascendance of a modern leisure ethic and the rise of the recreational middle landscape during the Gilded Age.[1]

Legitimating leisure and incorporating it into the landscape was no simple matter. The people of progress venerated the work ethic, attributing much of their success to it. Until well into the nineteenth century, the pursuit of leisure had been regarded as decadent at best and downright sinful at worst. As one contemporary observed, "the gospel of rest had not been preached." Writing shortly after the turn of the century, Leroy T. Carleton of Winthrop, Maine, added: "At the close of the Civil War, in 1865, the country at large had no outdoor sports recognized by refined and cultivated people as becoming and proper, and vacations, as we now understand that term, were an unknown quantity." What changed after mid-century were the mounting stresses of urban-industrial life. An epidemic of the "disease of modern civilization," a nervous disorder known as neurasthenia, plagued the people of progress. The recommended prescription was a dose of the three R's—rest, relaxation, and recreation, each of which could be found in abundance at resorts like Poland Spring.[2]

The proprietors did not disappoint those who regarded Maine as the "playground of the nation." The Rickers dotted the hilltop with athletic tracks, courts, courses, and diamonds and promoted the gospel of leisure with gusto. The message took hold. By 1897 the *Hill-Top* commanded patrons that the enjoyment of "out-door games" was "the duty of all." "The wheel, the lofter, the racket, or the bat" was the call to arms, with the attendant promise of a "beneficial effect" to follow. To the editors of the paper, the presence of "moving figures" lent "a picturesqueness to the landscape." A new recreational element had arrived on the scene and formed with the pastoral and natural complements a multilayered middle landscape of leisure.[3]

Like so much else at Poland Spring, the remarkable transformation from alarm about to legitimation of leisure grew out of the interplay between many of the same antimodern and modern themes repeatedly invoked by promoters of the resort. On the one hand, sports offered the chance for patrons to get out into nature and recall the nostalgic past. This produced the romantic recreation of outdoor, often noncompetitive, and frequently solitary sports such as fishing, boating, swimming, walking, running, and cycling. On the other hand, sports also provided many of the opportunities sought by modern man: to build individual character, to improve physical and mental health, to add to social status, to consume, and to partake of therapeutic pleasure. This produced the "rational recreation" of physical and often intermural competitive sports such as tennis, baseball, and golf. The triumph of the legitimation process culminated in the popularity of purely leisure recreation in the form of social and intramural competitive games such as croquet, bowling, and billiards.[4]

Those two ever-observant social analysts, the Poole brothers, attributed the leisure revolution to the taxing nature of contemporary life. They expressed concern that modern Americans were "all vitalness." Their brains were charged like lightning; their bodies were electric; and their pulses never slowed. The fast set, which the Pooles equated with businessmen, ate too fast, drank too fast, and consequently, died too fast. Most at risk was the New England Yankee, whom the pair likened to "an arrow in full flight, flying so fast that he sets himself on fire and burns himself into ashes by the fierce rapidity of his own motion." The brothers gravely warned: "Our business men must leave their business often or they will soon leave it once and forever." As salvation from this dismal fate, they recommended outdoor exercise. Exposure to sunshine, starlight, wind, and rain could bring "respite from toil, surcease of care and escape from pressure." No healthier place for rest and recreation existed, they believed, than the countryside. Consequently, the brothers counseled the fast set to find good horses and make haste for country roads where "the blessed memories of early days" would replace the concerns of business.[5]

"Healthful and Harmonious"

The Pooles' celebration of the "woody smells, the mossy rocks and old stone fences" demonstrates how promoters of the leisure revolution drew upon romantic images of nature and the past, especially as it was embodied in the countryside, to advance the cause of recreation. Such accounts starkly contrasted nostalgia for early days with anxiety over modern times. In addition, publicists pointed out that recreation offered the opportunity to leave behind the artificial world of the city for the natural world of the country. There, people could exchange sedentary life for strenuous life, therapeutic experience for authentic experience and enervation for revitalization. In essence, "healthful and harmonious" romantic recreation promised escape from the perils of progress.[6]

The traditional field sport of fishing provided the first recreational alternative to ox-cart rides on the hilltop. Once dismissed as an idle pastime of the rural indolent or a subsistence activity of marginal country folk, the romantic anglers of the Gilded Age transformed the activity into a "ritualized recreation" that built character, developed self-reliance, encouraged sportsmanship, and defined gentility. As early as 1876, a reporter cited "the attractiveness of the surrounding pond for fishing" as one of the leading assets of the resort. The *Hill-Top* claimed that the fishing opportunities in the vicinity of the Poland Spring House compared favorably to those found at any seaside hotel. For avid anglers such as Byron Moulton, the fine catches of trout and bass available for twenty miles around made the site a veritable paradise. Moulton went so far as to declare Upper Range Pond "the best fishing ground in the State" after he and a friend hauled in twenty black bass with a combined weight of over forty pounds in two hours during one summer day in 1894.[7]

The sport owed part of its appeal to nostalgia for a simpler past. Promoters invested fishing with the aura of noble antiquity by invoking the image of a premodern icon. Isaak Walton was an Englishman whose 1653 treatise, *The Compleat Angler*, became the bible of the sport. The *Hill-Top* credited him with inventing recreational fishing and teaching a philosophy that many centuries later still provided relief "to many a weary brain." In tribute to his enduring influence, the periodical labeled latter-day followers of "the high priest of anglers," Waltonites. The lead disciple at Poland Spring was Moulton's fishing partner, Joseph Sawyer, a man referred to as "our Isaak Walton."[8]

Within the state, one of the chief apostles of Walton and leading missionaries of angling was a woman, Cornelia T. Crosby of Phillips. Rejecting the physical inactivity of her staid Victorian predecessors and opening the outdoors to the vitality of the emerging New Woman, "Fly Rod" Crosby found her calling as a hunter in the Maine woods, angler on its lakes, and ambassador of its recreational offerings. During a visit to Poland Spring in July 1897, the *Hill-Top* described her as "a fine shot" and "the most expert woman fly caster in the world." "Fly Rod" attributed the fishing ability of women to a love of the sport that made them "more enthusiastic over it and better anglers than men." Rather than dividing the two sexes, she regarded the outdoors as the common ground where males and females could come closer together. Mindful of a different connotation of the romance of nature, Crosby observed: "life in the woods broadens women and makes them more companionable to men."[9]

The religion of such devoted "piscatorial enthusiasts" as Sawyer and Crosby drew some of its appeal from the range of experiences provided by the encounter with nature. The harsh reality of fishing included suffering through either soaking rain and wet feet or sweltering sun and blistered skin; pesky mosquitoes, swarming black flies, and smelly tar ointment; and creeping tiredness. As reward for enduring these trials, fishermen had the chance to enjoy the contrasting romantic side of angling. The *Hill-Top* vividly described as beautiful and almost poetic the sights and sounds of the sport. There was "the delicate curve of the slender rod" that produced "the graceful casting of the fly" and "the gentle hum of the long line," followed by "the noiseless tap" as it hit the water, culminating in "the mighty splash" of the victim. What began as an antimodern foray into romanticism, ended as a modern jolt of authentic experience. The scene climaxed in a Darwinian struggle during which the "art and artifice" of the human brain triumphed over the "vacuity" of "the witless denizen of the waters." The ultimate thrill came not from the catch itself, but instead from the energy that surged through the body of the angler, causing muscles to tense and blood to rush. Recalling the Pooles' reference to the electric vitality of the people of progress, the *Hill-Top* pointed out that "you get much the same combination of volts in fishing you get in driving a spirited horse."[10]

In a culture infatuated with the idea that life was a progressive evolutionary struggle only the fittest survived, sports served as yet another arena of competition. Fishermen cast their lines into the Range Ponds not only to engage in a Darwinian contest against bass, trout, pickerel, perch, and salmon, but also to prove who the ablest anglers were. Several guests vied for this distinction during the 1898 season, apparently with little regard for conserving the fishery. On July 25th, the team of Rose and Maginnis hauled in nine bass, a catch that tipped the scales at seventeen pounds. A few days later, two challengers brought in ten fish, only to find that they weighed a disappointingly paltry thirteen and a half pounds. On July 29th, Rose and Maginnis tried to better their own record, but fell two fish and a few pounds short. On the same day, Joseph Sawyer shattered the mark and demonstrated his fanaticism for fishing by catching 230 trout, a feat the *Hill-Top* compared to Admiral George Dewey's recent conquest of the Spanish at Manila Bay in the Philippines. Not to be outdone, a trio of guests from the resort hauled in 321 bass several days later while fishing on the Belgrade Lakes a few miles northwest of the state capital in Augusta.[11]

The pendulum of recreational experience swung back to the romantic side, as the modern competitive and efficiently machine-like fisherman became a boater. A local newspaper account in 1892 observed that a birch canoe on any one of the nearby lakes floated as "soft on the water as a floating leaf." Two years later, the *Hill-Top* compared the graceful movement of a canoe to dancing to summer music. Furthermore, it likened the exhilaration of drifting in a boat on a placid lake to the feeling of floating between heaven and earth. In contrast to the electric moment of landing a fish, which vitalized the body, this was a dreamy experience that touched the soul. When boating, unlike angling, the current of romanticism apparently only flowed upstream toward antimodernity. The *Hill-Top* compared the "poetry of motion" boaters found on Maine's lakes to the "jaunty buoyancy" they faced on the state's wild rivers. The nostalgic hero of this epic encounter with primeval nature was "the rough Maine woodsman." His steady eye and strong arms enabled him to navigate vessels unharmed through "rolling rapids" and "riotous cataracts." Noting the limits of modernity, the paper maintained that "no human art" could safely pilot modern steamers and cruisers through such wilderness hazards.[12]

There was something about being vigorous and being outdoors that lent itself to the romance of heroism. Another missionary who brought the gospel of recreation to the resort was Captain William H. Daily. Described as "one of the world's most famous swimmers," this athletic and powerfully built lifesaver had earned wide public acclaim and a gold medal from the

United States Congress for his "scores of heroic and daring deeds." In August 1895, Daily paid a visit to Poland Spring to put on a "Programme of Natation," which included demonstrations of diving, floating, swimming, and life-saving. At least two hundred spectators watched the exhibition he put on at Middle Range Pond. Daily offered to come back and give lessons to guests, so long as a minimum of fourteen people expressed interest in learning how to swim. His evangelism was unnecessary, for the activity had already caught on at the resort. During the summer of 1894, the resort bathhouses had been "used considerably" and swimming had been "indulged in to a great extent." Similarly, the *Hill-Top* reported in 1896 that "bathing in the middle lake has become very popular."[13]

Landlubbers who shunned the amusements of "Aquatic Poland" found other means of romantic recreation. Led by the active Byron Moulton, recreational walking became a popular form of exercise during the 1890s. His were not short strolls along the landscaped footpaths and Lovers' Lane of the hill-top. Forsaking the speed, comfort, and status of horse-drawn rides, Moulton and other "champion walkers of Poland" undertook long jaunts, requiring great stamina and endurance, over many of the same scenic routes traveled by the carriages. Accompanied by two young women, he walked one August day in 1894 from the Poland Spring House to White Oak Hill and then returned along the north shore of Middle Range Pond to the resort. By journey's end, the trio had traversed nearly seven miles. Other treks took walkers to the Shaker village and even all the way to Mechanic Falls and back, a fourteen-mile hike. Less fit guests accepted the invitation to try the "Mile Walk" and see "the many beauties of Poland." More energetic patrons ran. A "popular young 'Quaker'" went for "a five-mile spin in his running tights" early one morning during the summer of 1894. It was a sight that reportedly attracted a great deal of attention, especially from the "natives."[14]

Usually, the focus of romantic recreation was on the surrounding scenery, not on the athleticism of the participants or the tightness of their attire. It was the picturesqueness of the hill country that drew a group of "Matterhorners" off the veranda of the Poland Spring House and to the "mount-climbing" challenge they dramatically dubbed Mont Chat Noir. Known by the local "peasants" as Black Cat Mountain and rising all of four hundred feet, it was not nearly the fearsome and fatiguing "perilous experience" that the *Hill-Top* facetiously made it out to be. In fact, the "social recreation," toasted with bottles of *"Eau de Pologne"* uncorked at the conclusion of the ascent to the summit, probably better characterized the true spirit of the hike.[15]

What was more instructive about the conquest of Black Cat than the climb was how the hikers got to Raymond—on bicycles. During the early 1890s, the bike swiftly surpassed both the carriage and canoe as the most popular vehicle for flight from modernity, not only at Poland Spring, but also throughout the entire country. Bicycle production nationwide increased from 40,000 in 1890 to 1.2 million in 1896, while ridership rose from an estimated 150,000 to 4 million. In 1895 Marcia Jordan placed the number of bicycles in Portland at twelve hundred. A year later, the *Hill-Top* counted forty bikes at Poland Spring. Noting that the bicycle boom coincided with a period of economic depression and social turmoil in the United States, Richard Harmond has proposed that people turned to cycling as a means to escape the tension and strife of modern life. He has also pointed out the paradoxical attraction of the bicycle as "both a mechanism of progress and a vehicle of flight" from it. This made the device the ideal instrument for romantic recreationalists interested in traversing the middle landscape between antimodernity and modernity.[16]

Whatever the source of its popularity at the resort, the new sport of cycling quickly attracted the attention of the *Hill-Top*. In 1896 the paper described the world as "unanimously interested in" the activity, to the extent that it now could divide humans into three classes: the makers, the sellers, and the riders of bikes. The periodical responded to the craze by introducing a cycling column as a regular feature. The inaugural article took up the familiar plea of the organized biking community—for towns to "dress up" their highways. The second column described two routes cyclists at the resort might find of interest: Diamond Run, a five-mile circuit around Shaker Hill, and Spring Hill Run, a four-mile trip around Ricker Hill. It also directed guests eager to learn how to ride the wheel to the resort's resident expert cyclist, who happened to be the night clerk at the Poland Spring House.[17]

As with the carriage and canoe, the bicycle appealed to people in part because it brought them in closer contact with the outdoors. This explains why "a great admirer of nature" spent so much of his time on the hilltop driving, boating, and cycling. The admirer happened to be another of the self-made, socially ascendant, Franklinesque and Lapham-like characters who populated the resort so abundantly, the appropriately named Benjamin Franklin Keith. A New Hampshire lad who had gone on to Boston to seek his fame and fortune, Keith had already begun to build with his partner and fellow Poland Spring patron, Edward F. Albee, what became by the turn of the century the nation's leading theatrical empire. The so-called "Prince of Vaudeville" took his cycling very seriously, claiming the endeavor furnished "more exercise than all the rest put together." As the "star bicyclist" at the resort, Keith was best known for sprinting past horse teams on uphill stretches of roadway—a practice known as "scorching."[18]

The blend of romantic attention to nature and rational interest in exercise pursued by Keith exemplified the circuitous route the people of progress traveled in their search for order. Although reports in the Hill-Top verify that many bikers did seek to get away from urban environments, they also confirm that cyclists brought along an "overt pro-urban predilection" on their flights from progress. When urban bikers reached the countryside, they expected to find modern comforts. A dinner at the resort culminated many bicycle trips to Poland Spring. As for the ride, some cyclists preferred controlled contact with a middle landscape to freewheeling along rural roadsides. To meet this demand, the Rickers opened a three-mile track in 1897.[19]

Cyclists also exhibited their modernity by manifesting the same competitive spirit that pervaded Gilded-Age culture from the boardroom to the fishing hole. Their challenges were to outdo one another by riding ever-greater distances at ever-swifter speeds. Although the inaugural edition of the "Cyclist Column" specifically advised bikers to "ride for rest," not for distance, subsequent issues of the Hill-Top extolled the achievements of riders who undertook lengthy trips. The paper reported that three cyclists from Portland rode to the Mansion House, a distance of thirty miles, in two hours and thirty minutes on August 16, 1896. The following year, two bikers surpassed this feat by riding all the way from Boston. The honor of the longest bicycle trip to the resort went to Maurice Augustus Burbank. In August 1897, he journeyed from New Haven, Connecticut, to Poland Spring, Maine, covering nearly 250 miles of the total distance by bike. The first leg of the route Burbank followed ended in Palmer, Massachusetts, and came within seven miles of qualifying as a "century run," a ride of one hundred miles. From Palmer, Burbank took a train to Boston. From there, he biked 134 miles to Yarmouthville, Maine, in sixteen hours, stopping to rest along the way for only one hour. The ride to his ultimate destination added the final twenty miles to the trip.[20]

For the many cyclists who started out from Portland, the competitive challenge came from trying to lower the time it took to reach Poland Spring. The trip was a taxing one, as the grade heading inland away from the coast was uphill most of the way. Undaunted by the muscle-straining climbs that lay ahead, three groups of wheelmen set out from the coastal city in a race against the clock on June 27, 1897. A strong wind and the broken seat of one rider prevented the first six cyclists from making good time. The second group, composed of four members from the Portland Athletic Club, had a better run, which they capped off with dinner at the Poland Spring House. The third group turned in the swiftest time of the day. The two members of the League of American Wheelmen reached the resort in a speedy two hours and fifteen minutes.[21]

Women were not excluded from the bicycle craze. Calling for the same sort of physically active New Woman envisioned and embodied by "Fly Rod" Crosby, Marcia Jordan encouraged females to take to the roads. In an 1895 letter to the *Hill-Top*, she advised women to persevere in the face of obstacles such as dresses that threatened to wind around wheels and a "fatal magnetism" that seemed to draw riders toward collisions with watering troughs, holes in the ground, and other cyclists. Jordan resolved the first problem by replacing her ordinary clothes with "a dark blue serge short skirt and Norfolk jacket, black canvas leggins and dark straw hat." She recommended a wider outlook as the solution to the second pitfall. Jordan imagined that if a woman could endure the "lame muscles, black-and-blue decorations and the like honorable scars" that were inevitably a part of cycling, the time would arrive when "some fine day sees you, wrench in pocket, confidence in glance, spinning off past green fields, fascinated, bewitched, a creature with new powers and a fresh enchantment."[22]

The Favorite Outdoor Sport

As the various motivations of cyclists, both male and female, made clear, the appeal of recreation was more than romantic contact with nature and nostalgic escape from the dizzying present to the sedate past. While the distinctions between romantic and rational recreation are neither clear cut nor absolute, the rise of sports such as tennis, baseball, and golf at the Poland Spring resort during the 1890s did further alter the leisure ethic. Although fishing and cycling could be highly competitive, the new trio of sports added formality and organization to athletic endeavor. Rules and teams replaced informal challenges among friends. In addition, the new regime of sports emphasized athleticism. Physical prowess was more important for successful participation in rational sports than it was for the more accessible romantic athletic activities.[23]

The shift in emphasis from romantic to rational recreation paralleled the rise of the muscular Christianity ideology and strenuous life movement. The genesis of the transformation was the concern that modern society, with its mental stresses on the one hand and sedentary comforts on the other, was producing an enervated and even emasculated population. As a result, the belief arose among the people of progress that exercise, especially in pursuit of some Christian endeavor, was the path to physical, mental, and moral improvement. Athleticism had triumphed over asceticism. On a more secular level, the idea that the body was a dynamic system whose functioning improved with activity gained dominance during the late nineteenth century over the concept of it as a divinely predestined creation. Thus, exercise became a requirement for the maintenance of good health. In addition, proponents of rational recreation believed that competition built personal character and that sports provided training for success in modern society. This triathlon of muscular morality, healthy exercise, and character development furthered the legitimation of leisure at Poland Spring.[24]

The first rational recreation to come to the fore at the resort was tennis. In 1894 the *Hill-Top* reported that the activity had become one of "the favorite out-door sports." Six years later, the paper was still reporting that tennis was "quite the latest fad." The popularity of the pastime prompted the editors to sponsor a tennis tournament in 1894 to determine the best player at Poland Spring. The event attracted large crowds that enthusiastically cheered on the participants. After five rounds of "hard fought" matches, the final two competitors remained from the original field of fourteen—Ted Wakefield and Mortimer Singer. The eventual winner of the tennis tournament was Wakefield, who as a consequence of his victory, returned to college from his summer job on the hilltop with "a very handsome cup as a trophy."[25]

Frederick S. Wakefield was a twenty-year-old student about to head into his senior year at Bates College in Lewiston. Although he was not very physically imposing, standing only five feet nine inches and weighing a slight 150 pounds, Wakefield excelled at sports. In addition to his success on the tennis court, he was also a star on the diamond, playing second base on the resort's baseball team. Wakefield's admirable athletic qualities exemplified how the modern leisure revolution transformed sports into a paradigm for work. The *Hill-Top* described him as a "very brainy" athlete and "very conscientious worker." Wakefield displayed both traits on the tennis court, where he took great delight in making his opponents hustle for all they were worth by putting the ball just ever so tantalizingly and frustratingly out of reach.[26]

Wakefield's challenger for the tennis trophy, Mortimer M. Singer, came from a far more privileged social background. An heir to the sewing machine company established by his father, Isaac A. Singer, Mortimer was a Yale University undergraduate who did not have to work his way through school. Unlike Wakefield, Singer could afford to idle away a leisurely summer at the resort vacationing with his family. Apparently, the advantages of wealth had not spoiled Singer, as the *Hill-Top* characterized him as a "very popular" and "excellent young man." On the tennis court, he was a strong and steady player who had mastered the Lawford stroke, a baseline forehand shot popularized by the 1887 Wimbledon champion, Herbert Lawford. More important, he never became rattled and always played "from beginning to end in the same hard, faithful manner." Despite these sterling qualities, Singer met his match in Wakefield, who emerged as the resort tennis champion for the 1894 season in three straight sets.[27]

The emphasis placed on the determination exhibited by the two athletes rationalized recreation by portraying it more like worthwhile work than frivolous play. The *Hill-Top* even made watching tennis seem like hard work. It noted the *"tremendous* applause" that punctuated rallies, remarking: "it was enough to inspire the soul of a Carthaginian to even greater efforts." The intensity of one match so swept up one onlooker that she exuberantly tossed her summer bonnet into the air at the conclusion of one particularly hard-fought point. Only the glaring disapproval of the older set forestalled further outbursts of emotion by the "pretty young ladies" gathered round the court. The rules of gentility prevailed there just as strongly as they did almost everywhere else at the resort.[28]

"The Game of all Games"

The one group that consistently flouted the rules of gentility was the Poland Spring baseball team. Despite the romantic mythology and pastoral image of the sport's origins and infancy, the national pastime in its adolescence and ascendance was largely an urban game, with many of the attendant modern social issues attached to it. Thus, the wide following enjoyed by baseball owed more to the rational values it reinforced than to the romantic attributes it claimed or the recreational pleasures it provided. Baseball fans at the resort admired the competitive effort displayed by players and reveled in the feeling of community instilled by their team. In addition to the sense of identity that came from following the exploits of the home nine, the act of actively rooting allowed fans to participate in the masquerade of rational recreation with-

Before golf became king at Poland Spring, baseball was the center of the recreational playground. During the early 1890s, the diamond was located in front of the main hotel, where guests took advantage of the ample verandas and balconies to view games. *Maine Historic Preservation Commission.*

out any of the sweating. In short, watching baseball contests became the ideal form of Victorian virtual experience. Competition, community, identity, and spectation, these were the chief attributes that made baseball "the game of all games" at Poland Spring.[29]

Organized baseball came to the hilltop at least by 1892. In that year, players from Poland Spring won three games against challengers from Bates College. The following summer, guests decided to tap into the amusement fund to hire a permanent resort team. The Rickers agreed to support the project by letting members have free room and board. The *Hill-Top* described the group brought together for the 1894 season as "the strongest hotel nine in the country." The club played twice a week, usually on Wednesday and Saturday afternoons. So avid were the "base-ball enthusiasts," if no game was scheduled, they would travel to Lewiston to watch contests. When the home team did play, their fans could be found at the diamond near the front entrance of the Poland Spring House, a location that ensured plenty of shaded seats on the hotel veranda.[30]

Several of the recruits to this "salaried organization" were journeyman semiprofessionals. The first baseman was a shoemaker from Ipswich, Massachusetts, while one of the outfielders hailed from Haverhill, Massachusetts. College athletes formed the core of the team. Michael Powers, a catcher from Holy Cross in Worcester, Massachusetts, joined a pitcher from Bowdoin College in Brunswick, Maine, along with Ted Wakefield and three of his Bates College classmates. In addition to his prowess on the tennis court, Wakefield was a "dandy" ballplayer in the estimation of "the well-known base-ball magnate of the Hub," Arthur H. Soden, who owned Boston's entry in the National League. The star of the team was outfielder Louis Sockalexis, a Penobscot from Indian Island in Old Town, Maine, who embodied the ideal of athletic prowess. Dark-haired, clear-eyed, lithe-limbed, broad-shouldered, and swift-footed, "Soc" stood a shade under six-feet tall and weighed a solid two hundred pounds. One account written a few years later described him as "a massive man, with gigantic bones and bulging muscles." The person proudly referred to at Poland Spring as "our red man" also possessed a rifle-like right arm that made him "the best thrower in New England." According to legend, he had once won a bet by hurling a ball clear over the six-story main tower of the Poland Spring House. Despite his mighty athletic talents, Sockalexis was modest, even shy about his abilities.[31]

Given the collection of talent the amusement committee had assembled, the *Hill-Top* had high hopes for the team. The paper realized that attaining the distinction would require both concerted effort and clean play. Advocating the virtue of hard work, the editors railed against "lazy ball playing," warning the athletes that anyone who did not show life and energy on the field would risk losing his position. This was not a command to win at any cost, for the periodical also clearly defined the genteel sportsmanlike code of conduct expected of the ballplayers. They were to act "gentlemanly" and play fairly. "Dirty ball" had no place at Poland Spring. Supporters of the team would only tolerate "clean, manly contests for the supremacy of the diamond." In the competitive struggle of rational recreation, character counted for at least as much as conquest.[32]

Fans had their obligations to the cause of victory as well. The *Hill-Top* assured the ballplayers that so long as they gave their best, they would hear no complaints, win or lose. Indeed, the paper had instructed spectators to cheer "a good hit, a remarkable catch, a well-stolen base." The periodical expected nothing less than "hearty support," reminding rooters of the Poland nine that "applause costs nothing, but it has won many a game of ball." The final charge to the team was: "Boys, work! hustle! win if you can, but play ball all the time."

In case applause from the stands and encouragement from the newspaper were not sufficient motivations, the editors announced an added incentive. At the end of the season, prizes would be presented to the players with the highest batting average, most runs scored, and best fielding percentage.[33]

The 1894 baseball season got off to an auspicious start as the club decisively defeated New Auburn eleven to one. The players' "business like" approach to the game so impressed the *Hill-Top* that it immediately pronounced the home team "worthy of wearing the Poland uniform." The newspaper even dared to predict that the players "undoubtedly will prove themselves to be the best nine we have had here." Poland Spring won two more games before falling to a powerful club from Lewiston. Fans had anticipated the loss, since the opponents fielded the highest salaried team in the New England League. The paper did manage to find one positive outcome of the game—the ability of the team to prevent the challengers "from making a big score." The club quickly rebounded, reeling off two more victories to run its record to five and one. Confident that their baseball team could overpower most of the remaining local opposition, supporters looked to do battle against other New England resorts.[34]

The challenge was ill timed. The day before it appeared in the *Hill-Top*, the team suffered its second loss, a tight decision by the score of four to two to the Murphy Balsams. Unlike the earlier setback against Lewiston, defeat at the hands of the Portland club brought no honor. The Murphy Balsams had a reputation for being "as big a set of rowdies as were ever set loose." Much of the blame for the poor showing was placed squarely on the strong shoulders of Sockalexis. Although the rest of "the boys played good ball," they could not overcome their mate's two errors and four hitless tries at bat. While the paper excused the "off day" as something every athlete experienced, it also made clear that fans expected the team's star to redeem himself by hitting at least three home runs in the next game.[35]

A more debilitating setback befell the club a few days later. Three disgruntled players left the resort. The exact circumstances of their departure are unclear. Edward Ricker said he sent them home. The *Hill-Top* first reported that the trio departed in a dispute over club rules; then, it suggested several weeks later that the players had defected to "some strong team in the mountains or elsewhere." Another possible explanation came from the news making the rounds that one morning it had taken "three pails of water to awaken one of the ball players." This suggests that the temperance ideal that reigned on the hilltop might not have extended to the hard-drinking denizens of the diamond. Whatever the reason for the team's disruption, the incident confirmed the unflattering stereotype that baseball players often did not act like "Sunday School boys." It also highlighted the delicate social equilibrium that existed at Poland Spring among proprietors, patrons, and employees.[36]

The team eventually found replacements for the three defectors but the damage had already been done. Three successive losses in mid-August, coupled with injuries that sidelined the catcher with fractured ribs and two pitchers with unspecified ailments, led to the decision to disband the club. After a two-week hiatus, the Poland Spring nine was able to return to the field of play thanks to the addition of several substitutes. A pick-up team from Lewiston provided the first opposition for the new squad. The hero of the contest was Sockalexis, whose hitting powered his mates to an easy victory. In fact, the two home runs he hammered in the first inning nearly met the challenge the Hill-Top had made to him a month earlier.[37]

The climax of the season for the Poland Spring club was a fourth and final "combat" against the hated Balsams. Determined to avenge two earlier losses, Eddie Murphy had brought along a new team made up of players from the Portland League. In a "corker" of a contest filled with much excitement, Poland Spring rallied from an early deficit to take a late lead. Unfortunately for the home fans, rain shortened the game and the score reverted to a sixteen all tie. The hotel team played its final game of 1894 the following day in Rockland. The victory left the club with an overall record of ten wins, seven losses, and the one tie.[38]

Despite some dashed hopes along the way, the baseball contests brought patrons many hours of "solid enjoyment" during the summer. Fans joyfully celebrated the victories and sorrowfully mourned the defeats of the home team. In the process, allegiance to the club fostered a community spirit among guests. Each game placed the honor of the resort at stake. Each win brought glory not only to the players, but also to the loyal rooters who provided them with both financial and vocal support.[39]

Perhaps because of the troubles experienced with hired ball players, guests did not recruit a team in subsequent summers and enthusiasm for the sport soon faded. In 1895 a group called the Bell Boys played a few games. In later years, teams from surrounding towns sometimes came to the resort to play contests. On occasion, patrons took to the diamond. In 1899 a group of guests calling itself the Brooklyns defeated the rival Bostons by the score of fourteen to thirteen. The following summer, the Yanigans, a squad made up of older patrons, lost to the Poland Kids in a battle that brought distinction to the players and entertainment to the fans. A few days later, the Yanigans rebounded, defeating a team of resort employees, the Tillyslowboys.[40]

"Golf Is King at Poland Spring"

As interest in baseball waned, the popularity of golf teed off. In fact, about the spot of the pitcher's mound became the location of the first tee, as a golf course replaced the baseball diamond. The Rickers introduced the sport to Poland Spring in 1896. Despite early reports that golf had "taken a great hold upon the guests," few people actually played during the first season. In the years that followed, the ranks steadily grew as those patrons who learned the game at the resort joined those who came already knowing how to play. By 1898 the Hill-Top commented that wild horses could not stop most golfers once they took up the sport. Each day brought the arrival of more and more players. From morning until night, dozens of enthusiasts filled the course and from year to year, their skills improved.[41]

The reasons for golf's rapid ascendance during the last few years of the nineteenth century mirrored in microcosm the reasons for the leisure revolution that had taken place during the preceding two decades. Like other popular recreational activities of the era, golf offered the romance of a nostalgic past and close contact with nature. Appealing to more modern values, the sport also made available to rational recreationists ample opportunities to participate in both the strenuous life of exercise and the status-conscious culture of consumption. Indeed, the king of sports conferred upon golfers the elite status of sportsmen and women. Finally, golf provided the controlled competition upon which the people of progress thrived.[42]

While the game was new to Poland Spring in 1896, promoters of golf managed to hearken back to the past to burnish its novelty with the patina of romantic nostalgia. Although try as it might the Hill-Top could not link the sport to the classical world, golf still possessed the requisite antiquity to appeal to antimodernist inclinations. The paper did manage to trace "the 'Royal and Ancient Game' of Goff" back to the misty lochs and bucolic glens of sixteenth-century Scotland, where it found the sport's most celebrated popularizer, King James the Sixth. In a lighthearted moment, the editors imagined that Scotsmen Macbeth, Macduff, and Robert the Bruce had formed one of golf's first threesomes. Promoting an aristocratic view of the sport, the newspaper decreed in 1897: "Golf is King at Poland Spring." The motto not only acknowledged the primacy of golf's popularity; it also affirmed the status ambitions of golf's devotees. The implication was clear. The king of sports was, in turn, the sport of kings. Eagerly waiting to lay claim to the regal legacy of the links was the Gilded-Age leisure class.[43]

In modern times, a round of golf presented antimodern romantics with the opportunity to escape enclosed city buildings for open country fields. Holes named Woods, Birches, Spring, Hill, Lakeview, Grove, and Rockery served as unmistakable reminders of the natural surroundings. Moreover, the artistry of golf added to the beauty of the landscape. The *Hill-Top* explained that the "picturesque" sport gave to the grounds "a scheme of color the nodding heads of ripening grass of former days did not possess." The recreational middle landscape also improved upon its pastoral progenitor by adding "life, activity, and healthful animation" to the countryside.[44]

The man responsible for the design of the golf course was Arthur H. Fenn. Although he had only taken up the sport in 1893 while living in Aiken, South Carolina, Fenn had quickly become one of the nation's leading golfers, finest instructors, and most enthusiastic promoters. Certain that golf was "the most fascinating game of them all," he confidently predicted it "is here to stay and will always be played in this country hereafter, and will be more popular as it is better known." Infected with Fenn's enthusiasm, the Rickers prevailed upon him to come to Poland Spring in 1896 and lay out a course. Fenn not only came, he agreed to stay on as the resident golf professional and course supervisor, positions he continued to hold well into the twentieth century.[45]

Despite the romantic nature-inspired names assigned to most of the holes, Fenn approached the design of the course with an almost scientific outlook that called for thorough study of the overall layout and proper consideration of the placement of the hazards and bunkers. His guiding rule was "that a good stroke should never be punished." Therefore, the course should be neither too "hard and sporty" nor too easy. Additionally, it should feature neither too few nor too many obstacles. Another principle that Fenn strove for was variety. He believed different landscape features should be incorporated into the course and that the length of fairways should be varied within a range of 125 to 550 yards. His annual tinkering with his masterpiece lengthened the course from 2,465 yards with a par of thirty-eight in 1897 to 2,875 yards with a par of forty-one in 1900. All the while, work continued to improve the greens and bunkers. Three years of laying new sod and dumping tons of wood ash, along with careful nursing by human hands, constant tending with horse-drawn lawnmowers, and sporadic unleashing of the groundskeepers secret weapon, sheep, finally produced the perfect course — one virtually free of poor lies. Everyone who played the course agreed that no other resort could rival, let alone surpass, the "the best hotel links in the country."[46]

Although golf claimed historic origins and provided ample exposure to nature, modern values such as exercise, consumption, class-consciousness, and, most of all, competitiveness gave the sport its great appeal. Finding an activity that supplied just the right amount of physical exertion was no easy task for Gilded-Age Americans. Croquet was dismissed as "a game for children." Tennis, while suitable for adults, required participants who were "physically well qualified." Baseball was an even more demanding sport. To attain even an ordinary level of proficiency, players needed the muscles, speed, eyesight, and reflexes possessed only by young to middle-aged men. Having nearly exhausted all the possibilities, the *Hill-Top* concluded that the ideal sport for both sexes and all ages was golf.[47]

In its extensive coverage of the sport, the resort newspaper often emphasized the strenuous nature of the endeavor. Soon after the golf course opened, the periodical predicted: "there will be interesting games to follow, with goodly exercise, and hearty appetites resultant." Several years later, an article observed that the sport helped build "a healthy constitution and great vitality." "For the wiry, withy, nerveless, exact man of muscle and willowy suppleness," golf presented the opportunity for athletic supremacy. For "the athlete with avoirdupois," it offered the chance for physical activity and weight loss. Byron Moulton also championed the benefits of golf, praising the sport for providing "real healthful exercise" that developed strong muscles, lungs, hearts, and minds. Moreover, he credited golf with contributing to social well being by luring young men and women away from "questionable places of amusement."[48]

Lest readers get the mistaken impression that swinging clubs and strolling around the course demanded too much exertion, the *Hill-Top* tempered these testimonials with assurances that the sport offered "good exercise without being lively." To emphasize this point, the paper contrasted the pain brought about by sawing cord wood with the delight experienced while pounding "a small and unoffending ball over four miles of hill and dale, twice within a day." The periodical accounted for the difference, and thereby encapsulated the leisure revolution, with the explanation that the former activity was work, while the latter was play. The resort's golf professional put it another way. Fenn maintained the sport was popular with middle-aged businessmen, because "the exercise was moderate and all that was required." He elaborated that golf benefited men by diverting their attention away from "business cares" and toward pleasure. In accordance with this idea, Fenn concluded that the sport made "a splendid game for the summer visitors who are away for recreation or pleasure, as they get both at the same time."[49]

In addition to the healthful effects received from the mild exercise of golfing, the sport also built character. The *Hill-Top* attributed "the great development as a golf player" of one woman to "her tireless energy and perseverance." Similarly, it praised another lady golfer for the pluckiness she displayed on the course. Furthermore, the sport fostered Victorian gentility through its strict code of etiquette. With each scorecard handed out, players were "earnestly requested to observe the rules of golf." The ten commandments included neither moving nor talking while another player was preparing for a shot, not putting at a hole while a flag was still in it, and remembering to replace divots. The eighth commandment even covered the proper terminology golfers were to use for the reckoning of holes and strokes. To reinforce the importance of propriety on the links, the scorecard stated in bold letters: "these customs prevail everywhere and should be conscientiously observed."[50]

The customs of Victorian gentility and propriety also governed how golfers equipped and outfitted themselves. The sport ideally suited the culture of consumption that flourished at the resort and players consumed both conspicuously and conscientiously. One only needed to leaf through the *Hill-Top* to find sources for every piece of equipment imaginable. Tiffany and Company of New York City solicited mail orders for such indispensable golf baubles as silver scoring pencils, gold golf pins, leather scorebooks, and silver prize cups. A store in Portland advertised that it stocked complete lines of golf supplies marketed under the leading brand names. Consumers could cut out the middleman by ordering directly from A. G. Spalding, which stated that it carried "all the latest and newest things in Golf," including superior drivers, brassies, and clubs designed by and named for Arthur Fenn and Alexander Findlay.[51]

Advertisers offered to outfit as well as equip golfers. The fashionable sportsman or woman could send to Lewiston for golf suits, boots, stockings, belts, and white duck trousers. Players could also order "Everything the Golfer Needs," including red golf coats and sweaters, plain and vested capes, fancy flannels, and knit waistcoats from Boston. Commenting on the impact golf had on fashion, the *Hill-Top* quipped in 1897 that "it has been a great thing for the plaid manufacturers." Two years later, the paper joked that the time had finally arrived when the red coats of Old England were "a pleasing sight upon the green lawns of New England." As for the few portions of the golfer's body not covered by fashionable sportswear, Hinds' Honey and Almond Cream, on sale at the news counter in the Poland Spring House, promised to provide "soothing and excellent" protection from the summer sun.[52]

Golfers could win many of these accessories as prizes in competitions. The sorting and sifting process on the links included frequent jousts to determine the royalty of the king of sports. At the top of the hierarchy stood the resident golf professional, who from time to time took on a well-known cast of touring challengers. Below were the amateurs, in descending status, men, women, and children of varying talent. To rank their order, golfers competed in an assortment of skill challenges and host of tournament formats. To defend the honor of the resort, they competed against competitors representing other golf courses. Curiously, however, for all the focus on competition, the modern-day disciples of Darwinism devised through the golf handicap system a way to regulate the inevitable triumph of the fittest. Among the elite, the preference for social exclusivity at the resort was not confused with acceptance of athletic inequality on the golf course.

Save for occasional challenges by the true masters of golf, the undisputed king of the links at Poland Spring was Arthur Fenn. He became the standard by which other golfers at the resort charted their progress and prowess. Try as they might, no one could better any of Fenn's marks. From his inaugural round score of forty-seven strokes for nine holes on July 30, 1896, his mastery of the course enabled him to become the first player to shoot a round under par and to make a hole-in-one. By 1900 he lowered both of his course records—to thirty-four strokes for nine holes and to seventy-three strokes for a full round of eighteen. In search of greater challenges, Fenn spent the off-season traveling the country and participating in tournaments. During the fall of 1897, he entered nineteen open competitions, seventeen of which he won. Fenn's more than fifty championship trophies, many of which he displayed in the office of the Poland Spring House, attested to his distinction as "one of the bright particular stars of golfdom."[53]

The greatest competitive challenges for Fenn came in the form of exhibition matches arranged with other elite golfers. His most frequent foe was Alexander H. Findlay, an employee of a Boston sporting goods firm. Like Fenn, Findlay was one of the leading golfers in the land. Between 1897 and 1900, the two men played 1,333 holes of golf against one another on courses throughout the nation. After four years of head-to-head competition, Findlay held a slim lead of only six holes. At Poland Spring, the "very keen but friendly rivalry" between the pair drew large crowds. To heighten interest, guests sometimes put up a purse for the winner of their intense duels.[54]

If Findlay was Fenn's favorite and friendliest rival, then Harry Vardon was his toughest challenger. With three British Open titles to his credit in the past five years, the celebrated Englishman had gained by 1900 the reputation as "the greatest golfer in the world." Seeking to capitalize on Vardon's fame, Spalding began marketing a new golf ball named after the champion. To promote sales of the Vardon Flyer, the sporting goods company sponsored a tour throughout the United States by the product's namesake. Vardon's visit to Poland Spring became the athletic event of the season in 1900. His itinerary scheduled him to play exhibition matches against Fenn and Findlay in mid-August. Weeks beforehand, guests awaited the champ's arrival with great anticipation. Some even began to speculate about the success Vardon would have playing the course. Patrons wagered whether he would be able to hit a three-hundred-yard drive at the sixth tee or shoot under thirty-six strokes overall. When he finally showed up at the resort on August 12th, a crowd of ardent golf fans, many of whom had especially made the trip from Portland, greeted him.[55]

The next day, Vardon and Fenn faced off in a thirty-six-hole competition described as "one of the greatest golf matches played in America." Byron Moulton led the large gallery that followed the pair and marveled at the champ's wonderful talent. His drives were straight, his approaches direct, his putts skillful. Even more impressive, he seemed to play so effortlessly. In short, the machine-like Vardon wasted no energy, made few errors, and left no scars on the golf course. Despite having to slog through an intense rainstorm, the Englishman shot a "beautiful" round, lowering the course records for nine and eighteen holes. Unable to beat the challenger on his own, Fenn teamed up with Findlay on August 14th in a best-ball competition. The pair defeated Vardon in "one of the hardest matches" he faced while touring the United States. The struggle was so epic that it left the *Hill-Top* begging amateur photographers to part with shots of the competition so it could be properly documented in the newspaper. Before departing, the champ dazzled fans one last time by driving golf balls straight up into the air. Pleased by the enthusiastic reception he had received, Vardon accepted an invitation to return at the end of the month for another exhibition.[56]

For most golfers, tournaments proved to be the most popular form of competition. Permutations of the basic concept were wide-ranging and inventive in their creativity, making for a variety of possible contests. Tournaments followed many formats: male, female, and mixed fields; children and adult age levels; singles, pairs, and mixed pairs entries; nine, eighteen, and thirty-six holes; medal and match play. They also tested different skills. In addition to contests based upon a standard round of golf, the resort hosted driving, approaching, and putting tournaments. Driving contests rewarded golfers whose strength enabled them to hit the ball the farthest and straightest. The other two skill competitions favored those who played with accuracy and finesse. In an approach tournament, contestants played nine balls, three each from distances of eighty, forty, and twenty yards. The player who holed out all the balls with the fewest number of shots won. Putting tournaments made use of a miniature course laid out in front of the Poland Spring House in 1899. The objective was to complete a round in the least number of strokes.[57]

To the winners went the spoils. Besides the highly coveted prizes, there were the fiercely contested trophies, which in the words of the contemporary social critic of the leisure class, Thorstein Veblen, reflected "the desire of the successful men to put their prowess in evidence by exhibiting some durable result of their exploits." By 1899 golfers at the resort competed for the Maine State, Poland, and Mansion Cups. These three grand prizes grew out of a plan devised by several patrons to organize a "big golf tournament." Guests responded to the appeal for donations with great enthusiasm. In addition, some women at the resort took it upon themselves to subscribe for the purchase of a fourth prize. They established the Ladies' Cup to ensure that the golfer with the lowest gross score in the first stage of the competition received due recognition, regardless of whether his net score, the number after deducting the handicap, qualified him to continue play in later rounds.[58]

The use of handicaps in the biggest tournament of the season is instructive. For all the celebration of competition, the sport of golf, unlike any other, tried to minimize the risk of failure. For the athletic aristocracy that had worked so hard to attain its social status, too much pride and prestige was at stake to permit the routine triumph of the fittest. Thus, although they were loath to regulate competition in the economic arena, the people of progress devised all sorts of schemes to regulate competition on the golf course. For example, the best-ball format, which allowed a team to record the lower of two partners' scores on each hole, enabled Fenn and Findlay to defeat Vardon even though he had beaten or tied both players in every round. In the sport of golf, the principle of parity supplanted that of superiority. The goal was to share the awards, not to ensure that the best players always prevailed.

Even golf, however, was not all about competition. As the organizers of a "kickers" tournament in 1900 understood, some recreators were more interested in having fun than in winning. The kicker was that golfers were allowed to set their own handicaps. The incentive to inflate the number was removed by making the objective of the contest a range of scores, rather than the lowest net score. Also added to this system was the element of chance. The victor would be determined by drawing a number between eighty and ninety-five. Whoever had the corresponding net score would be declared the champion. Under these rules, the reward for golfing skill was greatly reduced and the competitive rational sport was transformed into an entertaining leisurely recreation.[59]

The arcane rules of the kickers tournament demonstrated a new trend the leisure class brought to the playing fields of the resort—the simple desire for fun. Despite the emphasis placed on the value of toughened character, healthy bodies, and earnest competition, commentators did not forget the purely pleasurable aspects of recreation. An article in a Lewiston newspaper made this point in 1892 by noting the "delectation" that play on the tennis courts, baseball field, and croquet grounds offered guests. A few years later, a promotional guide reiterated that the accommodations available for sailing, fishing, and outdoor games presented a great variety of opportunities for "entertainment and delectation." In 1894 the *Hill-Top* weighed in with the observation that the "healthful exercise" provided by games such as croquet, bowling, billiards, and pool added "fully fifty per cent to the enjoyment of the average guest."[60]

The leading idealizer of the ethic and landscape of recreational leisure at Poland Spring was Maine artist Scott Leighton. In at least two of his paintings from the 1890s, Ricker Hill and the Poland Spring House provided the backdrop for equestrian scenes set on nearby White Oak Hill. In "A Morning Ride," six finely attired gentlemen chat during a break in the hunt. Meanwhile in "At the Jump," a pack of hounds leads a dozen hunters in frenzied pursuit of an unseen quarry. Unless the activity emanated from Norton Pope's estate, where the transplanted Brooklyn businessman put the "Darwin theory" to the test breeding saddle, race, and coach horses; show and hunting dogs; and a menagerie of critters that included foxes, monkeys, and opossums, the scenes were probably imagined. At the time of Leighton's paintings, guests at the resort were more likely to take a morning ride in a

"At the Jump," Scott Leighton's depiction of the recreational landscape of leisure dates to circa 1890. Its mate, "A Morning Ride," was displayed in the Maine State Building. *Sherwood E. Bain, "N. W. Scott Leighton," Antiques, 115 (1979): 551. Photograph courtesy of Kennedy Galleries.*

carriage or on a bike than on a horse. Whether the artist painted factual or fictional scenes is not especially relevant. Their significance lies in the artist's vision. When Leighton gazed in his mind's eye across Middle Range Pond toward the hotel on the hilltop, he saw a recreational landscape, not the pastoral landscape seen by his former student, D. D. Coombs. He envisioned well-dressed equestrians, riding well-groomed horses, following well-trained hunting dogs, in imitation of the English aristocracy. He saw a "status community" that in large part defined its identity on the basis of the leisure recreations it pursued.[61]

To get from Byron Moulton's ox-cart ride in 1876 to Scott Leighton's horseback riders two decades later required a remarkable revolution in attitudes about recreation. In America's centennial year, the public still viewed leisure and the aristocrats who enjoyed it with deep suspicion. As the pace of work and life in urban industrial society quickened during the last quarter of the nineteenth century, free time gained first utility and then legitimacy. Nostalgia for simpler times, when work and play were less differentiated, and the desire to reconnect man with nature provided a romantic antimodern sanction to recreation. The arguments that exercise improved health and competition built character contributed a rational modern justification. As cultural constraints against leisure eroded further, even the pursuit of pure pleasure became an acceptable end of recreation. This revolution in thought gave birth to a new leisure class, whose participation in recreational activities helped define its identity and give its members their status. Moreover, acceptance of leisure's legitimacy added yet another layer to the appeal of the Poland Spring resort. Superimposed upon the pastoral landscape Byron Moulton found in 1876 was the recreational landscape Scott Leighton painted in the 1890s. The transformation from country farm to summer city was almost complete. Only one crowning and defining addition to the middle landscape of the city of vivid contrasts remained to be made.

The Maine State Building

Toward an Urban Vision

Scott Leighton's depiction of the recreational landscape, "A Morning Ride," hung for all Poland Spring patrons to view in another setting of cultured leisure, although this one mostly favored sedentary pursuits—the Maine State Building. Home to a museum, library, newspaper, and art gallery, the facility epitomized the ascendance of the modern urban values and vision that had transformed the hilltop over the course of four decades. Here guests could pass their leisure time in suitably genteel fashion: studying examples of natural history; reading books, literary magazines, and the resort newspaper; admiring paintings and sculptures; and examining the surrounding architecture. In short, here culture was king. No other building or landscape at the resort better symbolized the fruition of the transformation of the former country farm into a full-fledged summer city.[1]

The World's Columbian Exposition

The Maine State Building had its origin in a sprawling seven-hundred-acre fairground built on the shores of Lake Michigan to the south of downtown Chicago. The occasion for this ambitious project was the 1893 World's Columbian Exposition. More than a celebration of the past, the fair was really a tribute to progress and modernity. The White City and the barely half-century-old, still burgeoning city of Chicago stood as crowning achievements of "the consensus of American ideas, in the advancement of Art, Science, Engineering, Literature, [and] Mechanics" over the four centuries since the permanent arrival of Europeans in the New World. The event proved to be immensely popular. At the dedication of the Maine State Building, the president of Maine's Board of World's Fair Managers described the event as "the most gigantic and most magnificent exhibition that the world has ever known." Inspired by such superlatives, millions of Americans flocked to the fair. Paid attendance during the six-month run from May through October astoundingly surpassed twenty-seven million visitors in a nation of only sixty-three million citizens. The exposition was such a draw during the summer of 1893 that it depressed attendance at Poland Spring, despite the ten to fifteen thousand dollars Edward Ricker spent promoting the resort at the fair.[2]

Both the creation of the White City in Chicago and the transformation of the summer city at Poland Spring represented the convergence of architectural and landscape design trends that coalesced by the end of the nineteenth century into the ideal of the "city beautiful." Scattered projects of village improvement, urban park construction, outdoor municipal art, and city planning eventually evolved into a formal ideology and widespread movement whose fundamental premise was that a planned and orderly urban environment could produce social harmony and moral uplift. The model White City, which stood in counterpoise to the haphazardly evolved, typically problem-plagued host city, demonstrated the possibilities of coordinating space and structures, beauty and utility, and art and technology into urban design. The White City's planners acted out of the conviction that creating an orderly urban environment composed of attractive architecture and edifying institutions, interspersed with tranquil parks and inspiring monuments, could tame the teeming masses and transform them into a virtuous democratic citizenry. The hierarchical social structure implied by this conception of the quite literally reformed city and handed down from elite urban planners to a compliant public was apparent to the editors of the Hill-Top. They applauded the forum the Columbian Exposition provided for "the free exchange of ideas to the great advantage of all, from the most skilled to the most ignorant."[3]

Indeed, promoters of Poland Spring well understood the philosophy of the city beautiful movement. In 1897 the Hill-Top distilled its essence to the dictum: "Admire the beautiful, and make things beautiful that they may be admired." An editorial commented that "cities should be made beautiful as well as substantial; streets and roads should be made permanent and kept in perfect condition." The resort provided ample evidence of the beneficial effects of civic beauty. Although the hilltop became "quite a metropolitan center" as nine hundred to one thousand patrons and employees bustled about on any given day during the summer, it remained a city without disturbances, jails, policemen, or alarms. The paper attributed the absence of turmoil to the presence of "every other peaceful requirement of a city including a public library and art gallery."[4]

The connection between the White City and summer city was more than ideological. These two great exemplars of the city beautiful movement were also connected architecturally. In 1891 the nine-member committee of Maine's Board of World's Fair Managers entrusted a native son, Charles Sumner Frost, with the assignment to design a showcase for objects illustrating the state's "history, progress, moral and material welfare and future development." Born in Lewiston in 1856 and trained in architecture at the Massachusetts Institute of Technology, Frost had followed in 1881 the course of empire westward to Chicago, where he took up his trade. A decade later, Frost's plan for his home state's headquarters at the White City beat out five other submissions.[5]

The "Pavilion of Maine" was located with other state buildings across from the Palace of Arts at the northern end of the fairgrounds. Designed in the Queen Anne style, the octagonal building was constructed at a cost between eighteen and thirty thousand dollars from the finest native granite, slate, and wood supplied by fifteen Maine companies. The exterior elements included a triple-arched entrance, loggia balconies, four turrets, and a cupola. Each side of the octagon measured twenty-seven feet, giving the building an overall width of sixty-five feet. From ground to cupola, the structure stood eighty-seven feet in height. Finished in the colonial revival style, the interior featured a large rotunda surrounded by six rooms on the first floor for the relaxation of visitors; six exhibit spaces on the second floors for the presentation of "the natural and industrial products of the State"; and six alcoves on the unfinished third floor. Opposite the entrance and over the oak mantelpiece surrounding the fireplace appeared a contribution to the decor of the building from the Rickers—Leighton's equestrian painting that paid tribute to the leisure class.[6]

Given that one of the first meetings of Maine's World's Fair commissioners was held at the Poland Spring House, it is not surprising the family was so actively involved in the exposition. In addition to the painting and the display of prizewinning water, a souvenir booklet commissioned by the Board of Managers to promote "the unsurpassed summer resorts of Maine" highlighted the presence of Hiram Ricker and Sons in Chicago. The board's Committee on Summer Resorts had funded the project with a budget of one thousand dollars and contracted with George Haynes to produce thirty thousand copies of "a book illustrative and descriptive of Maine summer resorts, her manufacturing and industrial interests." Distributed at the fair, the publication became a "highly prized" souvenir.[7]

In *The State of Maine*, Haynes included a two-page spread on Poland Spring. It touched upon many of the themes that made the resort so appealing to Gilded-Age tourists—domesticity, luxury, health, and beauty. A montage of five illustrations filled the first page: one each of the Mansion, Poland Spring, and Spring Houses, as well as a scene of Middle Range Pond and Ricker Hill, and a view of the western Maine mountains from the hilltop. In the accompanying text, Haynes praised the Mansion House for its "home comforts." He identified the big hotel as "the Palace Summer Hotel of New England." He claimed that the water was "superior to any of the spas in Europe." He described the hilltop as "the centre of a beautiful and picturesque park." Finally, he depicted the mountain scenery as blue hills blended with "the azure heavens." Haynes's tribute to the site concluded with the assurance that "to be a guest of this famous and justly celebrated summer resort is to realize the ideal possibilities of health, rest and pleasure."[8]

The White City Comes to the Summer City

At the conclusion of the exposition, the Maine Board faced the vexing question of what to do with the building. When the Park Commissioners of Chicago rejected an offer to assume control of the facility, it seemed doomed to become "a white elephant." A devastating fire that swept through Jackson Park and leveled much of the White City in January 1894 increased the eagerness of the commissioners to be rid of most of the remaining buildings. Choosing from several options, the Maine managers enthusiastically accepted an ambitious plan submitted by the Rickers. The family proposed relocating the structure from Chicago to Poland Spring, where it would serve "as a memorial to the national fair" and "become the crowning feature of the opening of . . . the second century of the Ricker inns." In essence, the Maine State Building would become a huge trophy affirming that Poland Spring, the pre-eminent summer resort in the state, encapsulated what it meant to be from Maine.[9]

Facing a nineteen-day deadline to vacate the fair grounds, workmen had to disassemble the building hurriedly, while carefully adhering to a method of marking and cataloging the pieces that was described as "systematic in the extreme." Under the watchful supervision of Hiram W. Ricker, the crew identified each of the eleven rows of granite masonry by letter and each stone by number. They then loaded every single scrap of building material aboard sixteen Grand Trunk rail cars that carried the cargo on a three-day journey to Maine. The move was expensive, costing three thousand dollars. It was also fortuitous, as the structure made it off the fairgrounds shortly before Pullman rioters torched much of what remained of the White City in July 1894.[10]

Back on the hilltop, the Rickers chose a spot at the edge of the oak grove between the Mansion and Poland Spring Houses as the new home for the Maine State Building. There, "crowning the summit of this noble eminence," it would overlook "as fair and as grand a picture as that spread out about it in the 'White City.'" As the dog days of summer approached, work on the project was "being pushed rapidly." With the foundation nearly complete, the cornerstone was laid on August 14, 1894. The ceremony drew a large number of guests, who came to witness the burial of a time capsule filled with souvenirs of the resort and mementoes of the day. During the fall and winter and on into spring, the resort's head carpenter, Forrest Walker, oversaw the thorough reconstruction of the building. With the exception of the addition of dormer windows between three of the four corner turrets and commemorative black slate tablets on either side of the front entrance, the exterior was faithfully rebuilt. On the inside, workers slightly altered the arrangement of partitions on the first floor, converted the second floor into two three-room suites to accommodate additional guests, and finished off the third floor, making sure all the while to preserve the harmony of the original design. By the summer of 1895, the facility was ready to reopen.[11]

To commemorate the occasion, the Rickers organized "the greatest event that Poland ever witnessed." Dedication day, Monday July 1st, drew an overflow crowd of "men and women whose names are familiar in other walks of life." The ceremony commenced with the playing of a patriotic overture. As the tune trailed away, Joseph W. Symonds, a retired justice of the State Supreme Court, stepped forward as master of ceremonies to impart the introductory remarks. In keeping with the commemorative theme celebrating the centennial of the Rickers' arrival on the hilltop, the judge set the tone with his nostalgic comments. He recalled the "common splendor of the New England past" and the family's share "in the common glory of New England life." More than a geographic entity, New England was for him the bastion of gentility, "where liberty and learning, the graces of culture and refinement, strength and nobility of character, all the best results of civilization, have grown and flourished." "More than a mere monument of the past," the Maine

The dedication of the Maine State Building following its removal from the World's Columbian Exposition in Chicago took place before a large and distinguished gathering on July 1, 1895. Embodying the cultural ideals of the White City and city beautiful movement, the facility housed a museum, library, newspaper, and gallery for the intellectual edification and moral elevation of resort patrons. *Maine Historic Preservation Commission.*

State Building was for Symonds an extension of the values embodied in the White City and pointed "the way of the future."[12]

Sustaining the nostalgic mood of the introductory remarks, Senator William Frye reviewed the history of the Rickers in a "charming inimitable" address that "held the people entranced throughout the length." Having settled the Maine frontier at a time before schoolhouses and roads, when pioneers contended with wild forests, untamed beasts, and rocky soil, the family represented for Frye a quintessential study in success. In one century, the Rickers had transformed the site of "a mere cabin" into a resort featuring "the finest structure of a summer hotel in the United States of America." The Senator attributed the rise of the family to the archetypal virtues of several stock characters. To begin with, there were the labors of "the stern old Puritan of a father," Hiram. Next in order of importance came the lessons taught by the well-educated, firm-willed, wise, discreet, and blessed mother, Janette, who epitomized the Victorian cult of true womanhood. Finally, there was the industriousness of the three stalwart Ricker sons. Success was not entirely manmade, however. Frye ascribed much of the family's character development to the influence of nature, specifically to the hardships dealt by the geography of Maine. Among the most important "fruit gathered from the rocky hill-side farms of the dear old Pine Tree State," he contended, were a long litany of virtues, including hard work, economy, thrift, temperance, patience, perseverance, courage, and faith.[13]

It was left to the "fine flow of oratory" from General Augustus P. Martin to explain the romantic value of nature; beyond the lessons taught through the harsh realities it imposed. According to Martin, the State of Maine's reputation "as the most delightful and invigorating summer resort" on the continent confirmed the power of "unsurpassed natural scenery" to renew the health and strength of "the worn and weary all over the land." Furthermore, the clean air and fresh water in abundance on the hilltop demonstrated the "cleansing and purifying qualities" of nature. Contemptuously dismissing the "cold and scientific" modern approach to the natural world, the general called for a revival of the ancient understanding of nature as a "romantic story." His own romanticism led him to portray Poland Spring as a "grand cathedral of its Maker," where the soul became "purer, stronger, more enduring, more powerful, more helpful, and more hopeful."[14]

Martin's optimistic view of nature, based upon nostalgic memories of his childhood in New Gloucester, contrasted starkly with the pessimistic view of urban life he had formed during his tenure as a Boston Police Commissioner. Nature was spiritual, poetical, and ethereal. The city was a place of heartless materialism, daily drudgery, and mundane prosiness. The "calm sunshine," he believed, would make harried moderns "forget the battles, the downfalls, the cuts and scars of life's great fight." Sounding like an evangelist, Martin concluded with the fervent hope that his remarks would help awaken man's better nature and divert "the flow of his mind from the channel of his daily avocation into that higher, broader, purer sphere of life which shall know no change."[15]

Senator Eugene Hale expressed similarly antiurban sentiments in his speech, although with less gravity and more wit. Addressing the Maine State Building as his "young friend," he thanked the Lord that it had gotten out of Chicago safely, alluding to its potential fate at the hands of the Pullman arsonists. The senator likened the move to exchanging "an election riot in the lower streets of New York City" for "the placidity of a Shaker meeting here in the State of Maine." Turning to engage his subject directly, Hale advised the building that "you ought to be glad that you are rid of noise, my young friend, and temptation, and anarchists, my young friend, and that you have come down here where nature sits at her best and broods lovingly over such a scene as human eyes have rarely witnessed." The antimodern message to the people of progress was clear. Cities were places of danger, contention, commotion, disorder, and sin. The resort, in contrast, was a place of perfect tranquility.[16]

In unintentional rebuttal, two speakers, who focused on the origins of the Maine State Building in the idealized White City, blunted the harsh assessments of the Gilded-Age city. Representing the Governor of Massachusetts, Judge Advocate General Edgar R. Champlin recalled the Celestial City that had sprung up in Chicago "with the whiteness of the lily of the valley." It seemed entirely appropriate to him that the Maine pavilion now stood amid "a city upon a hill," for both cities manifested the achievements of planning and design. Marveling at the waterworks, electric-light station, beautiful buildings, and natural attractions at Poland Spring, he concluded: "This has not happened by chance. There has been one mind planning, one mind working, and that mind is the mind of the Rickers." True to the values of the city beautiful movement, he prophesied that in the years to come, the Maine State Building would better prepare visitors "for the duties of citizenship." Moreover, Champlin predicted that it would "impress on the minds and hearts of those who come here the great truths of American liberty and American freedom." Likewise, the mere sight of the structure transported Representative Charles A. Boutelle back to "that magical White City on the borders of Lake Michigan." He hoped that the salvaged remnant of the fair would radiate the influences of art and literature and would revivify the "spirit of Americanism."[17]

Despite the overtures to nostalgia and nature, and the undertow of antimodernism and antiurbanism, the real point of the dedication ceremony was a celebration of progress. The prime presenter of that message was Maine Governor Henry B. Cleaves, in whose estimation the upward ascendance of American civilization was both unambiguous and unabated. The theme was a favorite one of the governor. At the original dedication of the Maine State Building in Chicago, Cleaves had heralded the progress of "the good old mother State" and the American Republic. On this day, too, he paid tribute to "the rapid progress of this great North American Republic," which he described in forceful language that made "an excellent impression" on his audience as "the best, the grandest, the purest, the noblest republic that was ever given to the world." The governor also praised "the noble sons of Hiram Ricker" for their liberality, earnestness, energy, and most of all, progressiveness. By dedicating the Maine State Building to "the cause of education," the Cleaves contended, the Rickers made possible "streams of light, of brightness and wisdom" that would strengthen the home, the citizen, the town, the city, the commonwealth, and ultimately, the entire republic.[18]

The connection between progress and culture as embodied in the Maine State Building also served as the basis for remarks by Justice William P. Whitehouse of the Maine Supreme Court. In his opinion, the accomplishments of the "magnificent enterprise" at Poland Spring rivaled the "rushing tide of progress" witnessed in the fields of business, art, and science. He especially lauded the proprietors for advancing "the tide of intelligent social life" at the resort. Whitehouse reckoned the ability to combine successfully the contrasts of entertainment and culture as "the genius of the Ricker family." The judge complimented the proprietors for striving to intertwine nature and knowledge, as well as the contrasts of soul and mind, in the Maine State Building. Resorting to metaphorical prose, he imagined that thousands of guests would "breathe the air from the treasure rooms of literature and inhale learning as they walk amid the foliage of a well-filled library." Imbued with a less tempting ideal of the fruit of the tree of knowledge, Whitehouse enraptured the audience with imagery of "the odor of leather-scented volumes" that would be as "fragrant as the first bloom of those sciential apples that grew amid the happy orchard." In this idyllic vision, the Maine State Building would be a genteel paradise of books and paintings. In short, it would be an Eden of Culture.[19]

Collectively, the ten speakers who followed the master of ceremonies to the podium had laid out the central contrasts that had shaped the hilltop over the past one hundred years. As Representative Nelson Dingley, Jr., insightfully summarized the occasion, the resort was "a great transformation scene," where both "the lovers of learning and lovers of scenery" were accommodated. Some orations, informed by modern values, had appealed to the former group, as speakers paid homage to progress, culture, and the city beautiful. Other talks, containing strains of antimodernism, had resounded with the notes of nostalgia, romanticism, and antiurbanism that appealed to the rusticating inclinations of the latter group. The overarching goal of the reconstruction project was for the Maine State Building to "monumentalize the presence of culture." Defined during the Gilded Age as the pursuit of social refinement, aesthetic sensibilities, and higher learning, culture was the keystone of order. The facility promoted this ideal by providing a home for the leading institutions of genteel culture. The Rickers had the parlors, smoking rooms, and reception areas on the first floor converted into museum display spaces, reading rooms, a library, and a newspaper office. In addition, the previously unused third floor became an "admirably lighted and designed" gallery. Under the auspices and guidance of the proprietors of the Poland Spring resort, the building was set to encourage "the advancement and the perpetuation of Art and Literature."[20]

The Museum

The Maine State Building functioned in part as a museum, having as its principal purpose education. Wall and floor space under the rotunda gradually filled up with photographs of featured scenes from the World's Columbian Exposition, portraits of leading men of progress, and displays of interesting specimens of nature. It made for an instructive juxtaposition of the presumed progressive effects of Social and Scientific Darwinism. In addition to the tableaux to evolution, souvenirs and curios collected by the Rickers and donated by well-wishers decorated the room. Joining the mounted moose head above the fireplace was a stuffed American eagle, "a splendid specimen of our National Bird of Freedom." Near one of the stairwells stood an ornate and valuable Japanese vase presented by two officials of the Pennsylvania Insurance Company. Measuring five feet in height and over six feet in circumference at its widest, the object was appraised by a New York art dealer as "one of the largest ever brought to this country." Watching over all this was an autographed portrait of "the prince of showmen," Phineas T. Barnum, whose relatives were "staunch patrons of Poland Spring."[21]

The picture of the patron saint of the American museum and Victorian popular culture joined an impressive pantheon of respectable gentlemen. One wall honored Presidents Washington, Lincoln, and McKinley, as well as Vice President Garret A. Hobart, whose family regularly visited the resort. Most of the other portraits paid tribute to native sons of Maine. The nationally known prohibitionist Neal Dow, poet Henry Wadsworth Longfellow, and politicians Hannibal Hamlin, Thomas Brackett Reed, and James Blaine were prominently featured. They shared wall space with pictures of the entire congressional delegation of the state, nine of the eleven dedication day speakers, several members of the state judiciary, and one highly valued Maine-born guest, Crosby Noyes. These famous moderns watched over glass cases securing the relics of anonymous ancients that were part of "a large and valuable" display of local Indian artifacts.[22]

Abundant displays of flora also adorned the rotunda. Throughout the room stood jardinieres of wildflowers and cultivated plants purposefully placed with an eye toward providing patrons with many pleasing views. Complementing the floral arrangements was one entire room on the first floor devoted to botanical exhibits. The fern room, so named because of a decorative frieze located there, owed its existence to the work of Kate Furbish. An amateur botany enthusiast from Brunswick, Maine, Furbish had gained a reputation for the watercolor illustrations she painted of her discoveries. In 1893 the Rickers appointed Furbish the resort's resident botanist and furnished her with living quarters and studio space. In exchange, she had the duty of gathering samples of local wildflowers and preparing an instructional pamphlet for the benefit of guests. Somewhat skeptical of the assignment, Furbish had the impression that the real reason for her presence was to provide "for the amusement of the half invalid." Despite her reservations about the intent of the project, she faithfully recorded throughout the summer the location and flowering dates of the plant species found within a three-mile radius of the hilltop. By the end of her first collecting season, Furbish had catalogued 563 specimens in her journal.[23]

Having found "the flora of Poland very rich in rare plants," Furbish returned to the resort the next two summers and added to her inventory. By the time the Maine State Building opened, her herbarium had grown to over six hundred plants, each of which she had mounted and identified with a specially printed label. Described as "a labor of love," the "exquisitely-prepared" exhibit was sure "to delight the botanist," the Hill-Top predicted. It certainly delighted the paper, which promoted Furbish's work as "the only collection of 'wild flowers' ever on exhibition at any hotel in the world." Furbish never did complete the pamphlet assignment that had originally brought her to the resort. She did, however, head off to the Portland Museum of Natural History a few days after the dedication of the Maine State Building to present a pair of papers on the flora of Poland Spring to a gathering of nearly one hundred fellow botanical enthusiasts. In the years to come, Furbish continued to scour the countryside surrounding the hilltop until her finds numbered 732 different varieties of plants in all.[24]

Precisely as the Hill-Top had hoped, the herbarium did indeed attract "much interest." Furbish's specimens were exhibited forty-eight at a time and were rotated weekly. The display had the desired effect of developing patrons' appreciation for "Nature's garden." Soon after the opening of the Maine State Building, the newspaper reported that Mrs. B. F. Redfern had collected two previously uncataloged plants in West Poland. By the time of her return to Boston at the end of August, the appropriately named Redfern had made several more "valuable additions" to the museum collection. A few years later, another inspired guest added a unique discovery to the botanical display, two Sun-dew plants, whose glutinous beads trapped unsuspecting insects. Wildflowers were not the only specimens that comprised the herbarium. In 1897 Dr. Schuyler displayed some of the mushrooms he had gathered. Furbish joined the hunt, too. Responding to a guest who had shown "a little interest" in plant life, the resort's resident botanist prepared a list of over thirty mushrooms she had collected between 1896 and 1899 in the woods leading to the pumping station. Furbish closed her letter with a note of satisfaction, writing "it makes me very happy to learn that there is even one who enjoys these interesting plants."[25]

Besides botanicals, other specimens of the natural world demonstrated "the line of progression" at Poland Spring. To augment the displays in the fern room, the Hill-Top solicited donations of additional natural curiosities. In particular, the paper sought items from Maine's forests, quarries, and mines so that the hundreds of visitors who viewed the exhibits each summer would gain more familiarity with "the natural wealth of the state." The plea produced at least two contributions. One guest gave his butterfly collection to the museum. The second donation had no local connection, but was interesting nonetheless. It consisted of shark bones, teeth, and shells that a businessman from Wilmington, North Carolina, had retrieved from his artesian well.[26]

More in keeping with the request of the Hill-Top, three large cases "for the display of a magnificent collection of minerals of superior value" filled out the fern room. This exhibit, which "attracted a vast deal of attention," focused on the products of local mines such as tourmaline from Mt. Mica in Paris and quartz from Mt. Apatite in Auburn. Although the paper claimed that these common Maine gems rivaled "the diamond in beauty and brilliance," rarities such as a gold nugget from the Canadian Klondike, as well as meteorite fragments from Canyon Diablo in Arizona and the Sacramento Mountains of New Mexico were the more popular draws. Presiding over the minerals in much the same way Furbish did over plants was E. R. Chadbourn of Lewiston. Every Thursday during the summer of 1898, the mineralogist visited the Maine State Building to answer questions about the exhibit. He also supplied the *Hill-Top* with articles or with information for columns about minerals. In his absence, the curious could consult copies of the "Complete Mineral Catalogue" that Chadbourn offered for sale.[27]

As so often happened at Poland Spring, consumer culture soon competed with genteel culture. While Chadbourn tried to encourage appreciation for the scientific and aesthetic value of the gems, "the fortune-seeking appetite" generated much of their allure. Guests could purchase samples promoted as "attractive souvenirs—suitable for the cabinet, the mantel or the centre-table." Besides their appointed place in the Victorian curio cabinet back home, some minerals had utility as mundane domestic tools such as paperweights and letter openers. Their highest value, however, was as items of conspicuous consumption, the pieces of personal jewelry that sparkled and shone at the resort's banquets and balls.[28]

The marriage of nature and commerce also took place in the museum's quirky cork exhibit. Mounted in tribute to the celebrated stoppers used in Poland Water bottles, the display was described as "an object lesson in cork." Every imaginable form of the material was shown—curved, flattened, stripped, squared, clipped, and rounded; so, too, were the special knives and "other implements used in the service of manufacture." Surrounding the display were a series of photographs illustrating the steps that went into the production process. The most notable novelty of the display was "the whole history of cork" carved in relief, naturally, out of the wood. In the foreground, the tableaux showed workshops where the stages of stripping, boiling, cutting, rounding, sieving, sorting, baling, and carting took place. In the background were a grove of cork trees and a harbor scene of the Mediterranean city of San Feliu de Guixols, Spain, the source for the premier cork that kept Poland Water safe from impurities.[29]

The Library

Like the Maine State Building, the Rickers considered the library housed in it one of the unique features that set their resort apart from others. When the family acquired the structure in 1894, it gained 175 books in the bargain. Supplemented by ninety-seven donated volumes of "old works," this constituted the extent of the collection on opening day. The books were shelved in glass cases located in the first-floor room that also doubled as the librarian's quarters. The office was situated off the rotunda, where a long table contained "the current periodical literature of the day," twenty-two comfortable rattan chairs invited occupancy, and many pleasant nooks provided places to lounge and read. "A free circulation of air and a constant changing of the atmosphere" made possible by ample open space, added to the hospitable and refreshing ambience of the reading room.[30]

Spurred on by the contribution of 138 "standard" titles from General Augustus Martin, who backed up his idealistic rhetoric with philanthropic deeds, and another 75 classics from another generous donor, the library grew to 854 books by the end of the first season. Five years later, the count stood at almost three thousand. Nearly three hundred "interested guests," led by the generous General Martin and public-spirited Senator Frye, had donated virtually the entire collection. Another "highly prized feature of the institution" was its extensive periodical selection. The library subscribed to most of the "standard and current" magazines of the day, including the *Atlantic Monthly, Harper's Monthly, Ladies' Home Journal, London Illustrated News, New England Magazine, North American Review, Scientific American,* and *Youth's Companion.*[31]

Guests had access to the library between 9:00 A.M. and 9:00 P.M. on weekdays and 10:00 A.M. and 8:30 P.M. on Sundays. An honor system rather than rigid rules governed use of the facility. Because of the limited size of the collection and short duration of the season, patrons could only borrow one book at a time and had to return it within one week. Delinquents had little to worry about, however, as the library charged no fees, required no deposits, and collected no fines. In spite of the lax operating procedures, the system worked. Six years passed before the first book disappeared.[32]

Overseer of this relaxed and friendly operation was Frank Carlos Griffith. Hailing from Roxbury, Massachusetts, by way of his native Dixfield, Maine, Griffith served as the librarian for all but six summers between 1895 and 1929. During the remainder of the year, he was a theatrical agent, whose most famous client was actress Minnie Maddern Fiske. Between 1895 and 1900, a succession of assistants helped Griffith. In 1896 Mrs. Griffith joined her husband in the library. The following season, Robert Marsh, a grandson of Hiram and Janette Ricker, filled the role.[33]

Despite the informality of the library, Griffith meticulously attended to his duties. Arriving well before opening time, he raised the curtains to their proper height, dated the guest register, filled the inkwells, sharpened the pencils, unlocked the bookcases, straightened the shelves, and laid out the periodicals. On slow days, he had time to repair, rebind, and reshelve books. More often, though, he entertained a steady stream of visitors. This is how Griffith facetiously described a typical day on duty. The librarian had to ex-

The library was just one of the functions of the Maine State Building and responsibilities of Frank Carlos Griffith, who is pictured at work in his office. In addition to serving as librarian, he edited the resort newspaper, the *Hill-Top*, and assisted Nettie Ricker with the operation of the art gallery. *Maine Historic Preservation Commission.*

plain to an argumentative patron the reason for the book-borrowing limit. He had to find out for an inquisitive lady the maiden name of King Tut's wife. He had to explain to a skeptical stranger the origins of the Japanese vase in the rotunda. Finally, he had to help giggling girls come up with ideas for the upcoming costume party. It was all in a day's work for Griffith, who, judging by his long tenure, must have enjoyed his summer job despite the trials he mentioned.[34]

The demands of the job did not prevent Griffith from compiling detailed records. Befitting the mathematical bent of an efficiency-obsessed industrial age, he could supply an array of statistics calculated to impress. The busiest and slowest days of the week were Sunday and Tuesday in August 1897, but Saturday and Wednesday in June 1899. The circulation for the busiest single day was seventy-two books checked out on Monday, August 24, 1896. The record for the highest daily average circulation over an entire week was forty-three volumes per day during the fourth week of August in 1897. The total number of books checked out each month ranged from 1,107 in August 1896 to 1,452 in September and October 1900. Finally, the total volumes circulated each season nearly doubled from 2,574 in 1896 to 4,950 in 1900.[35]

The urge for order and efficiency also led Griffith to classify and account for each volume by subject matter. A slight majority of books fit into one of three categories: light fiction, classics, and public documents. The abundance of the last classification owed mainly to the large number of donations from Senator Frye. In addition to the top three, the other categories of books, accounting for anywhere from 38 to 46 percent of the entire library collection, were, in order, history, juvenile, magazines, miscellaneous, religion, poetry, biography, reference, and travel. The relative percentage of subject matter remained fairly constant between 1896 and 1900, with one notable exception. The number of fiction titles dramatically increased by nearly half, from 18 to 27 percent.[36]

Because it ran counter to the cultural objectives of the city beautiful movement, the growing popularity of light fiction, with its emphasis on entertainment and pleasure rather than education and elevation, caused concern. Reviewing the library's circulation figures in 1905, the *Hill-Top* reported that 80 percent of the books checked out fell into this classification, while only 13 percent were by standard writers and the remaining 7 percent represented all other categories. At a loss to explain the statistics, the paper termed the reading habits of the resort's patrons an enigma. By 1909 the concern flared into full-fledged alarm. An editorial dismissed light and interesting books as drugs that "dull the mind into a torpor of unnatural sentiment or excitement." Shifting metaphors, the guest editorialist then likened light fiction to sugar and the nutritious literary classics to broiled filet of beef. The essential ingredient distinguishing the two genres was realism. The writer viewed the book as "the guiding friend in whom we see the world as in a mirror." Its purpose was to uplift—to raise the reader above "the horizon of human existence." The anonymous literary critic, therefore, championed the merits of Irving, Hawthorne, Thackeray, Dickens, Balzac, and Scott, authors whose works would "reward some reader with cross-sections of real throbbing life."[37]

To a great extent, the popularity of light fiction stemmed from changes in the publishing field. Noting the power of commerce to overshadow art in modern times, the *Hill-Top* detailed the formula for publishing a successful novel. The first step was to create "an artistically designed cover." Next came the choice of an appealing title. Then followed the selection of a plain and distinct type font, making certain to use ample margins and generous spacing on each printed page. The final step in the production process was to make sure to include excellent illustrations. The actual story ranked very low in the list of priorities. A book "started rolling with good and well advised advertising," the paper cynically observed. Especially certain to gain the publication "a vogue many a better book will hunger for" was a testimonial from a well-known personality. Once again, modern consumer culture had supplanted Victorian genteel culture.[38]

The Newspaper

The Maine State Building also served as headquarters for the *Hill-Top*, the official chronicler, promoter, and arbiter of genteel culture at the resort. Conceived in 1894, the newspaper was the brainchild of two enterprising employees of the Poland Spring House, Harry T. Jordan, an office worker, and Don Freeman, the head bellman. The stated purpose of the original editors was to publish a paper that would serve "the interests of the Poland Spring Hotels and their visitors." To that end, they pledged in the first issue to "present a bright, clean, newsy, readable publication." In addition, they promised to tackle the challenge with "hard, faithful, conscientious work." Jordan and Freeman hoped that the result of their efforts would "be worthy of representing one of the grandest, most magnificent and liberally managed hotel resorts in the country."[39]

Many supporters assisted the endeavor. Maine author Holman Day wrote the lead article, "Facts and Fancies at Poland Spring," for the first issue. Benjamin Keith and Joseph Sawyer gathered newsworthy information on fellow guests. Nelson Dingley made the presses of his Lewiston newspaper available for printing the periodical. The editors were also grateful to the many local merchants who agreed to place ads in the untested publication. The main backer of the enterprise was Edward Ricker. He shrewdly agreed to buy $250 worth of advertising if, and only if, Jordan and Freeman published ten issues during the initial season, even one less and they would receive nothing in payment. The editors met the challenge and actually exceeded the quota by one. Suggesting how tight the resort's profit margin was, Ricker joked when he finally paid the bill that he would gladly trade the profits of the Poland Spring House for those of the *Hill-Top*.[40]

The editors put out issues for eleven weeks during the heart of the summer season from July to September. The deadline for submitting material was Thursday. As soon as the edited copy was ready, the resort's courier set out to the printers in Lewiston. Along the way, he also sought to make a little extra pocket money, while simultaneously promoting the paper, by offering to pick up items for guests from any store that advertised in the *Hill-Top*. If all went well, copies hit the newsstand on Sunday morning. Readers could purchase single issues for ten cents or they could subscribe for the season by paying one dollar. The latter option allowed guests who could not stay for the entire summer to keep up from home on all the social and cultural activities taking place at the resort.[41]

The paper was a success from the outset. Issues sold like "proverbial hot cakes," sometimes requiring second printings to meet the demand. The expanding length of the *Hill-Top* and the rising number of advertisers demonstrated its popularity. From twelve pages in 1894, the publication steadily expanded in increments of four pages, so that by 1899 each issue featured thirty-two pages. Advertisers increased annually from nineteen in 1894 to ninety-nine in 1900. Most of the 171 businessmen and companies that advertised during the seven-year span were located either in Poland, Auburn, Lewiston, Portland, Boston, or New York. Besides Hiram Ricker and Sons, four advertisers, architect George Coombs, jeweler H. A. Osgood, and physician Dr. Milton Wedgwood each of Lewiston, as well as accountant John O. Rice of Portland, appeared in issues during all seven years. The main categories of goods and services advertised covered the essentials of leisure-class consumer culture: hotels (23.4 percent), apparel (15.2 percent), furnishings (11.1 percent), foodstuffs (8.8 percent), medicine (8.2 percent), and transportation (8.2 percent).[42]

On a more subjective level, guest Terence McGowan, himself the editor of a periodical in Portland, provided this qualitative assessment: "there is no resort paper in America that quite equals the *Hill-Top*." As the editors proudly shared with their audience, the *National Hotel Reporter* concurred in the opinion. "The abundant high-class advertising given it," indicated to the trade journal "how well business men appreciate its merits." Praising the periodical for being "notably attractive, beautifully printed, and beautifully illustrated," the *Reporter* remarked that readers of the resort newspaper were not likely either to throw it away or regard it as useless.[43]

The format and content of the *Hill-Top* varied little over the years. As Jordan and Freeman had promised in the inaugural issue, each edition opened with "a regular illustrated article on some point of interest about Ricker Hill, or in the vicinity." The feature usually ran two to three pages in length. In addition to the advertisements, each issue also typically included an editorial and a list of the latest arrivals. "Bubbles," which in 1895 became known as "Tid-Bits," served as the combination society and gossip column, or in the more high-toned genteel language of the editors "as a medium of information concerning our guests." Indicating that the leisure class was far from idle, schedules for the many daily activities of the resort regimen dotted the paper's pages. Reports on "all dances, hops, and germans; boating, fishing, and riding parties; base-ball games, card parties, entertainments, etc." during the preceding week rounded out the remainder of each edition.[44]

The seemingly omnipresent fixture of the Maine State Building, Frank Griffith, succeeded Jordan and Freeman as a coeditor of the Hill-Top in 1895. He shared the post until 1906 with Nettie Ricker, although her role seems to have been nominal at best. In addition to fulfilling so capably the duties of librarian, Griffith became the real driving force behind the paper. During his long tenure, he wrote most of the copy for each issue, including the lead article, editorial, and art column, as well as many of the special features.[45]

Although the paper encouraged submissions from contributors, few guests accepted the invitation. Two who did were authors Jane Patterson and Marcia Jordan, both of whom contributed poems. In the eleventh issue of the Hill-Top in 1899, their works shared the same page in the children's section. Patterson titled her rhyme "Root of the Matter," while Jordan called hers "Little Bluebird." The paper had published two other examples of Patterson's verse, one each in 1897 and 1898. Jordan was more prolific, contributing nine poems in total between 1896 and 1900, as well as two articles in 1900. She eventually collected many of her poems into a booklet entitled "A Flush of June," which her friends the Rickers made sure was promoted extensively and enthusiastically in the Hill-Top and offered for sale at the newsstand in the Poland Spring House. Jordan showed her gratitude for the family's sponsorship of her literary career by dedicating a poem to Nettie Ricker, about whom she wrote: "The 'daybreaks' touched with rosy tint . . . whisper in my ear, / The generous loyal thought of her, Whose friendship I hold dear!"[46]

The Art Gallery

Whereas the museum had education and the newspaper information as their primary goals, the gallery had as its main objective the aesthetic elevation of patrons. As adherents of the city beautiful movement, the Rickers knew that art exhibitions were "the rule in all large cities." As architects of a summer city, the family realized it, too, needed to establish a facility "in the interest of advancement in art." Having a gallery at the resort would fill guests with pleasure, serve them up a mental feast, and impress them with "liberal feeling." The family dared hope it might even provide local residents with "an art education."[47]

The driving force behind the creation of the gallery was Nettie Ricker. When not involved with putting together the *Hill-Top*, she devoted her time to establishing an art facility "of high standard and merit." It was the perfect project for a frustrated artist. Like her mother and namesake before her, Nettie fancied herself a painter. She had studied at Cowles Art School in Boston and even carried her passion to the point of training with Robert Vonnoh and Abbott Graves, two accomplished and notable artists of the era. Lack of success in the field, eventually sent Nettie into a "decline" that culminated in outright depression. Her brothers tried to buoy the young woman's spirits by placing her in charge of the gallery in the Maine State Building, where they intended to display "representative work of representative American painters."[48]

Nettie eagerly took up the assignment. Unlike exhibition directors at many other galleries, she personally invited artists to contribute rather than accepting unsolicited submissions. As a consequence, Nettie spent her springtimes traveling to Boston and New York, negotiating with artists, selecting works, arranging for their shipment, overseeing their installation, and compiling an annual exhibition catalog with the help of Frank Griffith. The day-to-day operation of the gallery and entertainment of visiting artists filled her summers. With the arrival of fall came the tasks of returning the art and planning for the following year's display. Coupled with her involvement with the resort newspaper, it made for a busy year. Her reward was psychological satisfaction rather than riches. Nettie's labors as gallery director also eventually brought her the professional recognition she craved—associate membership in the Guild of Boston Artists. As her spirits improved, Nettie adopted almost a regal air about herself. Photographed one year in the velvet and ermine dress and ostrich-feather hat that she wore to an Artists' Ball in Boston, she looked like a queen on her throne. Interestingly, one of her hobbies in her younger years had been collecting cabinet and post cards of European royalty.[49]

Nettie's approach toward the inaugural exhibition was one of experimentation. When the Maine State Building opened in July, the six alcoves in the third-floor gallery contained thirty-nine pictures by eleven artists. Two months later, the display had grown to fifty-six official entries, three of which had already sold, by nineteen artists. Free catalogs available in the library informed viewers about the title and creator of each work. By day, natural sunlight streaming through glass skylights brightened the gallery. By night, artificial electric illumination spotlighted the pictures "to better advantage." Despite the pretensions of aesthetic enlightenment and moral elevation, market economics were never far away in the Gilded-Age gallery. Significantly, one of the ways the *Hill-Top* assessed the value of the inaugural exhibit was monetarily. The price tag for all the art works displayed in 1895 amounted to $13,715, an average of almost $250 per painting.[50]

In addition to the formal art exhibit, visitors to the gallery in 1895 viewed several familiar depictions of the hilltop that decorated the walls of the Maine State Building. On the first floor appeared "Presidential Range from the Poland Spring House" by S. P. Hodgsdon, as well as Leighton's "A Morning Ride." Ascending the stairway to the third level, "an excellent watercolor" of the Mansion House by William J. Bixbee and "a thoroughly excellent" painting of the old Ricker school house by Frank H. Shapleigh were displayed in the balcony area overlooking the rotunda. A landscape by Janette Wheeler Ricker, one of "a number of meritorious canvases" the matriarch of the resort painted during her lifetime, also graced the space. Included in the official exhibition were two works by her daughter, Nettie. One was a landscape, the other a still life, which the hardly impartial resort newspaper described as "an attractive little picture . . . quiet in its pretensions but effective, and true in its drawing and coloring."[51]

The *Hill-Top* preferred natural themes and invited weary guests to view the many images of "the sea, the sky, the flowers, the fruit, the woods, the shaded path" on display in the gallery. The reward for feeding the "inner sense" in this way, the periodical advised, would be "calm repose." To reinforce the point, the paper told the story of a "delightful gentleman," who owed his serenity and equanimity to the depictions of nature with which he surrounded himself. Pictures of a delightful woodland babbling brook and a "realistic representation of an Alaskan glacier" decorated his office. At his home, "nature's pleasing subjects" had replaced disquieting works by the old masters, which had included many scenes of suffering brought about by storms, shipwrecks, battles, and strife. Reportedly, the results had been beneficial.[52]

To ensure that the prosperous economic and respectable social elites became the competent cultural elite possessing the requisite knowledge to appreciate the works on display, the resort hosted a series of art history lectures soon after the gallery opened. In early August, Carolyn M. Field presented illustrated talks in the reading room of the Maine State Building. Excellent audiences turned out to learn about ancient, classical, and early Christian art, as well as Romanesque and Gothic architecture. Beginning in 1896, the regularly featured "Art Notes" in the *Hill-Top* did their part to educate guests about the virtues of art, craftsmanship of specific masterpieces, and backgrounds of selected artists.[53]

In the same year, forty-two artists contributed 136 works to the second annual exhibition. The growth in size reflected the Gilded Age's preference for abundance and Victorian culture's predilection for virtually floor-to-ceiling Salon-style displays designed to overwhelm viewers. The increase in the number of selections also demonstrated a more expansive view of art. Intending "to do everything possible to encourage the development" of the new photographic medium, the *Hill-Top* proposed the inclusion of photographs taken by guests. The many fine views of natural scenery, "interesting architectural features," "charming groups," and "elaborate turnouts" in the area presented a wealth of artistic possibilities for the owners of Kodak, Quad, Hawkeye, and Detective cameras. The paper made the suggestion more enticing by raising the possibility of awarding "elegant prizes" to the best entries.[54]

For the Ricker family, expanding the exhibit and opening it to photos paled in significance to a permanent addition made in 1896. As guests entered the gallery, "the gentle, sweet and refined features" of Janette Ricker greeted them. More than a dozen years after her death, Janette's influence still loomed large on the hilltop. Senator Frye had honored the memory of the "representative American *mother*" in his remarks at the dedication of the Maine State Building a year earlier. The day after the ceremony, sisters Cynthia and Sarah Ricker, accompanied by one of Janette's sisters, had made a pilgrimage to their mother's childhood home in Rumford, Maine. Now the patron saint of all things maternal and creative at Poland Spring had a more public, prominent, and permanent presence, where all could venerate her, guests as well as progeny. Both a tribute to her artistry and a shrine to her domesticity, the portrait of the "kindly New England mother" enabled the resort's matriarch to "add a welcome to all visitors, as she did while living."[55]

Between 1895 and 1900, the number of works included in the exhibitions fluctuated from a low of 35 in 1899 to a high of 139 in 1900, according to the shifting whims and criteria of curators Ricker and Griffith. Along the way, more than a little commercialism, in addition to elitism, crept into the agenda of cultural advancement. The *Hill-Top* not only frequently reminded guests of the availability of the works on display and the readiness of the librarian to quote prices, it also aggressively promoted art as a commodity. A bear art market in 1897 and 1898 caused the paper to urge readers to buy before the tariff on imported works and "the full return of Prosperity" forced prices back up again. During the 1900 season, the cumulative value of the exhibit totaled over thirty thousand dollars, surpassing all previous records, and presenting conspicuous consumers with "rare opportunities" to "add much to the value and attractiveness of private collections." The abundance of paintings priced at between fifty and one hundred dollars also afforded guests the chance to "beautify the home, gratify the taste for artistic work and advance art," all at a reasonable cost.[56]

The desire to advance American art provided much of the impetus for both the aesthetic and commercial appeals behind the promotional campaign. Although Europe undeniably possessed a far longer artistic heritage replete with "giants of the brush and palette" and unquestionably set the standards for recognition in the world of art, the *Hill-Top* still avidly championed the cause of native artists. They, too, could paint "good" pictures, with good defined as art that accurately represented nature and created atmosphere. "American Art," therefore, deserved "all the encouragement possible," the paper asserted in an outburst of cultural nationalism.[57]

Relatively few guests heeded the pleas. Nor did the warning that "some one will awake to the fact that the picture they had marked as theirs has been acquired by another" arouse much response. Patrons purchased less than 3 percent of the 586 paintings exhibited between 1895 and 1900. In addition to two paintings sold by D. D. Coombs, "November Twilight" by John Enneking was among the select few to find a taker, in this case, a resort patron from New Jersey, who bought the work for one hundred dollars in 1898. One of the most successful purveyors of artwork at Poland Spring was a former student of Enneking's, Boston painter Agnes Leavitt. The key to her success was the subject matter she favored—picturesque New England landscapes, especially ones associated with the surroundings of the resort. In 1897 she sold two of her works to a guest from St. Louis, Missouri. "Birch Tree a Century Old," a watercolor "full of the richness of color more commonly associated with oil," fetched Leavitt one hundred fifty dollars; while a New Hampshire scene, "Haying on the Lower Slope of Mt. Monadnock," brought forty dollars. Three years later, Leavitt placed two more watercolors of local scenes

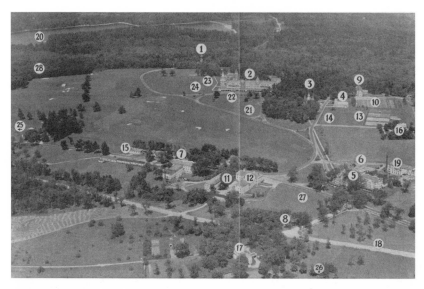

This aerial view of the Poland Spring resort from the mid-twentieth century shows the extent of the complex. In scope, as well as scale, the Ricker family transformed the hilltop into "a city of vivid contrasts." 1. Spring House and Bottling Plant. 2. Poland Spring House. 3. Maine State Building. 5. Mansion House. 20. Lower Range Pond. 24. Golf Course. *"Maine's 5000 Acre Natural Playground" (author's collection).*

on display. The resort newspaper judged them both superb and reminded readers they "would serve as excellent souvenirs." Apparently, Nettie Ricker agreed, as she purchased "Pine Grove in Poland" for the bargain price of thirty-five dollars.[58]

Given the smattering of paintings sold, the *Hill-Top* measured the popularity of the exhibitions in other ways. In 1897 the paper noted "a very largely increased interest" in the gallery. Similarly, it reported the following season that appreciation of and inquiries about pieces in the display grew daily. The interest had even spread beyond the confines of the resort. The periodical proudly proclaimed in 1898: "the Poland Spring Exhibition has taken its place among the annual collections of art work of the country, and in the few years it has been in progress it has attained a prominence which has been most flattering." A few years later, S. S. Miles affirmed the self-congratulations. Following a visit to Poland Spring on the occasion of the tenth annual exhibition, this "dean of Boston newspaper men" reported that "numerous art critics" from the hub of New England culture had given unanimous approval to the display. Praising the Ricker brothers for bringing "the educating interest" to the area, he described the gallery as a "Mecca" that saved Maine from "total art eclipse." His condescension concluded with the optimism characteristic of a faithful disciple of the city beautiful ideology: "the consequent education in art cannot be other than elevating and beneficial."[59]

As far as the snobbish Bostonian was concerned, the Rickers had succeeded in their goal of bringing a summer city of culture to the blighted backwoods of the Pine Tree state. They had successfully transformed the Maine State Building into a place the people of progress flocked to "by thousands" in order to partake of "fruits of the brain and hand of artists and literateurs." In addition to the gallery glimpsed by Miles, the museum, library, and newspaper each offered patrons scaled-down versions of the leading institutions of metropolitan society that defined modern urban culture. In the Maine State Building, they could experience the contrasts of resort life. They could admire gems of nature while calculating their value as jewels of fashion. They could surround themselves with official government publications, intellectual literary magazines, heroic histories, and informative reference works while they leisurely devoured light fiction. They could read about the prime features of the resort and local landmarks of the countryside while leafing through the *Hill-Top* to find the latest gossipy bubbles and tidbits. They could be inspired by works of art while envisioning how they would add to the decor of the parlor back home. In sum, within the capacious eight walls of the Maine State Building, guests of the Poland Spring resort could be comfortably, complexly, ambiguously, ambivalently, that is to say, thoroughly, modern.[60]

Conclusion

Poland Spring in 1900

The arrival of the 1900 season brought a wave of retrospection to the editors of the *Hill-Top*. The first issue of the summer looked back approvingly on the old dying century, regarding its marvels and advancements as evidence of the onward and upward progress of civilization. Several weeks later, the paper reviewed the "grand accomplishments" of the nineteenth century in more detail, but with a similar conclusion. Comfortable and swift trains had left stifling stages behind in the dust, while ancient clipper ships sailed in the wake of gigantic steamboats. Telegraphs encircled the globe and telephones connected moneyed representatives on Wall Street with wheat farmers in the Dakotas. Throughout the Western wilderness, modern pioneers now outnumbered savages and beasts. The revolutions in transportation and communication, as well as the improvements in medicine, annihilation of time, and proliferation of luxury, all pointed to the advancements of the past one hundred years. Faith in progress still reigned supreme at century's end.[1]

Nevertheless, the search for the ideal middle landscape continued. Although the force of progress had increasingly propelled the resort toward an urban vision after 1860, echoes of nostalgic escapism lingered on the hilltop four decades later. Pamphlets and brochures issued at the turn-of-the-century still highlighted the architectural contrasts on display at Poland Spring. The Mansion House retained its "colonial aspect," yet featured "every modern convenience"—electric lights, baths, and "the most scientific and modern sanitation." Epitomizing the ideal of the middle landscape, the building held the distinction of "being at one and the same time both the oldest . . . and the newest hotel in the United States." In contrast, the Poland Spring House was "the architectural opposite of the Mansion House." Rather than projecting the image of a noble past to colonial revivalists, the main hotel exhibited the bounty of the luxurious present for the leisure class. This building was heralded as containing up-to-date facilities, sumptuous furnishings, and "every comfort of the city home."[2]

A visit to the famous spring at the turn of the century placed guests in the midst of another layered middle landscape of vivid contrasts. Mention of the "old-time formation of primeval rock" through which the water flowed conjured up the pristine antiquity of the geological landscape. References to the "remnants of the primitive forest" that enshrouded the site paid tribute to the natural landscape. While nature instilled the water with purity, modern technology preserved its healing power. Thus, a new "perfected bottling plant," whose operation was a model of the industrial landscape, coexisted with the spring. Having spared no expense on the facility, the Rickers offered assurances that workers used as much care "as the modern surgeon practices in his clinical operations." Because everything was handled scientifically, everything was kept perfectly clean. Mechanical washing, sterilization, and pasteurization, combined with natural filtration, ensured that the final product reached consumers in the same condition it left the ground—absolutely pure.[3]

Additional technological improvements had modernized other elements of the Poland Spring landscape as well. The construction of immense barns and importation of productive herds had transformed a pastoral family farm into a modern milk factory. The erection of an extensive greenhouse had supplanted wild natural flora with modern cultivated floral culture. The addition of a sprinkler system had transformed a field into the finest recreational golf links in the land and consequently, into a fitting outlet for modern leisure culture. Finally, the reconstruction of the Maine State Building had transformed a pine grove into an urbane repository of modern literary and artistic culture. The cumulative result was transformation of a country farm into what publicists of Poland Spring referred to by the end of the century succinctly as a "summer city."[4]

The dialectic between antimodernity and modernity, between escape and progress, at the core of the transformation reflected the influence of many movements, patterns, and trends of Gilded-Age culture. The most obvious characteristics of antimodernity during the era were rampant nostalgia for the past, which was embodied most significantly in the colonial revival, and romantic attachment to nature, which gave rise to the back-to-nature movement. A less clear form of antimodernity was an ambivalent antiurbanism that rejected the horrific realities of the modern city exposed by reformer Jacob Riis and other Progressive muckrakers, while continuing to embrace the hopeful ideals of the city beautiful movement's master work, the White City. Subtler versions of antimodernity manifested themselves in many forms of cultural escapism, both physical and intellectual, such as a xenophobic nativism, which fueled the fervor for social exclusivity on the hilltop, and the arts and crafts movement, which made Indian and Shaker craftspeople welcome at Poland Spring.[5]

The most obvious attributes of modernity were fascination with technology and faith in progress, which was "raised almost to the level of a theology." The late-nineteenth-century cult of progress and materialism also contributed to a new activism that emerged during the 1890s in response to the stultifying order of urban-industrial life and most obviously took form as the strenuous-life movement. Coming to grips with material abundance added two other important tenets to the modern mentality—the legitimacy of consumption and leisure. During the Gilded Age, modern consumers made virtues out of traditional republican vices of luxury and conspicuous display. Likewise, the emergent leisure class elevated recreation and pursuits of pleasure from acts of moral decadence to ones of therapeutic necessity, all in the name of progress. Some have even argued that tourism itself became a hallmark of modernity.[6]

Drawn by new ideas of modernity, pleasant memories of past stays, and glowing descriptions presented in promotional pamphlets, several thousand visitors vacationed at the summer city in 1900. Fundamentally, the people of progress came to Poland Spring because the resort affirmed their social status, legitimated their desire for leisure, satiated their need to consume, and most important, revitalized their faith in progress. Part exclusive club, colonial homestead, social mecca, therapeutic spa, pastoral farm, natural Eden, recreational playground, and cultured city, the complex social, architectural, and natural landscapes provided patrons with ample opportunity to experience the best features of both antimodernity and modernity. At the resort, they could escape the grim social realities of life by retreating to the nostalgic past and romantic nature, while simultaneously embracing modern cultural ideals. Given the ascendance of the urban vision that increasingly shaped the resort, the antimodern appeals ultimately amounted to the most elaborate masquerade of all on the hilltop. It was symptomatic of the superficial gilding that served as the ultimate metaphor defining the age. As the people of progress evolved into Progressives, a succeeding generation of reformers would attempt to remove the masks, scour away the self-deceptions, and address more squarely the vexing problems of modernization that had played a part in transforming a country farm into a summer city over the last half of the nineteenth century.

As for the future of the Rickers and their "city of vivid contrasts," in many respects the Gay Nineties represented Poland Spring's zenith. While it remained a vibrant and viable vacation haven well into the Roaring Twenties, the forces of modernity further transformed transportation technology, the resort industry, the leisure class, and ultimately, the hilltop itself. During the early decades of the twentieth century, the introduction of the automobile, overexpansion by the Ricker Hotel Company, and a family succession crisis all undermined the Rickers' empire. The Great Depression, which ruined so many of the people of progress, the Rickers included, delivered the final fatal blow. That, however, is a tale for another time.

Appendixes

Appendix A

Ricker-Bolster Genealogy

Maturin Ricker (–1706)
  m. Rebecca Shaw
Joseph Ricker (1695–1771)
  m. Elizabeth Garland
Jabez Ricker (1742–1827)
  m. Molly Wentworth (1743–1838)
Wentworth Ricker (1768–1837)
  m. Mary Pottle (1764–1843)
    Mary Ricker
    Wentworth, Jr.
    Sophronia m. Eleazer Burbank
    Hiram
    Albert m. Charlotte Schillinger

Isaac Bolster (–1753)
  m. Hepsibah (–1742)
Isaac Bolster (1737–1825)
  m. Mary Dwinall (1739–1815)
Isaac Bolster, Jr. (1769–1835)
  m. Hannah Cushman (1777–1865)
Alvan Bolster (1795–1862)
  m. Cynthia Wheeler (1802–1879)
    Janette Wheeler Bolster
    William Wheeler
    John Quincy Adams
    Martha m. John Pulsifer
    Mary Josephine
    Cynthia Maria m. Ira Nay
    Sarah m. John Stockbridge
    Alvan Augustine

Hiram Ricker (1809–1893)
  m. **Janette Wheeler Bolster** (1821–1883)
    Edward Payson Ricker (1847–1928)
      m. Amelia A. Glancy (1860–1935)
    Alvan Bolster (1850–1933)
      m. Cora B. Sanders (1860–1922)
      Jane Jeffries (1880–1960)
    Cynthia Ella Ricker (1852–1937)
      m. Oliver Marsh (1835–1924)
    Hiram Weston Ricker (1857–1930)
      m. Vesta P. Folsom (1856–1936)
    Sarah Little (1860–1953)
    Janette Maria (1865–1944)

Appendix B

Origins of Poland Spring Guests

TABLE I. Origins of Poland Spring Guests by State

STATE	1894 #	1894 %	1901 #	1901 %
Massachusetts	488	33.6	663	27.2
New York	362	24.9	542	22.3
Maine	156	10.8	466	19.1
Pennsylvania	121	8.3	140	5.7
Rhode Island	42	2.9	31	1.3
Connecticut	32	2.2	40	1.6
New Jersey	30	2.1	78	3.2
Illinois	27	1.9	49	2.0
District of Columbia	25	1.7	38	1.6
Maryland	20	1.4	17	0.7
New Hampshire	14	1.0	12	0.5
Missouri	11	0.8	10	0.4
Louisiana	10	0.7	9	0.4
Ohio	8	0.6	34	1.4
Michigan	7	0.5	10	0.4
North Carolina	6	0.4	18	0.7
Georgia	5	0.3	6	0.2
Colorado	5	0.3	5	0.2
Florida	3	0.2	6	0.2
Minnesota	3	0.2	5	0.2
Delaware	3	0.2	2	0.1
California	2	0.1	15	0.6
Virginia	2	0.1	5	0.2
Wisconsin	2	0.1	5	0.2
Indiana	1		5	0.2
Iowa	1	0.2*	2	0.1
Alabama	1		0	
Texas	0		6	0.2
Nebraska	0		5	0.2

TABLE 1. *Continued*

STATE	1894 #	1894 %	1901 #	1901 %
Kentucky	0		2	0.1
Tennessee	0		2	0.1
Utah	0		2	0.1
Alabama	0		1	0.2*
Kansas	0		1	
Vermont	0		1	
West Virginia	0		1	
Foreign	24	1.7	29	1.2
Unclear	40	2.8	172	7.1
Total	1,451	100.0	2,435	100.0

SOURCES: *Hill-Top*, 1894, 1901.
*The cumulative percentage of the states that individually amount to less than 0.1.

TABLE 2. Leading Points of Origin for Guests

CITY	1894	%	CITY	1901	%
Boston, Mass.	311	21.4	New York, N.Y.	449	18.4
New York, N.Y.	277	19.1	Boston, Mass.	361	14.8
Philadelphia, Pa.	107	7.4	Portland, Maine	174	7.1
Portland, Maine	83	5.7	Philadelphia, Pa.	119	4.9
Brooklyn, N.Y.	50	3.4	Lewiston, Maine	85	3.5
Providence, R.I.	34	2.3	Auburn, Maine	69	2.8
Washington, D.C.	25	1.7	Brooklyn, N.Y.	52	2.1
Chicago, Ill.	23	1.6	Brookline, Mass.	50	2.1
Baltimore, Md.	20	1.4	Chicago, Ill.	40	1.6
Newton, Mass.	19	1.3	Washington, D.C.	38	1.6
Total	949	65.4	Total	1,437	59.0

TABLE 3. Origins of Guests by Size of Community

SIZE OF COMMUNITY	1894	%	CUM.*	1901	%	CUM.*
>1,000,000	407	28.0		656	26.9	
500,000 – 999,999	50	3.4	31.4	385	15.8	42.7
250,000 – 499,999	348	24.0	55.4	104	4.3	47.0
100,000 – 249,999	94	6.5	61.9	127	5.2	52.2
50,000 – 99,999	72	5.0	66.9	310	12.7	64.9
25,000 – 49,999	147	10.1	77.0	88	3.6	68.5
10,000 – 24,999	104	7.2	84.2	344	14.1	82.6
5,000 – 9,999	34	2.3	86.5	82	3.4	86.0
1,000 – 4,999	90	6.2	92.7	90	3.7	89.7
1 – 999	16	1.1	93.8	25	1.0	90.7
Unknown	89	6.1	100.0	224	9.2	100.0
Total	1,451			2,435		

*The cumulative percentage total as the reader looks down the table.

Appendix C

Population Trends in Poland and Surrounding Towns

TOWN	1860 POPULATION	1900	% CHANGE
Auburn	4,022	12,951	+222.0
Lewiston	7,424	23,761	+220.0
Oxford	1,281	1,331	+3.9
Poland	2,746	1,648	
Minot	1,799	808 [a]	−8.8
Mechanic Falls	—	1,687	
Gray	1,768	1,388	−21.5
New Gloucester	1,654	1,162	−29.7
Casco	1,116	783	−29.8
Raymond	1,229	823	−33.0
Otisfield	1,199	728	−39.3
Hebron	895	494	−44.8
Sabbathday Lake	103	41	−60.2

SOURCE: *Maine Register, State Year-Book and Legislative Manual* (Portland, Maine: Portland Directory, 1921), 381, 398–99, 421, 423–24, 509–10, 516, 521, 523, 597–98, 837, 845; Priscilla J. Brewer, *Shaker Communities, Shaker Lives* (Hanover, N.H.: University Press of New England, 1986), 238.

[a] Mechanic Falls was formed from sections of Poland and Minot in 1893.

Notes

Manuscript Collections

ABR: Alvan Bolster Ricker Memorial Library, Poland, Maine.
ACRD: Androscoggin County Registry of Deeds, Auburn, Maine.
AHS: Androscoggin Historical Society, Auburn, Maine.
CCRD: Cumberland County Registry of Deeds, Portland, Maine.
MHPC: Maine Historic Preservation Commission, Augusta, Maine.
MHS: Maine Historical Society, Portland, Maine.
MSL: Maine State Library, Augusta, Maine.
OCRD: Oxford County Registry of Deeds, Paris, Maine.
PSPS: Poland Spring Preservation Society, Poland Spring, Maine.
USS: Shaker Library, United Society of Shakers, New Gloucester, Maine.

Primary Sources

BDG: *Boston Daily Globe*
HT: *Hill-Top*
LEJ: *Lewiston Evening Journal*
LFJ: *Lewiston Falls Journal*
LJIM: *Lewiston Journal, Illustrated Magazine Section*
LSJ: *Lewiston Saturday Journal*
PC: *Poland Centennial*
PMSW: *Poland Mineral Spring Water*
PSC: *Poland Spring Centennial*
PSW: *Poland Spring Water*
WMV: *Wonderful Medicinal Virtues*

Introduction (pp. 1–4)

1. "A Trip to Poland and the Mineral Spring," *LFJ*, 20 July 1860; *Poland Spring House* (South Poland, Maine: Hiram Ricker and Sons, 1901), [48].

2. Historians have often used the concept of transformation to synthesize the events

of the Gilded Age; for examples, see: Allan Nevins, *The Emergence of Modern America* (New York: MacMillan, 1927), 75; Matthew Josephson, *The Robber Barons: The Great American Capitalists, 1861–1901* (New York: Harcourt, Brace, 1934), 29; Robert H. Walker, *Everyday Life in the Age of Enterprise, 1865–1900* (New York: G. P. Putnam's Sons, 1967), 13; John A. Garraty, *The New Commonwealth* (New York: Harper and Row, 1968), xiii; Daniel Walker Howe, ed., *Victorian America* (Philadelphia: University of Pennsylvania Press, 1976), 3; Gwendolyn Wright, *Moralism and the Model Home: Domestic Architecture and Cultural Conflict in Chicago, 1873–1913* (Chicago: University of Chicago Press, 1980), 3; T. J. Jackson Lears, *No Place of Grace: Antimodernism and the Transformation of American Culture, 1880–1920* (New York: Pantheon Books, 1981); Alan Trachtenberg, *The Incorporation of America: Culture and Society in the Gilded Age* (New York: Hill and Wang, 1982), 3; and Thomas J. Schlereth, *Victorian America: Transformations in Everyday Life, 1876–1915* (New York: Harper Collins, 1991), xii. Credit for the concept of resorts as metaphors for progress goes to: Jon Sterngass, *First Resorts: Pursuing Pleasure at Saratoga Springs, Newport and Coney Island* (Baltimore: Johns Hopkins University Press, 2001), 25.

3. Robert H. Wiebe, *The Search for Order, 1877–1920* (New York: Hill and Wang, 1967), xiii.

4. Edwin Lawrence Godkin, "Chromo-Civilization," chap. in *Reflections and Comments* (New York: Charles Scribner's Sons, 1895), 192–205.

5. Thorstein Veblen, *The Theory of the Leisure Class: An Economic Study of Institutions* (New York: Macmillan, 1899; reprint, New York: Dover, 1994).

6. Henry Adams, "The Dynamo and the Virgin," chap. in *The Education of Henry Adams: An Autobiography* (Boston: Houghton Mifflin, 1918), 379–90; Henry Adams, *The Tendency of History* (New York: MacMillan, 1919; reprint, New York: Book League of America, 1929), 3–4, 169–72.

7. Thomas Beer, *The Mauve Decade: American Life at the End of the Nineteenth Century* (New York: Alfred A. Knopf, 1926); Lewis Mumford, *The Brown Decades: A Study of the Arts in America, 1865–1895* (New York: Harcourt, Brace, 1931).

8. Vernon Louis Parrington, *The Beginnings of Critical Realism in America, 1860–1920* (New York: Harcourt, Brace, 1930), 3–5, 23–26; Charles A. and Mary R. Beard, "The Gilded Age," chap. in *The Rise of American Civilization* (New York: MacMillan, 1933), 383–479; Josephson, *Robber Barons*. For a more recent interpretation that emphasizes the class conflict of the era, see: Nell Irvin Painter, *Standing at Armageddon: The United States, 1877–1919* (New York: W. W. Norton, 1987), x–xliii.

9. Richard Hofstadter, *The Age of Reform: From Bryan to FDR* (New York: Vintage Books, 1955).

10. Mark Wahlgren Summers, *The Era of Good Stealings* (New York: Oxford University Press, 1993), 301.

11. Nevins, *Emergence of Modern America*; Arthur Meier Schlesinger, *The Rise of the City, 1878–1898* (New York: MacMillan, 1933); Samuel P. Hays, *The Response to Industrialism 1885–1914* (Chicago: University of Chicago Press, 1957); Blake McKelvey, *The Urbanization of America, 1860–1915* (New Brunswick, N.J.: Rutgers University Press, 1963).

12. Wiebe, *Search for Order*; Garraty, *New Commonwealth*; Louis Galambos, "The Emerging Organizational Synthesis in Modern American History," *Business History Review* 44 (1970): 279–90; Trachtenberg, *Incorporation of America*.

13. Most chroniclers of the Gilded Age have acknowledged the centrality of faith in progress during the era; see: Parrington, *Beginnings of Critical Realism*, xxv, 17–9; Beard and Beard, *Rise of American Civilization*, 407; Josephson, *Robber Barons*, 29, 149, 178; John Higham, "The Reorientation of American Culture in the 1890s," in *The Origins of Modern Consciousness*, John Weiss, ed. (Detroit, Mich.: Wayne State University Press, 1965), 34; Henry Nash Smith, "Introduction," in *Popular Culture and Industrialism, 1865–1900* (New York: New York University Press, 1967), x; Garraty, *New Commonwealth*, 310; Howard Mumford Jones, *The Age of Energy: Varieties of American Experience, 1865–1915* (New York: Viking, 1970), 156; and Lears, *No Place of Grace*, 7–26.

14. Thomas A. Chambers, "Tourism and the Market Revolution," *Reviews in American History* 30 (2002): 555–63.

Part I. The People of Progress (pp. 5–7)

1. H[enry] A. Poole and G[eorge] W. Poole, *History of Poland: Illustrated Embracing a Period of Over a Century* (Mechanic Falls, Maine: Poole Brothers, 1890), 7, 85, 94–97. Mechanic Falls separated from Poland in 1892.

2. Georgia Drew Merrill, ed., *History of Androscoggin County, Maine* (Boston: W. A. Ferguson, 1891), iii; W. A. Ferguson, "Auburn," in *History of Androscoggin County*, 599; Richard Herndon, comp., *Men of Progress: Biographical Sketches and Portraits of Leaders in Business and Professional Life in and of the State of Maine*, ed. Philip W. McIntyre and William F. Blanding (Boston: New England Magazine, 1897), 134, 481, 617; J. W. Penney, "Primitive Industry and Modern in the State of Maine," in *Three Able Addresses Delivered Before the State Board of Trade* (Portland, Maine: Marks Printing House, 1902), 34.

3. Nelson Dingley, Jr., "The Future of Our Country," in *Poland Centennial*, ed. Alvan B. Ricker, Bert M. Fernald and Hiram W. Ricker (Poland, Maine: Ricker, Fernald and Ricker, 1896), 30; Francis A. Walker, *A Compendium of the Ninth Census* (Washington, D.C.: Government Printing Office, 1872), 890–91; *Twelfth Census of the United States: Manufactures*, Part III, Vol. IX (Washington, D.C.: United States Census Office, 1902), 38, 747; *Twelfth Census of the United States: Manufactures*, Part IV, Vol. X (Washington, D.C.: United States Census Office, 1902), 2–4, 482–83; B. R. Mitchell, *International Historical Statistics: The Americas, 1750–1988*, 2d ed. (New York: Stockton Press, 1993), 528.

4. Richard Herndon, comp., *Men of Progress*, (1897), 591–92; Merrill, ed., *History of Androscoggin County*, 736, 738, 755; Poole and Poole, *History of Poland*, 91–93, 143; David B. Pillsbury, "History of the Atlantic and St. Lawrence Railroad Company" (M.A. thesis, University of Maine at Orono, 1962), 120.

5. Merrill, ed., *History of Androscoggin County*, 388–92, 629–34; Yves Frenette, "Factory Workers in Lewiston and Auburn," in *Maine: The Pine Tree State from Prehistory to the*

Present, Richard W. Judd, Edwin A. Churchill, and Joel W. Eastman, ed. (Orono: University of Maine Press, 1995), 457–59.

6. *Twelfth Census of the United States: Population*, Part I, Vol. I (Washington, D.C.: United States Census Office, 1901), 430–33, 482–83, 609–46.

7. *Maine Register, State Year-Book and Legislative Manual* (Portland, Maine: Grenville M. Donham, 1901), 245, 261, 361; Crosby S. Noyes, *The Crown of New England: The Grand Old Town of Minot* (Washington, D.C.: Judd and Detweiler, 1904), 5.

8. Poole and Poole, *History of Poland*, 34–35, 97.

Chapter 1. The Proprietors (pp. 9–23)

1. Aurelia G. Mace, Journal, New Gloucester, Maine, 1896–1907, 23–25 July 1896, USS.

2. For a review of the historiographical debate about when and how the notion of making the land pay originated in early America, see: Christopher Clark, "Economics and Culture: Opening Up the Rural History of the Early American Northeast," *American Quarterly* (1991): 279–97.

3. My understanding of the liberal capitalist development of the United States economy during the nineteenth century has been shaped by the following three works: James Willard Hurst, *Law and the Conditions of Freedom in the Nineteenth-Century United States* (Madison: University of Wisconsin Press, 1956); Richard Hofstadter, *The American Political Tradition: And the Men Who Made It* (New York: Vintage Books, 1948), v–xi, 45–67; and Charles Sellers, *The Market Revolution: Jacksonian America, 1815–1846* (New York: Oxford University Press, 1991).

4. Stephen A. Marini, *Radical Sects of Revolutionary New England* (Cambridge, Mass.: Harvard University Press, 1982), 27–39; *Poland Mineral Spring Water: The Story of Its History and Its Marvellous Curative Properties* (South Poland, Maine: Hiram Ricker and Sons, 1883), 5.

5. Deed, Jabez Ricker to Thomas Cushman, York, Mass., 9 November 1793, USS; Mace, Journal, 23–25 July 1896; Aurelia G. Mace, *The Aletheia: Spirit of Truth* (Farmington, Maine: Knowlton, McLeary, 1899; reprint, Sabbathday Lake, Maine: United Society of Shakers, 1992), 108–9.

6. "Poland Spring Celebrates 150 Years of Hospitality," *Tower*, 3 July 1943, 1; *Poland Spring Centennial: A Souvenir* (South Poland, Maine: Hiram Ricker and Sons, 1895), 21–22; "Poland Spring, The Paradise of New England," *LSJ*, 6 August 1892, 6.

7. *PSC*, 22, 24.

8. Ibid., 24–26; "Paradise of New England," *LSJ*, 6 August 1892, 6; "The Mansion House," *HT*, 6 September 1896, 2; *Mansion House* (South Poland, Maine: Hiram Ricker and Sons, [1899]), [4]; "Poland Spring Celebrates," *Tower*, 3 July 1943, 1–2.

9. Ibid.; *PSC*, 25–30; Poole and Poole, *History of Poland*, 22. For the lineage of the Ricker family, see Appendix A.

10. *PSC*, 34; Deed, Book 6, 13 June 1856, 148–50, ACRD.

11. "After a Long Life," *LEJ*, 6 June 1893, 7; A[rthur] G. S[taples], *The Inner Man* ([Lewiston, Maine]: Privately printed, 1923), 25; L. C. Bateman, "Before Poland Became Famous," *LJIM*, 1–5 February 1908, 8.

12. "Scenery in Maine," *Portland Transcript*, 5 October 1839; "Fought Way Across Plains," *HT*, 2 September 1922, 39; Poole and Poole, *History of Poland*, 22; *HT*, 1 July 1900, 24.

13. *PSC*, 34–35; Bateman, "Before Poland Became Famous," *LJIM*, 1–5 February 1908, 8.

14. *PSC*, 15–7; William B. Lapham, *History of Rumford, Oxford County, Maine, from Its First Settlement in 1779 to the Present Time* (Augusta, Maine: Press of the Maine Farmer, 1890), 249; "Hiram Ricker," New England Historical Publishing Company, 1903, TMs, AHS; Stuart F. Martin, *New Penacook Folks* (Rumford Point, Maine: Stuart F. Martin, 1980), 87, 228.

15. *PSC*, 18; Ricker, Fernald, and Ricker, *PC*, 24; Bateman, "Before Poland Became Famous," *LJIM*, 1–5 February 1908, 8; Lapham, *History of Rumford*, 258.

16. *PSC*, 19, 25–26; Lapham, *History of Rumford*, 258; "US Census—1850, Oxford County, Maine, Town of Rumford," *Population Schedules of the Seventh Census of the United States, 1850, Maine: Oxford County* (Washington, D.C.: National Archive and Record Service, General Services Agency, 1963), microfilm, roll 262.

17. Percy Leroy Ricker and Elwin R. Holland, *A Genealogy of the Ricker Family* (Bowie, Md.: Heritage Books, 1996), 382.

18. Poole and Poole, *History of Poland*, 7; Pillsbury, "History of the Atlantic and St. Lawrence," 50, 57, 79, 113; S[ylvester] B. Beckett, *Guide Book of the Atlantic and St. Lawrence, and St. Lawrence and Atlantic Rail Roads* (Portland, Maine: Sanborn and Carter, and H. J. Little, 1853), 38.

19. George Rogers Taylor, *The Transportation Revolution, 1815–1860* (New York: Rinehart, 1951); Donna-Belle Garvin and James L. Garvin, *On the Road North of Boston: New Hampshire Taverns and Turnpikes, 1700–1900* (Concord: New Hampshire Historical Society, 1988), 168–74; Poole and Poole, *History of Poland*, 82; Ricker, Fernald, and Ricker, *PC*, 16–7; "After a Long Life," *LEJ*, 6 June 1893, 7; *PSC*, 34; *National Cyclopaedia of American Biography*, vol. 2 (New York: James T. White, 1899), s. v. "Hiram Ricker," 61.

20. Deeds, Book 81, 8–9 December 1848, 223–24; Book 82, 12 January 1849, 143; Book 83, 9 December 1848, 147; Book 83, 13 December 1848, 189; Book 84, 4 February 1850, 463–64; Book 84, 10 December 1849, 472; Book 97, 14 June 1852, 141, OCRD; Bateman, "Before Poland Became Famous," *LJIM*, 1–5 February 1908, 8; Hiram Ricker, Correspondence, Portland, Maine, to A. H. Burbank, 5 December 1850, Private Collection.

21. Hiram Ricker, Correspondence, Portland, Maine, to F. O. J. Smith, 16 January 1851, Francis O. J. Smith Collection, Collection 28, MHS; Hiram Ricker, Correspondence, Portland, Maine, to F. O. J. Smith, 16 September 1851, Francis O. J. Smith Collection, Collection 38, Box 16, File 1, MHS; Thomas L. Gaffney, "Maine's Mr. Smith: A Study of the Career of Francis O. J. Smith, Politician and Entrepreneur" (Ph.D. diss., University of Maine at Orono, 1979), 441–47; Doug Hutchinson, *The Rumford Falls and Rangeley Lakes Railroad* (Dixfield, Maine: Partridge Lane Publications, 1989), 9.

22. Hiram Ricker, Correspondence, Poland, Maine, to F. O. J. Smith, 18 August 1852, Francis O. J. Smith Collection, Collection 38, Box 16, File 1; "After a Long Life," 6 June 1893, *LEJ*, 7; *Acts and Resolves of Maine* (1853), 160–62.

23. Bateman, "Before Poland Became Famous," *LJIM*, 1–5 February 1908, 8; Alfred Cole and Charles F. Whitman, *A History of Buckfield, Oxford County, Maine from the Earliest Explorations to the Close of the Year 1900* (Buckfield, Maine: C. F. Whitman, 1915; reprint, Bridgton, Maine: Coburn Press, 1977), 448; Martin, *New Penacook Folks*, 79; Hutchinson, *Rumford Falls and Rangeley Lakes Railroad*, 9; Norman A. Vashaw, *What Was Ain't What Is: A Picture History of Canton, Maine* (Canton, Maine: Norm Vashaw and Bob Barrett, 1995), 90–91.

24. Deed, Book 105, 20 September 1855, 428, OCRD; Bateman, "Before Poland Became Famous," *LJIM*, 1–5 February 1908, 8.

25. Deeds, Book 233, 17 October 1851, 455, CCRD; Book 4, 20 October 1856, 61; Book 6, 13 June 1856, 148–50; Book 16, 17 October 1851, 69, ACRD.

26. Peter B. Bulkley, "Horace Fabyan, Founder of the White Mountain Grand Hotel," *Historical New Hampshire* 30 (1975): 54–68; Guy Gosselin, "Going North — Transportation and Tourism in the White Mountains," *Historical New Hampshire* 50 (1995): 42–45; Dona Brown, *Inventing New England: Regional Tourism in the Nineteenth Century* (Washington, D.C.: Smithsonian Institution Press, 1995), 41–74; Bryant F. Tolles, Jr., *The Grand Resort Hotels of the White Mountains: A Vanishing Architectural Legacy* (Boston: David R. Godine, 1998), 47–75, 239–46; Louis Clinton Hatch, ed., *Maine: A History* (New York: American Historical Society, 1919; reprint, Somersworth, N.H.: New Hampshire Publishing, 1974), 904–12; Richard Rollins Wescott, "Economic, Social and Governmental Aspects of the Development of Maine's Vacation Industry, 1850–1920" (M.A. thesis, University of Maine at Orono, 1961), 4–31.

27. Poole and Poole, *History of Poland*, 44, 73, 93; Merrill, ed., *History of Androscoggin County*, 748, 750; "Court of County Commissioners Hearing on Petition," Poland, Maine, 12 September 1894, TMs, 197, ABR.

28. [Hiram Ricker], "Poland Spring," [1884], TMs, AHS, 1–2; Poole and Poole, *History of Poland*, 33; *PMSW*, (1883), 9; *PSC*, 38–39.

29. *PMSW* (1883), 8; [Ricker], "Poland Spring," 2–4; *PSC*, 35–38.

30. *Wonderful Medicinal Virtues of the Poland Mineral Spring Water*, (South Poland, Maine: Hiram Ricker and Sons, [1877]), 3–5; [Ricker], "Poland Spring," 4–5; *PSC*, 41–42; *PMSW* (1883), 9.

31. [Ricker], "Poland Spring," 5–8; "Trip to Poland," *LFJ*, 20 July 1860; *Poland Spring Hotels* (South Poland, Maine: Hiram Ricker and Sons, 1887), [11]; *PSC*, 43.

32. Randall H. Bennett, *The Mount Zircon Moon Tide Spring: An Illustrated History* ([Bethel, Maine:] Randall H. Bennett, 1997), 5–7; Wescott, "Development of Maine's Vacation Industry," 16; "Eagle Hotel," *Eastern Argus*, 2 July 1860, 1.

33. *National Cyclopaedia*, s. v. "Hiram Ricker," 61; Janette Ricker, Correspondence, Poland, Maine, to Guss [Bolster], 11 May 1862, Private Collection; "The Old Homestead," *HT*, 14 July 1895, 2; Bateman, "Before Poland Became Famous," *LJIM*, 1–5 Febru-

ary 1908, 9; James Harper, Sketchbook, New York, N.Y., 1863, AHS; "Poland Spring in the Past," *HT*, 15 July 1894, 2.

34. *Poland Mineral Spring Water* (South Poland, Maine: Hiram Ricker and Sons, [1876]), 2; *Annual Report of the Railroad Commissioners of the State of Maine* (Augusta, Maine: Sprague, Owen and Nash, 1872), 15; (Augusta, Maine: Sprague, Owen and Nash, 1878), 64; (Augusta, Maine: Sprague and Son, 1883), 30; *HT*, 2 July 1905, 8; Jeff Holt, *The Grand Trunk in New England* (Toronto: Railfare Enterprises, 1986), 39, 50, 66, 74, 83.

35. *PMSW* (1883), 73; *Poland Mineral Spring Water* (South Poland, Maine: Hiram Ricker and Sons, 1889), 75–76.

36. *PMSW* (1883), 73; *WMV*, inside front cover; *PMSW*, (1889), 76; Holt, *Grand Trunk*, 88.

Chapter 2. The Patrons (pp. 24–51)

1. For a general overview of the connection between Gilded-Age industrialization and urbanization and the rise of social exclusivity, see: John S. Gilkeson, Jr., *Middle-Class Providence* (Princeton, N.J.: Princeton University Press, 1986), 134–35, 353. The following histories identify social exclusivity as one of the leading characteristics of Gilded-Age resorts: Betsy Blackmar and Elizabeth Cromley, "On the Verandah: Resorts of the Catskills," In *Victorian Resorts and Hotels: Essays from a Victorian Society Autumn Symposium*, ed. Richard Guy Wilson (Philadelphia: Victorian Society of America, 1982), 56; Glenn Uminowicz, "Sport in a Middle-Class Utopia: Asbury Park, New Jersey, 1871–1895," *Journal of Sport History* 11 (1984): 62–64; William Barton McCash and June Hall McCash, *The Jekyll Island Club: Southern Haven for America's Millionaires* (Athens: University of Georgia Press, 1989), 10–11, 40; Brown, *Inventing New England*, 103; Dona L. Brown, "Purchasing the Past: Summer People and the Transformation of the Piscataqua Region in the Nineteenth Century," in *"A Noble and Dignified Stream": The Piscataqua Region in the Colonial Revival, 1860–1930*, ed. Sarah L. Giffen and Kevin D. Murphy (York, Maine: Old York Historical Society, 1992), 7–8; Stanford E. Demars, *Tourist in Yosemite, 1855–1985* (Salt Lake City: University of Utah Press, 1991), 15–17; Janet Elinor Schulte, "'Summer Homes': A History of Family Summer Vacation Communities in Northern New England, 1880–1940" (Ph.D. diss., Brandeis University, 1993), 1–10; Tolles, *Grand Resort Hotels*, 14–15; Sterngass, *First Resorts*, 212, 268; Thomas A. Chambers, *Drinking the Waters: Creating an American Leisure Class at Nineteenth-Century Mineral Springs* (Washington, D.C.: Smithsonian Institution Press, 2002), 84; and Susan R. Braden, *The Architecture of Leisure: The Florida Resort Hotels of Henry Flagler and Henry Plant* (Gainesville: University of Florida Press, 2002), 87, 106, 117, 132.

2. Stuart M. Blumin, *The Emergence of the Middle Class: Social Experience in the American City, 1760–1900* (Cambridge, England: Cambridge University Press, 1989), 11; Burton J. Bledstein, "Introduction: Storytellers to the Middle Class," in *The Middling Sorts: Explorations in the History of the American Middle Class*, ed. Burton J. Bledstein and Robert D. Johnson (New York: Routledge, 2001), 9–19. Defining class in United States history is a

difficult exercise due to the tendency either to deny the significance of class or to assume that American society has always been upwardly mobile and broadly middle class. Blumin has defined the emergent nineteenth-century middle class on the basis of common values manifested in the areas of work, consumption, residence, associations, and family. I place Poland Spring's clientele at the upper end of the class continuum because of their occupational status. There were few middling clerks, storekeepers, salesmen, and teachers among this crowd.

3. "Bubbles," *HT*, 16 September 1894, 9; "Hearing on Petition," 206; "Poland Guests," *HT*, 8 August 1897, 10; "Bubbles," *HT*, 2 September 1894, 9.

4. See Appendix B, Table 1.

5. "Paradise of New England," *LSJ*, 6 August 1892, 7. See Appendix B, Tables 2 and 3. The trend of a preponderantly urban clientele at Northern New England summer resorts is confirmed by the following studies: Peter B. Bulkley, "Identifying the White Mountain Tourist, 1853–1854: Origin, Occupation, and Wealth as a Definition of the Early Hotel Trade," *Historical New Hampshire* 35 (1980): 107–62; and Dona Brown, "Accidental Tourists: Visitors to the Mount Mansfield Summit House in the Late Nineteenth Century," *Vermont History* 65 (1997): 122–24.

6. Richard Herndon, comp. *Boston of To-day: A Glance at Its History and Characteristics*, ed. Edwin M. Bacon (Boston: Post Publishing, 1892), 180, 255–56, 294–95, 301, 393, 417–18, 449; E. Digby Baltzell, *Puritan Boston and Quaker Philadelphia: Two Protestant Ethics and the Spirit of Class Authority and Leadership* (Boston: Beacon Press, 1979), 259–61, 289, 359–60; E. Digby Baltzell, *Philadelphia Gentlemen: The Making of a National Upper Class* (Glencoe, Ill.: Free Press, 1958), 148, 168–69, 210, 322–24.

7. William Dean Howells, *The Rise of Silas Lapham* (Boston: Ticknor, 1885; reprint, New York: New American Library, 1963), 5–24; Brown, *Inventing New England*, 7–8; Sterngass, *First Resorts*, 213.

8. *WMV*, 33; Levi Perme, Correspondence, South Poland, Maine, 28 July 1878, Private Collection; George H. Haynes, *The Charming Inland Retreats of Maine* (Portland, Maine: Self-published, 1890), 11; "The Poland Spring Hotel," *Tea Table* 1 (May 1890), unpaginated; *Announcement Twenty-Third Annual Summer Season Poland Spring House* (South Poland, Maine: Hiram Ricker and Sons, 1898), 1; *Poland Spring House* (1901), [3]; "Hearing on Petition," 185.

9. "Paradise of New England," *LSJ*, 6 August 1892, 7; "Pictures at Poland," *LSJ*, 5 August 1893, 8; *HT*, 21 August 1904, 22; "Gossip," *HT*, 5 September 1909; "Of Personal Interest," *HT*, 28 July 1917, 4; "Poland Spring Personals," *HT*, 17 August 1918, 5; "Poland Spring Personals," *HT*, 17 July 1920, 5; "Of Social Interest," *HT*, 3 September 1921, 7; *HT*, 7 August 1926, 21; George Ricker and Rose Ricker, ed., *Poland Spring Remembered: Recollections of Catharine Lewis Lennihan* (Poland Spring, Maine: Poland Spring Preservation Society, 1988), 32–36.

10. T. A. Dwyer, "Recollections of My First Visit to Poland Springs," *HT*, 30 August 1896, 4.

11. *HT*, 12 August 1894, 5; "Sunday Services," *HT*, 14 July 1895, 2; "Tid-Bits," *HT*, 2 Au-

gust 1896, 8;"Sunday Services," *HT,* 22 August 1897, 8; "Sunday Services," *HT,* 9 July 1899, 16; "Sunday Services," *HT,* 13 August 1899, 3; "Sunday Service," *HT,* 15 July 1900, 2; *HT,* 30 August 1903, 15; "All Soul's Chapel Monument to Many," *Tower,* 31 July 1943, 2; Ricker and Ricker, ed., *Poland Spring Remembered,* 43;

12. "Tid-Bits," *HT,* 13 September 1896, 14; Jane Lippitt Patterson, *The Romance of the New Bethesda* (Boston: Universalist Publishing House, 1888), 284–86; Richard Herndon, comp., *Men of Progress: One Thousand Biographical Sketches and Portraits of Leaders in Business and Professional Life in the Commonwealth of Massachusetts,* ed. Edwin M. Bacon (Boston: New England Magazine, 1893), 510.

13. Judith S. Goldstein, *Crossing Lines: Histories of Jews and Gentiles in Three Communities* (New York: William Morrow, 1992), 166–78. In her study of Maine's most fashionable resort area, Goldstein describes how Joseph Pulitzer, Walter Damrosch, and Jacob Schiff navigated around anti-Semitic barriers on Mount Desert Island.

14. John Higham, *Strangers in the Land: Patterns of American Nativism, 1860–1925,* 2d ed. (New Brunswick, N.J.: Rutgers University Press, 1955; reprint, 1988), 26–27; Leonard Dinnerstein, *Antisemitism in America* (New York: Oxford University Press, 1994), 35–56; Stephen Birmingham, *"Our Crowd": The Great Jewish Families of New York* (New York: Harper and Row, 1967), 158–65.

15. Mel Robbins, *Poland Spring: An Informal History,* 5th ed., ([Poland Spring, Maine]: Privately printed, 1992), 17, 22, 24; Mary E. Bennett, ed., *Poland: Past and Present, 1795-1970* ([Poland, Maine]: Poland Anniversary Committee, 1970), 75–77; "Ricker Raps 'History' of Spa," *Maine Sunday Telegram,* 27 July 1975, 18; Dumas Malone, ed., *Dictionary of American Biography,* vol. 10, (New York: Charles Scribner's Sons, 1936), s. v. "Simon Wolf," 449; Simon Wolf, Correspondence, to Jeanette Ricker, 13 August 1917, 18 September 1917, Private Collection.

16. "Bubbles," *HT,* 22 July 1894, 3; John Boyd Thacher, Correspondence, Washington, D.C., to John T. Dickinson, 31 January 1894, AHS; *PSC,* 54; *Report of the Board of World's Fair Managers of Maine* (Augusta, Maine: Burleigh and Flynt, 1895), 16; "Chicago and Poland," *HT,* 29 July 1894, 8; "Poland Spring," *LSJ,* 22 July 1893, 9.

17. "Review of the Week," *LSJ,* 14 July 1894, 12; David Ray Papke, *The Pullman Case: The Clash of Labor and Capital in Industrial America* (Lawrence: University Press of Kansas, 1999), 17–35, 101–2.

18. *The Chicago Blue Book of Selected Names of Chicago and Suburban Towns* (Chicago: Chicago Directory Company, 1892), 345–46; "Chicago and Poland," *HT,* 29 July 1894, 8; Holt, *Grand Trunk,* 88–89; Catherine Cocks, *Doing the Town: The Rise of Urban Tourism in the United States, 1870–1915* (Berkeley: University of California Press, 2001), 42–58.

19. "Chicago and Poland," *HT,* 29 July 1894, 8.

20. "Col. John Thilman Dickinson," *The Biographical Dictionary and Portrait Gallery of Representative Men of Chicago, Minnesota Cities and the World's Columbian Exposition* (Chicago: American Biographical Publishing Company, 1892), 759; "Bubbles," *HT,* 19 August 1894, 9.

21. "Chicago and Poland," *HT,* 29 July 1894, 8; "Bubbles," *HT,* 26 August 1894, 9.

22. "The Hop," *HT*, 29 July 1894, 4; "Progressive Euchre," *HT*, 5 August 1894, 6; R. F. Foster, *Foster's Encyclopedia of Games* (New York: Frederick A. Stokes, 1897), 244–45.

23. "On the Poland Brake," *HT*, 5 August 1894, 1–2; "A True Story of the Facts in the Maginnis Strike," *Daily Item* (New Orleans, La.), 1 September 1894; "A Jolly Drive," *HT*, 5 August 1894, 2; "An August Outing," *HT*, 19 August 1894, 2; "Bubbles," *HT*, 9 September 1894, 3; "A Fair-well Drive," *HT*, 9 September 1894, 4.

24. "Wednesday's Launch Party," *HT*, 19 August 1894, 6; "Mother Goose," *HT*, 26 August 1894, 4; "A Merry Party," *HT*, 2 September 1894, 7.

25. "Bubbles," *HT*, 9 September 1894, 5.

26. Daniel J. O'Keefe, Correspondence, South Poland, Maine, 8 October 1895, AHS; "Hearing on Petition," 13, 222–23.

27. E. Digby Baltzell, *The Protestant Establishment: Aristocracy and Caste in America* (New York: Random House, 1964), 113–29.

28. "Hearing on Petition," 180, 222–23, 333, 351.

29. Ibid., 13, 115–17; "Coach Couldn't Pass," *LSJ*, 16 June 1894, 26.

30. Elizabeth Cromley, "Masculine/Indian," *Winterthur Portfolio* 31 (1996): 265–80; Charles Dudley Warner, "Their Pilgrimage," *Harper's New Monthly Magazine* 73 (1886): 933; "Hearing on Petition," 191–92, 223, 226.

31. "Tid-Bits," *HT*, 8 August 1897, 16; "The Indians," *HT*, 21 July 1895, 5; "Tid-Bits," *HT*, 19 July 1896, 8; "Indians," *HT*, 23 August 1896, 5; *HT*, 18 July 1897, 7.

32. "The Indians," *HT*, 21 July 1895, 5; "Tid-Bits," *HT*, 8 August 1897, 16.

33. *HT*, 2 August 1896, 4; "Hampton Students," *HT*, 16 August 1896, 14.

34. Louis R. Harlan and Raymond W. Smock, ed., *The Booker T. Washington Papers*, vol. 3 (Urbana: University of Illinois Press, 1984), 5, 379; "Booker T. Washington," *HT*, 21 July 1895, 2; "Tid-Bits," *HT*, 29 August 1897, 9; "Tid-Bits," *HT*, 28 August 1898, 6; "Booker T. Washington," *HT*, 12 August 1900, 24.

35. Patterson, *Romance of the New Bethesda*, 96–104; Mace, *Aletheia*, 64. Douglass did vacation at the Poland Spring resort in 1884.

36. "Editorial," *HT*, 13 July 1902, 8–9.

37. Patterson, *Romance of the New Bethesda*, 179; Menu, Poland Spring House [c. 1882], Author's Collection; O'Keefe, Correspondence, 8 October 1895. For a study of black workers at two leading Gilded-Age resort areas, see: Myra B. Young Armstead, *"Lord, Please Don't Take Me in August": African Americans in Newport and Saratoga Springs, 1870–1930* (Urbana: University of Illinois Press, 1999).

38. "The Masquerade," *HT*, 5 September 1897, 4–5.

39. "The Masquerade," *HT*, 26 August 1894, 5; "The Employees' Ball," *HT*, 1 September 1895, 3.

40. O'Keefe, Correspondence, 8 October 1895.

41. Hutchinson, *Rumford Falls and Rangeley Lakes Railroad*, 8–13; Herndon, comp., *Men of Progress* (1897), 275–77; John J. Leane, *A History of Rumford, Maine, 1774–1972* (Rumford, Maine: Rumford Publishing, 1972), 23–32.

42. "Hearing on Petition," 73–77, 86–89.

43. Ibid., 169–70.

44. Ibid., 77–79.

45. Ibid., 109, 193, 208–9, 221, 339–40; "An Unusual Real Estate Opportunity" [West Gloucester, Maine: Privately printed, 1893], 16; *Annual Report of the Railroad Commissioners of the State of Maine* (Augusta, Maine: Burleigh and Flynt, 1895), 17.

46. "The Stage Line Controversy," *Lewiston Daily Sun*, 22 June 1894.

47. "Hearing on Petition," 210, 220.

48. Ibid., 83–84, 219–20.

49. Ibid., 16–17, 52, 59–61, 114, 224, 310; Deeds, Book 148, 25 August 1892, 416–18; Book 151, 15 December 1892, 171–72; Book 155, 15 June 1893, 198–200; Book 155, 4 December 1893, 211–13, 267; Book 155, 27 February 1894, 560, ACRD.

50. "Stage Line Controversy," *Lewiston Daily Sun*, 22 June 1894; "Hearing on Petition," 83–84, 189–91, 194, 216–17, 319, 351; "Editorial," *HT*, 19 August 1894, 4.

51. "The War of the Stages," *LEJ*, 14 June 1894, 7; "Hearing on Petition," 84; "Coach Couldn't Pass," *LSJ*, 16 June 1894, 6.

52. Ibid.

53. "Hearing on Petition," 62, 84–85, 263.

54. "Fighting the Way," *LEJ*, 13 September 1894, 8.

55. "Hearing on Petition," 4–9.

56. Ibid., 13–15.

57. Ibid., 99–108.

58. Ibid., 110, 113.

59. Ibid., 169, 195, 202, 210, 218.

60. Ibid., 180, 205, 211–12.

61. Ibid., 286, 293, 305–13.

62. Ibid., 323, 328–30.

63. Ibid., 333–36, 344, 350–52.

64. Ibid., 345, 349–53.

65. "Editorial," *HT*, 16 September 1894, 4; "The Rickers Win," *LEJ*, 18 September 1894, 7; "State Chat," *LSJ*, 16 June 1894, 4; Mace, Journal, 18 January 1896; S[taples], *Inner Man*, 11 .

Part II. The Masquerade of Antimodernity (pp. 53–56)

1. "The Bal Masque," *HT*, 1 September 1895, 2.

2. "The Bal Poudre," *HT*, 7 August 1898, 7; Carroll Smith-Rosenberg, *Visions of Gender in Victorian America* (New York: Alfred A. Knopf, 1985), 50, 99–101; Sterngass, *First Resorts*, 2–4, 115–38, 265.

3. Lears, *No Place of Grace*, 312.

4. William G. McLoughlin, *The Meaning of Henry Ward Beecher: An Essay on the Shifting Values of Mid-Victorian America, 1840–1870* (New York: Alfred A. Knopf, 1970), 3–6, 102, 114; James Lincoln Collier, *The Rise of Selfishness* (New York: Oxford University Press,

1991), 4 –13; Louise L. Stevenson, *The Victorian Homefront: American Thought and Culture, 1860–1880* (New York: Twayne Publishers, 1991), xx–xxiii, 3 –7, 60; Anne C. Rose, *Victorian America and the Civil War* (Cambridge, England: Cambridge University Press, 1992), 3.

5. Demars, *Tourist in Yosemite*, 11– 20; Dean MacCannell, *The Tourist: A New Theory of the Leisure Class* (New York: Schocken Books, 1976), 1–15; John Urry, *The Tourist Gaze*, 2d ed. (London: Sage Publications, 2002), 150.

6. John F. Sears, *Sacred Places: American Tourist Attractions in the Nineteenth Century* (New York: Oxford University Press, 1989), vii, 4, 216; Anne Farrar Hyde, *An American Vision: Far Western Landscape and National Culture, 1820–1920* (New York: New York University Press, 1990), 7, 301– 4; Brown, *Inventing New England*, 7–12; Cindy S. Aron, *Working at Play: A History of Vacations in the United States* (New York: Oxford University Press, 1999), 3 – 5; Chambers, *Drinking the Waters*, xiii–xix.

7. John K. Walton, *The English Seaside Resort: A Social History, 1750–1914* (New York: Leicester University Press and St. Martin's Press, 1983), 225; Goldstein, *Crossing Lines*, 152; Schulte, "'Summer Homes,'" 391– 97; Brown, *Inventing New England*, 9 –13; Peter B. Bulkley, "A History of the White Mountain Tourist Industry, 1818 –1899" (M.A. thesis, University of New Hampshire, 1958), 46; Tolles, *Grand Resort Hotels*, 19, 77, 143; Janice Zita Grover, "Luxury and Leisure in Early Nineteenth-Century America: Saratoga Springs and the Rise of the Resort" (Ph.D. diss., University of California at Davis, 1973), 4, 9 – 10; Sterngass, *First Resorts*, vii, 6 –7, 35, 66 – 69, 143, 265; Chambers, *Drinking the Waters*, 30; Betsy Blackmar, "Going to the Mountains: A Social History," in *Resorts of the Catskills*, ed. Alf Evers, Elizabeth Cromley, Betsy Blackmar and Neil Harris (New York: St. Martin's Press for the Architectural League of New York and the Gallery Association of New York State, 1979), 77; Stefan Kanfer, *A Summer World: The Attempt to Build a Jewish Eden in the Catskills, from the Days of the Ghetto to the Rise of the Borscht Belt* (New York: Farrar, Straus and Giroux, 1989), 98; McCash and McCash, *Jekyll Island Club*, 13; Braden, *Architecture of Leisure*, 3; Hyde, *An American Vision*, 216; Sears, *Sacred Places*, 6; Aron, *Working at Play*, 9.

8. "Editorial," *HT*, 14 July 1895, 4.

9. Ibid.

10. Ibid.

Chapter 3. The Mansion House (pp. 57 – 78)

1. "Trip to Poland," *LFJ*, 20 July 1860.

2. Michael Kammen, *Mystic Chords of Memory: The Transformation of Tradition in American Culture* (New York: Alfred A. Knopf, 1991), 132– 45, 217–25, 294 –95; Karal Ann Marling, *George Washington Slept Here: Colonial Revivals and American Culture, 1876 – 1986* (Cambridge, Mass.: Harvard University Press, 1988), 39 – 52, 131; Celia Betsky, "Inside the Past: The Interior and the Colonial Revival in American Art and Literature, 1860 –1914," in *The Colonial Revival in America*, ed. Alan Axelrod (New York: W. W. Norton for The Henry Francis duPont Winterthur Museum, Winterthur, Del., 1985), 265 –

66; Sarah Burns, *Pastoral Inventions: Rural Life in Nineteenth-Century American Art and Culture* (Philadelphia: Temple University Press, 1989), 264–75.

3. David Lowenthal, *The Past Is a Foreign Country* (Cambridge, England: Cambridge University Press, 1985), 121–23; Alan Axelrod, "Preface," ix–x; Kenneth L. Ames, "Introduction," 10–15; and William Butler, "Another City upon a Hill: Litchfield, Connecticut, and the Colonial Revival," in *Colonial Revival in America*, 15–20; Marling, *George Washington Slept Here*, 42, 153; Joseph A. Conforti, *Imagining New England: Explorations of Regional Identity from the Pilgrims to the Mid-Twentieth Century* (Chapel Hill: University of North Carolina Press, 2001), 229.

4. *PSC*, 88.

5. G[eorge] W. Ricker, "The Ricker Family," *New England Historical and Genealogical Register* 5 (1851): 308–9.

6. Ibid., 309. In a footnote, the editor of the *New England Historical and Genealogical Register* suggested that Ricker based his ambush account on a misreading of *A Narrative of the Indian Wars in New England* by William Hubbard. Citing the journal of Rev. John Pike, the *Register* contended that the attack actually occurred on June 4, 1706, and led to the deaths of both brothers.

7. Sam Ricker, Amelia, Ohio, Correspondence, to Hiram Ricker, South Poland, Maine, February 1870, AHS; Percy Leroy Ricker, "The Ricker Genealogies," in *Genealogy of the Ricker Family*, iv.

8. Charles E. Nash, "William Berry Lapham," in *Collections of the Maine Historical Society*, 2d series, 5 (Portland: Maine Historical Society, 1894), 341; William B. Lapham, comp., *Records of Some of the Descendants of George and Maturin Ricker, Who Were Early at Dover, N.H.: and Who Were Killed by the Indians, June 4, 1706* (Augusta, Maine: Sprague, Owen and Nash, 1877), 1–2; [William B. Lapham], "Ricker Family," *Maine Genealogist and Biographer* 2 (1877): 105–6; "Paradise of New England," *LSJ*, 6 August 1892, 6; "Hiram Ricker," New England Historical Publishing Company, TMs, 1903; Stanley Russell Howe, "Historical Perspectives on Bethel Since Lapham," in *History of the Town of Bethel, Maine*, William B. Lapham (Augusta, Maine: Press of the Maine Farmer, 1891; reprint, Somersworth, N.H.: New England History Press, 1981), ii–iii.

9. [Lapham], "Ricker Family," *Maine Genealogist and Biographer* 3 (1877): 12, 16.

10. Nash, "William Berry Lapham," 341; *WMV*, 2, 13.

11. *PMSW*, (1883), 5–7.

12. W[illiam] H. H. Murray, "The Poland Spring Hotel," in *Poland Spring* (South Poland, Maine: Hiram Ricker and Sons', 1890), 2–5.

13. *Poland Spring Water: Nature's Great Remedy and Its Marvelous Curative Properties* (South Poland, Maine: Hiram Ricker and Sons, 1890), [5–6]. Similar themes and dates of publication suggest that Murray may have authored both "Poland Spring Hotel" and *Poland Spring Water*. A definite connection linking him to both pieces is the announcement for his book, *Lake Champlain and Its Shores*, which appears inside the front and back covers of each pamphlet.

14. "Paradise of New England," *LSJ*, 6 August 1892, 6.

15. Ibid.; Lears, *No Place of Grace*, 108–9; Rose Mellon, Channel Islands Family History Society, Correspondence, to Ms. Ricker-Bouchard, 17 August 1996, Private Collection.

16. M. F. Jasper, Correspondence, to Mr. [Frederick G.] Kalkhoff, [New York, N.Y.], 18 May 1892, AHS; M. F. J[asper], "Riker or Ricker," AHS; Percy Leroy Ricker "Armorial Bearings," in *Genealogy of the Ricker Family*, x; Lears, *No Place of Grace*, 188.

17. "The Souvenir," *HT*, 7 July 1895, 5.

18. "Home Personals," *LEJ*, 24 September 1883, 3; *PSC*, 6–7, 18. Hiram Ricker actually passed away on June 4, 1893.

19. *PSC*, 7, 9–21.

20. Ibid., 69–71; Rodris Roth, "The New England, or 'Old Tyme,' Kitchen Exhibit at Nineteenth-Century Fairs," in *Colonial Revival in America*, 159–83; Marling, *George Washington Slept Here*, 34–43; Burns, *Pastoral Inventions*, 266–67.

21. *PSC*, 78–79.

22. Ibid., 64–67, 80.

23. Ibid., 80, 82.

24. Ibid., 83–84; Sears, *Sacred Places*, 100–15.

25. *PSC*, 84–89.

26. Charles Frederic Goss, *Cincinnati, the Queen City: 1788–1912* (Chicago: S. J. Clarke, 1912), 707; Ellen Ricker Freeman, Locust Corner, Ohio, Correspondence, to Mr. Ricker, 18 April, 27 April, 1 May, 7 June, 19 August, 1 October, 12 November, 13 November 189[7]; Sara Ricker Simpson, Correspondence, n.p., n.d., Private Collection.

27. Ricker, "Ricker Genealogies," in *Genealogy of the Ricker Family*, iv; E[rnest] H. Ricker, Elgin, Ill., Correspondence, to Hiram W. Ricker, South Poland, Maine, 8 March 1897; C. E. Ricker, Gardiner, Ore., Correspondence, to Hiram Ricker and Sons, South Poland, Maine, 26 December 1898; H. P. Ricker, Black Creek, N.Y., Correspondence, 30 June 1902; John W. Hayley, Lowell, Mass., Correspondence, to H. W. Ricker, 3 April 1900; P[ercival] L. Ricker, Washington, D.C., Correspondence, to Mrs. Marsh, 19 October 1905, Private Collection. Percy Leroy Ricker's manuscript is the basis of *A Genealogy of the Ricker Family* co-authored by Elwin R. Holland and finally published in 1996.

28. John W. Hayley, *Genealogical Memoranda, Relating Chiefly to the Haley, Piper, Neal and Ricker Families of Maine and New Hampshire* (Lowell, Mass.: Courier-Citizen, 1900), 79–81, 93–95.

29. Ricker, Fernald, and Ricker, *PC*, 1, 25, 27; "Church Record," vol. 4, 11 September 1895, 367, USS. The Shakers reported that 2,200 people partook of the centennial day dinner.

30. Ricker, Fernald, and Ricker, *PC*, 1.

31. Bert M. Fernald, "Address of Welcome," in Ibid., 5–6.

32. W. W. McCann, "Oration," in Ibid., 12–14.

33. Ibid., 13, 21–22.

34. Ibid., 24, 26.

35. Ibid., 26.

36. Nelson Dingley, Jr., "The Future of Our Country," in Ibid., 27–32.

37. E. P. Ricker, in Ibid., 32–34.

38. J. Albert Libby, "1795–1895," in Ibid., 38–39.

39. J. W. Penney, "The Early Settlers," in Ibid., 78, 80.

40. Ibid., 80, 86.

41. Ibid., 90, 92.

42. "Unusual Real Estate Opportunity," 14; PSC, 60, 63; "The Mansion House," HT, 6 September 1896, 2; "Paradise of New England," LSJ, 6 August 1892, 8.

43. Ibid.

44. "Lecture and Sunday-School," HT, 30 August 1896, 5; "All Souls' Chapel," Tower, 31 July 1943, 1–2; Ricker and Ricker, ed., Poland Spring Remembered, 16–19; "Sunday-School Picnic," HT, 4 July 1897, 2.

45. "Paradise of New England," LSJ, 6 August 1892, 8; George H. Haynes, The State of Maine, in 1893 (New York: Moss Engraving Company, 1893), 41; "A Notable Improvement," HT, 3 July 1898, 2; Mansion House, [4]; "Hearing on Petition," 185, 198; Edmund S. Hoyt, comp., Maine State Year-Book (Portland: Hoyt, Fogg and Breed, 1869), 164.

46. "The Mansion House," HT, 6 September 1896, 2; "A Notable Improvement," HT, 3 July 1898, 2.

47. Mansion House, [4]; "A 'Parlor Car' Winter," HT, 10 September 1899, 3.

48. "Old Home Changes," HT, 1 July 1900, 1–2.

49. "Old Homes," HT, 5 August 1900, 1–2; Vincent J. Scully, Jr., The Shingle Style and the Stick Style: Architectural Theory and Design from Downing to the Origins of Wright, rev. ed., (New Haven, Conn.: Yale University Press, 1971), 28; Brown, "Purchasing the Past," 12; Braden, Architecture of Leisure, 10–11, 69–74; Susan Prendergast Schoelwer, "Curious Relics and Quaint Scenes: The Colonial Revival at Chicago's Great Fair," in Colonial Revival in America, 185–87; Celia Betsky, "Inside the Past," 265.

50. "Old Homes," HT, 5 August 1900, 2–3.

Chapter 4. The Poland Spring House (pp. 79–110)

1. PSC, 68; Chambers, "Tourism and the Market Revolution," 555–56.

2. "Trip to Poland," LFJ, 20 July 1860; Patterson, Romance of the New Bethesda, 47; S[taples], Inner Man, 27.

3. Ibid., 26–27; "After a Long Life," LEJ, 6 June 1893, 7; PSC, 63; Ricker, Fernald, and Ricker, PC, 67; Bateman, "Before Poland Became Famous," LJIM, 1–5 February 1908, 8; Deeds, Book 69, 10 July 1875, 453; Book 90, 20 January 1876, 195–97, ACRD.

4. Deed, Book 90, 20 January 1876, 195, ACRD; "Poland Mineral Spring," LEJ, 10 June 1876.

5. Ibid.; Deeds, Book 69, 10 July 1875, 453; Book 81, 10 July 1875, 75; Book 84, 5 May 1876, 65–7, ACRD; "Poland Once Again," HT, 2 July 1899, 2–3; S[taples], Inner Man, 27.

6. "The Fiftieth Anniversary," HT, 3 July 1926, 1; "Records," vol. 1, New Gloucester, Maine, 22 June 1876, 252, USS; "Poland Mineral Spring," LEJ, 10 June 1876; WMV, 13.

7. "Poland Mineral Spring," *LEJ*, 10 June 1876; "Dissolving Views of Poland," *HT*, 19 July 1903, 1.

8. Patterson, *Romance of the New Bethesda*, 51, 75, 131, 201, 252; Steven Mintz, *A Prison of Expectations: The Family in Victorian Culture* (New York: New York University Press, 1983), 11–12; Harvey Green, *The Light of the Home: An Intimate View of the Lives of Women in Victorian America* (New York: Pantheon Books, 1983), 36–37; Colleen McDannell, *The Christian Home in Victorian America, 1840–1900* (Bloomington: Indiana University Press, 1986), 7–8; Karin Calvert, "Children in the House, 1890 to 1930," in *American Home Life, 1880–1930: A Social History of Spaces and Services*, ed. Jessica H. Foy and Thomas J. Schlereth (Knoxville: University of Tennessee Press, 1992), 77–81; Katherine C. Grier, *Culture and Comfort: People, Parlors, and Upholstery, 1850–1930* (Rochester, N.Y.: Strong Museum, 1988), 4–5; Lori Anne Loeb, *Consuming Angels: Advertising and Victorian Women* (New York: Oxford University Press, 1994), 18–26.

9. McDannell, *Christian Home*, 25–28.

10. *PSC*, 71; *WMV*, 13; "Stages," *HT* 30 June 1895, 8; "Pleasure and Comfort at Poland Spring," *HT*, 16 September 1894, 5; "Paradise of New England," *LSJ*, 6 August 1892, 7–8; "Poland Spring," *HT*, 16 September 1894, 2; Louisa May Alcott, *Little Women* (Boston: Robert Brothers, 1869; reprint, New York: Barnes & Noble), 415. For more on the significance of the veranda, see: Elizabeth Cromley, "A Room with a View," in *Resorts of the Catskills*, 13–18; Blackmar and Cromley, "On the Verandah," 51–57; McDannell, *Christian Home*, 26–27; and Karen Halttunen, "From Parlor to Living Room: Domestic Space, Interior Decoration, and the Culture of Personality," in *Consuming Visions: Accumulation and Display of Goods in America, 1880–1920*, ed. Simon J. Bronner (New York: W. W. Norton and Company for the Henry Francis duPont Winterthur Museum, 1989), 167–68.

11. "Obituary: Leander Stevens," *Eastern Argus*, 28 November 1903; "Poland Mineral Spring," *LEJ*, 10 June 1876; Kenneth L. Ames, *Death in the Dining Room and Other Tales of Victorian Culture* (Philadelphia: Temple University Press, 1992), 7–43; *PSC*, 72; *Poland Spring Hotels* (1887), [6]; *HT*, 17 July 1898, 22.

12. *PSC*, 72; "Poland Once Again," *HT*, 2 July 1899, 2; Halttunen, "From Parlor to Living Room," 160–61; Ames, *Death in the Dining Room*, 177, 190–93; Katherine C. Grier, "The Decline of the Memory Palace: The Parlor after 1890," in *American Home Life*, 50–54; Grier, *Culture and Comfort*, 1–2, 66–67, 136, 219; Bradley C. Brooks, "Clarity, Contrast, and Simplicity: Changes in American Interiors, 1880–1930," in *The Arts and the American Home, 1890–1930*, ed. Jessica H. Foy and Karal Ann Marling (Knoxville: University of Tennessee Press, 1994), 15–21; McDannell, *Christian Home*, 49–50; Loeb, *Consuming Angels*, 26–32, Braden, *Architecture of Leisure*, 46.

13. Grier, *Culture and Comfort*, 56–57, 188; *Poland Spring Hotels* (1887), [6].

14. "Poland Mineral Spring," *LEJ*, 10 June 1876; Ricker and Ricker, ed., *Poland Spring Remembered*, 42; *WMV*, 13; *Poland Spring: Announcement* (South Poland, Maine: Hiram Ricker and Sons, 1892), unpaginated; "Poland Spring," *LSJ*, 6 August 1892, 7; Menu, Poland Spring House, South Poland, Maine, 1 June 1896, MHPC; "Tid-Bits," *HT*, 11 Au-

gust 1895, 12; "Drank Poland Water," *Boston Sunday Globe*, 14 June 1890; "Paradise of New England," *LSJ*, 6 August 1892, 7. For a more detailed account of the "rising standards of refinement" in the nineteenth-century dining room, see: Clifford E. Clark, Jr., "The Vision of the Dining Room: Plan Book Dreams and Middle-Class Realities," in *Dining in America, 1850–1900*, ed. Kathryn Grover (Amherst: University of Massachusetts Press and Rochester, N.Y.: Margaret Woodbury Strong Museum, 1987), 145–47; John Kasson, *Rudeness and Civility: Manners in Nineteenth-Century Urban America* (New York: Hill and Wang, 1990), 185–93, 204–11; and Cocks, *Doing the Town*, 72–75.

15. Menu, Poland Spring House, 14 September 1887, Author's Collection; "Our Cuisine," *HT*, 16 September 1894, 6; "What You Eat," *HT*, 4 August 1895, 1.

16. Ibid., 2; "Behind the Scenes," *HT*, 23 August 1896, 2; "Our Cuisine," *HT*, 16 September 1894, 6; Harvey A. Levenstein, *Revolution at the Table: The Transformation of the American Diet* (New York: Oxford University Press, 1988), 7–8, 22.

17. Advertisement, *HT*, 25 July 1897, 11; Alpheus Shaw, Bill, Portland, Maine, to W[entworth] Ricker, 1 December 1825, AHS; *PSC*, 16, 27–29; "Poland Mineral Spring," *LEJ*, 10 June 1876; "Poland Spring House," *Maine Temperance Record*, February 1904, [3].

18. "Poland Mineral Spring," *LEJ*, 10 June 1876; "Our Cuisine," *HT*, 16 September 1894, 6; A[lvan] B. Ricker, Notebook, South Poland, Maine, 1896–1903, MSL.

19. Ricker and Ricker, ed., *Poland Spring Remembered*, 40–42; Patterson, *Romance of the New Bethesda*, 183–84; "Poland Facts," *HT*, 11 August 1895, 3; "Pleasure and Comfort," *HT*, 16 September 1894, 5; "Tid-Bits," *HT*, 2 August 1896, 8.

20. "At Poland Spring," *Portland Daily Press*, 1889, in Scrapbook, John Calvin Stevens Collection #209, M 573–5, MHS; *Souvenir List of Employees* (Poland Spring, Maine: Hiram Ricker and Sons, 1900), [4–5]; Carrie F. Hubbard, Contract, Poland Spring House, South Poland, Maine, 26 April 1892, MHPC; *Twelfth Census of the United States*, "Schedule No. 1-Population," Poland, Androscoggin County, Maine, 28 June 1900, Series T623, Roll 588, 252–53; Patterson, *Romance of the New Bethesda*, 184.

21. Ibid.; Hubbard, Contract.

22. Elizabeth Collins Cromley, "A History of American Beds and Bedrooms, 1890–1930," in *American Home Life*, 120; *WMV*, 13; "Poland Spring," *LEJ-Trade Edition*, 2 February 1898; *PSC*, 69, 74.

23. *Poland Spring Hotels* (1887), [2, 4]; "Paradise of New England," *LSJ*, 6 August 1892, 8.

24. "Hearing on Petition," 122–23; *Obituary Record of the Graduates of Bowdoin College and the Medical School of Maine* (Brunswick, Maine: Bowdoin College Library, 1911), 368; *HT*, 30 June 1895, 8.

25. *PSC*, 66; Deeds, Book 98, 31 March 1879, 13–5; Book 104, 18 March 1881, 120–21, ACRD; C[harles] R. Milliken, Correspondence, Portland, Maine, to Albert Young, 26 April 1881, AHS.

26. "Dissolving Views," *HT*, 19 July 1903, 2; "Quarter Century," *BDG*, 4 March 1897.

27. Carlos E. Pinfield, "Music Throughout the Years at Poland Spring," *HT*, 25 August 1928, 5–6; Patterson, *Romance of the New Bethesda*, 81.

28. Pinfield, "Music Throughout the Years," *HT*, 25 August 1928, 6–7; "Paradise of New England," *LSJ*, 6 August 1892, 7–8; "Bubbles," *HT*, 12 August 1894, 3; "Pleasure and Comfort," *HT*, 16 September 1894, 5; Patterson, *Romance of the New Bethesda*, 265; "Our Orchestra," *HT*, 8 July 1894, 4; "Our Orchestra," *HT*, 29 July 1894, 2.

29. "The Music Hall," *HT*, 11 July 1897, 1–2; "Concert," *HT*, 1 August 1897, 7; "Last Sunday's Concert," *HT*, 21 July 1895, 4.

30. Lawrence Levine, *Highbrow/Lowbrow: The Emergence of Cultural Hierarchy in America* (Cambridge, Mass.: Harvard University Press, 1988), 119–46; Kasson, *Rudeness and Civility*, 215–56; Craig H. Roell, *The Piano in America, 1890–1940* (Chapel Hill: University of North Carolina Press, 1989), 14–17; Jessica H. Foy, "The Home Set to Music," in *Arts and the American Home*, 63.

31. "Mrs. Bailey's Lectures," *HT*, 28 July 1895, 3; "Gen. Martin's Talk," *HT*, 14 July 1895, 4; "Astronomical," *HT*, 25 August 1895, 7; "Lecture and Sunday School," *HT*, 30 August 1896, 5; "Tid-Bits," *HT*, 17 July 1898, 16; "Chamberlin-Lewis Concert," *HT*, 15 August 1897, 3; "Tuesday's Entertainment," *HT*, 24 July 1898, 3; "Harriet Evalyn Carter," *HT*, 14 August 1898, 3; "Brigham Lecture," *HT*, 9 September 1900, 8; "Alaska," *HT*, 11 August 1895, 9; "India," *HT*, 19 August 1900, 12; "Matterhorn," *HT*, 6 September 1896, 9; "Taminosian," *HT*, 4 August 1895, 5; Michael S. Graham, "The Sabbathday Lake Shakers and the Rickers of the Poland Spring Hotel: A Scrapbook History" (New Gloucester, Maine: United Society of Shakers, 2001), [6–7].

32. Deed, Book 133, 11 February 1889, 311–13, ACRD; "A Quarter Century at Poland Spring," *BDG*, 4 March 1897; Elizabeth Cromley, "Upward and Inward with Time: Catskills Resort Architecture," *Progressive Architecture* (1978): 46; Earle G. Shettleworth, Jr., "Turn-of-the-Century Architecture: from about 1880 to 1920," in *Maine Forms of American Architecture*, ed. Deborah Thompson (Camden, Maine: Downeast Magazine, 1976), 206; Tolles, *Grand Resort Hotels*, 21.

33. "At Poland Spring," *Portland Daily Press*, 1889; John Calvin Stevens, Correspondence, Boston, Mass., 19 March 1889, MHPC; "Dissolving Views," *HT*, 19 July 1903, 2.

34. "Paradise of New England," *LSJ*, 6 August 1892, 7; "At Poland Spring," *Portland Daily Press*, 1889; *Poland Spring Hotels* (South Poland, Maine: Hiram Ricker and Sons, 1889), 5; Herndon, *Boston of To-day*, 247; "Reed & Barton Silversmiths," *HT*, 29 August 1897, 11; Marina Moskowitz, "Public Exposure: Middle-Class Material Culture at the Turn of the Twentieth Century," in *Middling Sorts*, 170–73.

35. "At Poland Spring," *Portland Daily Press*, 1889; *Poland Spring Hotels* (1889), 9; "Bubbles," *HT*, 19 August 1894, 9.

36. Murray, "Poland Spring Hotel," 6–10.

37. Merrill, ed., *History of Androscoggin County*, 735; "Poland Spring," *HT*, 16 September 1894, 1; Geo[rge] H. Haynes, "Poland Spring," *HT*, 9 September 1894, 2; "Maine's Famous Resort," *HT*, 16 September 1894, 7; "Quarter Century," *BDG*, 4 March 1897; "Why Poland Thrives," *HT*, 30 July 1899, 2.

38. Aron, *Working at Play*, 82–92; Chambers, *Drinking the Waters*, 80–118; Braden, *Architecture of Leisure*, 1, 52–53.

39. Patterson, *Romance of the New Bethesda*, 13, 85; Perme, Correspondence, South Poland, Maine, 28 July 1878.

40. "Told on the Verandas," *HT*, 2 September 1894, 5.

41. Patterson, *Romance of the New Bethesda*, 265–66, 283; "Editorial," *HT*, 7 July 1895, 6.

42. Allen Johnson, ed., *Dictionary of American Biography*, vol. 3 (New York: Charles Scribner's Sons, 1929), s. v. "Benjamin Franklin Butler," by Carl Russell Fish, 357–59; John A. Garraty and Mark C. Carnes, ed., *American National Biography*, vol. 4 (New York: Oxford University Press, 1999), s. v. "Benjamin Franklin Butler," by Hans L. Trefouse, 91–93.

43. Summers, *The Era of Good Stealings*, 5–7; Kathryn Allamong Jacob, *Capital Elites: High Society in Washington, D.C., after the Civil War* (Washington, D.C.: Smithsonian Institution Press, 1995), 84–86; Parrington, *Beginnings of Critical Realism*, 13; "At Poland," *LEJ*, 17 June 1890, 1.

44. B[enjamin] F. Butler, Correspondence, to O. D. Barrett, Washington, D.C., 26 February 1887, Letter Book, 1887–1892, Special Collections, Miller Library, Colby College, Waterville, Maine; "Banqueting at Poland," *LEJ* 18 July 1887, 1; "Gen. Butler and Party at Poland Spring," *LEJ* 18 July 1887, 1.

45. "Reception and Promenade Concert," Program, 18 July 1887, Private Collection; "Poland Aglow," *LEJ*, 19 July 1887.

46. Karen Halttunen, *Confidence Men and Painted Women: A Study of Middle-Class Culture in America, 1830–1870* (New Haven, Conn.: Yale University Press, 1982), 174–86; Mary W. Blanchard, "Boundaries and the Victorian Body: Aesthetic Fashion in Gilded Age America," *American Historical Review* 100 (1995): 24–25; "Bal-Poudre," *HT*, 2 September 1894, 2; "Powder and Patches," *HT*, 5 August 1900, 13. For more on the cultural significance of the formality of Victorian dance, see: Green, *Light of the Home*, 13; Daniel Joseph Singal, "Towards a Definition of American Modernism," *American Quarterly* 39 (1987): 20; and Donna R. Braden, *Leisure and Entertainment in America* (Dearborn, Mich.: Henry Ford Museum and Greenfield Village, 1988), 154.

47. "The Hop," *HT*, 22 July 1894, 8; "The Mid-Summer Hop," *HT*, 25 August 1895, 7; "Beauty and Grace," *HT*, 8 August 1897, 18; "Pleasure and Comfort," *HT*, 16 September 1894, 5.

48. "Paradise of New England," *LSJ*, 6 August 1892, 8; Schulte, "'Summer Homes'," 267–333.

49. Patterson, *Romance of the New Bethesda*, 257, 282; Rose, *Victorian America*, 3, 17, 111–41, 175; McDannell, *Christian Home*, 153.

50. "The Amusement Fund," *HT*, 30 June 1895, 5; "Concert," *HT*, 12 August 1894, 2.

51. "The Music Hall," *HT*, 11 July 1897, 2; "Tid-Bits," *HT*, 17 July 1898, 16; "Zanoni," *HT*, 6 September 1896, 4; "Zanoni," *HT*, 3 September 1899, 5.

52. "Page, the Impersonator," *HT*, 3 September 1899, 28; "Tid-Bits," *HT*, 10 September 1899, 19; "Tuesday's Entertainment," *HT*, 24 July 1898, 3; *HT*, 29 August 1897, 10.

53. *Poland Spring Hotels* (1887), [6–7]; PSC, 67; *HT*, 23 July 1899, 29; *Poland Spring House* (South Poland, Maine: Hiram Ricker and Sons, 1899), 8.

54. "Bubbles," *HT,* 12 August 1894, 9; "Massage," *HT,* 18 July 1897, 4; "Massage," *HT,* 12 July 1896, 8; "Massage," *HT,* 26 July 1896, 13; *HT,* 17 July 1898, 5; "Tid-Bits," *HT,* 25 August 1895, 10; "Miss Haglund," *HT,* 9 July 1899, 19; *HT,* 16 July 1899, 3; *HT,* 6 August 1899, 24; *HT,* 20 August 1899, 19; *HT,* 19 August 1900, 6.

55. *HT,* 4 September 1898, 14; *HT,* 6 August 1899, 7; *HT,* 14 August 1898, 4; *HT,* 10 September 1899, 5; "Artistic Dressing of Hair," *HT,* 1 July 1900, 2; "Tid-Bits," *HT,* 22 July 1900, 14; *Souvenir List,* [2]; *HT,* 3 July 1904, 22.

56. "Quarter Century," *BDG,* 4 March 1897; "Dissolving Views," *HT,* 19 July 1903, 2; Shettleworth, "Turn-of-the-Century Architecture," 206.

57. "Tid-Bits," *HT,* 4 August 1895, 6; "Whisht," *HT,* 11 August 1895, 11; "Tid-Bits," *HT,* 23 August 1896, 9; "Progressive Whist," *HT,* 15 August 1897, 4; "Compass Whist," *HT,* 10 September 1899, 30.

58. "Progressive Euchre," *HT,* 7 August 1898, 4.

59. "Poland Mineral Spring," *LEJ,* 10 June 1876; *WMV,* 13; "The Springfield Gas Machine," *Manufacturer and Builder,* 8 (April 1876): 88; Maureen Ogle, *All the Modern Conveniences: American Household Plumbing, 1840–1890* (Baltimore: Johns Hopkins University Press, 1996), 35.

60. Ibid., 93–118; *Annual Report of the State Board of Health* (Waterville, Maine: Sentinel Publishing, 1913), 97; Herndon, comp., *Men of Progress* (1897), 154; *Poland Spring Hotels* (1887), [9, 18].

61. "Paradise of New England," *LSJ,* 6 August 1892, 7; A. G. Young, "A Comparative View of Sanitary Laws, and What Changes Are Needed in Those of Maine," in *Second Annual Report of the State Board of Health* (Augusta, Maine: Sprague and Son, 1886), 262; A. G. Young, "Summer Resorts," in *Second Annual Report,* 283–85; *Poland Spring Hotels* (1887), [17]; "Sanitation at Poland Springs," *Sanitary Inspector,* 10 (June 1897): 168–69.

62. *Poland Spring Hotels* (1887), [3–6]; *PMSW* (1883), 14; "At Poland Spring," *Portland Daily Press,* 1889; *PSC,* 75; *Announcement,* (1898), 3.

63. "Poland Once Again," *HT,* 2 July 1899, 1–3.

64. *PSC,* 67; "The Studio," *HT,* 8 July 1894, 5; "At Poland Spring," *Portland Daily Press,* 1889; "Bubbles," *HT,* 16 September 1894, 9; Schulte, "'Summer Homes,'" 335–36, 377–83; Urry, *Tourist Gaze,* 3.

65. "See for Yourself," *HT,* 3 July 1898, 22; *HT,* 20 August 1899, 3; *HT,* 11 September 1898, 3; "Mr. Denys Bourdon Returns," *HT,* 15 July 1922, 3; "The Studio," *HT,* 4 August 1895, 4; "Editorial," *HT,* 8 September 1895, 4; *HT,* 9 July 1899, 15; *HT,* 16 July 1899, 7; *HT,* 3 September 1899, 2; Andrea Volpe, "Cartes de Visite Portrait Photographs and the Culture of Class Formation," in *Middling Sorts,* 157–60; Madelyn Moeller, "Ladies of Leisure: Domestic Photography in the Nineteenth Century," in *Hard at Play: Leisure in America, 1840–1940,* ed. Kathryn Grover (Amherst: University of Massachusetts Press and Rochester, N.Y.: Strong Museum, 1992), 139.

66. Murray, "Poland Spring Hotel," 10. The historiography of the development of Gilded-Age consumer culture is extensive. Written amid the late-nineteenth-century consumer revolution, the seminal study of the subject remains Veblen's *Theory of the*

Leisure Class. Other leading works include: T. J. Jackson Lears and Richard Wightman Fox, ed., *The Culture of Consumption: Critical Essays in American History, 1880–1980* (New York: Pantheon Books, 1983); Daniel Horowitz, *The Morality of Spending: Attitudes Toward the Consumer Society in America, 1875–1940* (Baltimore: Johns Hopkins University Press, 1985); and Bronner, ed., *Consuming Visions*. The intersection of leisure and consumer culture is explored in Richard Butsch, ed., *For Fun and Profit: The Transformation of Leisure into Consumption* (Philadelphia: Temple University Press, 1990). The particular role resorts played in the commodification of leisure is addressed in Sterngass, *First Resorts*, 1, 30, 147, 157–61, 170–76, 270–71.

67. "Pleasure and Comfort," *HT*, 16 September 1894, 5; "The Green Bottle," *HT*, 2 August 1896, 1–2; "Baker's," Advertisement, *HT*, 14 August 1898, 23; *HT*, 7 July 1895, 5; *Poland Spring Hotels* (1889), 24; "Poland Mineral Spring," *LEJ*, 10 June 1876; *Poland Spring Hotels* (1887), [6].

68. "A Useful Article," *HT*, 11 August 1895, 5; "The Cooking Utensil," *HT*, 25 August 1895, 6; *HT*, 8 September 1895, 7.

69. Beverly Gordon, *Bazaars and Fair Ladies: The History of the American Fundraising Fair* (Knoxville: University of Tennessee Press, 1998), 1–33; Elizabeth Alice White, "Charitable Calculations: Fancywork, Charity, and the Culture of the Sentimental Market, 1830–1880," in *Middling Sorts*, 73–76; "Church Record," vol. 3, New Gloucester, Maine, 5 July–10 September 1888, 384–94, USS; Mace, Journal, 5 August 1896; "The Shakers of Sabbathday Lake," *HT*, 19 July 1896, 2; Chambers, *Drinking the Waters*, 100.

70. *HT*, 30 June 1895, 11; *HT*, 17 July 1898, 22; "The Art Store," 12 September 1897, 3; "The Store," *HT*, 11 July 1897, 13; "The Art Store," *HT*, 5 September 1897, 3; *HT*, 13 August 1899, 7; *HT*, 8 July 1900, 24; *HT*, 26 August 1900, 24; "The Art Store," *HT*, 25 July 1897, 7; "The Art Store," *HT*, 8 August 1897, 9; "The Art Store," *HT*, 29 August 1897, 4; Lears, *No Place of Grace*, 60–96.

71. *PSC*, 19; "The Leading Business Men of Maine," *LJIM*, (1899), 3; S[taples], *Inner Man*, 27–29; "Pictures at Poland," *LSJ*, 5 August 1893, 8.

72. Patterson, *Romance of the New Bethesda*, 37; "Leading Business Men," *LJIM*, (1899), 3; Edw[ard] P. Ricker, Correspondence, Boston, Mass., to [Alvan Bolster Ricker], 26 October 1896, Private Collection; Cha[rle]s. Sumner Cook, Correspondence, Portland, Maine, to E. P. Ricker, 27 May 1913, 1–3, AHS.

73. "Paradise of New England," *LSJ*, 6 August 1892, 8; *PSC*, 87; "Hearing on Petition," 170–72; Delmer C. Wilson, Diary, New Gloucester, Maine, 13 March 1899, USS; *Annual Report* (Poland, Maine: Town of Poland, 1902), 3, 17, 29.

74. "Bubbles," *HT*, 16 September 1894, 9; *Seventh Annual Report of the Bureau of Industrial and Labor Statistics for the State of Maine* (Augusta, Maine: Burleigh and Flynt, 1893), 9, 21; *Poland Spring* (South Poland, Maine: Hiram Ricker and Sons', [1893], 15; "Pictures at Poland," *HT*, 5 August 1893, 8; "Quarter Century," *BDG*, 4 March 1897; *Announcement*, (1898), 1; "Great Business," *HT*, 4 September 1898, 14; "Ever Young and Fair," *HT*, 4 July 1897, 2. For a comparison of room rates at other resorts, see: Roland Van Zandt, *The Catskill Mountain House* (New Brunswick, N.J.: Rutgers University Press, 1966), 343–45; and Braden, *Architecture of Leisure*, 93.

75. "Paradise of New England," *LSJ*, 6 August 1892, 7; "Unusual Real Estate Opportunity," 14–15. A useful analysis of revenue sources at a Virginia Springs resort is provided in Chambers, *Drinking the Waters*, 21.

76. Deeds, Book 98, 31 March 1879, 13–15; Book 104, 18 March 1881, 120–21; Book 110, 31 March 1884, 553; Book 116, 13 April 1885, 354; Book 130, 4 March 1892, 359–60; Book 133, 11 February 1889, 311–13; Book 145, 7 March 1892, 499–501; Book 159, 10 May 1892, 546–47; Book 178, 1 August 1898, 286–90; Book 222, 6 December 1911, 291, ACRD.

77. "Dissolving Views," *HT*, 19 July 1903, 2; Shettleworth, "Turn-of-the-Century Architecture," 206; "Poland Once Again," *HT*, 2 July 1899, 2.

Chapter 5. The Spring House (pp. 111–35)

1. "Trip to Poland," *LFJ*, 20 July 1860.

2. Murray, "Poland Spring Hotel," 2; [Holman Day], "Facts and Fancies at Poland Spring," *HT*, 8 July 1894, 2; "The *Hill-Top* Twenty-Six Years Ago," *HT*, 31 July 1920, 8. Although there was no attribution for "Facts and Fancies" at the time of publication, the 1920 article on the history of the *Hill-Top* credited it to Day. The Rickers referred to the water in three ways: Poland Mineral Spring Water, Poland Spring Water, and Poland Water. For the sake of consistency and economy, I have generally used the shortest title.

3. Nelson Manfred Blake, *Water for the Cities: A History of the Urban Water Supply Problem in the United States* (Syracuse, N.Y.: Syracuse University Press, 1956), 260–64; Earl Finbar Murphy, *Water Purity: A Study in Legal Control of Natural Resources* (Madison: University of Wisconsin Press, 1961), 24–30; Jon A. Peterson, "The Impact of Sanitary Reform upon American Urban Planning, 1840–1890," *Journal of Social History* 13 (1979): 84–91; Joel A. Tarr, *The Search for the Ultimate Sink: Urban Pollution in Historical Perspective* (Akron, Ohio: University of Akron Press, 1996), 103–24; Mitchell Okun, *Fair Play in the Marketplace: The First Battle for Pure Food and Drugs* (DeKalb: Northern Illinois University Press, 1986), 185–216, 251–86; *PMSW* (1883), 68–70; *Poland Spring Hotels* (1887), [9]; James Harvey Young, *Pure Food: Securing the Federal Food and Drugs Act of 1906* (Princeton, N.J.: Princeton University Press, 1989), 4–6, 293; Mary Douglas, *Purity and Danger: An Analysis of the Concepts of Pollution and Taboo* (London: Routledge and Keegan Paul, 1966), 2, 41–57, 161–63.

4. "To the Readers of the Tea Table," *Tea Table* 1 (May 1890): [1]; "Pure Olive Oil," *HT*, 7 August 1898, 7; "Veuve Chaffard," *HT*, 2 July 1899, inside cover; *HT*, 27 August 1899, 19; "Boston Chocolates," *HT*, 14 July 1901, 31; "Crystal Purity," *HT*, 11 August 1895, 6. Purity persists as a powerful promotional metaphor. For an analysis of the ways present-day Poland Spring water is marketed, see: Andy Opel, "Constructing Purity: Bottled Water and the Commodification of Nature," *Journal of American Culture* 22 (1999): 71–72.

5. "Paradise of New England," *LSJ*, 6 August 1892, 7; "After a Long Life," *LEJ*, 6 June 1893, 7; Ricker and Ricker, ed., *Poland Spring Remembered*, 28; *PSC*, 39.

6. *PMSW* (1883), 11; *PMSW* (1889), 12; "Paradise of New England," *LSJ*, 6 August

1892, 6; "Poland Spring in the Past," *HT*, 15 July 1894, 2; *PSC*, 45 – 50; *HT*, 1898, back cover; Roger L. Gowell, "The Rickers (Riccars) of Poland," 1972, TMs, photocopy, 3, AHS.

7. "Paradise of New England," *LSJ*, 6 August 1892, 7 – 8; *PSC*, 47; Sam Ricker, Amelia, Ohio, Correspondence, to Hiram Ricker, South Poland, Maine, February 1870, AHS.

8. "Paradise of New England," *LSJ*, 6 August 1892, 6; *PSC*, 63 – 66.

9. Ibid., 20, 66; *National Cyclopaedia*, vol. 24 (New York: James T. White, 1935), s. v. "Hiram Weston Ricker," 177; Hiram W. Ricker, Passport, United States Department of State, 1925, Private Collection.

10. O[liver] Marsh, Correspondence, to Ed[ward Ricker], 28 November 1880, AHS.

11. "Poland Spring," *LEJ*, 2 February 1898; *National Cyclopaedia*, s. v. "Hiram Weston Ricker," 177 – 78; S[taples], *Inner Man*, 125.

12. *PMSW* [1876], 3 – 4.

13. *PMSW* (1883), 4; *PSW*, [12, 14]. The same geological account in *Poland Mineral Spring Water* also appears in Poole and Poole, *History of Poland*, 31.

14. Murray, "Poland Spring Hotel," 1 – 2; Haynes, *Charming Inland Retreats*, 11.

15. "Do Not Forget," *HT*, 18 August 1895, 6; "Tid-Bits," *HT*, 25 July 1897, 3.

16. *Poland Mineral Spring Water: The Story of Its History and Its Marvellous Curative Properties* (South Poland, Maine: Hiram Ricker and Sons, 1891), 8 – 9; *PSC*, 8; "The Indians," *HT* 21 July 1895, 5; Bateman, "Before Poland Became Famous," *LJIM*, 1 – 5 February 1908, 8; Poole and Poole, *History of Poland*, 27; *PSW*, [10, 12]; *PMSW* (1883), 9 – 10, 16, 18; Bunny McBride and Harald E. L. Prins, "Walking the Medicine Line: Molly Ockett, a Pigwacket Doctor," in *Northeastern Indian Lives, 1632 – 1816*, Robert S. Grumet, ed. (Amherst: University of Massachusetts Press, 1996), 321 – 22.

17. *PSW*, [6, 10]; Haynes, "Poland Spring," *HT*, 9 September 1894, 2.

18. *WMV*, 2; [Ricker], "Poland Spring," 1.

19. "Poland Spring," *HT*, 15 July 1894, 1 – 2.

20. "A Drinking Song," *HT*, 28 July 1895, 3.

21. "Do Not Forget," *HT*, 18 August 1895, 6; Pal Vincent, *The Moses Bottle* (Poland Spring, Maine: Palabra Shop, 1969), 37; Ricker and Ricker, ed., *Poland Spring Remembered*, 43; "Spoony," *HT*, 1 September 1895, 4.

22. Vincent, *Moses Bottle*, 3, 37; Walt Humphrey, "Moses Bottles," *Western Collector* (1969): 50; *Poland Spring* [1893], 5; Patterson, *The Romance of the New Bethesda*, 11, 40, 90, 150, 180; "Bubbles," *HT*, 5 August 1894, 3.

23. Vincent, *Moses Bottle*, 13; *Poland Spring House* (1899), 28; *PSC*, 47.

24. "Poland Mineral Spring," *LEJ*, 10 June 1876.

25. "After a Long Life," *LEJ*, 6 June 1893, 7; [Ricker], "Poland Spring," 17 – 18, 35 – 36.

26. *WMV*, 10, 24 – 28.

27. Ibid., 15 – 17, 30; *PMSW* (1883), 44 – 46; [Ricker], "Poland Spring," 33.

28. *PSW*, [9, 16 – 19]; [Day], "Facts and Fancies," *HT*, 8 July 1894, 2.

29. *PMSW* (1883), 69 – 72.

30. *WMV*, 18, 33; [Ricker], "Poland Spring," 41; *PMSW* (1891), 82; "Bubbles," *HT*, 22 July 1894, 9.

31. PSC, 81; *Poland Spring: The Early History of This Wonderful Spring Its Growth and Development Illustrated* (South Poland, Maine: Hiram Ricker and Sons, 1914), [7]; *WMV*, 1; *Industries and Wealth of the Principal Points in Rhode Island* (New York: A. F. Parsons, 1892), 184.

32. J[esse] M. Libby, "Poland,"in *Atlas and History of Androscoggin County Maine*, E. F. Sanford and W. P. Everts, ed. (Philadelphia: Sanford Everts, 1873), 114 –15.

33. *WMV*, 1, 33; *PMSW* [1876], 18 –19; *PMSW* (1883), 54; *PSW*, [18].

34. "An Interesting Visitor," *HT*, 22 August 1897, 7; [Ricker], "Poland Spring," 7, 11– 12; *PMSW* (1891), 41; *Poland Spring* [1893], 41.

35. [Ricker], "Poland Spring," 5, 11, 37– 40; *WMV*, 22; *PMSW* (1883), 18.

36. *PSC*, 43; *PMSW* (1883), 16.

37. *WMV*, 23; *PMSW* (1883), 29; *Poland Spring Hotels* (South Poland, Maine: Hiram Ricker and Sons, 1888), 16; "Bubbles," *HT*, 5 August 1894, 9.

38. *Poland Mineral Spring Water* (South Poland, Maine: Hiram Ricker and Sons, [1879]), 12; *PMSW* (1883), 24 –27.

39. Donna J. Wood, *Strategic Uses of Public Policy: Business and Government in the Progressive Era* (Marshfield, Mass.: Pitman Publishing, 1986), 189; Chambers, *Drinking the Waters*, 55 – 63; *PSW*, [16]; *WMV*, 6; *PMSW* (1883), 21.

40. Bennett, *Mt. Zircon*, 13 –14; *Sixth Annual Report of the Secretary of the Maine Board of Agriculture* (Augusta, Maine: Stevens and Sayward, 1861), 453; *PMSW* [1876], 5–7; *WMV*, 6.

41. *Poland Spring: The Early History of this Wonderful Spring: Its Growth and Development Illustrated* (South Poland, Maine: Hiram Ricker and Sons, 1908), [18 –19]; *PSC*, 55; *Mansion House* [4]; "Poland Water Leads Them All," *HT*, 7 July 1895, 16; "Leads Them All!" *HT*, 1896, back cover.

42. *PMSW* (1883), 22.

43. Ibid., 18 –19.

44. *PSW*, [8, 14, 16, 18]; *Poland Spring House* (1899), 28.

45. *Poland Spring* [1893], 13 –14.

46. *Second Annual Report of the State Board of Health, 1886* (Augusta, Maine: Sprague and Son, 1887), 199, 283 – 85; *Fourth Annual Report of the State Board of Health, 1888* (Augusta, Maine: Burleigh and Flynt, 1889), 29 – 30; *Eleventh Report of the State Board of Health, 1898 – 99* (Augusta, Maine: Kennebec Journal Print, 1900), 4.

47. "Sanitation at Poland Springs," *Sanitary Inspector*, 168; "An Official Visit," *HT*, 4 July 1897, 10.

48. Wallace K. Oakes, Correspondence, to the Editors, *HT*, 9 July 1899, 16.

49. "Poland Water," *HT*, 8 September 1895, 1.

50. Peter Temin, *Taking Your Medicine: Drug Regulation in the United States* (Cambridge, Mass.: Harvard University Press, 1980), 12 –13, 31– 37, 198.

51. *WMV*, 33; *PMSW* [1879], 4; *PMSW* (1883), 2.

52. *PMSW* [1879], 2; *PMSW* (1883), 12, 22.

53. "Trip to Poland," *LFJ*, 20 July 1860; [Ricker], "Poland Spring," 8, 12 –16; *PMSW* [1879], inside front cover; *Poland Mineral Spring Water: The Story of Its History and Its Mar-

vellous Curative Properties (South Poland, Maine: Hiram Ricker and Sons, 1895), inside front cover; "Poland Water Leads Them All," *HT*, 7 July 1895, 16; *HT*, 13 September 1896, 4.

54. *WMV*, 1; Deed, Book 130, 12 December 1891, 341, ACRD; "Paradise of New England," *LSJ*, 6 August 1892, 8; *PSC*, 48; "Quarter Century," *BDG*, 4 March 1897; "Price List of Poland Water," Hiram Ricker and Sons, New York, [1895], MHS.

55. "The Poland Mineral Spring," *Gardiner Home Journal*, 16 May 1877; "Paradise of New England," *LSJ*, 6 August 1892, 6, 8; *PSC*, 28, 50; "Quarter Century," *BDG*, 4 March 1897; "Poland Water," *HT*, 8 September 1895, 1–3; "Sanitation at Poland Springs," *Sanitary Inspector*, 168–69.

56. *Poland Spring Hotels* (1887), [8]; "Unusual Real Estate Opportunity," 14; Merrill, ed., *History of Androscoggin County*, 736; *PSC*, 47.

57. John B. Bachelder, *Popular Resorts, and How to Reach Them* (Boston: John B. Bachelder, 1875), 176; John Hayward, *A Gazetteer of the United States of America* (Hartford, Conn.: Case, Tiffany, 1853), 670; Jonathan Paul DeVierville, "American Healing Waters: A Chronology (1513–1946) and Historical Survey of America's Major Springs, Spas, and Health Resorts Including a Review of Their Medicinal Virtues, Therapeutic Methods, and Health Care Practices" (Ph.D. diss., University of Texas at Austin, 1992), 123–41; Sterngass, *First Resorts*, 7–39; Chambers, *Drinking the Waters*, 185–208; [Ricker], "Poland Spring," 11; "A Talk with the Editor," *HT*, 12 August 1894, 4.

58. "Poland Spring Hotel," *Tea Table* 1 (May 1890); Haynes, *Charming Inland Retreats*, 11; "Bubbles," *HT*, 26 August 1894, 3; "Obey the Laws of Health," *HT*, 15 August 1897, 16; "Quarter Century," *BDG*, 4 March 1897; *HT*, 10 September 1899, back cover.

59. "Poland Mineral Spring," *LEJ*, 10 June 1876; [Ricker], "Poland Spring," 24–25, 36–37; *WMV*, 20–2; "Jottings," *HT*, 8 July 1922, 37.

60. *PMSW* (1891), 11; "Paradise of New England," *LSJ*, 6 August 1892, 6; *PSC*, 39–41; "Pictures at Poland," *LSJ*, 5 August 1893, 8; *PSW*, [20].

61. "The Perfect Tribute," *HT*, 28 July 1917, 1–3; Walter Graham, "Editorial," *HT*, 28 July 1917, 8.

Part III. The Search for a Middle Landscape (pp. 137–39)

1. Marcia B. Jordan, "Extract from a Summer Letter," *HT*, 17 July 1898, 4; M[arcia] B. J[ordan], "Vacation," *HT*, 14 July 1901, 6.

2. Jordan, "Summer Letter," *HT*, 17 July 1898, 4; "Many Vivid Contrasts," *HT*, 29 July 1922, 3; "Poland Spring," *LEJ*, 2 February 1898.

3. Leo Marx, *The Machine in the Garden: Technology and the Pastoral Ideal in America* (New York: Oxford University Press, 1964), 3–33, 354–65; Howard P. Segal, "Leo Marx's 'Middle Landscape': A Critique, a Revision, and an Appreciation," *Reviews in American History* 5 (1977): 137–41; Thomas Bender, *Toward an Urban Vision: Ideas and Institutions in Nineteenth-Century America* (Lexington: Published for the Organization of American Historians by the University of Kentucky Press, 1975), ix–xi, 73–92; Gunther Barth, *City People: The Rise of Modern City Culture in Nineteenth-Century America* (New

York: Oxford University Press, 1980), 4, 230–32. For examples of how the concept of the middle landscape has been applied to studies of other resorts, see: J. Ellis Voss, "Summer Resort: An Ecological Analysis of a Satellite Community" (Ph.D., diss., University of Pennsylvania, 1941), 139; Charles E. Funnell, *By the Beautiful Sea: The Rise and High Times of That Great American Resort, Atlantic City* (New York: Alfred A. Knopf, 1975), 77, 119–41; Andrea Rebek, "The Selling of Vermont: From Agriculture to Tourism, 1860–1910," *Vermont History* 44 (1976): 24; Stuart M. Blumin, *The Short Season of Sharon Springs: Portrait of Another New York*, in collaboration with Deborah Adelman Blumin (Ithaca, N.Y.: Cornell University Press, 1980), 30; and Sears, *Sacred Places*, 49, 64–65. The shift from complex pastoralism to a more urban vision of resort landscapes is explored in: Uminowicz, "Sport in a Middle-Class Utopia," 52–53, 71; Ellen Weiss, *City in the Woods: The Life and Design of an American Camp Meeting on Martha's Vineyard* (New York: Oxford University Press, 1987), 69–73, 109, 137–38; Armstead, *"Lord, Please Don't Take Me in August"*, xvii, 3, 9, 139; Chambers, *Drinking the Waters*, 28–29, 38; and Sterngass, *First Resorts*, 35–36, 113, 140.

4. James L. Machor, *Pastoral Cities: Urban Ideals and the Symbolic Landscape of America* (Madison: University of Wisconsin Press, 1987), xi–xiii, 8–14. My analysis of the city metaphor has been guided by the methodology of Rhys Isaac, *The Transformation of Virginia, 1740–1790* (New York: W. W. Norton, 1982), 5–6, 323–57; Bender, *Toward an Urban Vision*, ix–x; and Smith-Rosenberg, *Visions of Gender*, 42–52. For an example of how metaphors have been used to analyze leading Gilded-Age tourist destinations, see: Sterngass, *First Resorts*, 25, 138, 266. In the case of Poland Spring, interpreting the recurring metaphors of the city, progress, nobility, and purity is key to understanding the cultural significance of the resort.

Chapter 6. The Farm (pp. 141–65)

1. *Poland Spring Hotels* (1887), [3]; Burns, *Pastoral Inventions*, 8, 337.

2. Poole and Poole, *History of Poland*, 95; *Annual Report of the Bureau of Industrial and Labor Statistics* (Augusta, Maine: Burleigh and Flynt, 1891), 96–99. The problem of rural depopulation is covered in: Harold Fisher Wilson, *The Hill Country of Northern New England: Its Social and Economic History, 1790–1930* (New York: Columbia University Press, 1936), 97–138; Clarence Albert Day, *Farming in Maine, 1860–1940*, University of Maine Studies, 2d series, no. 78 (Orono: University of Maine Press, 1963), 171–79; Hal S. Barron, *Those Who Stayed Behind: Rural Society in Nineteenth-Century New England* (Cambridge, England: Cambridge University Press, 1984), 31–50; and Burns, *Pastoral Inventions*, 77–89. For population statistics of towns surrounding Poland, see Appendix C.

3. PSC, 71; William L. Bowers, *The Country Life Movement in America, 1900–1920* (Port Washington, N.Y.: Kennikat Press, 1974), 3–5, 132–34; David B. Danbom, *The Resisted Revolution: Urban America and the Industrialization of Agriculture, 1900–1930* (Ames: Iowa State University, 1979), vii–viii, 138–44.

4. "Trip to Poland," *LFJ*, 20 July 1860; *First Annual Report of the Secretary of the Maine Board of Agriculture* (Augusta, Maine: Stevens and Blaine, 1857), 56.

5. William Willis, *A Business Directory of the Subscribers to the New Map of Maine* (Portland, Maine: J. Chace, Jr., Sanborn and Carter, Bailey and Noyes, [1862]), 202–3; Poole and Poole, *History of Poland*, 98.

6. "Trip to Poland," *LFJ*, 20 July 1860; "Hearing on Petition," 204–5.

7. Libby, "Poland," in *Atlas and History of Androscoggin County Maine*, 114; Deed, Book 186, 23 June 1900, 216–18, ACRD; Poole and Poole, *History of Poland*, 116, 120; Merrill, ed., *History of Androscoggin County*, 726, 734; G[renville] M. Donham, *Maine Register, State Year-Book and Legislative Manual* (Portland, Maine: G. M. Donham, 1898), 281; "Poland Mineral Spring," *LEJ*, 10 June 1876. For accounts of the impact of tourism on agriculture in the Northeast, see: Wilson, *Hill Country*, 277–300; Howard S. Russell, *A Long, Deep Furrow: Three Centuries of Farming in New England* (Hanover, N.H.: University Press of New England, 1976), 278–80; David M. Gold, "Jewish Agriculture in the Catskills," *Agricultural History* 55 (1981): 31–49; Brown, *Inventing New England*, 135–67; Richard W. Judd, *Common Lands, Common People: The Origins of Conservation in Northern New England* (Cambridge, Mass.: Harvard University Press, 1997), 61–62, 77, 218; and Sterngass, *First Resorts*, 30.

8. Bennett, ed., *Poland: Past and Present*, 87, 90–92; S[taples], *The Inner Man*, 11, 13.

9. Poole and Poole, *History of Poland*, 63, 114; Bennett, ed., *Poland: Past and Present*, 84–87; Rexford Booth Sherman, "The Grange in Maine and New Hampshire, 1870–1940" (Ph.D. diss., Boston University, 1972), 145–78; S. Carlton Guptill, "The Grange in Maine from 1874–1940" (Ph.D. diss., University of Maine at Orono, 1973), 25–34, 173–77; Stanley Russell Howe, *"A Fair Field and No Favor": A Concise History of the Maine State Grange* (Augusta, Maine: Maine State Grange, 1994), 4, 62–66, 76.

10. *Statistics of the Industries of Maine* (Augusta, Maine: Sprague and Son, 1886), 30; *Agriculture of Maine* (Augusta, Maine: Burleigh and Flynt, 1888), 31–32; Poole and Poole, *History of Poland*, 23–24; Merrill, ed., *History of Androscoggin County*, 733; Deeds, Book 185, 28 October 1899, 3; Book 185, 6 November 1899, 19, ACRD; "The Poland Creamery," *HT*, 19 August 1900, 1–2; Bennett, ed., *Poland: Past and Present*, 63, 69; Poland Dairy Association, Advertisement, *HT*, 15 August 1897, 17; *Maine Register* (1900), 279.

11. Poole and Poole, *History of Poland*, 73, 88–90, 98; B[ert] M. Fernald, "Maine Canning Industry," in *Three Able Addresses*, 5; Day, *Farming in Maine*, 28–31; Bennett, ed., *Poland: Past and Present*, 44, 65, 90–92; Ricker, Fernald, and Ricker, *PC*, 111–12.

12. Bennett, ed., *Poland: Past and Present*, 65, 90; S[taples], *Inner Man*, 11; *Biographical Directory of the United States Congress, 1774–1989* (Washington, D.C.: Government Printing Office, 1989), 990–91; Christopher S. Beach, "Conservation and Legal Politics: The Struggle for Public Water Power in Maine, 1900–1923," *Maine Historical Society Quarterly* 32 (1993): 153–58.

13. "Poland Facts," *HT*, 11 August 1895, 3; "Poland Creamery," *HT*, 19 August 1900, 2; *Agriculture of Maine* (1888), 32; Poole and Poole, *History of Poland*, 24, 98.

14. Penney, "Primitive Industry," in *Three Able Addresses*, 32; "Poland Facts," *HT*, 11 August 1895, 3; Poole and Poole, *History of Poland*, 116; "Hearing on Petition," 158, 171, 247; *Thirty-Eighth Annual Report of the Secretary of the Board of Agriculture* (Augusta, Maine: Burleigh and Flynt, 1896), 69.

15. Merrill, ed., *History of Androscoggin County,* 731–32.

16. Poole and Poole, *History of Poland,* 17, 97–98.

17. Ibid., 95–97.

18. Ibid., 95–96, 114.

19. Edw[ard] P. Ricker, Correspondence, Boston, Mass., to [Alvan Bolster Ricker], 26–27 October 1896, Private Collection.

20. Edw[ard] P. Ricker, Correspondence, Boston, Mass., to Al[van Bolster Ricker], 26–27, 29 October 1896, Private Collection.

21. Edw[ard] P. Ricker, Correspondence, Boston, Mass., to Al[van Bolster Ricker], 27, 29, 30 October 1896, Private Collection.

22. Graham, "Shakers and the Rickers," [4]; Priscilla J. Brewer, *Shaker Communities, Shaker Lives* (Hanover, N.H.: University Press of New England, 1986), 238. For representative accounts of the numerous produce transactions between the Shakers and the Rickers, see: "Church Record," vol. 3, New Gloucester, Maine, 5–26 August 1889, 446–49; Delmer C. Wilson, Diary, New Gloucester, Maine, 25 May, 7 August 1895; and Delmer C. Wilson, Diary, New Gloucester, Maine, 14 May, 29 June, 3 August 1900, USS.

23. Merrill, ed., *History of Androscoggin County,* 750; "Unusual Real Estate Opportunity," 1–2.

24. *Portland Transcript,* 21 December 1887, 299; "Unusual Real Estate Opportunity," 5–15.

25. Poole and Poole, *History of Poland,* 40–41, 121; *HT,* 4 July 1897, 14; "Elmwood Farm," *HT,* 16 August 1896, 1–2; "Elmwood Farm," *HT,* 8 August 1897, 11; Herndon, comp., *Men of Progress,* 201; Bennett, ed., *Poland: Past and Present,* 12–13; Deeds, Book 98, 31 March 1879, 13–15; Book 98, 4 April 1879, 58; Book 120, 31 December 1885, 130–31; Book 122, 31 December 1885, 38, ACRD; William E. Pulsifer, comp., *Ancestry and Descendants of Jonathan Pulsifer and his wife Nancy Ryerson Pulsifer of Poland and Sumner, Maine* (Privately Printed, 1928), 28, 55; Ricker, Fernald, and Ricker, *PC,* 39.

26. Poole and Poole, *History of Poland,* 41–42; "Sanborn's Stock Farm," *HT,* 12 August 1894, 2; *HT,* 4 July 1897, 14.

27. Poole and Poole, *History of Poland,* 43–44.

28. Ricker, Fernald, and Ricker, *PC,* 112; "The Ideal Road Horse," *HT,* 30 June 1895, 10; *HT,* 4 July 1897, 14; "Elmwood Farm," *HT,* 8 August 1897, 11; "The Sanborn Exhibit," *HT,* 13 August 1899, 6; "Sanborn's," *HT,* 18 August 1901, 11.

29. Merrill, ed., *History of Androscoggin County,* 726; "Paradise of New England," *LSJ,* 6 August 1892, 6; "The Man Behind the Hotel," *HT,* 10 August 1902, 1–2.

30. *PSC,* 30; "Equine Poland," *HT,* 18 August 1895, 1–2.

31. "Our First Fire," *HT,* 26 August 1894, 6.

32. Ibid.; "Editorial," *HT,* 26 August 1894, 4; *PSC,* 30, 32.

33. Deeds, Book 169, 23 June 1896, 93–94, 152–53, ACRD.

34. "The Herd of Hiram Ricker and Sons," *Bureau of Industrial and Labor Statistics* (Augusta, Maine: Kennebec Journal Print, 1902), 52; "Our Cows," *HT,* 26 July 1896, 6; "Where Cows Abide," *HT,* 23 July 1899, 2; "Man Behind the Hotel," *HT,* 10 August 1902, 2; "Poland Spring as a Big Farming Establishment," *LJIM,* 14 October 1916, 8.

35. "Church Record," New Gloucester, Maine, vol. 5, 16 January 1899, 60, USS; "Where Cows Abide," *HT*, 23 July 1899, 1–3; "Man Behind the Hotel," *HT*, 10 August 1902, 2; "Barns," *Bureau of Industrial and Labor Statistics* (1902), 52; "Our Cows," *HT*, 26 July 1896, 6; "Cows, Milk, Cream, Butter-Official Health Certificate," *HT*, 25 July 1897, 8.

36. "Big Farming Establishment," *LJIM*, 8; *HT*, 31 July 1898, 14.

37. *PSC*, 4, 20; "The Ricker Without Whiskers," *Boston Globe*, 7 December 1933; Gowell, "Rickers of Poland," 4; R. E. Hilton, "Fond Memories," *Advertiser-Democrat (Norway, Maine)*, 1977; *National Cyclopaedia*, vol. 24, s. v. "Alvan Bolster Ricker," 178; "Big Farming Establishment," *LJIM*, 8; "Man Behind the Hotel," *HT*, 10 August 1902, 2.

38. "Poland Facts," *HT*, 11 August 1895, 1; *Souvenir List*, [11]; *HT*, 1 September 1895, 7; "We Abound in Sheep," *HT*, 4 September 1898, 1–2; "The Harvest," *HT*, 15 September 1901, 15; "Where Cows Abide," *HT*, 23 July 1899, 3.

39. "Church Record," vol. 4, 2 July 1895, 352; 11 August 1896, 422; "Church Record," vol. 5, 24 January 1899, 62.

40. "Church Record," vol. 5, 6–22 February 1899, 63–65, 73, 76; Deeds, Book 183, 26 May 1899, 144–49; Book 222, 27 February 1915, 521, ACRD. It actually took the Rickers sixteen years, not ten, to pay off the mortgage on the Poland Hill property.

41. Shaker Hill," *HT*, 9 July 1899, 2–3; "Big Farming Establishment," *LJIM*, 8; Bennett, ed., *Poland: Past and Present*, 75.

42. Barron, *Those Who Stayed Behind*, 31.

43. "Tid-Bits," *HT*, 18 August 1895, 5; *HT*, 3 July 1898, 22; "We Abound in Sheep," *HT*, 4 September 1898, 2; *HT*, 25 August 1895, 9; "Bubbles," *HT*, 26 August 1894, 9; Ellis Paxson Oberholtzer, *Philadelphia: A History of the City and Its People: A Record of 225 Years*, vol. IV, (Philadelphia: S. J. Clarke Publishing, [1912]), 548–52; Clarence H. Danhof, *Change in Agriculture: The Northern United States, 1820–1870* (Cambridge, Mass.: Harvard University Press, 1969), 228.

44. "Editorial," *HT*, 22 August 1897, 8; "We Abound in Sheep," *HT*, 4 September 1898, 2; "Editorial," *HT*, 1 September 1901, 8.

45. Wilson, *Hill Country*, 270–76; Dona Brown, "Purchasing the Past," 9; Brown, *Inventing New England*, 138–42; "Tid-Bits," *HT*, 7 July 1901, 21; Herndon, *Men of Progress*, (1897), 528–29; "Sons and Daughters of Maine," *HT*, 16 July 1905, 20; "Old School Days in Minot," *HT*, 1 September 1901, 19–20.

46. Noyes, *Crown of New England*, 3–4, 8, 10–11.

47. Peter J. Schmitt, *Back to Nature: The Arcadian Myth in Urban America* (Baltimore: Johns Hopkins University Press, 1969), 96–98; *HT*, 13 August 1899, 3; "An Agreeable Recognition," *HT*, 20 August 1899, 24; "Sunday Services," *HT*, 11 August 1901, 24; "Sunday Service," *HT*, 22 July 1900, 2; "Country Week," *HT*, 29 July 1900, 7.

48. "Sanborn's Stock Farm," *HT*, 12 August 1894, 1–2; "Old Oxford," *HT*, 7 August 1898, 2; "Editorial," *HT*, 1 August 1897, 8; "Perfect Poland," *HT*, 8 August 1897, 2.

49. Patterson, *Romance of the New Bethesda*, 13, 18, 22, 67–68, 71, 199.

50. *PSC*, 19; Edward P. Ricker, Correspondence, to [Alvan Augustus Bolster], Poland, Maine, 11 May 1862, Private Collection; S[taples], *Inner Man*, 25–26.

51. "Uncle Solon," *HT*, 10 July 1904, 30; Day, *Farming in Maine*, 36.

52. "Trained Steers," *HT*, 26 August 1900, 15; "Them Steers," *HT*, 1 September 1901, 7.

53. David C. Smith, "Virgin Timber: The Maine Woods as a Locale for Juvenile Fiction," in *A Handful of Spice: Essays in Maine History and Literature*, ed. Richard S. Sprague, University of Maine Studies, no. 88 (Orono, Maine: University of Maine Press, 1968), 189; Ronald G. Whitney, *The World of C. A. Stephens* (Springfield, Mass.: Waynor Publishing, 1976), 173; Mark W. Anderson, "Images of Nineteenth Century Maine Farming in the Prose and Poetry of R. P. T. Coffin and C. A. Stephens," *Agricultural History* 63 (1989): 121.

54. C[harles] A[sbury] Stephens, *A Great Year of Our Lives: At the Old Squire's* (Norway, Maine: Old Squire's Bookstore, 1912); 256–74.

55. [Delbert Dana Coombs], "D. D. Coombs, Artist," Account Book, [1869–1929], 30, 32, 37, Museum of Art, Olin Arts Center, Bates College, Lewiston, Maine; "Art Notes," *HT*, 29 August 1897, 3; "The Art Exhibition," *HT*, 5 July 1896, 2; "Art Notes," *HT*, 7 August 1898, 5; "The First Ones," *HT*, 11 August 1895, 3; "Mr. Sanborn's Housewarming," *HT*, 18 July 1897, 8.

56. "D. D. Coombs," Account Book, 32.

57. Ibid., 59; Burns, *Pastoral Inventions*, 6, 244; Raymond Williams, *The Country and the City* (New York: Oxford University Press, 1973), 120–41; "Editorial," *HT*, 30 July 1921, 6.

58. "Old Home Romances," *HT*, 9 August 1903, 1–3.

Chapter 7. The Grounds (pp. 166–88)

1. "Trip to Poland," *LFJ*, 20 July 1860; Sanford and Everts, ed., *Atlas and History of Androscoggin County*, 114; Poole and Poole, *History of Poland*, 22–23, 44; Bennett, ed., *Poland: Past and Present*, 63.

2. Hans Huth, *Nature and the American: Three Centuries of Changing Attitudes* (Berkeley: University of California Press, 1957), 30–53, 87–89; Van Zandt, *Catskill Mountain House*, 151–55; Roderick Nash, *Wilderness and the American Mind* (New Haven, Conn.: Yale University Press, 1967), 44–66; Bender, *Toward an Urban Vision*, 92, 172–80; Schmitt, *Back to Nature*, xviii–xix, 3–5, 177–79, 188–89; Kenneth Myers, *The Catskills: Painters, Writers, and Tourists in the Mountains, 1820–1895* (Yonkers, N.Y.: Hudson River Museum of Westchester, 1987), 18–19, 40, 49–51, 74; Brown, *Inventing New England*, 52–59; Judd, *Common Lands*, 197–205; Chambers, *Drinking the Waters*, 28–52.

3. *PMSW* (1883), 3–4; *PSC*, 70–71; "Poland Sunsets," *HT*, 29 July 1900, 2.

4. "The Top," *HT*, 21 August 1898, 2.

5. *HT*, 19 August 1900, 20; A. Hurlburt, "June Days," *HT*, 4 July 1897, 2; "Skip and Trip," *HT*, 25 July 1897, 5; "Tom and Jerry," *HT*, 2 July 1899, 15; "Editorial," *HT*, 1 September 1901, 8; A. H. H., "Reminiscence," *HT*, 12 August 1900, 26; "Country Roads," *HT*, 13 August 1899, 1–2.

6. "A Good Shot," *HT*, 7 July 1895, 10; "Last Look Around," *HT*, 12 September 1897, 18.

7. "The Rangeley Lake House," *HT*, 19 August 1900, 20; "A Trip to Camp Bemis," *HT*, 11 August 1901, 15.

8. Ibid.; Walter Berri, "Poland on the Rangeleys," *HT*, 16 August 1896, 2; Bennett, *Mount Zircon*, 19–20, 38; Jason Stone, "Chisholm's 'Folly,'" *Down East* (1992): 55–59.

9. "Editorial," *HT*, 1 August 1897, 8; Murray, "Poland Spring Hotel," 1–2; "Editorial," *HT*, 1 September 1901, 8; "Country Roads," *HT*, 13 August 1899, 2; "Autumn," *HT*, 10 September 1899, 2.

10. "Poland Mineral Spring," *LEJ*, 10 June 1876.

11. "June Days," *HT*, 4 July 1897, 2; "Autumn," *HT*, 10 September 1899, 1–2; "The Crown of Snow," *HT*, 9 September 1900, 1–2.

12. *Poland Spring Hotels* (1887), [2]; "Tid-Bits," *HT*, 18 July 1897, 6; "View," *HT*, 22 July 1900, 1; Louise M. Waterhouse, "Greeting to Poland," in *PC*, 50.

13. "A Summer Shrine," *HT*, 22 July 1894, 1–2.

14. *Poland Spring Hotels* (1887), [9]; Poole and Poole, *History of Poland*, 34; Merrill, ed., *History of Androscoggin County*, 735; "Summer Shrine," *HT*, 22 July 1894, 1; "Editorial," *HT*, 1 August 1897, 8.

15. "Summer Shrine," *HT*, 22 July 1894, 1; Haynes, "Poland Spring," *HT*, 9 September 1894, 1–2; Sears, *Sacred Places*, 6, 11; Grover, "Luxury and Leisure," 26, 114, 168.

16. "Editorial," *HT*, 1 August 1897, 8; "Country Roads," *HT*, 13 August 1899, 1; "Autumn," *HT*, 10 September 1899, 1; "Editorial," *HT*, 1 September 1901, 8.

17. "The Children in the Wood," *HT*, 27 August 1899, 1–2.

18. "Beneath the Pines," *HT*, 17 July 1898, 1–2.

19. Angela Miller, *The Empire of the Eye: Landscape Representation and American Cultural Politics, 1825–1875* (Ithaca, N.Y.: Cornell University Press, 1993), 148.

20. *National Cyclopaedia*, vol. 10 (New York: James T. White, 1900), s. v. "William Henry Harrison Murray," 230; Warder H. Cadbury, "Introduction," in *Adventures in the Wilderness*, ed. William K. Verner (Syracuse, N.Y.: Syracuse University Press and The Adirondack Museum, 1989), 32–39; David Strauss, "Toward a Consumer Culture: 'Adirondack Murray' and the Wilderness Vacation," *American Quarterly* 39 (1987): 271; Murray, "Poland Spring Hotel," 5–7. Murray's commentary on the natural surroundings of the resort also appeared without attribution in Poole and Poole, *History of Poland*, 35–39.

21. Murray, "Poland Spring Hotel," 8–10.

22. [George H. Haynes], *Specimens of Illustrations in Books Written by Geo. H. Haynes* (Portland, Maine: Self-published, [1893]), [cover, 2, 5]; Haynes, *Charming Inland Retreats*, 6, 9–14; George H. Haynes, "Ricker Family and Poland Spring," Portland, Maine, 21 October 1896, TMs, photocopy, 7–8, MHS. Haynes's remarks to the Genealogical Society were an amalgamation of verbatim extracts from William Murray's 1890 essay on the Poland Spring Hotel and from *Poland Spring Centennial*. Given his background as a descriptive writer, Haynes might have had a hand in preparing the latter work.

23. Haynes, "Poland Spring," *HT*, 9 September 1894, 1–2.

24. Libby, "1795–1895," in *PC*, 38–39; Waterhouse, "Greeting to Poland," in *PC*, 50–51.

25. "A Pleasant Prospect," *HT*, 10 July 1898, 2; [Day], "Facts and Fancies," *HT*, 8 July 1894, 2; "Summer Shrine," *HT*, 22 July 1894, 1–2; "Perfect Poland," *HT*, 8 August 1897, 2.

26. "Editorial," *HT*, 2 August 1896, 6.

27. "The Art Exhibition," *HT*, 5 July 1896, 2; "John J. Enneking," *HT*, 2 August 1896, 7; "Paintings in the Maine State Building," *HT*, 25 August 1895, 11; "Art Notes," *HT*, 3 July 1898, 3; "Art Notes," *HT*, 21 August 1898, 3.

28. *PMSW* [1879], 3; *Poland Spring Hotels* (1887), [6, 9]; *PSW* (1890), [4].

29. "Country Roads," *HT*, 13 August 1899, 1–2; "View," *HT*, 22 July 1900, 1–2.

30. "Poland Sunsets," *HT*, 29 July 1900, 1–2; Schmitt, *Back to Nature*, 146–49.

31. "Picturesque Maine," *HT*, 25 July 1897, 4; "Tuesday Evening, August 5th," *HT*, 1 August 1897, 5; "Picturesque Maine," *HT*, 8 August 1897, 9; *HT*, 7 August 1898, 12; *HT*, 11 September 1898, 4.

32. "Editorial," *HT*, 25 August 1895, 6.

33. "Poland Mineral Spring," *LEJ*, 10 June 1876; Patterson, *Romance of the New Bethesda*, 11, 80; "Hearing on Petition," 335; "The Drive to Poland," *HT*, 8 July 1900, 1.

34. Ibid., 1–2; "Paradise of New England," *LSJ*, 6 August 1892, 6; *PSC*, 70; Van Zandt, *Catskill Mountain House*, 72–73.

35. "An August Outing," *HT*, 19 August 1894, 2; "On the Poland Brake," *HT*, 5 August 1894, 1–2; Chambers, *Drinking the Waters*, 97.

36. Blackmar and Cromley, "On the Verandah," 51–53; "The Top," *HT*, 21 August 1898, 2; *WMV*, 13; "Poland Spring," *HT*, 16 September 1894, 2; [Day], "Facts and Fancies," *HT*, 8 July 1894, 2.

37. "Tid-Bits," *HT*, 18 August 1895, 5; *HT*, 7 August 1898, 12; E. L. J., "Lovers' Lane," *HT*, 29 July 1894, 6.

38. *Poland Spring Hotels* (1887), [13–14]; "Hearing on Petition," 107, 132, 144–45, 309.

39. "Poland Facts," *HT*, 11 August 1895, 1; "The Conservatory," *HT*, 18 July 1897, 1–2; *Souvenir List*, [11]; *Poland Spring House* (1899), 6, 8; Graham, "Shakers and Rickers," [4].

40. W. E. L. S., "Song Birds at Poland Spring," *HT*, 22 July 1900, 11–12; W. L. C. S., "More About Birds at Poland Spring," *HT*, 29 July 1900, 26; "The Bird in the Wonderful Mask," *HT*, 12 August 1900, 14–15; Schmitt, *Back to Nature*, 33–44.

41. "Butterflies at Poland," *HT*, 26 August 1900, 17; W. E. C. S., "Butterflies at Poland," *HT*, 2 September 1900, 11; "Poland Butterflies," *HT*, 9 July 1899, 15.

42. "Hearing on Petition," 97, 147; "Steam Launch," *HT*, 15 July 1894, 4; "Bubbles," *HT*, 29 July 1894, 3; *Annual Report of the Steamboat Inspectors for the State of Maine* (Augusta, Maine: Burleigh and Flynt, 1894), 6; "Yachting Party," *HT*, 19 August 1894, 1–2; *HT*, 9 September 1894, 7; "Editorial," *HT*, 12 August 1894, 4.

43. "The Lake Country," *HT*, 6 September 1903, 2; "View," *HT*, 22 July 1900, 1–2.

44. "Nameless Orphans," *HT*, 9 August 1903, 5; "Lake Country," *HT*, 6 September 1903, 1–2.

45. Patterson, *Romance of the New Bethesda*, 7–14.

46. Ibid., 18–21, 34, 69–74.

47. Ibid., 308–9.

48. Dwyer, "Recollections," *HT*, 30 August 1896, 4. The poem Dwyer quoted from was "The Vale of Avoca" by Tom Moore.

49. "Paradise of New England," *LSJ*, 6 August 1892, 6.

50. "Tid-Bits," *HT*, 8 August 1897, 10; "Tid-Bits," *HT*, 30 July 1899, 9; T. P. McGowan, "Picturesque Poland Spring," *HT*, 27 August 1899, 3.

51. Helen C. Weld, Diary, Jamaica Plain, Mass., 15–17 September 1891, Private Collection.

52. "To Poland Spring," *HT*, 22 August 1897, 18; "Poland Spring," *HT*, 16 September 1894, 2.

53. S[taples], *Inner Man*, 28; "A Trip to Rangeley," *HT*, 1 September 1901, 21.

Chapter 8. The Playing Fields (pp. 189–213)

1. "The Tournament of '99," *HT*, 27 August 1899, 14.

2. "Poland Spring," *LEJ*, 2 February 1898; Leroy T. Carleton, "Maine As a Vacation State," in *Three Able Addresses*, 11–13. For more on the nineteenth-century interplay between work and leisure, see: Dale Somers, "The Leisure Revolution: Recreation in the American City, 1820–1920," *Journal of Popular Culture* 5 (1971): 125–28; Daniel T. Rodgers, *The Work Ethic in Industrial America, 1850–1920* (Chicago: University of Chicago Press, 1978), 1–29; and Aron, *Working at Play*, 6–9, 34–43, 145–46, 258–59.

3. Penney, "Primitive Industry," in *Three Able Addresses*, 33; "Editorial," *HT*, 1 August 1897, 8.

4. Uminowicz, "Sport in a Middle-Class Utopia," 65; Urry, *Tourist Gaze*, 19.

5. Poole and Poole, *History of Poland*, 43.

6. Ibid.; Steven A. Riess, *City Games: The Evolution of American Urban Society and the Rise of Sports* (Urbana: University of Illinois Press, 1989), 61; Donald J. Mrozek, *Sport and American Mentality, 1880–1910* (Knoxville: University of Tennessee Press, 1983), 46–47; Lears, *No Place of Grace*, xii, xv–xvi; T. J. Jackson Lears, "From Salvation to Self-Realization: Advertising and the Therapeutic Roots of the Consumer Culture, 1880–1930," in *Culture of Consumption*, 6–17; "Editorial," *HT*, 1 August 1897, 8.

7. Judd, *Common Lands*, 182–84; Colleen J. Sheehy, "American Angling: The Rise of Urbanism and the Romance of the Rod and Reel," in *Hard at Play*, 78–86; "Poland Mineral Spring," *LEJ*, 10 June 1876; "Tid-Bits," *HT*, 25 July 1897, 3; "Paradise of New England," *LSJ*, 6 August 1892, 7–8; "Bubbles," *HT*, 5 August 1894, 9.

8. "Fishing," *HT*, 15 July 1900, 1–2; "The East Auburn Fish Hatcheries," *HT*, 2 September 1900, 1; "June Catches," *HT*, 3 July 1898, 3; "Just Fish," *HT*, 31 July 1898, 22.

9. Higham, "Reorientation of American Culture," 31; "Miss 'Fly Rod,'" *HT*, 4 July 1897, 4.

10. "Fishing," *HT*, 15 July 1900, 2.

11. "A Little Fish Story," *HT*, 7 August 1898, 22.

12. "Paradise of New England," *LSJ*, 6 August 1892, 7; "Notches on a Paddle-Blade," *HT*, 29 July 1894, 1–2.

13. "Capt. W. H. Daily," *HT*, 11 August 1895, 5; "A Real Hero," *HT*, 18 August 1895, 2;

"Editorial," *HT*, 30 August 1903, 8; "Bubbles," *HT*, 29 July 1894, 9; "Tid-Bits," *HT*, 16 August 1896, 9.

14. "Aquatic Poland," *HT*, 25 August 1895, 1; "Great Walking," *HT*, 19 August 1894, 6; "Tid-Bits," *HT*, 26 August 1900, 2; "Bubbles," *HT*, 12 August 1894, 9; "Bubbles," *HT*, 19 August 1894, 9.

15. "A Perilous Experience," *HT*, 25 July 1897, 4.

16. Richard Harmond, "Progress and Flight: An Interpretation of the American Cycle Craze of the 1890s," *Journal of Social History* 5 (1971–72): 236, 240–49; Gary Allan Tobin, "The Bicycle Boom of the 1890's: The Development of Private Transportation and the Birth of the Modern Tourist," *Journal of Popular Culture* 7 (1974): 839; M[arcia] B. J[ordan], Letter to the Editors, *HT*, 14 July 1895, 3; "Cyclist," *HT*, 9 August 1896, 5.

17. "Cyclist Column," *HT*, 26 July 1896, 5; "Cyclist Column," *HT*, 2 August 1896, 5.

18. "Bubbles," *HT*, 19 August 1894, 9; *HT*, 12 August 1894, 4; "Editorial," *HT*, 18 August 1901, 8; Charles W. Stein, ed., *American Vaudeville: As Seen by Its Contemporaries* (New York: Alfred A. Knopf, 1984), 4; Robert A. Smith, *A Social History of the Bicycle: Its Early Life and Times in America* (New York: American Heritage Press, 1972), 68, 192.

19. Tobin, "Bicycle Boom" 842–45; "Cyclist Column," *HT*, 4 July 1897, 3.

20. "Cyclist Column," *HT*, 26 July 1896, 5; "Cyclist Column," *HT*, 23 August 1896, 3; "Cyclist," *HT*, 11 July 1897, 7; "Tid-Bits," *HT*, 8 August 1897, 12; Smith, *Social History of the Bicycle*, 313.

21. "Cyclist Column," *HT*, 4 July 1897, 3.

22. J[ordan], Letter to the Editors, *HT*, 14 July 1895, 3. For more on the appeal of cycling to women, see: Harmond, "Progress and Flight," 252; Dale Somers, *The Rise of Sports in New Orleans, 1850–1900* (Baton Rouge: Louisiana State University Press, 1972), 233–36; and Smith, *Social History of the Bicycle*, 65, 76–80, 100.

23. Barth, *City People*, 149–50.

24. Harvey Green, *Fit for America: Health, Fitness, Sport and American Society* (New York: Pantheon Books, 1986), 181–215, 219–58; Uminowicz, "Sport in a Middle-Class Utopia," 65–71; Glenn Uminowicz, "Recreation in Christian America: Ocean Grove and Asbury Park, New Jersey, 1869–1914," in *Hard at Play*, 23–25; Mrozek, *Sport and American Mentality*, 189–225; Melvin L. Adelman, *A Sporting Time: New York City and the Rise of Modern Athletics, 1820–1870* (Urbana: University of Illinois Press, 1986), 270–86; Riess, *City Games*, 46–48, 253–54; Clifford Putney, *Muscular Christianity: Manhood and Sports in Protestant America, 1880–1920* (Cambridge, Mass.: Harvard University Press, 2001), 1–4, 20–39.

25. "Bubbles," *HT*, 26 August 1894, 9; "Tid-Bits," *HT*, 9 September 1894, 5; *HT*, 5 August 1900, 13; "Tennis Tournament," *HT*, 19 August 1894, 8; "Locals," *Bates Student* 22 (September 1894): 188.

26. "Statistics of the Class of '95," *Bates Student* 23 (June 1895): 162; Rodgers, *Work Ethic*, 108–9; "Tennis Tournament," *HT*, 19 August 1894, 8.

27. "Bubbles," *HT*, 5 August 1894, 3; E. Digby Baltzell, *Sporting Gentlemen: Men's Tennis from the Age of Honor to the Cult of the Superstar* (New York: Free Press, 1995), 44; "Tennis Tournament," *HT*, 19 August 1894, 8.

28. Ibid.

29. "Base-Ball," *HT*, 22 July 1894, 6; Riess, *City Games*, 68; Barth, *City People*, 160–91.

30. "Locals," *Bates Student* 20 (September 1892): 196–97; "Bubbles," *HT*, 8 July 1894, 3; "The Amusement Fund," *HT*, 8 July 1894, 5; "Coming Events," *HT*, 15 July 1894, 3; "Hearing on Petition," 189.

31. Ibid.; "The Amusement Fund," *HT*, 8 July 1894, 5; "Locals," *Bates Student*, 22 (September 1894): 188; "Our Baseball Team's Future," *HT*, 9 September 1894, 8; "Bubbles," *HT*, 8 July 1894, 3; "Base-Ball," *HT*, 22 July 1894, 7; Trina Wellman, *Louis Francis Sockalexis: The Life-story of a Penobscot Indian* (Augusta, Maine: Department of Indian Affairs, 1975), 2–12, 19; "Cleveland Chatter," *Sporting Life*, 27 March 1897, 3; Olen B. Rideout, "Playing Baseball in Houlton, Maine, with Louis Francis Sockalexis," *Down East* 12 (August 1965): 93.

32. "Base-Ball," *HT*, 22 July 1894, 6.

33. Ibid.

34. "Base-Ball," *HT*, 15 July 1894, 5; "Base-Ball," *HT*, 22 July 1894, 7; "Base-Ball," *HT*, 29 July 1894, 7.

35. "Hearing on Petition," 329; "Baseball," *HT*, 5 August 1894, 7.

36. "Hearing on Petition," 223, 328; "Bubbles," *HT*, 5 August 1894, 3; "Base-Ball," *HT*, 12 August 1894, 7.

37. Ibid.; "Bubbles," *HT*, 2 September 1894, 3; "Baseball," *HT*, 9 September 1894, 6.

38. Ibid.

39. "Base-Ball," *HT*, 22 July 1894, 6; "The Amusement Fund," *HT*, 8 July 1894, 5.

40. "Baseball," *HT*, 21 July 1895, 8; "Base-Ball of August 20th," *HT*, 28 August 1898, 22; "Great Base-Ball," *HT*, 20 August 1899, 16; "Base-Ball," *HT*, 19 August 1900, 20; "Base-Ball," *HT*, 26 August 1900, 15.

41. *HT*, 10 July 1926, 6; "Golf," *HT*, 30 August 1896, 3; "Golf," *HT*, 26 August 1900, 2; "Golf," *HT*, 3 July 1898, 22; "Golfiana," *HT*, 14 August 1898, 3; "Golf," *HT*, 11 September 1898, 16.

42. James M. Mayo, *The American Country Club: Its Origins and Development* (New Brunswick, N.J.: Rutgers University Press, 1998), 35–58.

43. "Briefly Put-Golf," *HT*, 25 July 1897, 1–2; "Golf," *HT*, 4 July 1897, 10; "Tid-Bits," *HT*, 1 August 1897, 6; "On Poland's Links," *HT*, 20 August 1899, 1; "Golf," *HT*, 26 August 1900, 1. For assessments of the relationship between sports and status, see: Veblen, *Theory of the Leisure Class*, 53, 145, 156–65; Somers, *Rise of Sports in New Orleans*, 23–51; Hardy, *How Boston Played*, 139–41; Mrozek, *Sport and American Mentality*, 118–26; and Riess, *City Games*, 54–60.

44. "On Poland's Links," *HT*, 20 August 1899, 2.

45. "Arthur H. Fenn," *HT*, 26 August 1900, 18; A. H. Fenn, "Golf," *HT*, 11 July 1897, 4.

46. Ibid.; "Golf," *HT*, 2 August 1896, 13; "Golf," *HT*, 15 August 1897, 10; "On Poland's Links," *HT*, 20 August 1899, 3; "Golf," *HT*, 1 July 1900, 5; "Golf," *HT*, 11 September 1898, 16.

47. "On Poland's Links," *HT*, 20 August 1899, 2.

48. "Golf," *HT,* 2 August 1896, 13; "Golf," *HT,* 26 August 1900, 2; "Presentation of the Vardon Cup," *HT,* 2 September 1900, 14.

49. "Golf," *HT,* 2 August 1896, 13; "Briefly Put-Golf," *HT,* 25 July 1897, 2; "On Poland's Links," *HT,* 20 August 1899, 2; "Golfiana," *HT,* 14 August 1898, 1; A. H. Fenn, "Golf," *HT,* 11 July 1897, 4.

50. *HT,* 31 July 1898, 7; "In Honor of Miss Lockwood," *HT,* 2 September 1900, 5; *Poland Spring Golf Links* [South Poland, Maine: Hiram Ricker and Sons, n. d.], AHS.

51. *HT,* 30 August 1896, 5; *HT,* 1 July 1900, 5, 24; *HT,* 3 July 1898, 23. The relationship between sports and consumer culture is explored in: Somers, *Rise of Sports in New Orleans,* 280–82; Stephen Hardy, *How Boston Played: Sport, Recreation, and Community, 1865–1915* (Boston: Northeastern University Press, 1982), 148–66; and Mrozek, *Sport and American Mentality,* 103–35.

52. *HT,* 28 August 1898, 15; *HT,* 8 July 1900, 9; "Golf," *HT,* 4 July 1897, 10; "On Poland's Links," *HT,* 20 August 1899, 3; *HT,* 17 July 1898, 7; "Golf," *HT,* 4 September 1898, 11.

53. "Seen from the Tower," *HT,* 5 September 1897, 2; "Golf," *HT,* 13 August 1899, 10–11; "Golf," *HT,* 9 July 1899, 10; "Arthur H. Fenn," *HT,* 26 August 1900, 18; "Golf," *HT,* 22 July 1900, 5; "Golf," *HT,* 26 August 1900, 2.

54. Stephen Hardy, "'Adopted by All the Leading Clubs': Sporting Goods and the Shaping of Leisure, 1800–1900," in *For Fun and Profit,* 79–80; "Golf," *HT,* 22 August 1897, 3; "Golf," *HT,* 5 August 1900, 5.

55. "Golf," *HT,* 19 August 1900, 13; Herbert Warren Wind, *The Story of American Golf: Its Champions and Its Championships* (New York: Farrar, Straus, 1948), 55–56; "Golf," *HT,* 5 August 1900, 5; "Golf," 12 August 1900, 5; 19 August 1900, 6, 9.

56. "Golf," *HT,* 19 August 1900, 13; "Golf," *HT,* 26 August 1900, 2; "To Amateur Photographers," *HT,* 26 August 1900, 13.

57. "Golf," *HT,* 10 September 1899, 22; "Golf," *HT,* 2 July 1899, 18.

58. Veblen, *Theory of the Leisure Class,* 16; "Golf, *HT,* 20 August 1899, 10–11; "The Tournament of '99," *HT,* 27 August 1899, 14.

59. "Golf," *HT,* 12 August 1900, 5.

60. "Paradise of New England," *LSJ,* 6 August 1892, 7; *PSC,* 84; "Bubbles," *HT,* 19 August 1894, 9.

61. The paintings appear as illustrations in: "Poland Spring," *HT,* 16 September 1894, 1; and Sherwood E. Bain, "N. W. Scott Leighton," *Antiques,* 115 (1979): 551. Poole and Poole, *History of Poland,* 120–21; "Church Record," vol. 4, 16 August 1894, 293; Mrozek, *Sport and American Mentality,* 105–7; Benjamin: G. Rader, "The Quest for Subcommunities and the Rise of American Sport," *American Quarterly* 29 (1977): 357–66.

Chapter 9. The Maine State Building (pp. 214–38)

1. *PSC,* 76.

2. "Maine State Building," *HT,* 30 June 1895, 2; Trachtenberg, *Incorporation of America,* 208–9; *Report of the Board of World's Fair Managers,* 26; Harold W. Dutch, ed., *Maine*

State Building at Poland Spring, Maine: Centennial, 1895–1995 (Poland Spring, Maine: Poland Spring Preservation Society, 1995), 18; "Pictures at Poland," *LSJ*, 5 August 1893, 5.

3. Trachtenberg, *Incorporation of America*, 209–18; Mel Scott, *American City Planning Since 1890* (Berkeley: University of California Press, 1969), 43–46, 66–80; Jon A. Peterson, "The City Beautiful Movement: Forgotten Origins and Lost Meanings," *Journal of Urban History* 2 (1976): 415–16, 424–25; William H. Wilson, *The City Beautiful Movement* (Baltimore: Johns Hopkins University Press, 1989), 1–4, 53–64, 75–87; "The Maine State Building," *HT*, 30 June 1895, 2.

4. "Editorial," *HT*, 8 August 1897, 8; "Editorial," *HT*, 11 August 1895, 6.

5. *Report of the Board of World's Fair Managers*, 4–6; Thomas C. Jester, "Charles Sumner Frost, 1856–1931," *A Biographical Dictionary of Architects in Maine* 6 (1991): [1].

6. Hubert Howe Bancroft, *The Book of the Fair*, vol. 1 (Chicago: Bancroft, 1893), 54–55; Jester, "Charles Sumner Frost," in *Biographical Dictionary of Architects*, [1, 3]; "Maine State Building," *HT*, 30 June 1895, 2; *PSC*, 68; Dutch, ed., *Maine State Building*, 46–47; "The Maine World's Fair Building," *LSJ*, 23 July 1892, 3; *Report of the Board of World's Fair Managers*, 12.

7. "At Poland Springs Will Governor Burleigh and World's Fair Commission Meet," *Kennebec Journal*, 7 July 1891, 1; *Report of the Board of World's Fair Managers*, 15, 23.

8. Haynes, *State of Maine*, 40–41.

9. Joseph P. Bass, "Address," in *Addresses at the Dedication of Maine State Building* (Lewiston, Maine: Lewiston Journal, 1895), 38; Dutch, ed., *Maine State Building*, 26; "A Poland Institution," *HT*, 3 September 1899, 1; *Report of the Board of World's Fair Managers*, 14; *PSC*, 67–68.

10. Dutch, ed., *Maine State Building*, 25–26; "Maine State Building," *HT*, 30 June 1895, 2–3.

11. Ibid.; *PSC*, 75; *HT*, 12 August 1894, 6; "Laying of Corner-Stone," *HT*, 19 August 1894, 4; Dutch, ed., *Maine State Building*, 41–42.

12. "Dedication of the Maine State Building," *HT*, 7 July 1895, 1–3; Joseph W. Symonds, "Address," in *Addresses at the Dedication*, 4.

13. Mace, *Aletheia*, 106–7; "Dedication of the Maine State Building," *HT*, 7 July 1895, 3; William P. Frye, "Address," in *Addresses at the Dedication*, 17–23.

14. Mace, *Aletheia*, 107; Augustus P. Martin, "Address," in *Addresses at the Dedication*, 40–43.

15. Ibid., 41–44.

16. "Dedication of the Maine State Building," *HT*, 7 July 1895, 3; Eugene Hale, "Address," in *Addresses at the Dedication*, 14.

17. Edgar R. Champlin, "Address," in *Addresses at the Dedication*, 9–12; "Dedication of the Maine State Building," *HT*, 7 July 1895, 2; Charles A. Boutelle, "Address," in *Addresses at the Dedication*, 29–30.

18. *Report of the Board of World's Fair Managers*, 28–30; Henry B. Cleaves, "Address," in *Addresses at the Dedication*, 8; "Dedication of the Maine State Building," *HT*, 7 July 1895, 1.

19. William P. Whitehouse, "Address," in *Addresses at the Dedication*, 34 – 35.

20. Nelson Dingley, Jr., "Address," in Ibid., 24; Trachtenberg, *Incorporation of America*, 143 – 44; *PSC*, 78; "The Reading Room," *HT*, 26 July 1896, 1.

21. "Some Valuable Presents," *HT*, 29 August 1897, 5; *PSC*, 76; "Poland Spring's Treasure-House," *HT*, 23 August 1903, 1 – 2.

22. Ibid., 2; "The Library," *HT*, 18 August 1901, 2.

23. "The Reading Room," *HT*, 26 July 1896, 1; "A Poland Institution," *HT*, 3 September 1899, 1 – 2; *HT*, 30 June 1895, 4; Ada Graham and Frank Graham, Jr., *Kate Furbish and the Flora of Maine* (Gardiner, Maine: Tilbury House, 1995), 111 – 12; Marcia Myers Bonta, *Women in the Field: America's Pioneering Women Naturalists* (College Station: Texas A & M University Press, 1991), 78 – 83; *PSC*, 86.

24. "Botanical," *HT*, 21 July 1895, 5; Graham and Graham, *Kate Furbish*, 114 – 21; "Reading Room," *HT*, 26 July 1896, 3; "The Only One," *HT*, 4 August 1895, 8; "Library," *HT*, 18 August 1901, 2.

25. "Tid-Bits," *HT*, 25 August 1895, 10; "Library," *HT*, 18 August 1901, 2; "Botanical," *HT*, 28 July 1895, 2; "Botanical," *HT*, 31 July 1898, 14; "Tid-Bits," *HT*, 5 September 1897, 12; Kate Furbish, "Mushrooms," *HT*, 12 August 1900, 3.

26. "A Suggestion," *HT*, 4 July 1897, 2; "Natural Curiosities," *HT*, 4 September 1898, 3; James H. Chadbourn, Correspondence, to Hiram Ricker and Sons, Wilmington, N.C., 24 August 1898, AHS; "Library," *HT*, 18 August 1901, 2.

27. "Minerals," *HT*, 2 July 1899, 19; "Poland Institution," *HT*, 3 September 1899, 2; "Minerals," *HT*, 25 July 1897, 7; "The Minerals," *HT*, 18 July 1897, 10; "Mineral Exhibit Notes," *HT*, 21 August 1898, 3; *HT*, 8 July 1900, 15; "Minerals About Poland," *HT*, 19 August 1900, 11; "Mineral Exhibit Notes," *HT*, 4 September 1898, 3.

28. "Minerals About Poland," *HT*, 19 August 1900, 11; "Minerals," *HT*, 18 July 1897, 10; "Maine Gems," *HT*, 1 August 1897, 3; "Mineral Exhibit Notes," *HT*, 28 August 1898, 3.

29. "The Bottle and the Cork," *HT*, 4 August 1901, 3.

30. "Library," *HT*, 18 August 1901, 1 – 2; *HT*, 7 July 1895, 5; "Reading Room," *HT*, 26 July 1896, 1.

31. "Poland Springs Library," *HT*, 13 September 1896, 2; "Library," *HT*, 18 August 1901, 2; "Maine State Building," *HT*, 28 July 1895, 3; "Reading Room," *HT*, 26 July 1896, 3.

32. "Poland Springs Library," *HT*, 13 September 1896, 2; "Library," *HT*, 18 August 1901, 2.

33. "Out of the Misty Past," *HT*, 31 July 1926, 5; Frank C. Griffith, Copybook, "Poland Spring Library, Maine State Building," Poland Spring, Maine, 1902 – 1903, 348, Private Collection; "Mrs. Fiske and Mary of Magdala," *HT*, 30 August 1903, 14 – 15.

34. "The Librarian's First Hour," *HT*, 25 August 1923, 3.

35. "Just Figures," *HT*, 12 September 1897, 3; "The Library," *HT*, 16 July 1899, 28; "Library," *HT*, 18 August 1901, 2.

36. Ibid.

37. "Some Library Enigmas," *HT*, 13 August 1905, 18; EBS, "Editorial," *HT*, 11 July 1909, 8 – 9; Jean-Christophe Agnew, "A House of Fiction: Domestic Interiors and the Commodity Aesthetic," in *Consuming Visions*, 133 – 55; Anne Scott MacLeod, "Reading

Together: Children, Adults, and Literature at the Turn of the Century," in *Arts and the American Home*, 111–23; Linda M. Kruger, "Home Libraries: Special Spaces, Reading Places," in *American Home Life*, 94–119.

38. "Editorial," *HT*, 27 July 1902, 10.

39. "Editorial," *HT*, 8 July 1894, 4.

40. [Day], "Facts and Fancies," *HT* 8 July 1894, 1–2; "The Hill-Top Twenty-Six Years Ago," *HT*, 31 July 1920, 8.

41. "Editorial," *HT*, 8 September 1895, 4; "Bubbles," *HT*, 8 July 1894, 3.

42. *HT*, 2 September 1894, 8. Miscellaneous categories accounted for another 23.4 percent of the 171 advertisers and unidentified categories for the remaining 1.8 percent.

43. *HT*, 25 August 1901, 24; "You're Another," *HT*, 20 August 1899, 3.

44. "Editorial," *HT*, 8 July 1894, 4; Sterngass, *First Resorts*, 63, 170, 178.

45. "Editorial," *HT*, 3 September 1905, 8.

46. Jane L. Patterson, "Root of the Matter," *HT*, 10 September 1899, 18; Marcia Bradbury Jordan, "Little Bluebird," *HT*, 10 September 1899, 18; *HT*, 11 September 1898, 12; M. B. J[ordan], "To N. M. R.," *HT*, 6 September 1903, 10.

47. "Art and Artists," *HT*, 30 July 1899, 3; "Art at Poland," *HT*, 12 August 1900, 1, 3; "The Art Exhibition," *HT*, 4 July 1897, 4; "Art and Artists," *HT*, 20 August 1899, 5.

48. *PSC*, 78; Dutch, ed., *Maine State Building*, 33; *Annual Exhibition of Paintings by Prominent Artists at the Poland Springs Art Gallery* (South Poland, Maine: Hiram Ricker and Sons, 1897), 15; Ricker and Ricker, ed., *Poland Spring Remembered*, 19.

49. "Pictures," *HT*, 11 September 1898, 2; Ricker and Ricker, ed., *Poland Spring Remembered*, 20–21. Family descendants still possessed twenty-seven images of European royalty from Janette M. Ricker's collection as recently as the late 1990s.

50. "Art at Poland," *HT*, 12 August 1900, 1–3; "Paintings," *HT*, 7 July 1895, 9; "Paintings in the Maine State Building," *HT*, 25 August 1895, 11; "The Art Gallery," *HT*, 13 September 1896, 3; "The Art Exhibition," *HT*, 5 July 1896, 1–3; "Art Notes," *HT*, 29 August 1897, 3; "Nine Poland Exhibitions," *HT*, 6 September 1903, 7. In 1903 the *Hill-Top* reported that the first exhibition contained sixty-six pictures by twenty-five artists.

51. "Paintings," *HT*, 7 July 1895, 9; "Paintings in the Maine State Building," *HT*, 25 August 1895, 11; *PSC*, 18; "The Art Exhibition," *HT*, 5 July 1896, 2–3; "Pictures, Souvenirs and Ricker Family Heirlooms That Casual Visitors of Poland Spring Never See," *LJIM*, 1 May 1920, 1.

52. "Perfect Poland," *HT*, 8 August 1897, 2; "Editorial," *HT*, 28 July 1901, 8.

53. "Complimentary Art Talks," *HT*, 11 August 1895, 10.

54. "Nine Poland Exhibitions," *HT*, 6 September 1903, 7; "Art at Poland," *HT*, 12 August 1900, 2; "A Photographic Exhibition," *HT*, 5 July 1896, 3.

55. "Art Gallery," *HT*, 12 July 1896, 3; "Dedication of the Maine State Building," *HT*, 7 July 1895, 3; "Echoes," *HT*, 7 July 1895, 5.

56. *Annual Exhibition*, (1899); *Annual Exhibition*, (1900); "Nine Poland Exhibitions," *HT*, 6 September 1903, 7; "Art at Poland," *HT*, 12 August 1900, 3; "The Art Exhibition," *HT*, 26 August 1900, 11; "Pictures," *HT*, 26 August 1900, 10.

57. "The Art Exhibition," *HT,* 1 July 1900, 3; "Pictures," *HT,* 11 September 1898, 2.

58. "Art Notes," *HT,* 7 August 1898, 5; "Picture Sales," *HT,* 22 August 1897, 2; *Annual Exhibition* (1898), 35; "The Art Exhibition," *HT,* 4 July 1897, 4; "Pictures Sold from Art Exhibitions," TMs, PSPS; "Art Notes," *HT,* 10 July 1898, 14; "The Art Exhibition," *HT,* 2 September 1900, 16.

59. "Art Notes," *HT,* 22 August 1897, 2; "Art Notes," *HT,* 7 August 1898, 5; "Pictures," *HT,* 11 September 1898, 2; "The Art Exhibition," *HT,* 17 July 1904, 18.

60. "Art," *HT,* 21 July 1901, 1.

Conclusion (pp. 239–42)

1. "Editorial," *HT,* 1 July 1900, 8; "Editorial," *HT,* 12 August 1900, 8.

2. *Poland Spring: America's Leading Spa* (South Poland, Maine: Hiram Ricker and Sons, 1900), [1]; *Poland Spring House* (1899), 4.

3. Ibid., 29.

4. *Poland Spring House* (1901), [9, 12, 48]; *Poland Spring House* (1899), 31.

5. Schmitt, *Back to Nature,* xix, 3–4; Lears, *No Place of Grace,* xi–xx.

6. George Cotkin, *Reluctant Modernism: American Thought and Culture, 1880–1900* (New York: Twayne Publishers, 1992), 123–25, 144; Higham, "Reorientation of American Culture," 26–27; Sterngass, *First Resorts,* 5; Urry, *Tourist Gaze,* 4. The distinctions between modern (a temporal designation), modernity (a cluster of cultural characteristics), modernism (a system of intellectual beliefs), and modernization (an economic process) are set forth in Singal, "Towards a Definition of American Modernism," 7–26. See also: Kenneth Cmiel, "Destiny and Amnesia: The Vision of Modernity in Robert Wiebe's *The Search for Order,*" *Reviews in American History* 21 (1993): 353–58.

Select Bibliography

Manuscript Collections

ABR: Alvan Bolster Ricker Memorial Library, Poland, Maine.
ACRD: Androscoggin County Registry of Deeds, Auburn, Maine.
AHS: Androscoggin Historical Society, Auburn, Maine.
CCRD: Cumberland County Registry of Deeds, Portland, Maine.
MHPC: Maine Historic Preservation Commission, Augusta, Maine.
MHS: Maine Historical Society, Portland, Maine.
MSL: Maine State Library, Augusta, Maine.
OCRD: Oxford County Registry of Deeds, Paris, Maine.
PSPS: Poland Spring Preservation Society, Poland Spring, Maine.
USS: Shaker Library, United Society of Shakers, New Gloucester, Maine.

Primary Sources

Addresses at the Dedication of Maine State Building. Lewiston, Maine: Lewiston Journal, 1895.
Announcement Twenty-Third Annual Summer Season Poland Spring House. South Poland, Maine: Hiram Ricker and Sons, 1898.
Annual Exhibition of Paintings by Prominent Artists at the Poland Spring Art Gallery. South Poland, Maine: Hiram Ricker and Sons, 1896–1900.
Annual Report of the Bureau of Industrial and Labor Statistics for the State of Maine. Augusta, Maine: Burleigh and Flynt, 1891, 1893; Kennebec Journal Print, 1902.
Annual Report of the Railroad Commissioners of the State of Maine. Augusta, Maine: Sprague, Owen and Nash, 1871–1878; Sprague and Son, 1883; Burleigh and Flynt, 1895.
Annual Report of the Secretary of the Maine Board of Agriculture. Augusta, Maine: Stevens and Blaine, 1857; Stevens and Sayward, 1861; Sprague, Owen and Nash, 1873; Burleigh and Flynt, 1896.
Annual Report of the State Board of Health. Augusta, Maine: Sprague and Son, 1886, 1887; Burleigh and Flynt, 1889; Kennebec Journal Print, 1900, 1906; Waterville, Maine: Sentinel Publishing, 1913.

Annual Report of the Steamboat Inspectors for the State of Maine. Augusta, Maine: Burleigh and Flynt, 1894.

Beckett, S[ylvester] B. *Guide Book of the Atlantic and St. Lawrence, and St. Lawrence and Atlantic Rail Roads*. Portland, Maine: Sanborn and Carter, and H. J. Little, 1853.

"Church Record." Vol. 3, New Gloucester, Maine, 25 March 1884 – 31 December 1889; vol. 4, 1890 – 1897; vol. 5, 1898 – 1906. USS.

Colby's Atlas of the State of Maine. 5th ed. Houlton, Maine: Colby and Stuart, 1884.

[Coombs, Delbert Dana]. "D. D. Coombs, Artist." Account Book, [1869 – 1929]. Museum of Art, Olin Arts Center, Bates College, Lewiston, Maine.

"Court of County Commissioners Hearing on Petition." Poland, Maine, 12 September 1894. TMs. ABR.

Deeds. Books 4, 6, 15 – 17, 22, 25, 33, 51, 58, 61, 63 – 65, 68 – 69, 74, 79, 81, 83 – 84, 90, 95, 98, 100, 104 – 5, 110 – 12, 114, 116, 120, 122, 124 – 25, 130, 132 – 33, 138, 140, 142, 145, 148, 150 – 51, 153, 155, 159 – 60, 167, 169, 178, 180 – 81, 183, 185 – 86, 191, 205, 217, 222 – 23, 247, 260, 307, 355. ACRD.

Deeds. Books 155, 192, 233. CCRD.

Deeds. Books 81 – 84, 97, 105. OCRD.

Godkin, Edwin Lawrence. "Chromo-Civilization." In *Reflections and Comments*. New York: Charles Scribner's Sons, 1895.

Griffith, Frank Carlos and Nettie M. Ricker, eds. *Poland Spring and About There*. South Poland, Maine: Hiram Ricker and Sons, 1903.

———. Copybook. "Poland Spring Library, Maine State Building." Poland Spring, Maine, 1902 – 1903. Private Collection.

Harlan, Louis R. and Raymond W. Smock, eds. *The Booker T. Washington Papers*. Urbana: University of Illinois Press, 1984.

Hayley, John W. *Genealogical Memoranda, Relating Chiefly to the Haley, Piper, Neal and Ricker Families of Maine and New Hampshire*. Lowell, Mass.: Courier-Citizen, 1900.

Haynes, George H. *The Charming Inland Retreats of Maine*. Portland, Maine: Self-published, 1890.

———. *Maine's Health, Pleasure and Sporting Resorts*. New York: A. H. Kellogg, 1894.

———. "Ricker Family and Poland Spring." Portland, Maine. 21 October 1896. TMs [photocopy]. MHS.

[———]. *Specimens of Illustrations in Books Written by Geo. H. Haynes, Descriptive Writer*. Portland, Maine: Self-published, [1892, 1893].

———. *The State of Maine, in 1893*. New York: Moss Engraving Company, 1893.

Herndon, Richard, comp. *Boston of To-day: A Glance at Its History and Characteristics*. Edited by Edwin M. Bacon. Boston: Post Publishing, 1892.

———, comp. *Men of Progress: Biographical Sketches and Portraits of Leaders in Business and Professional Life in and of the State of Maine*. Edited by Philip W. McIntyre and William F. Blanding. Boston: New England Magazine, 1897.

———, comp. *Men of Progress: One Thousand Biographical Sketches and Portraits of Leaders in Business and Professional Life in the Commonwealth of Massachusetts*. Edited by Edwin M. Bacon. Boston: New England Magazine, 1893.

Hill-Top (Poland Spring, Maine). 1894–1905, 1909, 1917–1918, 1920–1924, 1926, 1928.

"Hiram Ricker." New England Historical Publishing Company, 1903. TMs. AHS.

Howells, William Dean. *The Rise of Silas Lapham*. Boston: Ticknor, 1885; reprint, New York: New American Library, 1963.

Ladd, William. "Annals of Bakerstown, Poland and Minot." In *Collections of the Maine Historical Society*. 1st Series, Vol. II. Portland: Maine Historical Society, 1847.

Lapham, William B. *History of Rumford, Oxford County, Maine, from Its First Settlement in 1779 to the Present Time*. Augusta, Maine: Maine Farmer, 1890.

———. *History of the Town of Bethel, Maine*. Augusta, Maine: Press of the Maine Farmer, 1891; reprint, Somersworth, N.H.: New England History Press, 1981.

———, comp. *Records of Some of the Descendants of George and Maturin Ricker, Who Were Early at Dover, N.H.: and Who Were Killed by the Indians, June 4, 1706*. Augusta, Maine: Sprague, Owen and Nash, 1877.

[———]. "Ricker Family." *Maine Genealogist and Biographer* 2 (1877): 105–12; 3 (1877): 9–16; 3 (1877): 45–48.

Mace, Aurelia G. *The Aletheia: Spirit of Truth*. Farmington, Maine: Knowlton, McLeary, 1899; reprint, Sabbathday Lake, Maine: United Society of Shakers, 1992.

———. Journal, New Gloucester, Maine, 1896–1907. USS.

Mansion House. South Poland, Maine: Hiram Ricker and Sons, [1899].

Merrill, Georgia Drew, ed. *History of Androscoggin County, Maine*. Boston: W. A. Ferguson, 1891.

Murray, William H. H. *Adventures in the Wilderness*. Boston: Fields, Osgood, 1869. Reprint, edited by William K. Verner. Syracuse, N.Y.: Syracuse University Press and The Adirondack Museum, 1989.

Nash, Charles E. "William Berry Lapham." In *Collections of the Maine Historical Society*, 2d series, 5 (Portland: Maine Historical Society, 1894): 336–44.

Noyes, Crosby S. *The Crown of New England: The Grand Old Town of Minot*. Washington, D.C.: Judd and Detweiler, 1904.

Patterson, Jane Lippitt. *The Romance of the New Bethesda*. Boston: Universalist Publishing House, 1888.

Poland Mineral Spring Water. South Poland, Maine: Hiram Ricker and Sons, [1876, 1879].

Poland Mineral Spring Water: The Story of Its History and Its Marvellous Curative Properties. South Poland, Maine: Hiram Ricker and Sons, 1883, 1888, 1889, 1891, 1893, 1895.

Poland Spring. South Poland, Maine: Hiram Ricker and Sons, 1890, [1893].

Poland Spring: America's Leading Spa. South Poland, Maine: Hiram Ricker and Sons, 1900.

Poland Spring: Announcement. South Poland, Maine: Hiram Ricker and Sons, 1892.

Poland Spring: The Early History of This Wonderful Spring: Its Growth and Development Illustrated. South Poland, Maine: Hiram Ricker and Sons, 1908, 1914.

Poland Spring: Souvenir. Poland Spring, Maine: Hiram Ricker and Sons, [1885].

Poland Spring Centennial: A Souvenir. South Poland, Maine: Hiram Ricker and Sons, 1895.

Poland Spring Hotels. South Poland, Maine: Hiram Ricker and Sons, 1887–1889.

Poland Spring House. South Poland, Maine: Hiram Ricker and Sons, 1898–1899, 1901.

Poland Spring Water: Nature's Great Remedy and Its Marvelous Curative Properties. South Poland, Maine: Hiram Ricker and Sons, 1890.

Poole, H[enry] A. and G[eorge] W. Poole. *History of Poland: Illustrated: Embracing a Period of Over a Century.* Mechanic Falls, Maine: Poole Brothers, 1890.

Q[uint], H. A. "Ricker Pedigree—Corrections." *New England Historical and Genealogical Register* 5 (1851): 308–10.

Ralph, Julian. *Chicago and the World's Fair.* New York: Harper & Brothers, 1893.

"Records," vol. 1, New Gloucester, Maine, January 1872–30 September 1877. USS.

Report of the Board of World's Fair Managers of Maine. Augusta, Maine: Burleigh and Flynt, 1895.

Ricker, A[lvan] B. Notebook, South Poland, Maine, 1896–1903. MSL.

Ricker, Alvan B., Bert M. Fernald and Hiram W. Ricker. *Poland Centennial.* Poland, Maine: Ricker, Fernald and Ricker, 1896.

Ricker, George and Rose Ricker, eds. *Poland Spring Remembered: Recollections of Catharine Lewis Lennihan.* Poland Spring, Maine: Poland Spring Preservation Society, 1988.

Ricker, G[eorge] W. "The Ricker Family." *New England Historical and Genealogical Register* 5 (1851): 308–10.

[Ricker, Hiram]. "Poland Spring." [1884], TMs, AHS.

Ricker, Mary Elizabeth Arthur. Interview by Elizabeth Ring and Earle G. Shettleworth, Jr., 20 September 1971. Transcript. MHPC.

Ricker, Percy Leroy and Elwin R. Holland. *A Genealogy of the Ricker Family.* Bowie, Md.: Heritage Books, 1996.

Sanford, E. F. and W. P. Everts, eds. *Atlas and History of Androscoggin County Maine.* Philadelphia: Sanford Everts, 1873.

Souvenir List of Employees. Poland Spring, Maine: Hiram Ricker and Sons, 1900.

S[taples], A[rthur] G. *The Inner Man.* [Lewiston, Maine]: Privately printed, 1923.

Stephens, C[harles] A[sbury]. *A Busy Year at the Old Squire's.* Norway, Maine: Old Squire's Bookstore, 1922.

———. *A Great Year of Our Lives: At the Old Squire's.* Norway, Maine: Old Squire's Bookstore, 1912.

Three Able Addresses Delivered Before the State Board of Trade. Portland, Maine: Marks Printing House, 1902.

Tower (Poland Spring, Maine). 1943.

Twain, Mark and Charles Dudley Warner. *The Gilded Age: A Tale of Today.* Hartford, Conn.: American Publishing, 1873.

"An Unusual Real Estate Opportunity." [West Gloucester, Maine: Privately printed, 1893].

Veblen, Thorstein. *The Theory of the Leisure Class: An Economic Study of Institutions.* New York: Macmillan, 1899; reprint, New York: Dover, 1994.

Warner, Charles Dudley. "Their Pilgrimage." *Harper's New Monthly Magazine* 73 (1886): 933–52.

Wilson, Delmer C. Diaries, New Gloucester, Maine, 1889, 1895, 1899, 1900. USS.

Wonderful Medicinal Virtues of the Poland Mineral Spring Water. South Poland, Maine: Hiram Ricker and Sons, [1877].

Secondary Sources

Adams, Henry. *The Education of Henry Adams: An Autobiography.* Boston: Houghton Mifflin, 1918.

———. *The Tendency of History.* New York: MacMillan, 1919; reprint, New York: Book League of America, 1929.

Adelman, Melvin L. *A Sporting Time: New York City and the Rise of Modern Athletics, 1820–1870.* Urbana: University of Illinois Press, 1986.

Allen, Robert C. "B. F. Keith and the Origins of American Vaudeville." *Theatre Survey* 21 (1980): 105–15.

Ames, Kenneth L. *Death in the Dining Room and Other Tales of Victorian Culture.* Philadelphia: Temple University Press, 1992.

Anderson, Mark W. "Images of Nineteenth Century Maine Farming in the Prose and Poetry of R. P. T. Coffin and C. A. Stephens." *Agricultural History* 63 (1989): 120–29.

Armstead, Myra B. Young. *"Lord, Please Don't Take Me in August": African Americans in Newport and Saratoga Springs, 1870–1930.* Urbana: University of Illinois Press, 1999.

Aron, Cindy S. *Working at Play: A History of Vacations in the United States.* New York: Oxford University Press, 1999.

Axelrod, Alan, ed. *The Colonial Revival in America.* New York: W. W. Norton for The Henry Francis duPont Winterthur Museum, Winterthur, Del., 1985.

Bain, Sherwood E. "N. W. Scott Leighton," *Antiques,* 115 (1979): 544–51.

Baltzell, E. Digby. *Philadelphia Gentlemen: The Making of a National Upper Class.* Glencoe, Ill.: Free Press, 1958.

———. *The Protestant Establishment: Aristocracy and Caste in America.* New York: Random House, 1964.

———. *Puritan Boston and Quaker Philadelphia: Two Protestant Ethics and the Spirit of Class Authority and Leadership.* Boston: Beacon Press, 1979.

———. *Sporting Gentlemen: Men's Tennis from the Age of Honor to the Cult of the Superstar.* New York: Free Press, 1995.

Barron, Hal S. *Those Who Stayed Behind: Rural Society in Nineteenth-Century New England.* Cambridge, England: Cambridge University Press, 1984.

Barth, Gunther. *City People: The Rise of Modern City Culture in Nineteenth-Century America.* New York: Oxford University Press, 1980.

Beach, Christopher S. "Conservation and Legal Politics: The Struggle for Public Water Power in Maine, 1900–1923." *Maine Historical Society Quarterly* 32 (1993): 150–73.

Beard, Charles A. and Mary R. Beard. *The Rise of American Civilization.* New York: MacMillan, 1930.

Beer, Thomas. *The Mauve Decade: American Life at the End of the Nineteenth Century.* New York: Alfred A. Knopf, 1926.

Bender, Thomas. *Toward an Urban Vision: Ideas and Institutions in Nineteenth-Century America.* Lexington: University of Kentucky Press for the Organization of American Historians, 1975.

Bennett, Mary E., ed. *Poland: Past and Present, 1795–1970.* [Poland, Maine]: Poland Anniversary Committee, 1970.

Bennett, Randall H. *The Mount Zircon Moon Tide Spring: An Illustrated History.* [Bethel, Maine:] Randall H. Bennett, 1997.

Birmingham, Stephen. *"Our Crowd": The Great Jewish Families of New York.* New York: Harper and Row, 1967.

Blake, Nelson Manfred. *Water for the Cities: A History of the Urban Water Supply Problem in the United States.* Syracuse, N.Y.: Syracuse University Press, 1956.

Blanchard, Mary W. "Boundaries and the Victorian Body: Aesthetic Fashion in Gilded Age America." *American Historical Review* 100 (1995): 21–50.

Bledstein, Burton J. and Robert D. Johnson, ed. *The Middling Sorts: Explorations in the History of the American Middle Class.* New York: Routledge, 2001.

Bluestone, Daniel. "From Promenade to Park: The Gregarious Origins of Brooklyn's Park Movement." *American Quarterly* 39 (1987): 529–50.

Blumin, Stuart M. *The Emergence of the Middle Class: Social Experience in the American City, 1760–1900.* Cambridge, England: Cambridge University Press, 1989.

———. *The Short Season of Sharon Springs: Portrait of Another New York.* In collaboration with Deborah Adelman Blumin. Ithaca, N.Y.: Cornell University Press, 1980.

Bonta, Marcia Myers. *Women in the Field: America's Pioneering Women Naturalists.* College Station: Texas A & M University Press, 1991.

Bowers, William L. *The Country Life Movement in America, 1900–1920.* Port Washington, N.Y.: Kennikat Press, 1974.

Boyer, Paul S. *Purity in Print: The Vice–Society Movement and Book Censorship in America.* New York: Charles Scribner's Sons, 1968.

———. *Urban Masses and Moral Order in America, 1820–1920.* Cambridge, Mass.: Harvard University Press, 1978.

Braden, Donna R. *Leisure and Entertainment in America.* Dearborn, Mich.: Henry Ford Museum and Greenfield Village, 1988.

Braden, Susan R. *The Architecture of Leisure: The Florida Resort Hotels of Henry Flagler and Henry Plant.* Gainesville: University of Florida Press, 2002.

Brewer, Priscilla J. *Shaker Communities, Shaker Lives.* Hanover, N.H.: University Press of New England, 1986.

Bridenbaugh, Carl. "Baths and Watering Places of Colonial America." *William and Mary Quarterly* 3 (1946): 151–81.

Bronner, Simon J., ed. *Consuming Visions: Accumulation and Display of Goods in America, 1880–1920.* New York: W. W. Norton and Company for the Henry Francis duPont Winterthur Museum, 1989.

Brown, Dona. "Accidental Tourists: Visitors to the Mount Mansfield Summit House in the Late Nineteenth Century." *Vermont History* 65 (1997): 117–30.

———. *Inventing New England: Regional Tourism in the Nineteenth Century.* Washington, D.C.: Smithsonian Institution Press, 1995.

Bulkley, Peter B. "A History of the White Mountain Tourist Industry, 1818–1899." M.A. thesis, University of New Hampshire, 1958.

———. "Horace Fabyan, Founder of the White Mountain Grand Hotel." *Historical New Hampshire* 30 (1975): 52–77.

———. "Identifying the White Mountain Tourist, 1853–1854: Origin, Occupation, and Wealth as a Definition of the Early Hotel Trade." *Historical New Hampshire* 35 (1980): 107–62.

Burns, Sarah. *Pastoral Inventions: Rural Life in Nineteenth-Century American Art and Culture.* Philadelphia: Temple University Press, 1989.

Butsch, Richard, ed. *For Fun and Profit: The Transformation of Leisure into Consumption.* Philadelphia: Temple University Press, 1990.

Cadbury, Warder H. "Introduction." In *Adventures in the Wilderness*, ed. William K. Verner, 11–75. Syracuse, N.Y.: Syracuse University Press and The Adirondack Museum, 1989.

Cayleff, Susan E. *Wash and Be Healed: The Water-Cure Movement and Women's Health.* Philadelphia: Temple University Press, 1987.

Chambers, Thomas A. *Drinking the Waters: Creating an American Leisure Class at Nineteenth-Century Mineral Springs.* Washington, D.C.: Smithsonian Institution Press, 2002.

———. "Tourism and the Market Revolution." *Reviews in American History* 30 (2002): 555–63.

Clark, Christopher. "Economics and Culture: Opening Up the Rural History of the Early American Northeast." *American Quarterly* (1991): 279–301.

Cmiel, Kenneth. "Destiny and Amnesia: The Vision of Modernity in Robert Wiebe's *The Search for Order.*" *Reviews in American History* 21 (1993): 352–68.

Cocks, Catherine. *Doing the Town: The Rise of Urban Tourism in the United States, 1870–1915.* Berkeley: University of California Press, 2001.

Cole, Alfred and Charles F. Whitman. *A History of Buckfield, Oxford County, Maine from the Earliest Explorations to the Close of the Year 1900.* Buckfield, Maine: C. F. Whitman, 1915; reprint, Bridgton, Maine: Coburn Press, 1977.

Collier, James Lincoln. *The Rise of Selfishness.* New York: Oxford University Press, 1991.

Conforti, Joseph A. *Imagining New England: Explorations of Regional Identity from the Pilgrims to the Mid-Twentieth Century.* Chapel Hill: University of North Carolina Press, 2001.

Cotkin, George. *Reluctant Modernism: American Thought and Culture, 1880–1900.* New York: Twayne Publishers, 1992.

Cromley, Elizabeth. "Upward and Inward with Time: Catskills Resort Architecture," *Progressive Architecture* (1978): 46–51.

Danbom, David B. *The Resisted Revolution: Urban America and the Industrialization of Agriculture, 1900–1930.* Ames: Iowa State University Press, 1979.

Danhof, Clarence H. *Change in Agriculture: The Northern United States, 1820–1870.* Cambridge, Mass.: Harvard University Press, 1969.

Day, Clarence Albert. *Farming in Maine, 1860–1940.* University of Maine Studies, 2d series, no. 78. Orono: University of Maine Press, 1963.

Demars, Stanford E. *Tourist in Yosemite, 1855–1985.* Salt Lake City: University of Utah Press, 1991.

DeVierville, Jonathan Paul. "American Healing Waters: A Chronology (1513–1946) and Historical Survey of America's Major Springs, Spas, and Health Resorts Including a

Review of Their Medicinal Virtues, Therapeutic Methods, and Health Care Practices." Ph.D. diss., University of Texas at Austin, 1992.

Dinnerstein, Leonard. *Antisemitism in America*. New York: Oxford University Press, 1994.

Domosh, Mona. *Invented Cities: The Creation of Landscape in Nineteenth-Century New York and Boston*. New Haven, Conn.: Yale University Press, 1996.

Dorsey, Leslie and Janice Devine. *Fare Thee Well: A Backward Look at Two Centuries of Historic American Hostelries, Fashionable Spas and Seaside Resorts*. New York: Crown Publishers, 1964.

Douglas, Mary. *Purity and Danger: An Analysis of the Concepts of Pollution and Taboo*. London: Routledge and Keegan Paul, 1966.

Dutch, Harold W., ed. *Maine State Building at Poland Spring, Maine: Centennial, 1895–1995*. Poland Spring, Maine: Poland Spring Preservation Society, 1995.

Evers, Alf, Elizabeth Cromley, Betsy Blackmar and Neil Harris. *Resorts of the Catskills*. New York: St. Martin's Press for the Architectural League of New York and the Gallery Association of New York State, 1979.

Flood, Ernest C. *Empire Grove: The First 150 Years*. Poppenberg Press, 1983.

Foy, Jessica H. and Karal Ann Marling, eds. *The Arts and the American Home, 1890–1930*. Knoxville: University of Tennessee Press, 1994.

——— and Thomas J. Schlereth, eds. *American Home Life, 1880–1930: A Social History of Spaces and Services*. Knoxville: University of Tennessee Press, 1992.

Frederic, Paul B. *Canning Gold: Northern New England's Sweet Corn Industry*. Lanham, Md.: University Press of America, 2002.

Funnell, Charles E. *By the Beautiful Sea: The Rise and High Times of That Great American Resort, Atlantic City*. New York: Alfred A. Knopf, 1975.

Gaffney, Thomas L. "Maine's Mr. Smith: A Study of the Career of Francis O. J. Smith, Politician and Entrepreneur." Ph.D. diss., University of Maine at Orono, 1979.

Galambos, Louis. "The Emerging Organizational Synthesis in Modern American History." *Business History Review* 44 (1970): 279–90.

Garraty, John A. *The New Commonwealth*. New York: Harper and Row, 1968.

Garvin, Donna-Belle and James L. Garvin. *On the Road North of Boston: New Hampshire Taverns and Turnpikes, 1700–1900*. Concord: New Hampshire Historical Society, 1988.

Giffen, Sarah L. and Kevin D. Murphy. *"A Noble and Dignified Stream": The Piscataqua Region in the Colonial Revival, 1860–1930*. York, Maine: Old York Historical Society, 1992.

Gilkeson, John S., Jr. *Middle-Class Providence*. Princeton, N.J.: Princeton University Press, 1986.

Ginger, Ray. *Age of Excess: The United States from 1877 to 1914*. New York: MacMillan Publishing, 1965.

Gold, David M. "Jewish Agriculture in the Catskills." *Agricultural History* 55 (1981): 31–49.

Goldstein, Judith S. *Crossing Lines: Histories of Jews and Gentiles in Three Communities*. New York: William Morrow, 1992.

Gordon, Beverly. *Bazaars and Fair Ladies: The History of the American Fundraising Fair*. Knoxville: University of Tennessee Press, 1998.

Gowell, Roger L. "The Rickers (Riccars) of Poland." 1972, TMs, photocopy, AHS.

Graham, Ada and Frank Graham, Jr. *Kate Furbish and the Flora of Maine*. Gardiner, Maine: Tilbury House, 1995.

Graham, Michael S. "The Sabbathday Lake Shakers and the Rickers of the Poland Spring Hotel: A Scrapbook History." New Gloucester, Maine: United Society of Shakers, 2001.

Green, Harvey. *Fit for America: Health, Fitness, Sport and American Society*. New York: Pantheon Books, 1986.

————. *The Light of the Home: An Intimate View of the Lives of Women in Victorian America*. New York: Pantheon Books, 1983.

Gregory, Kristin. "The History of Poland Spring Bottling." [1995], TMs, photocopy. PSPS.

Grier, Katherine C. *Culture and Comfort: People, Parlors, and Upholstery, 1850–1930*. Rochester, N.Y.: Strong Museum, 1988.

————, ed. "Gendered Spaces and Aesthetics: A Special Issue." *Wintherthur Portfolio* (1996): 199–302.

Grover, Janice Zita. "Luxury and Leisure in Early Nineteenth-Century America: Saratoga Springs and the Rise of the Resort." Ph.D. diss., University of California at Davis, 1973.

Grover, Kathryn, ed. *Dining in America, 1850–1900*. Amherst: University of Massachusetts Press and Rochester, N.Y.: Margaret Woodbury Strong Museum, 1987.

————, ed. *Hard at Play: Leisure in America, 1840–1940*. Amherst: University of Massachusetts Press and Rochester, N.Y.: Margaret Woodbury Strong Museum, 1992.

Guptill, S. Carlton. "The Grange in Maine from 1874–1940." Ph.D. diss., University of Maine at Orono, 1973.

Haley, Bruce. *The Healthy Body and Victorian Culture*. Cambridge, Mass.: Harvard University Press, 1978.

Halttunen, Karen. *Confidence Men and Painted Women: A Study of Middle-Class Culture in America, 1830–1870*. New Haven, Conn.: Yale University Press, 1982.

Hardy, Stephen. *How Boston Played: Sport, Recreation, and Community, 1865–1915*. Boston: Northeastern University Press, 1982.

Harmond, Richard. "Progress and Flight: An Interpretation of the American Cycle Craze of the 1890's." *Journal of Social History* 5 (1971–72): 235–57.

Hatch, Louis Clinton, ed. *Maine: A History*. New York: American Historical Society, 1919; reprint, Somersworth, N.H.: New Hampshire Publishing, 1974.

Hays, Samuel P. *The Response to Industrialism 1885–1914*. Chicago: University of Chicago Press, 1957.

Higham, John. "The Reorientation of American Culture in the 1890's." In *The Origins of Modern Consciousness*, ed. John Weiss, 25–48. Detroit: Wayne State University Press, 1965.

————. *Strangers in the Land: Patterns of American Nativism, 1860–1925*. 2d ed. New Brunswick, N.J.: Rutgers University Press, 1955; reprint, 1988.

Historic Lewiston: Franco-American Origins. [Lewiston, Maine]: Lewiston Historical Commission, 1974.

Hofstadter, Richard. *The Age of Reform: From Bryan to FDR.* New York: Vintage Books, 1955.

――――. *The American Political Tradition: And the Men Who Made It.* New York: Vintage Books, 1948.

Holt, Jeff. *The Grand Trunk in New England.* Toronto: Railfare Enterprises, 1986.

Horowitz, Daniel. *The Morality of Spending: Attitudes toward the Consumer Society in America, 1875–1940.* Baltimore: Johns Hopkins University Press, 1985.

Howe, Daniel Walker, ed. *Victorian America.* Philadelphia: University of Pennsylvania Press, 1976.

Howe, Stanley Russell. *"A Fair Field and No Favor": A Concise History of the Maine State Grange.* Augusta, Maine: Maine State Grange, 1994.

Humphrey, Walt. "Moses Bottles." *Western Collector* (1969): 48–52.

Hunter, Julia A. *Fly Rod Crosby: The Woman Who Marketed Maine.* Gardiner, Maine: Tilbury House for Friends of the Maine State Museum, 2000.

Hurst, James Willard. *Law and the Conditions of Freedom in the Nineteenth–Century United States.* Madison: University of Wisconsin Press, 1956.

Hutchinson, Doug. *The Rumford Falls and Rangeley Lakes Railroad.* Dixfield, Maine: Partridge Lane Publications, 1989.

Huth, Hans. *Nature and the American: Three Centuries of Changing Attitudes.* Berkeley: University of California Press, 1957.

Hyde, Anne Farrar. *An American Vision: Far Western Landscape and National Culture, 1820–1920.* New York: New York University Press, 1990.

Isaac, Rhys. *The Transformation of Virginia, 1740–1790.* New York: W. W. Norton, 1982.

Jacob, Kathryn Allamong. *Capital Elites: High Society in Washington, D.C., after the Civil War.* Washington, D.C.: Smithsonian Institution Press, 1995.

Jester, Thomas C. "Charles Sumner Frost, 1856–1931." *A Biographical Dictionary of Architects in Maine* 6 (1991): [1–6].

Jones, Howard Mumford. *The Age of Energy: Varieties of American Experience, 1865–1915.* New York: Viking, 1970.

Josephson, Matthew. *The Robber Barons: The Great American Capitalists, 1861–1901.* New York: Harcourt, Brace, 1934.

Judd, Richard W. *Common Lands, Common People: The Origins of Conservation in Northern New England.* Cambridge, Mass.: Harvard University Press, 1997.

――――, Edwin A. Churchill, and Joel W. Eastman, eds. *Maine: The Pine Tree State from Prehistory to the Present.* Orono: University of Maine Press, 1995.

――――. "Reshaping Maine's Landscape: Rural Culture, Tourism, and Conservation, 1890–1929." *Journal of Forest History* 32 (1988): 180–90.

Kammen, Michael. *Mystic Chords of Memory: The Transformation of Tradition in American Culture.* New York: Alfred A. Knopf, 1991.

Kanfer, Stefan. *A Summer World: The Attempt to Build a Jewish Eden in the Catskills, from the Days of the Ghetto to the Rise of the Borscht Belt.* New York: Farrar, Straus and Giroux, 1989.

Kasson, John. *Amusing the Million: Coney Island at the Turn of the Century.* New York: Hill and Wang, 1978.

———. *Rudeness and Civility: Manners in Nineteenth-Century Urban America.* New York: Hill and Wang, 1990.

Leane, John J. *A History of Rumford, Maine, 1774–1972.* Rumford, Maine: Rumford Publishing, 1972.

Lears, T. J. Jackson and Richard Wightman Fox, eds. *The Culture of Consumption: Critical Essays in American History, 1880–1980.* New York: Pantheon Books, 1983.

———. *No Place of Grace: Antimodernism and the Transformation of American Culture, 1880–1920.* New York: Pantheon Books, 1981.

Levenstein, Harvey A. *Revolution at the Table: The Transformation of the American Diet.* New York: Oxford University Press, 1988.

Levine, Lawrence. *High Brow/Low Brow: The Emergence of Cultural Hierarchy in America.* Cambridge, Mass.: Harvard University Press, 1988.

Loeb, Lori Anne. *Consuming Angels: Advertising and Victorian Women.* New York: Oxford University Press, 1994.

Lowenthal, David. *The Past Is a Foreign Country.* Cambridge, England: Cambridge University Press, 1985.

McBride, Bunny and Harald E. L. Prins, "Walking the Medicine Line: Molly Ockett, a Pigwacket Doctor." In *Northeastern Indian Lives, 1632–1816,* ed. Robert S. Grumet, 321–47. Amherst: University of Massachusetts Press, 1996.

MacCannell, Dean. *The Tourist: A New Theory of the Leisure Class.* New York: Schocken Books, 1976.

McCash, William Barton and June Hall McCash. *The Jekyll Island Club: Southern Haven for America's Millionaires.* Athens: University of Georgia Press, 1989.

McDannell, Colleen. *The Christian Home in Victorian America, 1840–1900.* Bloomington: Indiana University Press, 1986.

McKelvey, Blake. *The Urbanization of America, 1860–1915.* New Brunswick, N.J.: Rutgers University Press, 1963.

McLoughlin, William G. *The Meaning of Henry Ward Beecher: An Essay on the Shifting Values of Mid-Victorian America, 1840–1870.* New York: Alfred A. Knopf, 1970.

Machor, James L. *Pastoral Cities: Urban Ideals and the Symbolic Landscape of America.* Madison: University of Wisconsin Press, 1987.

Marini, Stephen A. *Radical Sects of Revolutionary New England.* Cambridge, Mass.: Harvard University Press, 1982.

Marling, Karal Ann. *George Washington Slept Here: Colonial Revivals and American Culture, 1876–1986.* Cambridge, Mass.: Harvard University Press, 1988.

Martin, Stuart F. *New Penacook Folks.* Rumford Point, Maine: Stuart F. Martin, 1980.

Marx, Leo. *The Machine in the Garden: Technology and the Pastoral Ideal in America.* New York: Oxford University Press, 1964.

Matthews, Christopher N. "The Maginnis Cotton Mill Site: Site History." http://www.uno.edu/~cmatthew/MagHist.htm. 9 December 2003.

Mayo, James M. *The American Country Club: Its Origins and Development.* New Brunswick, N.J.: Rutgers University Press, 1998.

Meeks, Harold A. "Stagnant, Smelly, and Successful: Vermont's Mineral Springs." *Vermont History* 47 (1979): 5–20.

Miller, Angela. *The Empire of the Eye: Landscape Representation and American Cultural Politics, 1825–1875.* Ithaca, N.Y.: Cornell University Press, 1993.

Mintz, Steven. *A Prison of Expectations: The Family in Victorian Culture.* New York: New York University Press, 1983.

Mrozek, Donald J. *Sport and American Mentality, 1880–1910.* Knoxville: University of Tennessee Press, 1983.

Mumford, Lewis. *The Brown Decades: A Study of the Arts in America, 1865–1895.* New York: Harcourt, Brace, 1931.

Murphy, Earl Finbar. *Water Purity: A Study in Legal Control of Natural Resources.* Madison: University of Wisconsin Press, 1961.

Myers, Kenneth. *The Catskills: Painters, Writers, and Tourists in the Mountains, 1820–1895.* Yonkers, N.Y.: Hudson River Museum of Westchester, 1987.

Nash, Roderick. *Wilderness and the American Mind.* New Haven, Conn.: Yale University Press, 1967.

Nevins, Allan. *The Emergence of Modern America.* New York: MacMillan, 1927.

Ogle, Maureen. *All the Modern Conveniences: American Household Plumbing, 1840–1890.* Baltimore: Johns Hopkins University Press, 1996.

Okun, Mitchell. *Fair Play in the Marketplace: The First Battle for Pure Food and Drugs.* DeKalb: Northern Illinois University Press, 1986.

Opel, Andy. "Constructing Purity: Bottled Water and the Commodification of Nature." *Journal of American Culture* 22 (1999): 67–76.

Openo, Woodard Dorr. "The Summer Colony at Little Harbor in Portsmouth, New Hampshire, and Its Relation to the Colonial Revival Movement." Ph.D. diss., University of Michigan, 1990.

Painter, Nell Irvin. *Standing at Armageddon: The United States, 1877–1919.* New York: W. W. Norton, 1987.

Papke, David Ray. *The Pullman Case: The Clash of Labor and Capital in Industrial America.* Lawrence: University Press of Kansas, 1999.

Parker, Alison M. *Purifying America: Women, Cultural Reform, and Pro-Censorship Activism, 1873–1933.* Urbana: University of Illinois Press, 1997.

Parrington, Vernon Louis. *The Beginnings of Critical Realism in America, 1860–1920.* New York: Harcourt, Brace, 1930.

Peterson, Jon A. "The City Beautiful Movement: Forgotten Origins and Lost Meanings." *Journal of Urban History* 2 (1976): 415–34.

———. "The Impact of Sanitary Reform upon American Urban Planning, 1840–1890." *Journal of Social History* 13 (1979): 83–103.

Pillsbury, David B. "History of the Atlantic and St. Lawrence Railroad Company." M.A. thesis, University of Maine at Orono, 1962.

Pivar, David J. *Purity Crusade: Sexual Morality and Social Control, 1868–1900.* Westport, Conn.: Greenwood Press, 1973.

Putney, Clifford. *Muscular Christianity: Manhood and Sports in Protestant America, 1880 – 1920.* Cambridge, Mass.: Harvard University Press, 2001.

Rader, Benjamin G. "The Quest for Subcommunities and the Rise of American Sport." *American Quarterly* 29 (1977): 355 – 69.

Rebek, Andrea. "The Selling of Vermont: From Agriculture to Tourism, 1860 –1910." *Vermont History* 44 (1976): 14 – 27.

Rhoads, William Bertolet. "The Colonial Revival." 2 vols. Ph.D. diss., Princeton University, 1974.

Riess, Steven A. *City Games: The Evolution of American Urban Society and the Rise of Sports.* Urbana: University of Illinois Press, 1989.

Robbins, Mel. *Poland Spring: An Informal History.* 5th ed. Poland Spring, Maine: Privately printed, 1992.

———— and Cyndi Robbins. *Poland Spring: Walk Hand in Hand with History, 1790s to Today.* Poland Spring, Maine: Privately printed, [2003].

Rodgers, Daniel T. *The Work Ethic in Industrial America, 1850 –1920.* Chicago: University of Chicago Press, 1978.

Roell, Craig H. *The Piano in America, 1890 –1940.* Chapel Hill: University of North Carolina Press, 1989.

Rose, Anne C. *Victorian America and the Civil War.* Cambridge, England: Cambridge University Press, 1992.

Russell, Howard S., *A Long, Deep Furrow: Three Centuries of Farming in New England.* Hanover, N.H.: University Press of New England, 1976.

Schlereth, Thomas J. *Victorian America: Transformations in Everyday Life, 1876 –1915.* New York: Harper Collins, 1991.

Schlesinger, Arthur Meier. *The Rise of the City, 1878 –1898.* New York: MacMillan, 1933.

Schmitt, Peter J. *Back to Nature: The Arcadian Myth in Urban America.* Baltimore: Johns Hopkins University Press, 1969.

Schulte, Janet Elinor. "'Summer Homes': A History of Family Summer Vacation Communities in Northern New England, 1880 –1940." Ph.D. diss., Brandeis University, 1993.

Scott, Mel. *American City Planning Since 1890.* Berkeley: University of California Press, 1969.

Scully, Vincent J., Jr. *The Shingle Style and the Stick Style: Architectural Theory and Design from Downing to the Origins of Wright.* Rev. ed. New Haven, Conn.: Yale University Press, 1971.

Sears, John F. *Sacred Places: American Tourist Attractions in the Nineteenth Century.* New York: Oxford University Press, 1989.

Segal, Howard P. "Leo Marx's 'Middle Landscape': A Critique, a Revision, and an Appreciation." *Reviews in American History* 5 (1977): 137 – 50.

Sellers, Charles. *The Market Revolution: Jacksonian America, 1815 –1846.* New York: Oxford University Press, 1991.

Sherman, Rexford Booth. "The Grange in Maine and New Hampshire, 1870 –1940." Ph.D. diss., Boston University, 1972.

[Shettleworth, Earle G., Jr.]. "Poland Spring House." [c. 1970], TMs, photocopy. MHPC.

Singal, Daniel Joseph. "Towards a Definition of American Modernism." *American Quarterly* 39 (1987): 7–26.

Sloane, David Charles. *The Last Great Necessity: Cemeteries in American History*. Baltimore: Johns Hopkins University Press, 1991.

Smith, David C. "Virgin Timber: The Maine Woods as a Locale for Juvenile Fiction." In *A Handful of Spice: Essays in Maine History and Literature*, ed. Richard S. Sprague, University of Maine Studies, no. 88, 187–201. Orono, Maine: University of Maine Press, 1968.

Smith, Henry Nash. "Introduction." In *Popular Culture and Industrialism, 1865–1900*. New York: New York University Press, 1967.

Smith, Lincoln. *The Power Policy of Maine*. Berkeley: University of California Press, 1951.

Smith, Robert A. *A Social History of the Bicycle: Its Early Life and Times in America*. New York: American Heritage Press, 1972.

Smith-Rosenberg, Carroll. *Visions of Gender in Victorian America*. New York: Alfred A. Knopf, 1985.

Somers, Dale. "The Leisure Revolution: Recreation in the American City, 1820–1920." *Journal of Popular Culture* 5 (1971): 125–47.

———. *The Rise of Sports in New Orleans, 1850–1900*. Baton Rouge: Louisiana State University Press, 1972.

Stein, Charles W., ed. *American Vaudeville: As Seen by Its Contemporaries*. New York: Alfred A. Knopf, 1984.

Sterngass, Jon. *First Resorts: Pursuing Pleasure at Saratoga Springs, Newport and Coney Island*. Baltimore: Johns Hopkins University Press, 2001.

Stevens, John Calvin, II, and Earle G. Shettleworth, Jr. *John Calvin Stevens: Domestic Architecture, 1890–1930*. Scarborough, Maine: Harp Publications, 1990.

Stevenson, Louise L. *The Victorian Homefront: American Thought and Culture, 1860–1880*. New York: Twayne Publishers, 1991.

Strauss, David. "Toward a Consumer Culture: 'Adirondack Murray' and the Wilderness Vacation," *American Quarterly* 39 (1987): 270–86.

Summers, Mark Wahlgren. *The Era of Good Stealings*. New York: Oxford University Press, 1993.

Tarr, Joel A. *The Search for the Ultimate Sink: Urban Pollution in Historical Perspective*. Akron, Ohio: University of Akron Press, 1996.

Taylor, George Rogers. *The Transportation Revolution, 1815–1860*. New York: Rinehart, 1951.

Temin, Peter. *Taking Your Medicine: Drug Regulation in the United States*. Cambridge, Mass.: Harvard University Press, 1980.

Thompson, Deborah, ed. *Maine Forms of American Architecture*. Camden, Maine: Downeast Magazine, 1976.

"Those Glorious 1890s: Maine's Golden Decade." *Down East* 38 (January 1992): 1–80.

Tobin, Gary Allan. "The Bicycle Boom of the 1890s: The Development of Private Transportation and the Birth of the Modern Tourist." *Journal of Popular Culture* 7 (1974): 838–49.

Tolles, Bryant F., Jr., ed. "The Grand Resort Hotels and Tourism in the White Mountains, Proceedings of the Third Mount Washington Observatory Symposium." *Historical New Hampshire* 50 (1995): 1–144.

———. *The Grand Resort Hotels of the White Mountains: A Vanishing Architectural Legacy.* Boston: David R. Godine, 1998.

Trachtenberg, Alan. *The Incorporation of America: Culture and Society in the Gilded Age.* New York: Hill and Wang, 1982.

Uminowicz, Glenn. "Sport in a Middle-Class Utopia: Asbury Park, New Jersey, 1871–1895." *Journal of Sport History* 11 (1984): 51–73.

Urry, John. *The Tourist Gaze.* 2d ed. London: Sage Publications, 2002.

Valenza, Janet. "'Taking the Waters' at Texas Spas." *Journal of Cultural Geography* 11 (1990): 57–70.

Van Zandt, Roland. *The Catskill Mountain House.* New Brunswick, N.J.: Rutgers University Press, 1966.

Vashaw, Norman A. *What Was Ain't What Is: A Picture History of Canton, Maine.* Canton, Maine: Norm Vashaw and Bob Barrett, 1995.

Vincent, Pal. *The Moses Bottle.* Poland Spring, Maine: Palabra Shop, 1969.

Voss, J. Ellis. "Summer Resort: An Ecological Analysis of a Satellite Community." Ph.D., diss., University of Pennsylvania, 1941.

Walker, Robert H. *Everyday Life in the Age of Enterprise, 1865–1900.* New York: G. P. Putnam's Sons, 1967.

Walton, John K. *The English Seaside Resort: A Social History, 1750–1914.* New York: Leicester University Press and St. Martin's Press, 1983.

Weiss, Ellen. *City in the Woods: The Life and Design of an American Camp Meeting on Martha's Vineyard.* New York: Oxford University Press, 1987.

Wellman, Trina. *Louis Francis Sockalexis: The Life-story of a Penobscot Indian.* Augusta, Maine: Department of Indian Affairs, 1975.

Wescott, Richard R. "Early Conservation Programs and the Development of the Vacation Industry in Maine, 1865–1900," *Maine Historical Society Quarterly* 27 (1987): 2–13.

———. "Economic, Social and Governmental Aspects of the Development of Maine's Vacation Industry, 1850–1920." M.A. thesis, University of Maine at Orono, 1961.

Whitney, Ronald G. *The World of C. A. Stephens.* Springfield, Mass.: Waynor Publishing, 1976.

Wiebe, Robert H. *The Search for Order, 1877–1920.* New York: Hill and Wang, 1967.

Williams, Raymond. *The Country and the City.* New York: Oxford University Press, 1973.

Wilson, Harold Fisher. *The Hill Country of Northern New England: Its Social and Economic History, 1790–1930.* New York: Columbia University Press, 1936.

Wilson, Richard Guy, ed. *Victorian Resorts and Hotels: Essays from a Victorian Society Autumn Symposium.* Philadelphia: Victorian Society of America, 1982.

Wilson, William H. *The City Beautiful Movement.* Baltimore: Johns Hopkins University Press, 1989.

Wood, Donna J. *Strategic Uses of Public Policy: Business and Government in the Progressive Era.* Marshfield, Mass.: Pitman Publishing, 1986.

Wright, Gwendolyn. *Moralism and the Model Home: Domestic Architecture and Cultural Conflict in Chicago, 1873–1913.* Chicago: University of Chicago Press, 1980.

Young, James Harvey. *Pure Food: Securing the Federal Food and Drugs Act of 1906.* Princeton, N.J.: Princeton University Press, 1989.

Revisiting New England: The New Regionalism

SERIES EDITORS

Siobhan Senier, University of New Hampshire
Darren Ranco, Dartmouth College
Adam Sweeting, Boston University
David H. Watters, University of New Hampshire

This series presents fresh discussions of the distinctiveness of New England culture. The editors seek manuscripts examining the history of New England regionalism; the way its culture came to represent American national culture as a whole; the interaction between that "official" New England culture and the people who lived in the region; and local, subregional, or even biographical subjects as microcosms that explicitly open up and consider larger issues. The series welcomes new theoretical and historical perspectives and is designed to cross disciplinary boundaries and appeal to a wide audience.

Richard Archer, *Fissures in the Rock: New England in the Seventeenth Century*

Judith Bookbinder, *Boston Modern: Figurative Expressionism as Alternative Modernism*

Donna M. Cassidy, *Marsden Hartley: Race, Region, and Nation*

Nancy L. Gallagher, *Breeding Better Vermonters: The Eugenics Project in Vermont*

Sidney V. James, *The Colonial Metamorphoses in Rhode Island: A Study of Institutions in Change*

Christopher J. Lenney, *Sightseeking: Clues to the Landscape History of New England*

Donald W. Linebaugh, *The Man Who Found Thoreau: Roland W. Robbins and the Rise of Historical Archaeology in America*

Pauleena MacDougall, *The Penobscot Dance of Resistance: Tradition in the History of a People*

Diana Muir, *Reflections in Bullough's Pond: Economy and Ecosystem in New England*

James C. O'Connell, *Becoming Cape Cod: Creating a Seaside Resort*

Priscilla Paton, *Abandoned New England: Landscape in the Works of Homer, Frost, Hopper, Wyeth, and Bishop*

Jennifer C. Post, *Music in Rural New England Family and Community Life, 1870–1940*

David L. Richards, *Poland Spring: A Tale of the Gilded Age, 1860–1900*

Mark J. Sammons and Valerie Cunningham, *Black Portsmouth: Three Centuries of African-American Heritage*

Adam Sweeting, *Beneath the Second Sun: A Cultural History of Indian Summer*

Becoming Modern: New Nineteenth-Century Studies

SERIES EDITORS

Sarah Sherman, Department of English, University of New Hampshire
Janet Aikins, Department of English, University of New Hampshire
Rohan McWilliam, Anglia Polytechnic University, Cambridge, England
Janet Polasky, Department of History, University of New Hampshire

This book series maps the complexity of historical change and assesses the formation of ideas, movements, and institutions crucial to our own time by publishing books that examine the emergence of modernity in North America and Europe. Set primarily but not exclusively in the nineteenth century, the series shifts attention from modernity's twentieth-century forms to its earlier moments of uncertain and often disputed construction. Seeking books of interest to scholars on both sides of the Atlantic, it thereby encourages the expansion of nineteenth-century studies and the exploration of more global patterns of development.

Stephen Carl Arch, *After Franklin: The Emergence of Autobiography in Post-Revolutionary America, 1780–1830* (2001)

Justin D. Edwards, *Exotic Journeys: Exploring the Erotics of U.S. Travel Literature, 1840–1930* (2001)

Edward S. Cutler, *Recovering the New: Transatlantic Roots of Modernism* (2002)

Margaret M. Mulrooney, *Black Powder, White Lace: The du Pont Irish and Cultural Identity in Nineteenth-Century America* (2002)

William M. Morgan, *Philanthropists in Disguise: Gender, Humanitarianism, and Complicity in U.S. Literary Realism* (2004)

Piya Pal-Lapinski, *The Exotic Woman in Nineteenth-Century British Fiction and Culture: A Reconsideration* (2004)

Patrick H. Vincent, *The Romantic Poetess: European Culture, Politics and Gender, 1820–1840* (2004)

Betsy Klimasmith, *At Home in the City: Urban Domesticity in American Literature and Culture, 1850–1930* (2005)

David L. Richards, *Poland Spring: A Tale of the Gilded Age, 1860–1900* (2005)

Angela Sorby, *Schoolroom Poets: Childhood, Performance, and the Place of American Poetry, 1865–1917* (2005)

Index